Misalignment of Exchange Rates

A National Bureau
of Economic Research
Project Report

Misalignment of Exchange Rates: Effects on Trade and Industry

Edited by Richard C. Marston

The University of Chicago Press

Chicago and London

Richard C. Marston is the James R. F. Guy Professor of Finance and Economics in the Wharton School of the University of Pennsylvania and a research associate of the National Bureau of Economic Research.

The University of Chicago Press, Chicago 60637
The University of Chicago Press, Ltd., London

Printed in the United States of America
97 96 95 94 93 92 91 90 89 88 5 4 3 2 1

Library of Congress Cataloging-in-Publication Data

Misalignment of exchange rates : effects on trade and industry /
edited by Richard C. Marston.
p. cm.
"Proceedings of a conference . . . sponsored by the National Bureau of Economic Research and held in Cambridge, Massachusetts, on 7–8 May, 1987"—Pref.
Includes bibliographies and indexes.
ISBN 0-226-50723-8
1. Foreign exchange problem—Congresses. I. Marston, Richard C.
II. National Bureau of Economic Research.
HG203.M57 1988
332.4′56—dc19 87-37387
CIP

Relation of the Directors to the Work and Publications of the National Bureau of Economic Research

1. The object of the National Bureau of Economic Research is to ascertain and to present to the public important economic facts and their interpretation in a scientific and impartial manner. The Board of Directors is charged with the responsibility of ensuring that the work of the National Bureau is carried on in strict conformity with this object.

2. The President of the National Bureau shall submit to the Board of Directors, or to its Executive Committee, for their formal adoption all specific proposals for research to be instituted.

3. No research report shall be published by the National Bureau until the President has sent each member of the Board a notice that a manuscript is recommended for publication and that in the President's opinion it is suitable for publication in accordance with the principles of the National Bureau. Such notification will include an abstract or summary of the manuscript's content and a response form for use by those Directors who desire a copy of the manuscript for review. Each manuscript shall contain a summary drawing attention to the nature and treatment of the problem studied, the character of the data and their utilization in the report, and the main conclusions reached.

4. For each manuscript so submitted, a special committee of the Directors (including Directors Emeriti) shall be appointed by majority agreement of the President and Vice Presidents (or by the Executive Committee in case of inability to decide on the part of the President and Vice Presidents), consisting of three Directors selected as nearly as may be one from each general division of the Board. The names of the special manuscript committee shall be stated to each Director when notice of the proposed publication is submitted to him. It shall be the duty of each member of the special manuscript committee to read the manuscript. If each member of the manuscript committee signifies his approval within thirty days of the transmittal of the manuscript, the report may be published. If at the end of that period any member of the manuscript committee withholds his approval, the President shall then notify each member of the Board, requesting approval or disapproval of publication, and thirty days additional shall be granted for this purpose. The manuscript shall then not be published unless at least a majority of the entire Board who shall have voted on the proposal within the time fixed for the receipt of votes shall have approved.

5. No manuscript may be published, though approved by each member of the special manuscript committee, until forty-five days have elapsed from the transmittal of the report in manuscript form. The interval is allowed for the receipt of any memorandum of dissent or reservation, together with a brief statement of his reasons, that any member may wish to express; and such memorandum of dissent or reservation shall be published with the manuscript if he so desires. Publication does not, however, imply that each member of the Board has read the manuscript, or that either members of the Board in general or the special committee have passed on its validity in every detail.

6. Publications of the National Bureau issued for informational purposes concerning the work of the Bureau and its staff, or issued to inform the public of activities of Bureau staff, and volumes issued as a result of various conferences involving the National Bureau shall contain a specific disclaimer noting that such publication has not passed through the normal review procedures required in this resolution. The Executive Committee of the Board is charged with review of all such publications from time to time to ensure that they do not take on the character of formal research reports of the National Bureau, requiring formal Board approval.

7. Unless otherwise determined by the Board or exempted by the terms of paragraph 6, a copy of this resolution shall be printed in each National Bureau publication.

(Resolution adopted October 25, 1926, as revised through September 30, 1974)

Contents

Preface

This volume presents the proceedings of a conference "The Misalignment of Exchange Rates: Effects on Trade and Industry," sponsored by the National Bureau of Economic Research and held in Cambridge, Massachusetts, on 7–8 May 1987.

I would like to express my appreciation to the authors, discussants, and panel members whose contributions are published here for their participation in the conference and their willingness to keep to a tight publication schedule.

On behalf of the NBER, I would like to thank the Ford Foundation and the Andrew W. Mellon Foundation for providing financial support for the conference. I also thank Debbie Mankiw of the NBER for organizing a second conference in Washington at which many of the papers that appear in this volume were presented to a wider audience of economists, business leaders, and government officials. Kirsten Foss and Ilana Hardesty displayed their usual efficiency, combined with patience and good humor, in making arrangements for both conferences. Finally, I thank Martin Feldstein and Geoffrey Carliner of the NBER for their encouragement and support of this project from its outset.

This volume is dedicated to a long-time research associate of the NBER, Irving Kravis. Irv, who retired this June from his professorship at the University of Pennsylvania, has been an active researcher at the NBER for over thirty years. He has always had a keen interest in issues of international competitivenesss, and has published a series of influential studies, including his NBER study *Price Competitiveness in World Trade* (written jointly with Robert Lipsey), which have set a high standard for empirical research in this area. Irv was unable to participate in the conference because of illness, but his influence on the research published in this volume is pervasive.

Richard C. Marston

Introduction

Richard C. Marston

Economists writing on flexible exchange rates in the 1960s contemplated neither the magnitude nor the persistence of the changes in real exchange rates that have occurred in the last 15 years. Swings in real exchange rates of over 30% have occurred in the case of several currencies. Movements in relative prices of this magnitude lead to sharp changes in exports and imports, disrupting normal trading relationships and causing shifts in employment and output in the export- and import-competing sectors of the countries concerned.

Real disturbances such as the sharp increases in the relative price of oil in 1973–74 and 1978–79 have been responsible for some of these changes in real exchange rates. When real disturbances occur, changes in real exchange rates may play a useful role in facilitating the adjustment of the world economy to such shocks. But many of the largest changes in real exchange rates experienced recently do not represent the equilibrium adjustments of relative prices to real disturbances. Instead, these changes represent the temporary, but sustained, departure of real rates from their long-run equilibrium levels. It is these departures of real exchange rates from equilibrium which we refer to as "misalignment."

Many explanations for misalignment have been suggested by experts. In the case of the dollar's misalignment in the early 1980s, these explanations have ranged from the tight monetary policies instituted after Paul Volcker became Federal Reserve chairman in 1979 or the expansionary fiscal policies of the Reagan administration to the shifts in investor sentiment towards dollar securities attributed to "safe haven" motives or to a speculative "bubble," the latter having been said to occur during the few months leading up to the dollar's peak in February 1985. Misalignment thus may be associated with shifts in monetary policy or financial disturbances which change real exchange rates only because wages and prices are imperfectly flexible in the short run. Or misalignment may be associated with shifts in fiscal policy, which can change real exchange rates even when wages and prices are flexible, if those shifts are unsustainable in the long run, as many experts claimed about the fiscal policies of the Reagan administration.

The papers in this volume address a series of questions concerning misalignment. First, what causes exchange rates to be misaligned, and to what extent are observed movements in real exchange rates attributable to misalignment? The causes of misalignment are investigated both empirically within the context of the experiences of individual countries and theoretically in models of imperfect competition. The second set of questions concerns the effects of misalignment. How severe are these effects on employment and production in the countries concerned? Several of the papers provide detailed estimates of the effects of changes in real exchange rates on individual industries. Note that these estimates are not confined solely to cases of misalignment, since many of the same adjustment costs are incurred in response to real disturbances. Charles Bean, for example, analyzes the effects of sterling's rise in the late 1970s even though the appreciation of sterling was due at least in part to a real disturbance, the discovery of North Sea oil. Several papers ask whether these effects are reversible once exchange rates return to earlier levels, since some economists have contended that there is significant "hysteresis" in the adjustment of employment and production to changes in real exchange rates. Finally, several papers ask how misalignment might be avoided, or at least controlled, by macroeconomic policy. The panel on exchange rate policy also discusses this issue in detail.

In the first paper of the volume, William Branson advances an explanation for the dollar's misalignment in the 1980s that centers on fiscal policy and the associated federal budget deficits. He develops a model that explains the real exchange rate and real interest rate in terms of portfolio behavior and savings-investment behavior. Branson argues that the 1981 budget program of the Reagan administration led to a "crowding out" of foreign demand for U.S. products, as well as private domestic demand. This crowding out occurred through higher real interest rates and an appreciating real exchange rate for the dollar. The resulting current account deficits, however, had to eventually lead to a lower real value for the dollar as foreigners accumulated dollar claims. Branson uses his model to trace out the initial rise in exchange rates and interest rates, as well as the subsequent fall in the exchange rate as dollar claims accumulated. He then examines what happens when fiscal expansion is reversed. He attributes at least part of the recent fall of the dollar to the Gramm-Rudman-Hollings legislation of 1985, which set a timetable for the gradual reduction of the deficit.

Charles Bean investigates the misalignment of the pound sterling and its effects on British trade. In the first part of the paper, he uses a small-scale model of the British economy to study alternative explanations of the appreciation in the real exchange of the pound by 23% between 1978 and 1981. He finds that the discovery of North Sea oil and the subsequent rise in its price as a result of the Iranian revolution can explain 12% of the appreciation. Some of the remaining fraction of the appreciation can be attributed to tight monetary policy, but less than other experts have found. Bean attributes the rest of the appreciation to adverse supply-side factors (which raise domestic prices relative to foreign prices). In the second half of the paper, Bean turns to the question of whether sterling's appreciation may have long-term effects on the British ecomony that persist even after the appreciation has been reversed. Bean searches for evidence of such hysteresis in both demand and supply behavior. On the demand side, for example, temporary appreciations may allow foreign firms to establish a beachhead in a particular market because consumers develop loyalties to particular brands of a product. On the supply side, foreign firms may find it profitable to invest in a distribution network which will remain in place when the appreciation is reversed. Although Bean finds only tentative evidence of such hysteresis, his statistical analysis is interesting in itself from a methodological point of view.

Misalignment may be less of a problem for countries in the European Monetary System (EMS), because countries in the EMS are committed to fixing bilateral exchange rates between member currencies. Paul De Grauwe and Guy Verfaille present evidence showing that this is indeed the case; countries in the EMS have experienced less misalignment than those outside the system. The variability of real effective exchange rates within the EMS, moreover, has been reduced relative to the variability of rates outside the EMS and of rates among the EMS countries before the EMS was founded. Yet trade among EMS members has grown less rapidly since the beginning of the EMS. Trade among non-EMS countries, moreover, has increased twice as fast as that among EMS countries despite the greater exchange rate variability outside the EMS. De Grauwe and Verfaille attempt to explain this growth pattern for trade by estimating a cross-section model of trade flows among EMS and non-EMS members. The results show that low growth in output among EMS countries held down the growth of trade even while lower exchange rate variability had a significant effect in expanding trade among EMS members. The net result was lower trade growth in the EMS. De Grauwe and Verfaille cannot explain the low growth of output itself, however, so the ultimate cause of lower growth in trade remains to be investigated.

The Japanese economy benefited more than any other from the dollar's misalignment, and now that the dollar has fallen relative to the yen, the Japanese economy must bear much of the burden of adjustment. Bonnie Loopesko and Robert Johnson analyze how well that adjustment is proceeding in a wide-ranging study covering such topics as the measurement of equilibrium exchange rates for the yen, the extent of currency pass-through, the adjustment of Japanese trade to price changes, and the effects of Japanese and American fiscal policies on income and trade. The authors review how previous studies have measured equilibrium exchange rates and show why there is so much disagreement among economists about what would constitute an equilibrium exchange rate for the yen. They then ask why more adjustment has not occurred in response to the fall in the yen-dollar rate. They show some tentative evidence that Japan's trade surplus has begun to adjust to the lower dollar, but also show that this adjustment is proceeding more slowly than historical experience would suggest. One reason for the slow pace of trade adjustment, according to Loopesko and Johnson, is that the yen's appreciation has been passed through to export prices less than in the past, and retail prices in Japan have also adjusted much less than the fall in import prices would suggest. They present some interesting econometric evidence suggesting that this pass-through behavior may follow an asymmetric pattern that helps to protect Japanese market shares when the yen appreciates.

Rounding out the first set of papers is a panel on exchange rate policy consisting of Stanley Black, Dale Henderson, and John Williamson. Black begins by reviewing a list of problems associated with the present system and then discusses proposals for reform. He suggests that the most important failing of the present system of floating rates is that it allows a wide divergence in the monetary and fiscal policies of different countries. Yet international policy coordination is difficult to achieve, because governments disagree on objectives and often even employ different models to analyze the effects of policy initiatives on these objectives. He views target zones as an indirect method for achieving coordination, since departures from the zones would signal the need for changes in monetary and fiscal policies (although in a target zone system, these policy changes would not be mandated). Black argues that exchange rates can be managed with a combination of policies including sterilized intervention, at least when intervention is used in support of equilibrium exchange rates.

Dale Henderson reviews arguments for exchange rate policy in the case of four common types of shocks. He points out how difficult it is to identify some shocks even when current interest rates and exchange rates are used to pinpoint their source. According to Henderson, however, it is not difficult to identify the fiscal shock which led to the appreciation of the dollar. Henderson argues that the appreciation of the dollar helped to mitigate the effects of the U.S. fiscal expansion and foreign fiscal contraction which occurred in the early 1980s, and that a policy of fixing the exchange rate would have been "a disaster." He is skeptical about the argument that an international agreement to fix exchange rates would have helped to constrain U.S. fiscal policy or that of any other country.

The third member of the panel, John Williamson, observes that recent trade legislation proposed in the U.S. Congress calls on the president to push for an international agreement on exchange rates. For an international agreement to be successful, experts must be able to identify an equilibrium set of exchange rates which can serve as targets for the system. Williamson cites his earlier work showing how equilibrium rates might be calculated, then describes his more recent research (with Hali Edison and Marcus Miller) where he outlines a system of intermediate targets for international coordination. His proposed system requires that fiscal policies as well as monetary policies be coordinated, an important stipulation for those who believe the dollar's misalignment was largely attributable to fiscal policies.

The panel was followed by four papers examining the causes and effects of misalignment at the industry level. Joshua Aizenman's paper provides an analysis of how prices become misaligned. He specifies a model of overlapping labor contracts which ensures that current monetary shocks lead to the overshooting of exchange rates and to temporary misalignments. The novel feature which he introduces to the labor contract model is an imperfectly competitive goods market in which the prices charged may differ from firm to firm. A monetary shock leads to immediate wage adjustments only for those firms with contracts negotiated in the current period, so the prices charged by firms differ according to the vintage of the labor contract. This model thus can explain the presence of misalignment due to pure monetary shocks, although the duration of the misalignment is limited to the longest labor contract (since once all contracts are renegotiated, the real exchange rate returns to equilibrium). Aizenman also investigates how structural factors such as the degree of substitutability in the goods market can influence misalignment, and how the volatility of real and monetary shocks affects the contract length and therefore the persistence of misalignment.

Louka Katseli investigates one form of imperfect competition where firms choose prices on the basis of partial information about aggregate price movements. Katseli wishes to explain why the response of domestic prices to changes in exchange rates differs depending upon whether these changes occur in small increments or as a large-scale devaluation or revaluation. She specifies a model where an individual firm tries to estimate the aggregate price level on the basis of observing the prices of neighboring firms. When a devaluation occurs, the variance of aggregate price movements increases relative to firm-specific price movements, so any individual firm weights more heavily any price increases that it observes. As a result, the price level as a whole increases more than it would if the same change in the exchange rate occurred in a series of small movements. Katseli then uses Greek data to estimate how the variance of the exchange rate affects the overall inflation rate for Greece. She finds that the exchange rate variance has an influence on inflation quite apart from the direct effect of the rate of depreciation on inflation.

J. David Richardson examines one key industry in the United States where international competition has been steadily increasing, the auto industry. He develops a unique set of disaggregated data to assess how changes in exchange rates, factor costs, and voluntary export restraints have affected recent price competitiveness. Among these series is an "auto"dollar, the effective exchange rate for the dollar obtained by using auto import weights either with or without Canada (with whom the United States has an automobile trade agreement). He then adjusts this auto dollar for changes in relative unit labor costs in the manufacturing sectors of the United States and foreign countries to form a real exchange rate series measuring the relative costs of production. This series shows the United States suffered a marked loss of competitiveness beginning even before the dollar started appreciating in 1981 as unit labor costs rose faster in the United States than in its trading partners. The second part of the paper shows that this trend in relative unit labor costs was not matched by a corresponding change in the relative prices of U.S. and foreign automobiles. In fact, the dollar prices of Japanese automobiles sold in the United States actually rose relative to U.S. auto prices in the early 1980s. Richardson suggests that the voluntary restraint agreements (VRAs) which constrained Japanese sales may account for this price behavior. With quotas on units sold, the Japanese firms raised the yen export prices of cars sold to the United States enough to keep dollar prices rising despite an appreciation of the dollar.

The U.S. manufacturing sector as a whole was hit hard by the dollar's misalignment. William Branson and James Love estimate the effects of changes in the real exchange rate on 20 sectors of manufacturing in the United States. In most sectors, changes in the real exchange rate have significant effects on employment regardless of the period over which the equations are estimated. Branson and Love then use the estimates to calculate the effects of the dollar's misalignment in the period from 1980 to 1985. The misalignment is estimated to have reduced employment in the manufacturing sector by almost a million jobs. In the primary metals and nonelectrical machinery industries, the loss in employment was over 10%. They also estimate separate equations for production workers and other workers in each sector. They calculate that most of the job loss has been sustained by production workers, thus suggesting that manufacturing firms have moved production offshore while maintaining nonproduction staffs in the United States. They speculate that this pattern of employment loss may not be easily reversed now that the dollar has depreciated from its previous highs.

Paul Krugman's paper investigates three possible long-run consequences of a strong dollar. First, the current account deficits of the Reagan years have led to an accumulation of dollar debt that must be serviced. But Krugman argues that the burden of servicing this debt should be quite manageable (on the order of $10 billion/year) as long as foreigners are willing to maintain a fixed ratio of dollar debt to GNP. (In that case, the current account need not be balanced, but the growth of nominal debt is limited by the growth of nominal GNP.) The buildup of debt would pose serious problems only if foreigners insisted on significantly reducing their holdings of dollar securities. The second long-run consequence of a strong dollar is the reallocation of capital from the tradables to nontradables sectors. If a strong dollar causes a shift of investment from the tradables sector to the nontradables sector, this may require a corresponding depreciation for the movement to be reversed. Krugman finds, however, that there is little evidence of a decline in investment in manufacturing over this period, perhaps because there was increased military spending and an improvement in investment incentives due to the new tax law. Krugman also investigates whether the sustained appreciation has induced foreign firms to undertake fixed investment in marketing and distribution which may lead to permanent beachheads in the American market. Krugman estimates export and import demand equations to determine if there is any evidence of such irreversible changes in the markets for these products, but finds no such evidence. Thus he reaches the tentative conclusion that the dollar's appreciation has caused less long-term damage to U.S. industry (though not necessarily to U.S. employment) than was originally feared.

In a commentary on new directions for research, Rudiger Dornbusch identifies three areas where research on exchange rates might prove fruitful. The first is the application of imperfect competition models to the question of exchange rate pass-through. Dornbusch uses Salop's circle model to examine how domestic and foreign prices respond when domestic currency depreciations raise the local costs of foreign firms. He then applies Pindyck's irreversible investment model to issues of labor demand and investment in response to changes in real exchange rates. Finally, he sketches a model of exchange rate overshooting where current changes in the money supply are extrapolated into the future by private agents. It is hoped that this volume will help to stimulate further research on exchange rates along these and other lines.

1 Sources of Misalignment in the 1980s

William H. Branson

1.1 Introduction and Summary

The prolonged appreciation of the dollar that ended in early 1985 began in the spring of 1981. The data for the real effective foreign exchange value of the dollar (e) and the real long-term interest rate (r) are shown in figures 1.3 and 1.7 below. From the fourth quarter of 1980 to the fourth quarter of 1981, the real long-term interest rate rose from 1.3 to 8.3% and the dollar appreciated by 13% in real effective terms. Since then, long-term real interest rates have remained in the range of 5–10%. The dollar appreciated further in a series of steps, reaching a peak in early 1985 with a real appreciation of about 55% relative to 1980. It has declined by about 25% since then (as of December 1986), but remains 23% above its 1980 level. In this paper I lay out the argument that the rise in real interest rates and the dollar were largely due to the budget program that was announced in March 1981 and was subsequently executed. In particular, the shift in the high-employment—or "structural," as the responsible parties have taken to calling it—deficit by some $200 billion requires an increase in real interest rates and a real appreciation to generate the sum of excess domestic saving and a current account deficit to finance it. The argument is a straightforward extension of the idea of "crowding out" at full employment to an open economy. The decline in real interest rates and the dollar since mid-1985 has coincided with the passage of the Gramm-Rudman-Hollings (GRH) Act, which predicts with perhaps limited credibility the closure of the structural deficit. The evidence, it will turn out, is

William H. Branson is professor of economics and international affairs at Princeton University and director of the Program in International Studies and research associate of the National Bureau of Economic Research.

clear. The expansionary shift in the structural deficit pushed real interest rates and the dollar up; closing the deficit will bring them down.

The current situation of mid-1987, with a continuing structural deficit estimated by the Congressional Budget Office to be $175 billion, or 4% of GNP, is not sustainable, however. It is a "temporary equilibrium," to use the jargon of macroeconomic dynamics. If the deficit is not eliminated, eventually international investors will begin to resist further absorption of dollars into their portfolios, so U.S. interest rates would have to rise again, and the dollar will have to depreciate. This process may have begun as early as mid-1985. It will continue until the current account is back in approximate balance, and the entire load of deficit financing is shifted to excess U.S. saving. This paper describes the links from shifts in the structural deficit to real interest rates and the real exchange rate, and the dynamic mechanism that will bring the dollar back down again.

The present paper draws heavily on Branson, Fraga, and Johnson (1986) for analysis of the effects of the 1981 budget program. The technical details of the analysis are given there; here I simply lay out the logic and the implications for policy. Sections 1.2 and 1.3 of the paper present the "fundamentals" framework of the analysis. These sections draw on the discussion in Branson (1985a). The framework is fundamental in the sense that it emphasizes the variables, such as the high-employment deficit or the oil price, that the market should look to when it is forming expectations about movements in interest rates or the exchange rate. The focus is on real interest rates and the real (effective) exchange rate; these are the variables whose movements have been surprising. The argument that the shift in the budget can explain the rise in real interest rates and the dollar is presented in these two sections.

The role of expectations and the timing of the jump in interest rates and the dollar is discussed in section 1.4. The Economic Recovery Tax Act of 1981 provided a credible announcement of a future expansion in the high-employment budget deficit. The financial markets reacted by raising interest rates and the dollar well in advance of the actual fiscal shift, contributing to the recession of 1981–82. The Gramm-Rudman-Hollings legislation of 1985 announced a future contraction of the deficit. The markets reacted with a reduction of real interest rates and the dollar, again well in advance of the actual fiscal shift.

Finally, in section 1.5, I summarize recent econometric evidence, presented by Martin Feldstein (1986), that the shift in the structural budget deficit in the United States indeed explains the real appreciation of the dollar, leaving little room for the alternative explanations. Feldstein's econometrics for the exchange rate between the dollar and the

German deutsche mark show insignificant effects of the German budget position, so I will stick with a simple model of the U.S. economy here.

1.2 Short-Run Equilibrium in a Fundamentals Framework

A good start for my discussion of the causes of the movements of the dollar in the 1980s is exposition of a framework that describes the determination of movements in real interest rates and the real exchange rate. The focus is on real interest rates, because these have been the source of surprise and concern. If nominal interest rates had simply followed the path of expected or realized inflation and the exchange rate had followed the path of relative prices, the world would be perceived to be in order. It is the movement of interest rates and the exchange rate relative to the price path that is of interest here. So I begin by taking the actual and expected path of prices as given, perhaps determined by monetary policy, and I focus on real interest rates and the real exchange rate.

In this section I develop a framework that integrates goods markets and asset markets to describe simultaneous determination of the interest rate and the exchange rate. It is "short run" in the sense that I take existing stock of assets as given. Movement in these stocks will provide the dynamics of section 1.3. It is a fundamentals framework because it focuses on the underlying macroeconomic determinants of movements in rates, about which the market will form expectations. The latter are discussed in section 1.4. The framework is useful because it permits us to distinguish between external events such as shifts in the budget position (the deficit), shifts in international asset demands (the "safe haven effect"), and changes in tax law or financial regulation by analyzing their differing implications for movements in the interest rate and the exchange rate. It also permits me to analyze the effects of exogenous shifts in the current account balance due to savings in the oil price on exchange rates and interest rates. This will be useful in discussing the effect of the fall in the oil price on the yen after mid-1985. I begin with the national income, or flow-of-funds, identity that constrains flows in the economy, then turn to the asset-market equilibrium that constrains rates of return, and finally bring the two together in figure 1.1.

1.2.1 Flow Equilibrium: The National Income Identity

The national income identity that constrains flows in the economy is generally written as $Y = C + I + G + X = C + S + T$, with the usual meanings of the symbols, as summarized in table 1.1. Note here that for simplicity X stands for net exports of goods and services, the

Table 1.1 Definitions of Symbols

Symbol	Definition
National Income Flows (all in real terms)	
Y	= GNP
C	= Consumer expenditure
I	= Gross private domestic investment
G	= Government purchases of goods and services
X	= Net exports of goods and services, or the current account balance
S	= Gross private domestic saving
T	= Tax revenue
NFI	= Net foreign investment by the United States
NFB	= Net foreign borrowing = $-NFI$
Prices and Stocks	
r	= Real domestic interest rate
i	= Nominal domestic interest rate
r^*	= Real foreign interest rate
i^*	= Nominal foreign interest rate
e	= Real effective exchange rate (units of foreign exchange per dollar); an increase in e is an appreciation of the dollar
$\hat{e}$	= Expected rate of change of e
$\hat{P}$	= Expected rate of inflation
ρ	= Risk premium on dollar-denominated bonds
B	= Outstanding stock of government debt

current account balance. All flows are in real terms. We can subtract consumer expenditure C from both sides of the right-hand equality and do some rearranging to obtain a useful version of the flow-of-funds identity:

$$G - T = (S - I) - X. \tag{1}$$

In terms of national income and product flows, equation (1) says the total (federal, state, and local) government deficit must equal the sum of the excess of domestic private saving over investment less net exports.

Let us now think of equation (1) as holding at a standardized high-employment level of output, in order to exclude cyclical effects from the discussion. This allows us to focus on shifts in the budget at a given level of income. A deficit or surplus in this high-employment budget has come to be called the "structural" deficit in the 1980s. The OECD also calls it the "cyclically-adjusted" budget deficit. From here on I will refer to it as the "structural budget."

If we take a shift in this structural deficit $(G - T)$ as external, or exogenous to the economy, equation (1) emphasizes that this shift requires some endogenous adjustment to excess private saving $(S - I)$ and the current account X to balance the flows in income and product. In particular, if $(G - T)$ is increased by \$200 billion, roughly the actual increase in the structural deficit after 1981, a combination of an increase in $S - I$ and a decrease in X that also totals \$200 billion is required.

Standard macroeconomic theory tells us that for a given level of income, $(S - I)$ depends positively on the real interest rate r, and X depends negatively on the real exchange rate e (units of foreign exchange per dollar, adjusted for relative price levels).[1] So the endogenous adjustments that would increase $S - I$ and reduce X are an increase in r and in e. Some combination of these changes would restore balance in equation (1), given an increase in $G - T$.

We can relate this national income view of the short-run adjustment mechanism to the more popular story involving foreign borrowing and capital flows by noting that net exports X is also net national foreign investment from the balance of payments identity. Since national net foreign investment is minus national net foreign borrowing (NFB), so that $X = NFI = -NFB$, the flow-of-funds equation (1) can also be written as

$$(2) \qquad (G - T) = (S - I) - NFI = (S - I) + NFB.$$

This form of the identity emphasizes that an increase in the deficit must be financed either by an increase in excess domestic saving or an increase in net foreign borrowing (decrease in net foreign investment). One way to interpret the adjustment mechanism is that the shift in the deficit raises U.S. interest rates, increasing $S - I$. The high rates attract foreign capital or lead to a reduction in U.S. lending abroad, appreciating the dollar, that is, raising e. This process continues, with r and e increasing, until the increase in $S - I$ and the decrease in X add up to the originating shift in the deficit.

The actual movements in the government deficit, net domestic saving $(S - I)$, and net foreign borrowing, and the associated movements in the real long-term rate r and the real exchange rate e (indexed to 1985 = 100) are shown in table 1.2. The combined federal, state, and local deficit was roughly zero at the beginning of 1981. It expanded to a peak of \$167 billion in the bottom of the recession in the fourth quarter of 1982 and then shrank in the recovery. But the shift in the federal budget position left the total government deficit at \$155 billion at the end of 1985, after three years of recovery. Initially the deficit was financed mainly by net domestic saving, which also peaked at the bottom of the recession. But since 1982 the fraction financed by net foreign borrowing has risen; by the end of 1985 nearly all of the government deficit was financed by foreign borrowing.

The movements in the real interest rate and the real exchange rate roughly reflect this pattern of financing. The real interest rate jumped from around 2.0% to over 8% in 1981, fell during the recession, and rose in the recovery, staying in the 5–10% range since mid-1983. The

Table 1.2 **Savings and Investment Flows, Interest Rates, and Exchange Rates, United States, 1979:I–1986:II (Billions of Dollars Unless Otherwise Specified)**

Period	Net Foreign Investment[a]	Excess Domestic Savings[b]	Total Budget Surplus[c]	Federal Budget Surplus (% of GNP)	Real Interest Rate for 20-Year Treasury Bonds (%)[d]	Real Exchange Rate Index (Jan 85 = 100)[e]
1979:I	5.8	−15.0	20.7	−0.4	−1.3	62.7
1979:II	−1.9	−20.6	18.6	−0.2	−5.4	64.0
1979:III	4.5	−3.6	8.1	−0.8	−4.8	62.8
1979:IV	−2.6	−1.1	−1.4	−1.1	−2.0	63.6
1980:I	0.1	12.3	−12.1	−1.4	−4.7	65.4
1980:II	12.1	54.2	−41.9	−2.4	−4.7	64.3
1980:III	27.9	76.5	−48.6	−2.7	3.2	63.7
1980:IV	6.7	42.2	−35.5	−2.4	1.3	65.7
1981:I	16.3	30.9	−14.6	−1.6	1.7	69.1
1981:II	4.9	19.7	−14.8	−1.6	3.9	73.5
1981:III	5.5	31.7	−26.2	−2.0	2.6	77.2
1981:IV	11.2	74.2	−63.0	−3.1	8.3	74.4
1982:I	7.3	83.3	−76.0	−3.5	10.9	77.7
1982:II	16.5	94.3	−77.7	−3.6	7.5	79.4
1982:III	−12.3	110.3	−122.5	−5.0	5.2	83.4
1982:IV	−15.4	151.4	−166.8	−6.3	9.9	83.3
1983:I	−2.1	147.2	−149.2	−5.7	11.1	82.5
1983:II	−27.7	98.3	−126.0	−5.1	5.7	84.4
1983:III	−46.7	79.5	−126.2	−5.1	6.9	87.7
1983:IV	−57.4	55.5	−112.9	−4.8	8.4	88.1
1984:I	−73.7	13.8	−87.5	−4.2	7.7	88.3
1984:II	−92.1	1.9	−93.9	−4.4	8.7	90.1
1984:III	−92.7	12.0	−104.8	−4.5	8.5	95.0
1984:IV	−104.3	15.7	−119.9	−4.9	8.8	98.2
1985:I	−83.8	12.8	−96.6	−4.1	9.1	100.8
1985:II	−112.0	43.6	−155.6	−5.4	6.3	98.8
1985:III	−121.2	16.7	−138.0	−4.9	7.8	92.9
1985:IV	−143.8	11.3	−155.1	−5.3	6.6	88.5
1986:I	−128.6	−3.6	−121.5	−4.7	7.9	83.6
1986:II	−143.0	30.3	−173.3	−5.6	8.6	80.9

[a]Net foreign investment in the national income accounts summed with the national capital grants received by the United States.

[b]Gross private domestic savings minus gross private domestic investment, adjusted for statistical discrepancy.

[c]Combined federal, state, and local government budget deficits.

[d]Twenty-year Treasury bond yield less current CPI inflation.

[e]Feldstein and Bacchetta (1987).

real effective exchange rate shows an initial rise of about 13% in 1981, a more gradual increase beginning in early 1982, and an acceleration in 1984. The standard lags in adjustment of net exports to changes in the exchange rate can explain the slow reaction of net exports (net foreign borrowing) to the dollar appreciation.

The data in table 1.2 are consistent with the story of maintenance of the flow-of-funds equilibrium in equation (1), with one big exception and one major loose end. The exception is that interest rates and exchange rates jumped in 1981, while the structural deficit only began actually to emerge in 1982. Below in section 1.4 I argue that this reflects the market's anticipation of the shift in the budget. The loose end is that nothing has been said about what determines the precise mix or combination of rise in r and e that achieves short-run equilibrium. For this we turn to the financial markets.

1.2.2 Financial Market Equilibrium and the Rate of Return

We can obtain a relationship between the real interest rate r and the real exchange rate e that is imposed by financial market equilibrium by considering the returns that a representative U.S. asset holder obtains on domestic and foreign assets of the same maturity. The real interest rate on domestic assets r is the nominal interest rate i less the expected rate of inflation $\hat{P}$. The latter is taken here to be exogenous. The real exchange rate e is defined as the nominal rate E times the ratio of home price level P to the foreign price level P^*: $e = \frac{E\,P}{P^*}$. This means that changes in the real exchange rate are given by

$$(3) \qquad \hat{e} = \hat{E} + \hat{P} - \hat{P}^* .$$

Now we can define the real return on the domestic asset as r. The return, from the U.S. investor's point of view, on the foreign asset is the foreign nominal interest rate less expected depreciation $i^* - \hat{E}$ in nominal terms, and $i^* - \hat{E} - \hat{P}$, or $i^* - (\hat{E} + \hat{P})$, in real terms. From equation (3), this foreign real return is also given by $i^* - \hat{P}^* - \hat{e}$, or $r^* - \hat{e}$, where r^* is the foreign real interest rate. So from the representative U.S. investor's point of view, the real return on a U.S. asset is r, and on a foreign asset is $r^* - \hat{e}$. In equilibrium, the difference between the two real returns must be equal to the market-determined risk premium $\rho(B)$ on dollar assets. Here we assume that dollar-denominated bonds are imperfect substitutes for foreign-exchange-denominated bonds, so that the risk premium on dollar bonds increases with their supply: $\rho'(B) > 0$. The equilibrium condition for rates of return in real terms is then

$$(4) \qquad r - (r^* - \hat{e}) = \rho(B).$$

Next we need to relate the expected rate of change of the exchange rate to the actual current rate. If we denote the perceived long-run equilibrium real exchange rate that sets the full-employment current account balance at zero as $\bar{e}$, one reasonable assumption is that the current rate is expected to return gradually toward long-run equilibrium. This assumption can be written as a proportional adjustment mechanism:

$$\hat{e} = \theta(\bar{e} - e). \tag{5}$$

If e is below the long-run equilibrium, it is expected to rise, and vice versa. If we put this expression for $\hat{e}$ into the equilibrium condition (4) and rearrange a bit, we obtain the financial-market equilibrium relationship between e and r:

$$e = \bar{e} + \frac{1}{\theta}(r - r^* - \rho(B)). \tag{6}$$

This condition says that for given values of the bond stock B, the foreign real interest rate r^*, and the long-run equilibrium real exchange rate $\bar{e}$, an increase in r requires an increase in e to maintain equilibrium in financial markets. Why? If the U.S. interest rate rises, equilibrium can be maintained for a given foreign rate only if the dollar is expected to fall. From equation (6), this means that the actual current rate must rise to establish $\hat{e} < 0$. In terms of how the market works, the rise in the domestic real rate r causes sales of foreign assets and purchases of dollar assets. This in turn raises e until equilibrium is reestablished. This is essentially what happened in 1981 with the announcement of a path of future deficits. This did not substantially change the long-run e that would balance the current account, but it did move r and e.

1.2.3 Interest Rates and the Exchange Rate

We can now join the flow equilibrium condition, equation (1), and the rate-of-return condition, equation (6), to form the short-run framework for simultaneous determination of r and e. Let us rewrite equation (1) to show the dependence of S and I on r, and of X on e and a shift parameter α, which represents exogenous improvements in the trade balance due to events like a fall in the oil price:

$$G - T = S(r) - I(r) - X(e, \alpha). \tag{7}$$

For a given level of the full-employment budget, the trade-off between r and e that maintains flow equilibrium is given by the negatively sloped IX curve in figure 1.2.[2] For a given $G - T$, an increase in r, which increases $(S - I)$, requires a reduction in e, which increases X, to maintain flow equilibrium. An increase in $G - T$ or in α will shift the

IX curve up or to the right, requiring some combination of a rise in *r* and *e* to maintain flow equilibrium.

The rate-of-return condition (6) gives us the positively sloped *FM* curve in figure 1.1, for given *B*, r^*, and $\bar{e}$. Its slope is θ, the speed-of-adjustment parameter for expectations. An increase in the risk premium ρ, due to a rise in the supply of U.S. bonds *B*, will shift the *FM* curve up and to the left, requiring an increase in *r* for any given value of *e*.

In the short run, equilibrium *r* and *e* are reached at the intersection of the *IX* and *FM* curves in figure 1.1; there both equilibrium conditions are met. For the purposes of the analysis here, we assume that initially $e = \bar{e}$, with no expected movement in exchange rates. This is taken to represent the equilibrium around 1980, before the surge in interest rates and the exchange rate that I explain using the model of figure 1.1.

1.2.4 Effects of a Shift in the Budget

A shift in the structural budget towards deficit shifts the *IX* curve up, as shown in figure 1.2. The real interest rate and the real exchange rate rise, as described earlier. The composition of these movements is determined by the slope of the *FM* curve, representing financial market equilibrium. The movement of *r* and *e* from E_0 to E_1 raises excess domestic saving ($S - I$) and reduces net exports *X* by a sum equal to the shift in $G - T$. This also produces the short-run equilibrium financing of the shift in the deficit by domestic saving and foreign borrowing. The results of the shift in $G - T$ are the movements in excess domestic saving and foreign borrowing, and in *r* and *e*, that are shown in table 1.2. Thus the framework of figure 1.2 roughly captures the movements of *r* and *e* from 1981 to 1985.

The Gramm-Rudman-Hollings legislation of 1985, if effective, would have shifted the *IX* curve in figure 1.2 back down. By eventually re-

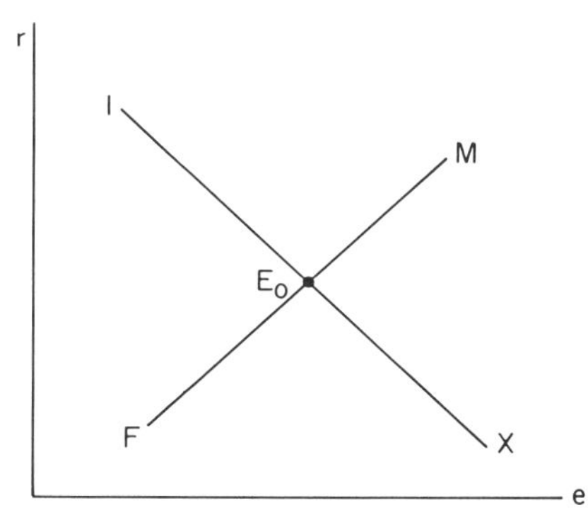

Fig. 1.1 Equilibrium *r* and *e*.

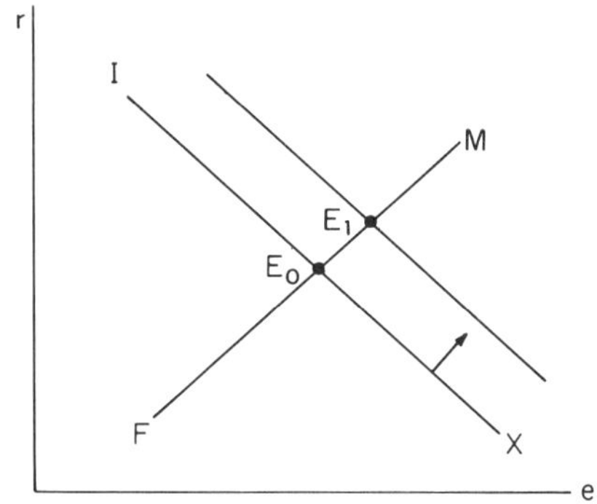

Fig. 1.2 Shift in the structural deficit.

ducing the structural deficit, it would create room in the high-employment economy for an increase in investment and net exports. This would be generated by a fall in *r* and *e* along the *FM* line in figure 1.2 as *IX* shifts down. This could explain some of the fall in *r* and *e* since mid-1985.

1.2.5 Extension to Several Countries

The short-run model presented here can be extended easily to a several-country setting. Good examples are the models of Krugman (1985) and McKibbin and Sachs (1986). In their models the effect on the exchange rate is dictated by the relative fiscal shift, while the effect in the real interest rate depends on world saving versus investment. An increase in the U.S. structural deficit relative to that in Europe or Japan would generate appreciation of the dollar against the ECU or the yen.

The movements in the structural budgets since 1981 are shown in table 1.3 for the major OECD countries. The others among the major six are Canada, France, Italy, and the United Kingdom. The numbers

Table 1.3 **Change in Structural Budget Balance (As Percentage of Nominal GDP)**

	1981	1982	1983	1984	1985	1986
United States	+0.9	−1.0	−0.8	−0.7	−0.5	−0.2
Japan	+0.6	+0.4	+0.6	+0.5	+1.0	+0.9
Germany	+0.1	+1.4	+1.2	+0.4	+0.5	0.0
Average of major six, excluding U.S.	+0.2	+0.6	+0.3	+0.2	+0.5	+0.4

Source: OECD Economic Outlook, December 1984, June 1985.

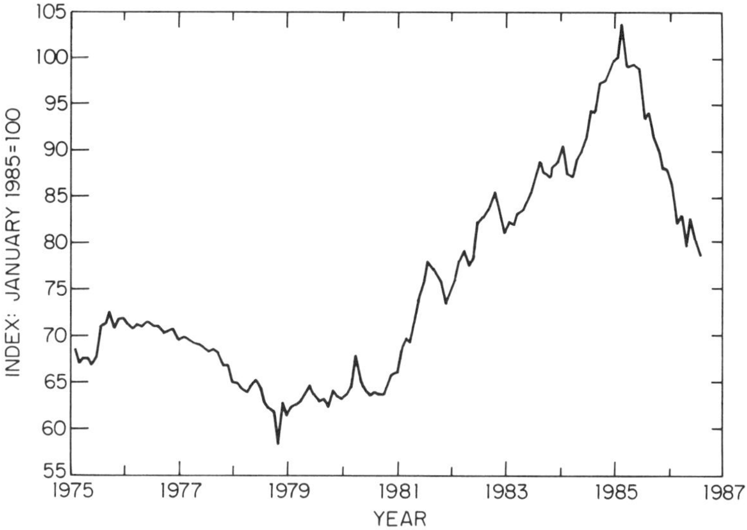

Fig. 1.3 Real trade-weighted exchange rate. Source: Feldstein and Bacchetta (1987).

in the table give the change in the structural surplus as a percentage of GDP each year. So the table shows the U.S. structural deficit increasing each year from 1982 to 1986 and the German and Japanese structural deficits decreasing each year. The fact that the positive entries for the average for the major six are smaller than for Germany and Japan implies that on average the other four had increasing structural deficits. In a sense, the true picture is Japan and Germany tightening and everyone else easing, led by the United States.

These fiscal shifts caused the real appreciation of the dollar shown in figures 1.3 and 1.4. Figure 1.3 is the effective dollar rate across 80 countries calculated by Feldstein and Bacchetta (1987).[3] Up is real appreciation of the dollar. In effective real terms, in figure 1.3 the dollar appreciated by about 55% from late 1980 to mid-1985. Figure 1.4 is the real dollar-yen exchange rate, taken from IMF data (*IFS* data tape). Again up is appreciation of the dollar. There we see the appreciation of the dollar by approximately 30% from 1980 to 1985. The movement of the real exchange rate makes room in equation (1) for the fiscal shift by decreasing X, making it negative in the U.S. case and increasing it in Japan.

The rapid appreciation of the yen against the dollar since the beginning of 1985 is in part due to the fall in the oil price. If we interpret for a moment figure 1.2 as representing Japan, a fall in the oil price increases $X(e, \alpha)$ and shifts the IX curve up. To maintain aggregate

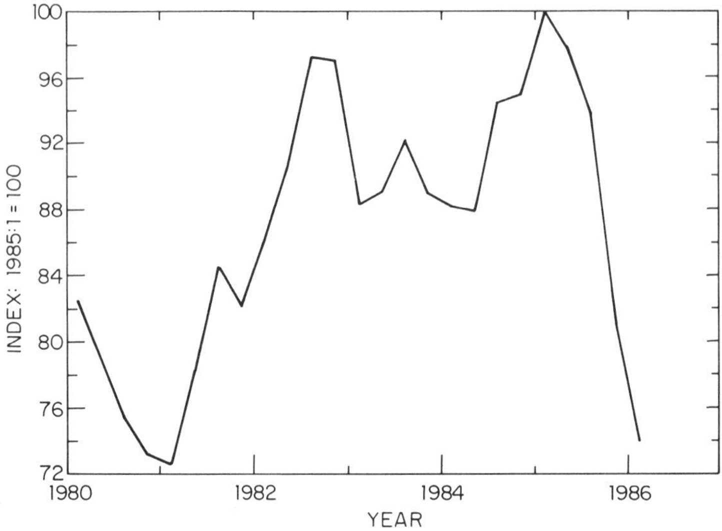

Fig. 1.4 Real dollar-yen exchange rate (up is dollar appreciation). Source: IFS data tape.

demand equal to full-employment output, the real interest rate in Japan should rise and the yen should appreciate.

The extensions to several countries show the importance of relative fiscal shifts for movements in the real exchange rate. But the results do not contradict the simple one-country model of figure 1.2, as long as we remember that it shows the effects of a fiscal shift in the United States relative to abroad. So for most of the paper I will stick with the simpler single-country version of the model.

1.3 Dynamic Adjustment to Long-Run Equilibrium

In figure 1.2, point E_0 is taken to represent the initial equilibrium of 1980, before the shift in the structural deficit, and point E_1 represents the economy in 1984 or 1985, after the full shift in the budget was completed. The next question that arises is: is the equilibrium E_1 sustainable in the absence of further legislation eliminating the deficit? The short answer is no. This takes us to the dynamics of debt accumulation.

1.3.1 Effects of a Continuing Deficit

At point E_1 in figure 1.2, the economy is running a substantial current account deficit, perhaps \$150 billion at the end of 1986. This adds, on balance, that amount each year to the holdings of dollar-denominated assets in international portfolios. Either the United States is borrowing abroad to finance partially the budget deficit, or it is reducing its lending as U.S. asset holders shift into government debt. In either case, the net foreign position in dollar-denominated assets is growing. This will lead eventually to international resistance to the absorption of further increases in dollar-denominated assets and to a rise in U.S. interest rates and the exchange rate.

At any given set of interest rates and exchange rates such as point E_1 in figure 1.2, international investors will have some desired distribution of their portfolio demands across currencies. This will depend, of course, on a whole array of expectations as well as current market prices. As the U.S. current account deficit adds dollars to these portfolios from the supply side, this disturbs the initial portfolio balance, shifting the distribution towards dollar assets. In order to induce investors to hold the additional dollar assets, either U.S. interest rates have to rise or the dollar must fall, thus offering investors a higher expected rate of return on dollars. As the dollar depreciates, the current account deficit will shrink. As the deficit shrinks, the rate at which international portfolio distributions are changing is reduced, and so is the rate at which the dollar depreciates. Eventually the economy returns to a long-run equilibrium where the current account is again balanced, and excess domestic saving finances the budget deficit. The dynamics of this adjustment mechanism in a fundamentals model were described in detail in Branson (1977); the version with a rational expectations overlay is given in Branson (1983).

This adjustment mechanism has a straightforward interpretation in the fundamentals framework of section 1.2. Consider the position of the economy at point E_1, reproduced in figure 1.5. Remember that $\bar{e}_0$ was the initial value of the real exchange rate that produced current account balance. At point E_1, the current account is in deficit, and dollar-denominated debt in international portfolios is increasing. This

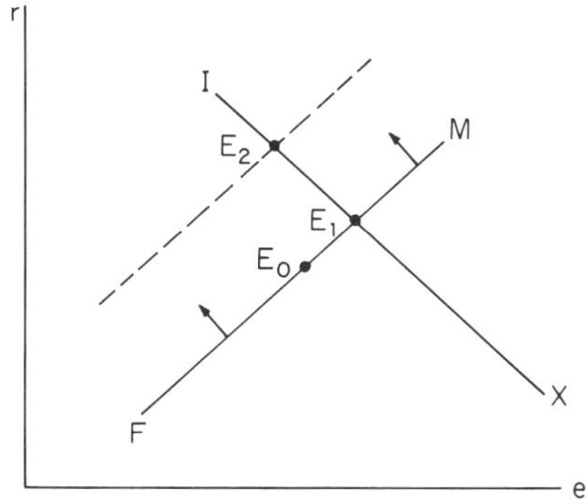

Fig. 1.5 Accumulation of dollar-denominated debt.

tends to raise the equilibrium U.S. interest rate *r* and reduce the exchange rate *e*. In figure 1.5 this is captured by a continuing upward drift in the *FM* curve. In equation (5) for rate-of-return equilibrium, the bond stock *B* is growing. This raises the risk premium, shifting *FM* up.[4] As *FM* shifts up, driven by the current account deficit, the interest rate rises and the exchange rate falls along *IX*. This movement continues until the current balance is again roughly zero, at point E_2 in figure 1.5. There the real interest rate has risen enough that $S - I = G - T$ at high employment.

If most of the increase in $S - I$ has come from a reduction in investment, the E_2 equilibrium will have a significantly lower growth path than the original E_0 equilibrium. Through the shift in the budget, the economy will have traded an increase in consumption (including defense) for a reduction in investment. The point E_2 in figure 1.5 has an exchange rate below $\bar{e}_0$, suggesting that in the new equilibrium the dollar will have depreciated in real terms relative to its initial 1980 position. Why? In the transition from E_1 to E_2, the United States is running a substantial current account deficit. This will reduce the U.S. international investment position. In fact, it is shifting this position from net creditor to net debtor. The consequence of this shift in the international credit position of the United States is a reduction in the investment income item in the current account. The former positive flow of investment income has become a negative flow of debt service.

At the original E_0 equilibrium, with a surplus on investment income and the service account, the current account balanced with a trade deficit. The deficit on trade in goods offset the surplus in services. But at the new E_2 equilibrium, the service account will be in deficit, requiring a trade surplus to produce current account balance. The real exchange rate at E_2 will have to be lower than at E_0 to produce the required shift in the trade balance from deficit to surplus. It should be clear that the result does not depend on the investment income account actually becoming negative. A series of current account deficits that reduce the investment income surplus would lead to a new equilibrium with a smaller trade deficit and therefore a higher value for *e*. This consequence of the dynamic adjustment through current account imbalance was discussed in Branson (1977).

1.3.2 Closing the Deficit: Gramm-Rudman-Hollings

How do we fit the Gramm-Rudman-Hollings (GRH) legislation that would, if effective, close the deficit by 1992 into the dynamic model? To see the answer, let us assume that GRH takes the *IX* curve back to its original I_0X_0 position of figure 1.2, running through the original equilibrium E_0. Will the economy then go back to that initial equilibrium? The answer is no. The accumulation of U.S. government debt and the shift in the U.S. international position from lender to borrower

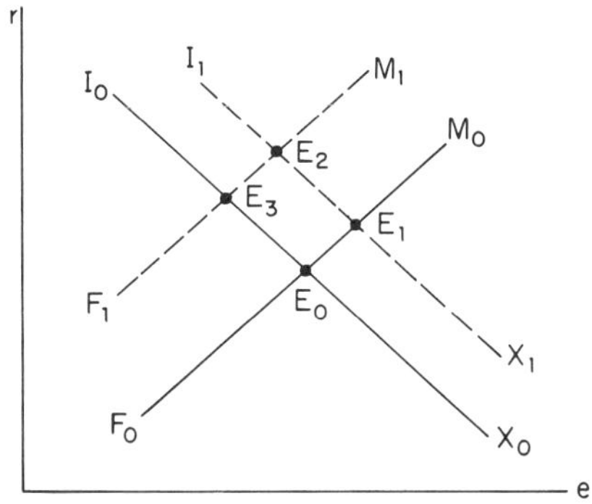

Fig. 1.6 Eventual reduction of the deficit.

has shifted the *FM* curve up, so the economy cannot return to the original equilibrium.

This result is shown in figure 1.6. The *IX* curve is back at its original I_0X_0 position of figure 1.2, but the debt accumulation has increased the risk premium $\rho(B)$ in equation (5), shifting the *FM* curve up to F_1M_1. So the new equilibrium with the budget deficit finally eliminated is at E_3, with a higher real interest rate and lower value for the dollar than at E_0. The higher real interest rate is due to the increased risk premium, and the lower value of the dollar is needed to produce the trade surplus needed to pay for U.S. debt service.

The reversal of the movement of the dollar that began in spring 1985 reflects a mixture of portfolio resistance, represented by movement from E_1 toward E_2 in figures 1.5 and 1.6, supplemented by GRH, which would push the equilibrium toward E_3. The dollar peaked in early 1985 and has fallen by about 25% in real terms since then (up to December 1986). Real interest rates have remained around 5%, which could be represented by a movement from E_1 to E_3 in figure 1.6. In addition, the mix of financing of the current account deficit has shifted from U.S. foreign borrowing towards a reduction in U.S. bank lending abroad. This may signal the rise in foreign resistance to further lending in dollars. So there is some evidence that the movement from equilibrium E_1 toward E_2 began in 1985, and that passage of GRH moved the equilibrium along to an eventual E_3. The long-run equilibrium with a shift in the U.S. international position from lender to borrower will require that the real interest rate in the United States be higher and the real value of the dollar lower than in the original equilibrium of 1980. This is the comparison of E_3 to E_0 in figure 1.6.

1.4 Expectations and Timing

Sections 1.2 and 1.3 of this paper presented the fundamentals framework for analyzing the determinants of movements in real interest rates and the exchange rate, both in a short run with asset stocks fixed and in a longer run in which the budget and the current account gradually change the country's international investment position. This framework suggests that agents in financial markets should form expectations about the exogenous variables that move the *IX* and *FM* curves—the flow and stock equilibrium loci—in order to anticipate movements in real interest rates and the exchange rate. The timing of the jump in these variables in 1981 and again in 1985 suggests that this is indeed the case.

The Economic Recovery Tax Act of 1981 had one particular aspect that is unusually useful for macroeconomic analysis. It provided an example of a clear-cut and credible announcement of future policy actions at specified dates. A three-stage tax cut was announced in the Tax Act in March 1981. Simultaneously, a multistage buildup in defense spending was announced. This implied a program of future structural deficits, beginning late in 1982. The fundamentals framework tells us that this would begin a process which starts with the *IX* curve shifting up, to E_1 in figures 1.2 and 1.5 causing a rise in real interest rates and appreciation of the dollar. It then continues with a current account deficit, a further rise in interest rates, and a real depreciation of the dollar toward a new long-run equilibrium E_2. If the budget deficit is eventually closed, the equilibrium would move further to E_3 in figure 1.6. The initial movement to E_1 is more certain than the eventual convergence to E_2 or E_3. If the tax changes were enacted when they were announced, British style, we would expect to see the jump in real interest rates and the exchange rate come on the heels of the tax changes.

But in the U.S. case, the 1981 announcement implied a forecast of a growing high-employment deficit beginning in 1982. During the period from March to June of 1981, projections of the likely structural deficit emerged from sources such as Data Resources, Inc., and Chase Econometrics and circulated through Washington and the financial community. This meant that the financial markets could look ahead to the shift in the budget (and the *IX* curve) and anticipate its implications for bond prices and interest rates.

The expected emergence of a persistent structural deficit provided a prediction that real long-term interest rates would rise (moving from E_0 to E_1 in figure 1.2), and bond prices fall. Once that expectation took hold in the market, the usual dynamics of asset prices tells us that long rates should rise immediately, in anticipation of the future shift in the budget. Indeed, in the early fall of 1981 the long rate moved above the short rate, and has remained there since, through recession and recovery. This is consistent with the bond market anticipating the movement not only to E_1 as the budget shifts but also toward E_2 as the effects

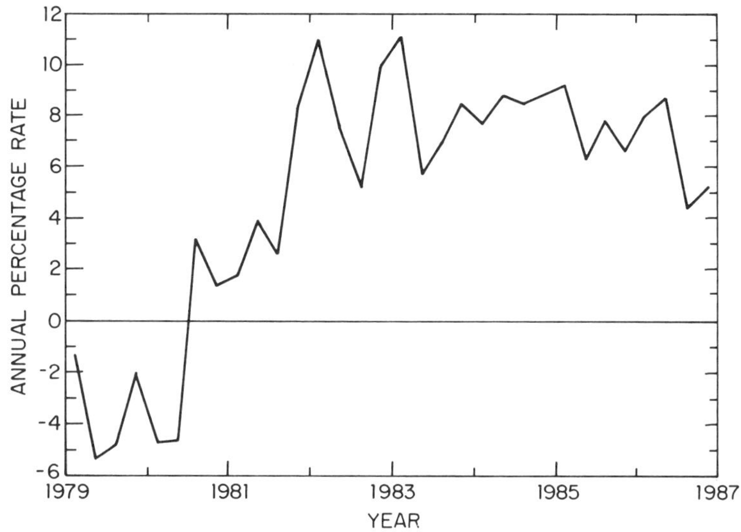

Fig. 1.7 Real long-term bond rate. 20-year Treasury bond less CPI inflation.

of debt accumulation are felt. In 1981, legislation closing the deficit was over the horizon.

The markets could also anticipate an appreciation of the dollar, that is, the rise in e from E_0 to E_1 in figures 1.2 and 1.5, as the structural deficit emerged. This expectation could have been derived from national income reasoning or from thinking about capital movements. One could ask the series of questions: (1) What will have to be crowded out to make room for the deficit? Answer: investment and net exports. (2) How will net exports get crowded out? Answer: dollar appreciation. Or one could reason that the rise in interest rates would attract financing from abroad, leading to appreciation of the dollar. Section 1.2 showed that these are two views of the same adjustment mechanism. Either says that the dollar would appreciate. Once that expectation takes hold, the dollar should be expected to jump immediately.

Indeed, the steepest appreciation of the dollar came across 1981, well before the emergence of the structural deficit. The deficit data are summarized in table 1.4, taken from the 1984 Council of Economic Advisers *Annual Report*. Real interest rates and the dollar show their major movements across 1981; the structural deficit begins to appear in 1982. This is consistent with the view that the markets anticipated the shift in the budget position when they understood the implications of the program that was announced in 1981. The anticipation of the shift in the budget by real interest rates and the real exchange rate in

Table 1.4 **Cyclical and Structural Components of the Federal Budget Deficit, Fiscal Years 1980–1989**

Fiscal Year	Total	Cyclical	Structural
Actual:			
1980	60	4	55
1981	58	19	39
1982	111	62	48
1983	195	95	101
Estimates (current services):			
1984	187	49	138
1985	208	44	163
1986	216	45	171
1987	220	34	187
1988	203	16	187
1989	193	−4	197

Sources: Budget of the United States Government Fiscal Year 1985 and Council of Economic Advisers.

1981 provide an important example of the effect of credible announcements and expectations in financial markets.

The implied reversal of the path of the real exchange rate as the fundamentals model moves from E_0 to E_1 to E_2 or E_3 also has its influence through expectations. If—as the dollar appreciates from E_0 toward E_1 in figures 1.2 and 1.5—agents in the market believe that the movement will eventually be reversed towards E_2 or E_3, this anticipated depreciation of the dollar will temper their increase in demand for dollar assets as real interest rates in the United States rise. This would tend to reduce the magnitude of the appreciation from E_0 to E_1 and the subsequent depreciation to E_2 or E_3. The dampening of price fluctuations is a general property of rational expectations analysis (it used to be called "stabilizing speculation"). An example is given in Branson (1983).

The upward jump in the exchange rate from E_0 to E_1 and gradual movement back toward E_2 are also consistent with market agents' anticipating the shift in the U.S. international position from creditor to debtor. This is implied by a sufficiently long period of current account deficits to finance the budget deficit. This in turn requires an initial appreciation of the dollar. But eventually the dollar must fall again, to a point somewhat below its original position. In anticipation of this swing, the market would generate an initial jump smaller than the one from E_0 to E_1, smoothing the path somewhat. Thus, expectations of the implications of, first, the shift in the budget position, and, second, the implied switch of the United States from international creditor to debtor would generate the movements in real interest rates and the exchange rate that we saw from 1980 to 1985. In particular, anticipation of the budget shift based on the March 1981 program can account for the movements on rates that came before the actual emergence of the structural deficit. Finally, it should be noted that anticipations of reversals as the path of asset market prices (generally known as "overshooting") reduce the magnitude of their fluctuations. It is shifts in the fundamentals that cause the fluctuations; in general, expectations can be expected to stabilize.

1.5 Econometric Evidence

The size and timing of the movements in the structural deficit and the real exchange rate in the first half of the 1980s strongly support the view that the shift in the expected deficit moved the exchange rate. Here I summarize some econometric evidence that corroborates this view. Rudiger Dornbusch and Jeffrey Frankel (1987) present an estimate of the sensitivity of the current account balance to a change in the real effective exchange rate. We can use that to check the consistency between the size of the shift in the current account and the structural deficit and the exchange rate from tables 1.2 and 1.4 above. Martin Feldstein (1986) studies the effect of shifts in the expected U.S. deficit on the deutsche-mark-dollar real exchange rate. His results are summarized below. John Campbell and Richard Clarida (1987) present time-series econometrics of exchange rates and interest differentials that suggest that the market's view of the long-run equilibrium real exchange rate was changing. This would be the case if the original shift in the budget was unanticipated and expected to be permanent, and likewise with GRH.

First, in table 1.2 we saw the increase in the total budget deficit from near zero in early 1981 to around $150 billion in 1985, with the federal deficit growing from 1.6% of GNP to a little over 5%. In table 1.4 we see the estimated structural federal deficit growing from about $40 billion in 1981 to $200 billion by 1989. These numbers point to an estimated increase in the expected structural federal budget deficit of around $150 billion, beginning in 1981.

This increase must be split between a reduction in the current account balance, identified as net foreign investment in table 1.2, and excess domestic savings, $S - I$ in equation (1) above, also shown in table 1.2. The burden of financing the deficit will shift from domestic sources in the short run to foreign borrowing in the medium run. This is a standard conclusion from Mundell in the 1960s. This implies a movement toward a trade deficit of $125–150 billion, building up from 1981 to 1985. Thus the current account balance fell from near zero in 1981 to around a

$150 billion deficit in 1985, providing the major share of finance for the structural deficit by then.

What about the real exchange rate? The index in table 1.2 rises from around 65 in 1980 to 100 in the first half of 1985, an increase of a bit over 50%. We compare 1981–85 on the current account balance to 1980–84 for the exchange rate to allow for lags in adjustment of trade flows behind the exchange rate. Using these data, it appears that a 50% appreciation was needed to generate a $150 billion reduction in the current account balance, about 4% of GNP. The ratio of these two numbers gives us an apparent semielasticity of the current account balance with respect to the real exchange rate of about 3—a 1% appreciation yields a $3 billion deterioration in the balance on current account.

This semielasticity is the current conventional wisdom number as reported by Stephen Marris (1985), and it is supported by the econometrics of Dornbusch and Frankel. Their regression shows that a 13.5% real appreciation will reduce the trade balance by 1% of GNP, so a 4% reduction would require a 54% appreciation. So if we ask the question: how big an exchange-rate change would be needed to generate the shift in the current account that we have observed? we get plausible econometric results.

The timing of the exchange-rate movement has already been discussed. The movement began sharply across 1981, as the expected full-employment deficit shifted. This takes us to Feldstein's study. He reports econometric equations that show directly the effects of a measured shift in the expected structural deficit on the real deutsche-mark-dollar exchange rate. So Feldstein turns the question around to ask how big the effect of the shift is on the deficit on the exchange rate, uses measures of the expected deficit, and focuses on the bilateral deutsche-mark-dollar rate.

I summarize Feldstein's results in table 1.5. Let me describe more precisely the econometrics. The dependent variable in the regressions is the deutsche-mark (DM) price of the dollar, adjusted for the ratio of GNP deflators and indexed to 1980 = 1.0. The independent variables in the equation shown in table 1.5 are the following. DEFEX is the ratio of the expected Federal structural deficit to GNP over the next five years. Here estimates of the actual deficit are used up to 1984, and projections are used after that. This implies that the shift in the budget after 1981 began to enter expectations in 1977. The expected deficit series begins to rise then. This underestimates the sharpness of the change in 1981.

The variable MBGRO is the ex post annual rate of change of the U.S. monetary base, which I take to be a predictor of the change in the future level of the U.S. money stock relative to that abroad. An

Table 1.5 **Econometric Estimates of Deutsche-Mark-Dollar Equations, 1973–84**

Independent Variable	Coefficient (Standard Error)	Elasticity in 1984
DEFEX	0.343 (.107)	0.67
MBGRO	−0.067 (.043)	0.32
PDLINF	−0.094 (.037)	—
DUM80+	−0.174 (.146)	—
$\bar{R}^2$	0.87	—
D-W	1.72	—

Source: Feldstein (1986), table 2, equation 2.6.
Note: Dependent variable: DM-Dollar Real Exchange Rate Index, 1980 = 1.0

increase in this variable should cause the dollar to depreciate. The variable PDLINF is a polynomial-distributed log on past rates of inflation on the GNP deflator, taken as a predictor of future inflation. An increase in this variable should also produce a depreciation. The variable DUM80+ is a dummy variable, unity from 1980 on and zero before, to capture other effects after 1980.

Feldstein reports many variants of the regression of table 1.5. In particular, he adds the German expected deficit and money growth and finds them insignificant. He adds a variable measuring the effects of changes in the tax laws on the after-tax rate of return, and it takes on the wrong sign. This leaves the DUM80+ variable as a rough measure of safe-haven effects.

In table 1.5 I show the coefficients and standard errors of the independent variables, with end-of-period elasticities for the expected deficit and money growth. The coefficient for the expected deficit is positive and highly significant. In Feldstein's data, which he shows in his appendix table A.1, the expected structural deficit as a fraction of GNP approximately doubled from 1.6% in 1978 to 3.3% in 1984. I use a base of 1978 to allow for the gradual way he introduces the expected deficit. The exchange-rate index rose by 70% from 1980 to 1984 (remember this is the DM-dollar rate, not the effective dollar rate of table 1.2). With an elasticity of 0.67, a 100% increase in the deficit would by Feldstein's estimate account for nearly all of the actual rise in the dollar. This is consistent with the Dornbusch-Frankel evidence cited earlier.

The coefficient of money growth is negative as expected, but not significant. Its significance varies across Feldstein's equations, but it is consistently negative. The inflation coefficient is negative, also as expected, and the safe-haven variable is quite insignificant.

Feldstein's econometrics on the DM-dollar rate thus fully supports the basic argument of this paper. The shift in the structural deficit was responsible for most of the rise in the real value of the dollar over the period 1980–85, and the timing is consistent with the shift in the expected deficit moving the actual real exchange rate.

Notes

1. Here for simplicity I ignore changes in the term structure of interest rates and focus on the real rate. See Branson, Fraga, and Johnson (1986) for the analysis of relative movements of short and long rates consistent with the story being told here.

2. The slope is given by $X_e/(I' - S')$.

3. The Feldstein-Bacchetta index uses multilateral trade weights and relative Consumer Price Indexes for the 80 countries for which data are available. These represent 89% of non-Soviet, non-U.S. trade.

4. The vertical measure of the shift is just $\rho'(B)$.

References

Branson, William H. 1977. Asset markets and relative prices in exchange-rate determination. *Sozialwissenschaftliche Annalen* 1: 69–89; also Reprints in International Finance no. 20, 1980. Princeton: Princeton University Press.

———. 1983. Macroeconomic determinants of real exchange risk. In Richard J. Herring, ed., *Managing foreign exchange risk*, pp. 33–74. Cambridge: Cambridge University Press.

———. 1985a. Causes of appreciation and volatility of the dollar. In Federal Reserve Bank of Kansas City, *The U.S. dollar: Recent developments, outlook, and policy*. Kansas City.

———. 1985b. The dynamic interaction of exchange rates and trade flows. In T. Peeters, P. Praet, and P. Reding, eds., *International trade and exchange rates*, pp. 133–60. Amsterdam: North-Holland.

Branson, William H., Arminio Fraga, and Robert A. Johnson. 1986. Expected fiscal policy and the recession of 1982. In M. H. Peston and R. E. Quandt, eds., *Prices, competition, and equilibrium*, pp. 109–26. New York: Barnes & Noble.

Buiter, Willem H. 1984. Comment on William H. Branson: Exchange rate policy after a decade of "Floating." In John F. Bilson and Richard C. Marston, eds., *Exchange rate theory and practice*, pp. 108–12. Chicago: University of Chicago Press.

Campbell, John Y., and Richard H. Clarida. 1987. The dollar and real interest rates. NBER Working Paper no. 2151, February.

Dornbusch, Rudiger, and Jeffrey Frankel. 1987. Macroeconomics and the dollar. In R. M. Stern, ed., *U.S. trade policies in a changing world economy*, pp. 77–130. Cambridge: MIT Press.
Feldstein, Martin S. 1986. The budget deficit and the dollar. In S. Fischer, ed., *NBER Macroeconomics Annual 1986*, pp. 355–92. Cambridge: MIT Press.
Feldstein, Martin S., and Phillipe Bacchetta. 1987. How far has the dollar fallen? NBER Working Paper no. 2122, January.
Krugman, Paul R. 1985. Fiscal policy, interest rates, and exchange rates: Some simple analytics. MIT mimeo, August.
Marris, Stephen N. 1985. The decline and fall of the dollar: Some policy issues. *Brookings Papers on Economic Activity* 1: 237–44.
McKibbin, Warwick J., and Jeffrey D. Sachs. 1986. Coordination of monetary and fiscal policies in the OECD. NBER Working Paper no. 1800.

Comment Maurice Obstfeld

William Branson has advanced an explanation of the U.S. dollar's recent behavior that centers on fiscal policy and the associated federal budget deficits. Prospective and actual American fiscal expansion pulled the dollar up starting in 1981, Branson argues; prospective and actual fiscal contraction, possibly reinforced by an increasing foreign reluctance to accumulate dollar claims, has pushed the dollar down since 1985. To make his case, Branson sets out a partial-equilibrium model of the "real" U.S. economy and demonstrates the model's ability to mimic the dollar's behavior when perturbed by fiscal policies similar to those enacted under the Reagan administration. By implication, the paper also explains U.S. real interest rates largely in terms of the government budget.

The paper's model is squarely in the tradition of the dynamic Mundell-Fleming approach, of which Branson was a pioneer. An increased government budget deficit is assumed to raise the demand for national savings; equilibrium is restored by a rise in the real interest rate (which encourages saving and reduces the flow supply of capital assets) and a real currency appreciation (which reduces the current account surplus—the flow of national saving into foreign assets). Alternatively, and I think more usefully, this mechanism can be viewed as maintaining equilibrium in the domestic output market. An increase in the fiscal deficit creates excess demand for home output, but the higher real

Maurice Obstfeld is a professor of economics at the University of Pennsylvania and a research associate of the National Bureau of Economic Research.

Helpful suggestions by William Branson, Alberto Giovannini, and Dale Henderson have been incorporated into this discussion. All errors and opinions, however, are the author's own. Financial support from the National Science Foundation and the Alfred P. Sloan Foundation is acknowledged with thanks.

interest rate shifts private demand to the future and the real currency appreciation shifts it abroad.

Like Branson, I believe that fiscal policy is of central importance in explaining the dollar's fluctuations in the 1980s; for that reason, I made a two-country version of the Mundell-Fleming model the centerpiece of my own 1985 review of recent exchange rate experience. Nonetheless, Branson's diagnosis of U.S. macroeconomic experience and prospects seems incomplete to me for two reasons.

First, Branson's contention that fiscal policy alone can explain most foreign exchange developments is not backed up by any persuasive empirical evidence. No serious attempt is made to assess the effects of other factors, notably monetary policy, on real exchange rates and interest rates. Calculations reported in my 1985 paper indicate that shifts in OECD (Organization for Economic Cooperation and Development) fiscal positions cannot account completely for the dollar's real appreciation between 1980 and 1985.

Second, the model Branson employs is ill-equipped to illuminate convincingly the longer-term effects of public budgetary policies in a growing world economy. In particular, the model treats only vaguely the intertemporal links that restrict the joint evolution of government debts, cross-border debts, outside asset supplies, and expectations.

Both of these difficulties are easier to raise than to resolve. The following comments therefore review some relevant facts and models with the aim of placing Branson's analysis in a broader perspective.

Monetary Policy, Interest Rates, and Exchange Rates

In a 1986 paper written with Arminio Fraga and Robert Johnson, Branson suggested that tighter U.S. monetary policy after 1979 contributed to the dollar's appreciation and to the recession that began in 1981. A reader of the present paper, however, comes away with the impression that a monocausal theory is being espoused. A review of the data shows that monetary policy must be included in any explanation of OECD exchange-rate and interest-rate behavior in the 1980s.

Table 1.6 shows recent nominal money supply growth rates for the United States, Germany, and Japan; table 1.7 shows corresponding real monetary growth rates.[1] In late 1979 in the United States and Germany,

1. The choice of M1 growth as the key indicator of monetary ease is of course open to debate; broader monetary aggregates such as M2 tell a different story. My defense is the usual one, that M1 seems to be the best available approximation to the notion of liquid balances. An additional problem relates to shifts in money demand, particularly those associated with financial deregulation. In spite of these drawbacks of the M1 indicator, I believe it still offers a rough picture of the stance of monetary policy. Figures on regulation-adjusted M1 generally confirm the story told by the tables; see Obstfeld (1985).

Table 1.6 **Monetary Growth Rates in the Big Three Industrialized Countries, 1978–86 (Percentage per Year)**

Country	1978	1979	1980	1981	1982	1983	1984	1985	1986
U.S.	8.2	7.5	7.5	5.1	8.7	10.4	5.3	11.9	16.7
Germany	14.2	3.7	4.2	−0.8	6.6	8.1	5.9	5.3	8.2
Japan	13.4	3.0	−2.0	10.0	5.7	−0.1	6.9	4.5	10.4

Note: Data from International Monetary Fund, *World Economic Outlook,* April 1986 (table 25), and *International Financial Statistics,* April 1987. Figures are percentage increases in the end-of-year money stock M1 over the corresponding value for the previous year.

Table 1.7 **Real Monetary Growth Rates in the Big Three Industrialized Countries, 1978–86 (Percentage per Year)**

Country	1978	1979	1980	1981	1982	1983	1984	1985	1986
U.S.	0.9	−1.3	−1.6	−4.5	2.2	6.6	1.4	8.6	14.1
Germany	9.9	−0.3	−0.6	−4.8	2.2	4.9	4.0	3.1	4.9
Japan	8.6	0.0	−5.8	6.8	3.8	−0.9	5.6	3.1	8.6

Note: M1 growth rate (from table 1.6) minus annual percentage change in GDP deflator, from International Monetary Fund, *World Economic Outlook,* April 1986 and April 1987.

and in early 1980 in Japan, short- and long-term nominal interest rates rose, and short-term rates jumped far above long-term rates as monetary growth slowed. According to the expectations theory of the term structure, this pattern is consistent with a liquidity squeeze that is expected to lead to lower inflation and lower nominal short-term rates in the future. Because inflation expectations cannot be measured with precision, the relation between these nominal interest rate changes and contemporaneous real interest rate changes is difficult to assess.[2]

Branson identifies the first half of 1981 as the period in which expected U.S. fiscal expansion set off the rise in U.S. real interest rates. Tables 1.6 and 1.7 show, however, that U.S. and German monetary growth dropped sharply in that year; at the same time, real interest rates at all maturities (as defined by Branson) rose in both countries,

2. The nominal interest-rate plots on which my account is based are in the International Monetary Fund's *World Economic Outlook,* April 1985, pp. 126–27. Branson defines short- and long-term real interest rates alike as nominal rates minus current CPI inflation; on this definition, the differences between the short and long nominal rates shown in the IMF plots are also differences between short and long real rates. It is unlikely, however, that Branson's definition of real interest rates is appropriate, particularly in the case of the long rate. Surely market participants used more information than the current inflation rate in forecasting inflation over the following 20 years.

with short rates rising most sharply and remaining above long rates for most of the year. By comparison, the long-term real rate rose only moderately in Japan (and the short-term real rate showed little change) in the face of that country's easy 1981 monetary stance.

A good case can thus be made that monetary factors were an important cause of the global interest rate developments of 1981 (a conclusion also reached by Blanchard and Summers 1984). In addition, other events reinforced American fiscal plans and tight money in pushing up interest rates. Between 1981 and 1982, for example, the OPEC surplus disappeared, reducing the flow of saving in the world economy.

Shifts in term-structure slopes in the early 1980s are also consistent with a monetary interpretation. Late in 1982, short-term interest rates fell decisively below long-term rates in the United States and Germany as their central banks became more expansionary. (This change had occurred in Japan the year before.) Under the expectations theory, this term-structure pattern is consistent with short-term rates that are temporarily low because of monetary ease and recession; an explanation does not have to rely on fiscal policy.

Even if monetary factors are key to explaining interest rate movements in the early 1980s, their relevance for exchange rates is less clear from the data. In evaluating the evidence, however, it should be remembered that 1978 was a year of crisis for the dollar: markets expected runaway U.S. money growth and massive future depreciation. These expectations led Germany and Japan to expand their money supplies rapidly in 1978 to support the dollar in the foreign exchange market. While the Federal Reserve's October 1979 shift in operating procedures had a small immediate impact on U.S. nominal monetary growth, the accompanying shift in market expectations about future money growth was probably significant. The expectation of a monetary regime change was reinforced by the election of an apparently anti-inflation U.S. president in November 1980.

The role of money in promoting the dollar's decline since early 1985 seems quite clear-cut. Branson again attributes the change largely to American fiscal legislation, this time restrictive. While some fiscal tightening has occurred and is likely to continue, the magnitudes involved are too small to explain plausibly the dollar's sharp descent from its peak. In contrast, a glance at tables 1.6 and 1.7 shows that U.S. monetary policy was extraordinarily loose in 1985 and 1986. (As in the late 1970s, Germany and Japan became less restrictive in 1986 to slow down the dollar's depreciation.) Without a rapid correction of the U.S. budget problem, growing inflation will eventually erode the recent increase in American competitiveness. One possibility that must worry the foreign exchange market is that U.S. policymakers will mistakenly saddle monetary policy alone with the assignment of eliminating the current account deficit.

Fiscal Deficits in the Long Run: An Analytical Framework

Branson's model offers a long-run analysis of fiscal deficits and the exchange rate, but it does not explicitly incorporate the essential intertemporal objectives and constraints that determine the evolution of asset stocks over time. In a 1987 paper, I develop a more complete framework geared to analyzing the medium- and long-term effects of budget deficits in a growing world economy. A modified small-country version of that model addresses many of the issues raised by Branson.[3]

The economy's labor force grows at rate μ and produces a homogeneous domestic output using a Ricardian technology with labor productivity parameter ω. Households in this economy can own foreign or domestic bonds, both of which are denominated in the export good, are perfect substitutes, and pay an interest rate r determined externally.[4]

The feature of the model that gives public debt policy its real effects comes from an insightful paper by Weil (1985). Every household is immortal, but newly born households are not connected to existing ones by ties of altruism and are born without financial wealth. Thus, a household born at time $v \leq t$ maximizes $\int_t^\infty \{\alpha \log[c^x(v,s)] + (1 - \alpha)\log[c^m(v,s)]\}\, e^{-\delta(s-t)}ds$, where $c^x(v,t)$ and $c^m(v,t)$ are the household's own consumption of exports and imports, respectively. Household size and labor endowment are normalized to 1, as is the total labor force at time $t = 0$. If $f(t)$ is the economy's per capita stock of net foreign claims and $d(t)$ its per capita stock of domestic government debt (both measured in exports), then the export value of aggregate per capita spending on the two goods, $c(t)$, is given by $c(t) = \delta[f(t) + d(t) + \omega/r + \int_t^\infty \tau(s)e^{-r(s-t)}ds]$, where $\tau(t)$ denotes time-t per capita transfer payments from the government. Let $e(t)$ be the real exchange rate, the price of domestic goods in terms of foreign goods. Per capita demand for the exported good is $\alpha c(t)$, while per capita demand for imports is $(1 - \alpha)e(t)c(t)$.

The rest of the world also grows at rate μ. Foreign demand for domestic output is $x^*[e(t)]$ (per domestic household), a decreasing function of $e(t)$. The home output market therefore clears when supply equals demand,

$$\alpha c(t) + x^*[e(t)] + g(t) = \omega. \tag{1}$$

Above, $g(t)$ is the home government's per capita consumption (devoted entirely to home goods).

The dynamics of the economy are described by the two differential equations

3. Alternative and complementary analyses of long-run fiscal policy effects in stationary economies are given by Frenkel and Razin (1986), Buiter (1986), and Giovannini (forthcoming).

4. The model assumes that $r > \mu$, so that the economy is dynamically efficient.

$$\dot{c}(t) = (r - \delta)c(t) - \mu\delta[f(t) + d(t)],$$
$$\dot{f}(t) = (r - \mu)f(t) + \omega - c(t) - g(t).$$

Under the assumption of saddlepath stability, the equilibrium average consumption level is

(2) $$c(t) = \delta\{f(t) + \omega/r + \int_t^\infty[\mu d(s) - g(s)]e^{-r(s-t)}ds\}.$$

A key feature of this solution is that consumption responds positively to current and future increases in the per capita government debt when $\mu > 0$. As emphasized by Weil (1985), government bonds are net wealth in this model, because some of the taxes that service them will be levied on other households that have not yet been born.

Equations (1) and (2) support an important element of the Branson thesis: a rise in expected future deficits, which raises expected future per capita debt levels, leads to an immediate jump in consumption. To eliminate the resulting excess demand for domestic output, $e(t)$ must therefore rise and crowd out foreign demand. The transmission mechanism is, however, quite different from the one Branson postulates. Anticipated fiscal policy has a direct impact on consumption and thus on the output market. Equilibrium in that market is restored by the exchange rate change.

The model's long-run implications for consumption and foreign claims are straightforward and are illustrated in figures 1.8 and 1.9 for the model's two possible configurations. In either case, a permanent unanticipated increase in the steady-state per capita public debt causes consumption to jump immediately from its initial equilibrium at point A to point B on the new saddlepath. Consumption and foreign assets both fall in the subsequent transition to the new steady state at point A'. As the figures show, a permanent increase in the steady-state public debt always leads to a long-run fall in both consumption and foreign assets per capita. According to (1), the consumption decline is associated with a lower steady-state real exchange rate—yet another case of the transfer problem.[5]

These results are broadly in line with Branson's predictions, but the inclusion of economic growth makes it clear that only permanently higher budget deficits—such as those associated with increases in the steady-state public debt—will have permanent effects on the economy.

5. This result is similar to one found by Branson, but again the mechanism is different. Branson relies on the hypothesis that an increasing risk premium must be offered to foreign investors as their holdings of dollar debt rise. In my model, a long-run real depreciation is necessary to preserve domestic goods-market equilibrium after a transfer of wealth abroad (given a standard assumption that foreigners have the greater marginal propensity to spend on their own output).

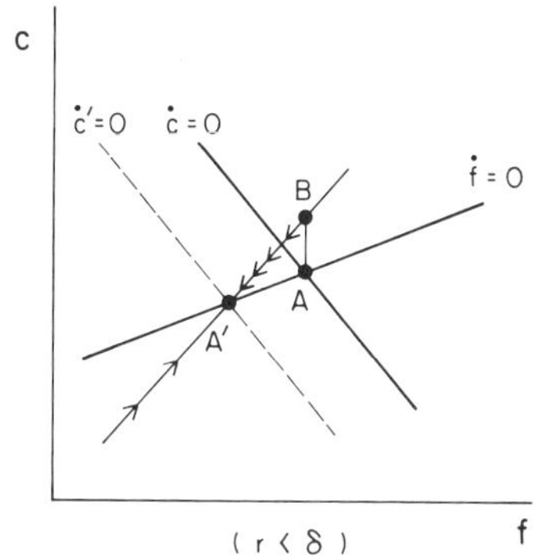

Fig. 1.8 Effects of an increased per capita public debt when the domestic time-preference rate exceeds the world interest rate.

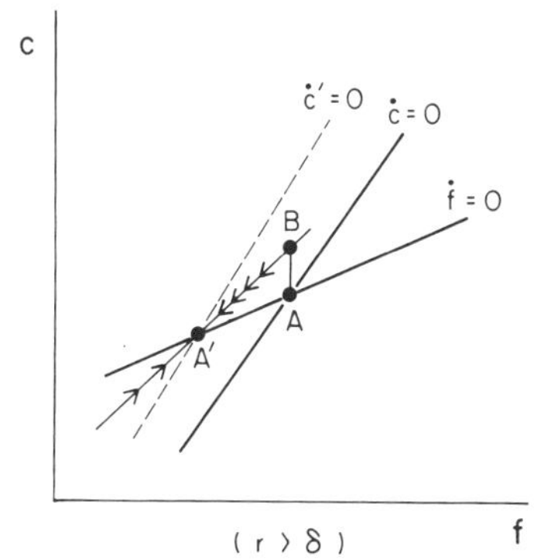

Fig. 1.9 Effects of an increased per capita public debt when the world interest rate exceeds the domestic time-preference rate.

Notice also that the economy does not return to its original current account position after a rise in the steady-state public debt. Only a lower long-run current account surplus is consistent with a lower long-run per capita foreign-asset level. Perhaps surprisingly, the long-run current account surplus is lower in spite of the fall in the relative price of domestic goods.

Conclusion

An explicitly intertemporal analysis of a model based on Mundell-Fleming assumptions confirms some central results of Branson's less formal treatment. In the short run, expected as well as current increases in the government deficit raise the real exchange rate and worsen the current account. Fiscal policies that cause the national debt to rise permanently relative to GNP depress both "outside" national wealth and the real exchange rate in the long run.

While these results are consistent with the view that fiscal policy has been central in determining the dollar's external value in the 1980s, factors other than fiscal policy appear to have had significant effects. The most important of these factors is monetary policy. U.S. monetary policy since 1985 has tried to reduce the severity of the international trade problem by forcing the dollar down. In spite of the dollar's sharp depreciation, little progress has been made in restoring external balance or defeating the protectionist threat. Unless expenditure-reducing policies are brought into play more quickly, part of the gain in U.S. competitiveness since 1985 is likely to be dissipated by higher inflation.

References

Blanchard, Olivier J., and Lawrence H. Summers. 1984. Perspectives on high world real interest rates. *Brookings Papers on Economic Activity* no. 2: pp. 273–324.

Branson, William H., Arminio Fraga, and Robert A. Johnson. 1986. Expected fiscal policy and the recession of 1982. In *Prices, competition, and equilibrium,* ed. M. H. Peston and R. E. Quandt. New York: Barnes and Noble.

Buiter, Willem H. 1986. Fiscal policy in open, interdependent economies. In *Economic policy in theory and practice,* ed. A. Razin and E. Sadka. London: Macmillan.

Frenkel, Jacob A., and Assaf Razin. 1986. Fiscal policies in the world economy. *Journal of Political Economy* 94 (June): 564–94.

Giovannini, Alberto. Forthcoming. The real exchange rate, the capital stock, and fiscal policy. *European Economic Review.*

Obstfeld, Maurice. 1985. Floating exchange rates: Experience and prospects. *Brookings Papers on Economic Activity* no. 2: pp. 369–450.

———. 1987. Fiscal deficits and relative prices in a growing world economy. Mimeographed. University of Pennsylvania, May.

Weil, Philippe. 1985. Overlapping families of infinitely lived agents. Mimeographed. Harvard University, April.

2 Sterling Misalignment and British Trade Performance

Charles R. Bean

2.1 Introduction

The possibility of Britain's participation in the Exchange Rate Mechanism of the European Monetary System has once again been the subject of speculation. In many respects this would represent the quite natural outcome of a continued evolution towards a more pragmatic approach to the conduct of monetary policy which has increasingly emphasized a broader range of financial indicators, including the exchange rate. This retreat from the purist monetarist perspective of the early years of Mrs. Thatcher's administration has been prompted on one hand by the difficulties encountered in controlling the original target aggregate, £M3, and on the other by the excessive volatility of the exchange rate and accompanying swings in competitiveness. The aim of this paper will be, first, to try to shed a little light on the reasons for this exchange rate volatility and, second, to ask whether it has done any lasting damage to British industrial performance.

Table 2.1 presents data on the nominal and real exchange rate (measured by relative producer prices) since the advent of floating, together with a number of other macroeconomic indicators. The 17% nominal appreciation of sterling between 1978 and 1981 in particular stands out. Associated with this there was a 23% deterioration in competitiveness and a contraction in manufacturing output of 14%. While manufacturing output has since recovered somewhat as competitiveness has improved, it is still well below its 1978 peak. The reduction in overall economic growth is, by contrast, less pronounced, and national income now stands

Charles R. Bean is a reader in economics at the London School of Economics and a research fellow of the Centre for Economic Policy Research, London.

Table 2.1 **Selected Macroeconomic Indicators**

	Nominal Effective Exchange Rate (1975 = 100)	Relative Producer Prices (1980 = 100)	GDP at Factor Cost (1980 Prices, 1980 = 100)	Manufacturing Output (1980 = 100)	Gross Oil Production (1980 prices, as % of GDP)	Unemployment (U.K.) (%)	Retail Price Inflation (%)
1973	111.8	75.7	94.5	114.2	—	2.4	9.1
1974	108.3	75.7	92.9	112.8	—	2.4	16.0
1975	100.0	79.0	92.0	105.0	0.0	3.7	24.2
1976	85.7	74.2	94.4	107.0	0.5	5.0	16.5
1977	81.2	79.0	96.9	109.0	1.6	5.3	15.9
1978	81.5	81.7	99.7	109.7	1.8	5.2	8.3
1979	87.3	89.4	102.4	109.5	2.7	4.8	13.3
1980	96.1	100.0	100.0	100.0	3.7	6.0	18.1
1981	95.3	100.8	98.7	94.0	4.9	9.3	11.9
1982	90.7	97.7	100.3	94.2	6.2	10.9	8.7
1983	83.3	91.0	103.8	96.9	6.3	11.9	4.6
1984	78.8	87.7	106.7	100.7	7.2	12.4	5.0
1985	78.7	90.0	110.5	103.9	6.7	12.9	6.1

Sources: Central Statistical Office, *Economic Trends Annual Supplement 1987* and *Petroleum Economist*.

more than 11% above its 1979 value. Unemployment, however, has risen remorselessly and only very recently has shown signs of falling.

While the facts of the recession are clear, its causes are open to debate. The appreciation of sterling and the associated squeeze on the tradable sector could be the result of at least two forces. First, it coincided with the adoption of contractionary fiscal and, more particularly, monetary policies by the newly elected Conservative administration. In a world of sluggish wage or price adjustment, an unexpected reduction in monetary growth is likely to produce an initial overappreciation of the exchange rate and a contraction that is concentrated in the tradables sector (see Dornbusch 1976 and Buiter and Miller 1981a, for instance). Buiter and Miller (1981b) cite this as a primary cause of the downturn beginning in 1979. On this explanation the appreciation of sterling was a temporary misalignment associated with the transition to a new, low-inflation, growth path.

The second explanation lays the blame on sterling's growing importance as a petrocurrency. The figures for gross oil production in table 2.1 show that between 1978 and 1982 the share of oil increased fourfold.[1] Indeed, by 1985 the United Kingdom, with 6% of free-world output, had become the fourth largest producer in the non-Communist world, after the United States, Saudia Arabia, and Mexico. In the space of ten years, the United Kingdom had been transformed from total dependence on imported oil into a significant net oil exporter. Further, the doubling of oil prices in the wake of the Iranian revolution significantly increased the value of this oil wealth. The "Dutch disease" literature suggests that the discovery and exploitation of such natural wealth will require an appreciation of the real exchange rate if the benefits of the resource discovery are to be enjoyed. The result will be a contraction in the output of nonoil tradables coupled with an expansion in nontradables production. Forsyth and Kay (1980), among others, have attributed the strength of sterling at the start of the 1980s to the importance of oil. On this explanation the appreciation of the exchange rate represented a reassessment of underlying fundamentals, rather than a temporary misalignment, and the accompanying unemployment was a purely temporary phenomenon associated with the process of structural change.[2]

In an attempt to disentangle the relative importance of these two explanations for the dramatic movements in the real exchange rate, I have conducted a few counterfactual simulations with a small empirical macroeconomic model of the United Kingdom. The results, presented in the first part of the paper, suggest that the presence of oil and the second oil price shock can account for something like a 12-percentage-point appreciation of both nominal and real exchange rates between 1978 and 1980. Contractionary monetary policy alone does not seem capable of explaining the rest, however. A combination of restrictive monetary policy and adverse supply-side movements can, on the other hand, provide an explanation of both the appreciation and the rise in unemployment.

Whatever the causes of the appreciation, it still prompts questions about the magnitude of the costs imposed on the economy. To the extent that demand and activity are transitorily reduced below equilibrium levels, there is a temporary welfare loss. However, temporary fluctuations in exchange rates may well have permanent effects on the economy. Such hysteresis effects have recently attracted attention in the context of labor markets (see Blanchard and Summers 1986, Gregory 1986, and Lindbeck and Snower 1986, for instance). In these models the current "natural rate" of unemployment may depend on the past history of the unemployment rate; for example, because the currently employed ("insiders") do not take account of the wishes of the unemployed ("outsiders"), or because firms use the unemployment history of a worker as a screening device, or simply because the human capital of the unemployed depreciates.

Similar hysteresis effects could arise in traded-goods markets for a number of reasons. On the demand side, customers may develop brand loyalty through purchasing a commodity and thus be more inclined to repeat the purchase. On the supply side, producers may experience significant costs in entering export markets, for example, in setting up distribution networks (see Baldwin and Krugman 1986) or more generally in increasing their market share. Once producers have left the market it may be difficult to reenter. In the face of a temporary appreciation, producers may then be inclined to cut margins and even incur losses in order to maintain market share. Both casual empiricism and the available aggregate data suggest that this was indeed the case during the 1979–82 period.

The view that hysteresis effects may be important in traded goods markets has also been voiced by industrialists themselves. Thus Vickers, in giving evidence to a House of Lords Select Committee set up to investigate the decline in British manufacturing, expressed the view that "The withdrawal by the UK from a number of important sectors of manufacturing industry represents a permanent loss to the UK economy. . . . Once a company, or country, has opted out of a particular industry it is virtually impossible ever to reenter."

The second half of this paper supplements this superficial evidence of the importance of hysteresis effects with econometric evidence concerning U.K. export performance since 1900. I find evidence of such effects on both the demand and supply side of the market. The paper concludes with a brief discussion of some of the policy implications.

2.2 The 1979–81 Appreciation: Oil or Tight Money?

It is not my intention to provide a comprehensive survey and assessment of the Thatcher years in general and the 1979–81 recession in particular. That has been done by others, for example, Buiter and Miller (1981b, 1983) and Matthews and Minford (1987). Rather I want to focus on the behavior of the exchange rate, supplementing existing, often informal, discussions with some pseudoeconometric evidence from a small annual macroeconometric model of the United Kingdom. The model lies somewhere between the small analytical and numerical simulation models with plausible parameter values on the one hand, and the large empirical macroeconomic forecasting models on the other. The former frequently lack realism, while the latter often lack theoretical coherence. It is not possible here to give a complete description of the model and of the econometric estimates, which are fully reported in Bean, Dinenis, and Probyn (1985), but a brief overview follows. The linearized version used for the simulations is, however, reported in full in the Appendix.

2.2.1 An Overview of the Econometric Model

The model is best thought of as a more developed version of the rational expectations with sluggish wage-price adjustment models in the tradition of Dornbusch (1976), Blanchard (1981), and Buiter and Miller (1981a). Supply is disaggregated into three sectors: manufacturing (corresponding to nonoil tradables), nonmanufacturing (corresponding to nontradables), and oil and gas (exogenous). Firms operate in a monopolistically competitive environment treating factor prices, initial holdings of inventories, and the capital stock as given. Technologies are of the CES variety. On the basis of factor prices and expectations about the level of demand and competitors' prices, they choose appropriate levels of factor inputs, price, and output. The elasticity of demand, and hence the mark-up, is constant. If sales expectations are not realized, then there is an unanticipated buildup or rundown of inventories of finished goods. There is no rationing in the goods market.

The wage equation, which thus determines the level of unemployment via labor demand, is of the Sargan (1964) real-wage-resistance type. Consequently, changes in the wedge between the consumption and product wage will affect the NAIRU. However, in the short run the nominal wage is predetermined, and an acceleration in inflation will produce a fall in real wages.

Domestic demand comprises consumption, investment, and government spending, which is exogenous. The consumption function is based on a standard life-cycle permanent-income model, implicitly with backward-looking expectations formation. It relates consumption to post-tax nonproperty income, interest rates, and net worth (including housing). A noteworthy feature of the results is the very strong negative impact of nominal rather than real interest rates (see Bean 1987, which also reports tests of Ricardian debt neutrality). This appears to be a rather robust feature of the data. It presumably reflects the interaction of credit rationing effects with the increased front-end loading of real mortgage repayments as interest rates rise (see Jackman and Sutton 1982).

Investment depends on "Tobin's Q," but the equations are rather novel in incorporating time-to-build lags. These make investment a function, not of the current real stock price, but of lagged expectations of the current stock price (see Dinenis 1985).

To obtain the demand for domestically produced goods, two further equations are added describing the split of domestic and foreign demand between domestic manufacturing, domestic nonmanufacturing, and foreign producers. The arguments in these equations are the various relative prices, as well as domestic and foreign demand.

The financial sector of the model comprises a conventional demand for (outside) money equation and a series of arbitrage relationships equating short-term interest rates with the expected returns on long bonds, equities, and foreign assets. Rational expectations in asset markets are assumed throughout.

The model was estimated on postwar annual data by both single equation and systems instrumental variables techniques. The complete model has 25 state variables, 21 of which are predetermined and 4 of which are non-predetermined (the exchange rate, the long interest rate, and manufacturing and nonmanufacturing stock prices). The simulations reported here were carried out using Buiter and Dunn's (1982) SADDLEPOINT program for simulating linear rational expectations models, which itself is based on the methods of Blanchard and Kahn (1980).

2.2.2 North Sea Oil

I start by considering the impact of oil on the exchange rate. However, before presenting the numerical results, it is worthwhile briefly summarizing the salient points of the theoretical literature (see Bean 1987 for an extensive bibliography). This falls into two parts, one of which deals with the medium- and long-term equilibrium implications, and the other of which deals with the problem of short-run adjustment when factor markets do not clear.

As far as the equilibrium implications are concerned, there are two primary channels through which the discovery of a natural resource affects the economy. The first is via a spending effect, whereby the resulting increased demand for consumer goods falls partly on nontradables and domestically produced tradables. The result is a rise in the price of nontradables to tradables and, if domestic and foreign tradables are imperfect substitutes, an improvement in the terms of trade. Associated with this will be a shift in resources from tradables to nontradables production.

The second channel is a resource effect whereby changes in the demand for factors of production lead to changes in factor rewards and a consequent change in supply in different parts of the economy. The magnitude and direction of this effect depends critically on the mobility of labor and capital and the capital intensity of the industries involved. However, for the case of North Sea oil this channel is likely to be relatively unimportant, since oil extraction utilizes very little labor, and the required capital can be obtained from abroad.

As far as short-run adjustment is concerned, Eastwood and Venables (1982) have discussed the issue in a Dornbusch-style model. They point out that one would not expect the discovery of oil to lead to a general recession because the requisite deterioration in competitiveness occurs instantaneously via a nominal exchange rate appreciation rather than domestic price adjustment. Only if there is a lag between discovery and the resulting increase in demand will a recession occur, because forward-looking behavior in exchange markets brings forward the competitiveness deterioration ahead of the increase in demand. In view of the backward-looking nature of the consumption function in the model used for the simulations and the fact that the government did not deliberately cut taxes and increase the budget deficit ahead of extraction, this is an important proviso.

Table 2.2 presents the results of a counterfactual simulation designed to answer the question: How did the discovery of oil and the increase in oil prices affect the exchange rate and the level of activity? In the base case oil production is set to zero, and real oil prices are held at their 1973 level. The table then gives the percentage changes in some key variables from this base scenario as a result of the discovery of oil and the two oil price hikes. I have assumed that the volume of reserves and production were correctly evaluated (their value, net of extraction costs, varies with the oil price and the exchange rate and is assumed to be zero prior to the first oil price shock); each of the two oil price shocks were unanticipated and regarded as permanent; real government spending and tax rates are kept constant (so the budget deficit and the stock of government debt vary endogenously); monetary

Table 2.2 **Effects of North Sea Oil and Oil Price Shocks (Percentage Changes)**

	1974	1975	1976	1977	1978	1979	1980	1981	1982	1983	1984
Nominal exchange rate	6.2	7.0	7.4	8.4	9.5	10.6	22.7	23.4	24.3	24.6	25.0
Real exchange rate	8.2	7.7	7.1	7.2	7.4	7.9	19.3	19.5	20.4	20.7	20.7
Manufacturing employment	1.0	−2.0	−0.5	−0.1	−0.1	−0.2	1.3	−1.8	−1.4	−1.7	−1.7
Services employment	−1.0	−0.5	−0.8	−0.7	−0.6	−0.5	0.3	1.0	1.2	1.1	1.1
Consumer price inflation	1.2	−1.1	−1.2	−1.0	−0.8	−0.7	−1.9	−0.5	0.0	−0.1	−0.1

policy is nonaccommodatory; and effects on world activity and interest rates are ignored. The assumptions on fiscal and monetary policy are certainly debatable, but it is not clear what other assumptions would be more appropriate.

Turning to the figures themselves, we see that the effect of the second oil price shock is to produce an 11% appreciation of the real exchange rate (12% nominal) in 1980, that is, it explains a little less than half of the real appreciation that actually occurred. This is in the same ball park as many previous estimates (see Bean 1987 for a survey), although rather smaller than those furnished by Forsyth and Kay in their seminal piece. There is no subsequent depreciation, but this is because the real oil price has been held constant after 1980. In practice, of course, it has now roughly halved. The model suggests that a permanent 10% fall in oil prices produces a real depreciation of 1.25%, so that around a 7% real depreciation since 1981 could be expected from the subsequent decline in oil prices. The simulation also displays an Eastwood-Venables-style recession in the interregnum between discovery and exploitation. In the post-1980 period, when most fields had come on stream, we find the classic Dutch-disease scenario of a contraction in manufacturing output and an expansion in services employment. (The rather peculiar increases in manufacturing employment in 1974 and 1980 are due to the fact that the model treats oil and labor as substitutes in production and that a deterioration in competitiveness only affects demand with a lag—a somewhat dubious property of the model.) Thus while the discovery and exploitation of oil and sterling's status as a petrocurrency help to explain the decline in manufacturing, they do not seem to adequately explain the overall increase in unemployment. One possibility is that the model simply underestimates the problems of absorbing unemployed workers from manufacturing into the services sector because of skill and regional mismatch. The other explanation lies in the contractionary policies pursued by the Conservative government, a question to which I now turn.

2.2.3 Monetary Policy and the Exchange Rate

The 1980 appreciation of sterling is frequently attributed to the adoption of a more restrictive monetary stance by the authorities as part of a wider counterinflationary strategy involving both a reduction in government expenditure and a reduction in the government deficit. Buiter and Miller (1981b) provide an eloquent exposition of this viewpoint. If inflation adjusts sluggishly, a reduction in monetary growth will, they claim, lead to an increase in domestic real interest rates and a temporary appreciation of the real exchange rate. On this view, the reduction in current and future monetary growth announced as part of the government's Medium Term Financial Strategy (MTFS) provided the immediate catalyst for the appreciation of sterling and the attendent recession (contractionary fiscal policy had a role to play here as well). Buiter and Miller attribute the lion's share of the blame here and ascribe only a subsidiary role for oil.

How well does this story stand up? To begin with, there is some debate over whether monetary policy was indeed contractionary. As table 2.3 makes clear, the growth of £M3, the government's chosen target aggregate, was actually fairly rapid through 1980 and 1981, and certainly well above the target ranges of 7–11% and 6–10%, respectively. However, the growth rate of M1, and especially the monetary base, was much more modest. Coupled with the rise in short-term interest rates that occurred, it is difficult not to believe that some monetary deceleration had taken place and that the disparate signals given by the various monetary aggregates was the result of innovations taking place within the financial sector (such as changes in the saving behavior of the private sector and in the pattern of corporate finance). The ex post reduction in nominal GDP growth also supports this view.

While it is not difficult to sustain the argument that a monetary deceleration had indeed occurred, the consequences of it are more debatable. Buiter and Miller (1983) note that there are problems in their earlier view inasmuch as the ex post real interest rate differential actually moved significantly against the United Kingdom in this period (see table 2.4).[3] Further, the question arises as to whether there is enough nominal rigidity in the economy to explain the facts.

Table 2.4 presents the estimated effects on the same set of key variables of the (unanticipated) introduction of a disinflationary program in which the rate of monetary growth is reduced by 1 percentage point per year for five years (starting in 1980), after which the rate of monetary growth is permanently lower by 5 percentage points. This sort of gradualist approach represents the intention, if not necessarily the execution, of the monetary side of the MTFS. It is assumed that the program is credible, so that agents in financial markets, who are endowed with rational expectations, correctly foresee the implications. This is not, of course, true of wage bargainers who have backward-looking inflationary expectations. The nominal exchange rate appreciates 17% on impact, but the real exchange rate appreciation is a more modest 9%. The overshoot predicted by the Dornbusch-Buiter-Miller approach is present, but it is not very pronounced. More noticeable is the significant reduction in inflation and a modest expansion in overall employment (although manufacturing employment shows a small decline after the first year as J-curve effects work through). The reason for this is that although there is a degree of nominal inertia in the wage equations, it is really not that significant. Wage demands moderate

Table 2.3 Selected Monetary Indicators

	Rate of Growth of Monetary Base	Rate of Growth of M1	Rate of Growth of £M3	3-Month Interest Rates	Rate of Growth of Nominal GDP	Ex Post Real Interest Differential
1978	15.0	16.3	15.6	11.9	15.4	—
1979	10.1	9.1	13.2	16.5	15.1	1.4
1980	5.6	4.0	18.7	13.6	16.4	7.4
1981	1.1	11.0	13.5	15.4	9.2	2.5
1982	3.8	11.3	14.6	10.0	8.5	−0.3
1983	6.4	8.4	5.9	9.0	9.2	—

Sources: Financial Statistics (various issues), *Economic Trends Annual Supplement*, 1987, and Buiter and Miller (1983).

Table 2.4 Effects of Progressive Reduction in the Rate of Monetary Growth (Percentage Changes)

	1980	1981	1982	1983	1984
Nominal exchange rate	17.2	21.9	25.8	31.0	36.4
Real exchange rate	9.2	7.7	7.9	7.0	7.0
Manufacturing employment	1.2	−1.1	−0.6	−0.6	−0.8
Services employment	0.5	1.2	1.5	1.8	1.9
Consumer price inflation	−9.0	−5.2	−5.3	−5.3	−5.4

along with the fall in import prices, resulting in a further fall in consumer prices and a decline in nominal interest rates. Because nominal rather than real interest rates influence consumer demand (see above), the latter actually rises. A long-run real appreciation is necessary to accommodate this increase in consumer demand. While the simulation therefore goes some way to explaining the behavior of the exchange rate, it does not seem to capture the rise in unemployment. Thus, on the basis of this simulation at least, monetary policy does not seem capable of bearing the full weight of the story.[4]

A central feature of the argument is obviously the low degree of nominal inertia in wage-setting behavior. A considerable amount of recent research has confirmed the view that the European economies in general, and the United Kingdom in particular, suffer from real, rather than nominal, wage rigidity (see for instance Branson and Rotemberg 1980, Grubb, Jackman, and Layard 1983, and Newell and Symons 1986). Indeed, Layard and Nickell (1986), in one of the most complete recent studies of United Kingdom labor market behavior, actually find no nominal inertia whatsoever in their annual wage equation. If anything, the degree of nominal inertia present in the model used here is actually rather greater than independent evidence suggests.

Of course one can always appeal to Lucas critique type arguments for doubting the relevance of econometric estimates for simulating policy shifts in the face of a change in regime. However, one would normally have expected them to overstate, rather than understate, the amount of nominal inertia in the face of an announced, credible, program of disinflation. I am therefore rather inclined to discount this explanation.

An alternative view is to lay the blame not solely at the door of restrictive monetary policy, but to a combination of restrictive monetary policy and adverse developments on the supply side. The winter of 1978–79 saw the breakdown of the Labor government's "social contract" with the unions and a wave of strikes, particularly in the public sector, resulting in significant wage increases for large groups of workers. While this winter of discontent was a major political factor leading to the election of Mrs. Thatcher, the Conservatives agreed to honor the increases granted to public sector workers. This in turn led to further private sector wage demands, and the result was a significant acceleration in the growth of average earnings from an annual rate of 12.3% over 1976–78 to 17.2% over 1978–80. The growth in real earnings was less marked—around 2% in 1979 and 1980—but since then the real incomes of those in work have continued to rise, along with the level of unemployment.

Layard and Nickell (table 10) estimate that between 1975–79 and 1980–83 the NAIRU rose by around 2 percentage points, a significant part of which is attributed to the breakdown in incomes policy, a resurgence in union militancy, and increased structural mismatch. Now one would expect an adverse movement in aggregate supply such as this to lead not only to a decline in employment, but also to a crowding out of net exports via an appreciation of the real exchange rate. Table 2.5 therefore reports the effects of a permanent fall in the NAIRU of 2 percentage points, starting in 1979. The result is a 12% appreciation of both real and nominal exchange rates (with a small overshoot), as well as a decline in employment which is heavily concentrated in the traded goods sector.

I conclude from this that while the monetary contraction alone does not seem to be a major factor behind the sterling appreciation, a combination of tight monetary policy and a deteriorating supply-side position can explain a real appreciation of upwards of 12%, to add to the 12% or so attributed to oil. Together this is of the same order of magnitude as that actually experienced. Most of this movement is, however, due to changes in underlying fundamentals, and only a very small part represents a temporary misalignment due to Dornbusch-style overshooting.

However, aside from any qualms one might entertain about the model—and there are many—one must also feel rather uncomfortable with this sort of ex post historical exercise, because there are just too many degrees of freedom around in the way of exogenous shocks and expectations of future variables to impose much discipline on the researcher. By a judicious choice of these, one can always fit the facts.

Table 2.5 **Effects of a 2 Percentage Point Increase in the NAIRU (Percentage Changes)**

	1979	1980	1981	1982	1983
Nominal exchange rate	11.6	11.1	10.1	9.5	9.2
Real exchange rate	11.6	12.4	11.9	10.4	9.6
Manufacturing employment	−1.1	−5.2	−4.9	−4.3	−4.1
Services employment	−0.8	−1.7	−2.4	−2.6	−2.4
Consumer price inflation	−1.2	1.1	0.3	−0.3	−0.5

Consequently I remain cautious about the conclusion that overshooting due to the monetary contraction was not a major feature of the appreciation. Rather the results represent just a little bit more evidence to add to the growing pile on exchange rate misalignment and the economic consequences of Mrs. Thatcher.

This analysis ignores the possibility of a misalignment other than as a result of the interaction of a contractionary monetary policy and nominal inertia. An alternative viewpoint is that the appreciation of sterling was simply the consequence of a bubble (rational or otherwise). There is now an extensive empirical literature rejecting uncovered interest parity (see, e.g., Fama 1984 and the references therein), although the absence of a well-formulated alternative hypothesis makes it difficult to know how bad an assumption it is or how to interpret the findings of Meese and Rogoff (1983) that a random-walk model of the exchange rate seems to dominate any other explanation. Evans (1986) does, however, report evidence that at least in the 1981–84 period the sterling-dollar rate was subject to a bubble, and Meese (1986) also reports evidence suggesting that both the sterling-dollar and dollar-deutschemark rates have been subject to bubbles since the advent of floating. Finally, Frankel and Froot (1985) construct an account of the 1981–84 period, which in part relies on irrational speculation. Consequently it would be rash to conclude that the greater portion of the 1979–80 sterling appreciation was necessarily a response to movements in fundamentals. While a bubble could account for the behavior of the exchange rate, however, it does not simultaneously seem capable of explaining the concomitant rise in unemployment given the limited nominal inertia in wage setting.

2.3 Permanent Effects from Transitory Exchange Rate Fluctuations

Whatever the cause of a movement in the real exchange rate, it will usually be accompanied by changes in the real economy. The 1979–81 real appreciation has now been largely reversed, but the possibility remains that it may have had a lasting impact on British trade performance. In this section I shall examine the empirical evidence for such hysteresis effects.

2.3.1 Demand Effects

Quotes like that of Vickers in their evidence to the House of Lords Select Committee and the observation that industrialists attach a great deal of significance to maintaining their market share suggest that hysteresis effects in goods markets are likely to be important. Within the industrial organization literature there is a considerable body of work discussing the advantages that accrue to incumbent firms. On the demand side one can think of at least three arguments as to why hysteresis effects might arise. First, incumbents may produce such a wide variety of differentiated products that it may be difficult for new entrants to find a niche (Schmalensee 1978). Second, uncertainty about product quality may lead consumers to stick with products that they have already purchased, rather than trying out the brands of new firms (Schmalensee 1982). Finally, there may be significant costs in some industries in switching suppliers (Klemperer 1987). All of these suggest that the demand for a firm's product may depend on its previous level of sales.

Rather than subscribe to any one particular theory for such state dependence, I shall use an eclectic, although rather ad hoc, approach and simply assume that consumer tastes are related to the past history of consumption. To motivate matters, suppose a representative consumer's tastes over the domestic product, X, and the foreign product, X^*, are given by:

$$(1) \qquad U = A(X_{-1})X^{\rho} + B(X^*_{-1})X^{*\rho} \qquad (\rho < 1)$$

with A', B' >0. Then, assuming the consumer ignores the effect of current choices on future tastes,[5] the relative demands are given by:

$$(2) \qquad (X/X^*) = (A/B)^{\sigma}(P^*/P)^{\sigma}$$

where P and P^* are the prices of the two products and $\sigma = 1/(1 - \rho)$ is the elasticity of substitution. It remains to parameterize A and B. It is convenient to write $A = A_0X^{\theta}$, $B = B_0X^{*\theta}$, in which case:

$$(3) \qquad \Delta(x - x^*) = \sigma(a_0 - b_0) + \sigma(p^* - p) + (\sigma\theta - 1)(x_{-1} - x^*_{-1})$$

where Δ denotes the difference operator and lowercase letters will henceforth be used to denote logarithms. Thus when $\theta = 1/\sigma$, we have pure hysteresis, and a transitory increase in the relative price of X will have a permanent effect on its share.

Because we are interested in the question of whether transitory shocks have durable effects, it makes sense to look at evidence over as long a time period as possible. Confining attention to just a few years of data is likely to severely limit the precision with which one can make inferences about such long-run effects. Further, very short-lived fluctuations, for example, lasting a month or so, are unlikely to affect trade permanently, because they can be insured against in the forward market. Rather one is interested in the effect of movements that last, say, a year or two. To this end I shall present estimates using (annual) data on British export performance going back to the beginning of the century taken from Alford et al. (1971). Although the arguments above could equally well apply to the home market, attention is restricted to export markets, because it is impossible to disaggregate the imports of goods data for most of the period between raw materials and intermediate inputs on the one hand and finished goods on the other. By contrast, British visible exports are almost exclusively finished goods (prior to North Sea oil) and hysteresis arguments seem most relevant to this market.

Thus X is the volume of British nonoil visible exports, while as a proxy for X^*, consumption of foreign products in the rest of the world, I use United States GNP (consumption of British products is, of course, only a tiny fraction of this). P is the associated UVI (AVI prior to 1950) converted into dollars at the prevailing exchange rate, whilst P^* is the dollar UVI for world manufactured exports (UN series). Since much of British trade in the early years of the century was concentrated in the colonies and more latterly has been directed to Europe, the use of U.S. data to proxy X^* is obviously less than perfect, but it is impossible to obtain a suitable world GNP variable for most of the period. However, to control for this and the changing structure of British export markets, I have included as an additional exogeneous variable, S, the share of exports to the United States in the total value of British exports. To control for the increasing integration of world markets since the Second World War, I have also included the ratio of world trade in manufactures to world manufacturing output, Z, (both UN series).

The ratio of United Kingdom nonoil exports to United States GNP is plotted in figure 2.1, while the price of United Kingdom exports relative to that of world manufacturers is plotted in figure 2.2. (Note that for convenience the series have been rescaled for the earlier periods.) Figure 2.2 reveals another benefit in looking at a long historical data set; while the 1979–80 appreciation is perhaps the most pro-

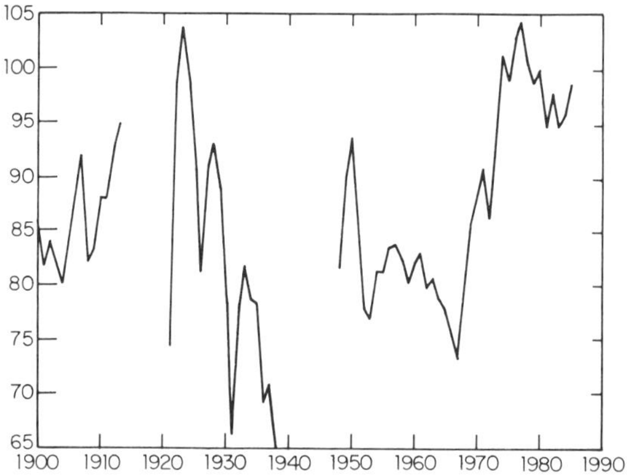

Fig. 2.1 U.K. export share.
Note: 1980 = 33 for data 1900–1913.
1980 = 66 for data 1921–38.
1980 = 100 for data 1948–85.

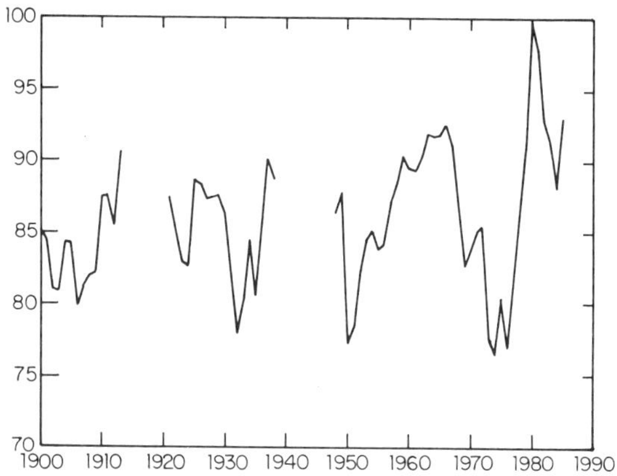

Fig. 2.2 Relative U.K. export prices.
Note: 1980 = 130 for data 1900–1913.
1980 = 100 for data 1921–38 and 1948–85.

nounced fluctuation, there are other periods when relative prices have moved quite sharply. Thus inferences are not likely to be unduly influenced by the experience of a single historical period (and moreover one when many aspects of both the British and the world economy were in a state of flux).

We begin by considering the stochastic properties of the various series in the demand equation. Table 2.6 reports the coefficient φ from the first-order autoregression:

(4) $$\Delta y = \text{constant} + \pi.\text{trend} + \varphi y_{-1}$$

where $y = x, x^*, x - x^*, p - p^*, s, z$. (In practice we also allow for different intercepts either side of the world wars.) Although the t-statistic on φ does not in fact have a t-distribution under the null hypothesis that $\varphi = 0$, it can nevertheless be used to test this hypothesis if the critical values reported in Dickey and Fuller (1981) are used instead. On the basis of these results, one would probably conclude that x, x^*, and z can reasonably be treated as nonstationary stochastic processes, while $x - x^*$, $p - p^*$, and s are best treated as stationary processes around a deterministic trend.

Having established this, it is then natural to ask whether x, x^*, and z are cointegrated. Two or more series, which are themselves nonstationary, are said to be cointegrated (Engle and Granger 1987) if some linear combination of them is stationary. It is clear from (3) that if $(p - p^*)$ is a strongly exogenous stationary stochastic process and $\theta = 1/\sigma$, then x and x^* cannot be cointegrated. Engle and Granger consider various ways of testing whether two or more nonstationary series are cointegrated. One procedure, which I follow here, is to regress one of the series

Table 2.6 Stochastic Properties of Various Time Series

Series	φ
x	−0.103
	(1.64)
x^*	−0.119
	(2.08)
x-x^*	−0.264
	(2.83)
p-p^*	−0.278
	(3.02)
s	−0.334
	(3.77)
z	0.005
	(0.10)

Notes: Sample: 1901–13, 1922–37, 1949–85; t-statistics in parentheses.

on the others and then test whether the residual from that regression is stationary using either the Durbin-Watson statistic (it should be zero under the null hypothesis of no cointegration) or a Dickey-Fuller type test.

The results of carrying out this procedure are presented in table 2.7. Equation (1) gives estimates of the long-run relationship between x, x^*, and z, while equation (2) presents a Dickey-Fuller type test of whether the residual in equation (1), $\tilde{x}$, is stationary, as would be the case if x, x^*, and z are cointegrated. This test is based on the t-statistic of $\tilde{x}_{-1}$, although once again cognizance must be taken of the fact that it does not have a t-distribution when $\tilde{x}$ is a random walk, and that $\tilde{x}$ is also a generated regressor. Engle and Granger provide Monte Carlo evidence on the distribution of both the Durbin-Watson statistic in equation (1) (their ξ_1 statistic) and the coefficient on $\tilde{x}_{-1}$ in equation (2) (their ξ_2 statistic). Using their results we are able to accept, at the 95% level, the hypothesis that x, x^*, and z are indeed cointegrated.

However, the finding that x and x^* are cointegrated does not necessarily imply the absence of hysteresis effects in export markets if $(p - p^*)$ is not strongly exogenous. This may be seen by considering the following example. Suppose that the demand equation is given by:

$$(5) \qquad \Delta(x - x^*) = \alpha\,(p^* - p) + u \qquad (\alpha > 0)$$

where u is some stationary stochastic process, and supply is given by:

$$(6) \qquad (p^* - p) = \beta(x^* - x) + v \qquad (\beta > 0)$$

where v is another stationary stochastic process. Then it is straightforward to show that

$$(7) \qquad (x - x^*) = (u + \alpha v)/[(1 + \alpha\beta) - L]$$

Table 2.7 **Cointegration Test for x, x^*, and z**

(1)
$$x = -\underset{(0.88)}{0.65} + \underset{(3.93)}{0.62D_1} + \underset{(1.06)}{0.11D_2} - \underset{(0.46)}{0.0016t} + \underset{(5.86)}{0.854x^*} + \underset{(5.13)}{0.517z}$$

Sample period: 1900–1913, 1921–37, 1948–85;
Standard error (%) = 7.64; Durbin-Watson = 0.88.

(2)
$$\Delta\tilde{x} = \underset{(0.39)}{0.0029} - \underset{(4.72)}{0.481\tilde{x}_{-1}}$$

Sample period: 1901–1913, 1922–37, 1949–85;
Standard error (%) = 6.12; Durbin-Watson = 1.37.

Notes: t-statistics in parentheses. D_1 = 1 in 1900–1913 and 0 otherwise. D_2 = 1 in 1921–37 and 0 otherwise. $\tilde{x}$ is the residual from regression 1.

where L is the lag operator. Thus $(x - x^*)$ is a stationary stochastic process even though (5) exhibits a hysteresis effect.

Table 2.8 presents instrumental variable estimates of the export demand equation itself, treating the current relative price as endogenous. Since the United Kingdom is a small supplier at the global level, it seems reasonable to treat p^* as (weakly) exogenous, and so the additional instruments are those factors determining United Kingdom export prices vis-à-vis current and lagged values of wages and raw material prices, relative to the foreign price level, and (economywide) productivity. In addition there are the shift variables s and z, as well as a number of dummies to take account of special factors. These are a dummy for the impact of the general strike (1 in 1926, −1 in 1927); a dummy to take account of the 1972 dock strike (1 in 1972, −1 in 1973); a dummy to partial out the effect of the Korean war (1 in 1951 and 1952); and a dummy to partial out the effects of widespread introduction of restrictive trade measures at the onset of the Great Depression (0.5 in 1930 and 1 in 1931). One might expect this last effect to be picked up by the ratio of world trade in manufactures to world manufacturing output, z, which drops precipitously at this time, but it does not seem to capture everything. In addition, 1908 is clearly an outlier, for some unidentifiable reason, and a dummy taking the value 1 in 1908 and 0 elsewhere is also included. The coefficients on these dummies and the intercepts, which differ each side of the world wars, are omitted from table 2.8 for brevity. I have also generalized the dynamic structure slightly by introducing additional lags on the exogenous variables to produce an error-feedback model.

Table 2.8 **Estimates of Export Demand Equation (Dependent variable: $\Delta(x - x^*)$)**

Sample period: 1901–13, 1923–37, 1949–85.

	Equation (1)	Equation (2)
$\Delta(p^* - p)$†	0.388	0.386
	(2.34)	(2.53)
$(p^* - p)$†	0.267	0.255
	(2.86)	(2.79)
Δx^*	−0.636	−0.654
	(4.23)	(5.61)
x^*	0.055	
	(1.17)	
Δs	−0.016	−0.034
	(0.33)	(0.70)
s	−0.053	
	(1.32)	
Δz	0.216	0.151
	(2.07)	(1.47)
z	−0.029	
	(0.38)	
$(x - x^*)_{-1}$	−0.13	
	(1.46)	
Standard error (%)	3.25	3.23
Durbin-Watson	2.15	1.97
Serial Correlation ($\chi^2(2)$)	7.96	3.63
Instrument validity ($\chi^2(m)$)	7.76	12.75
	(m = 5)	(m = 9)

Notes: t-statistics in parentheses. A dagger (†) denotes an instrumented variable. Additional instruments are $(p_m - p^*)$, $(p_m - p^*)_{-1}$, $(w - p^*)$, $(w - p^*)_{-1}$, log (government spending + investment) − log (labor force), log (manufacturing productivity)$_{-1}$, $(p^* - p)_{-1}$. Coefficients on constants and dummies are omitted for brevity. The instrument validity test is due to Sargan (1964), and the LM test for serial correlation is due to Breusch and Godfrey (1982).

Equation (1) of table 2.8 reveals a statistically significant levels effect from relative prices, but the error-feedback term $(x - x^*)_{-1}$ is small in magnitude and rather insignificant. This is certainly very suggestive of a hysteresis effect. Equation (2) omits the error-feedback term, as well as the levels terms in x^*, z, and s. This is easily accepted ($\chi^2(4) = 4.99$) and the coefficient on the level of prices remains highly significant, implying that a transitory movement in relative prices has a permanent effect on the export share. The results in this column imply that each point-year of overvaluation of the exchange rate results in a permanent loss of export share of 0.25%. Thus a 20% overvaluation sustained for two years would result in a loss of share of 10%. This is a pretty large effect, and one might feel hesitant in pinning so much faith in the statistical significance of the error-feedback coefficient. However, even if one settles for equation (1), in which there are no long-run effects from transitory fluctuations in the real exchange rate, adjustment is still very slow—the mean lag is over five years—and from a practical point of view there may be little to choose between pure hysteresis and just very long lags.

2.3.2 Supply Effects

The possibility of hysteresis effects on the supply side of the goods market has been suggested recently by Baldwin and Krugman (1986). They show how significant fixed costs of entry into a market, for example, the cost of setting up a distribution network, can mean that large temporary exchange rate movements have permanent effects on the pattern of trade. To illustrate the argument, suppose the maximum level of profits the firm can earn at any point in time, π_t, is driven by a white-noise process, and the fixed entry cost is N. Let $V_I(V_o)$ be the expected present value to the firm of being in (out) of the market. Then the firm will enter if $\pi > \pi_I$ where $\pi_I = N + \delta(V_o - V_I)$ and δ is the (constant) real discount factor. Similarly the firm will exit if $\pi < \pi_o$, where $\pi_o = \delta(V_o - V_I)$. Clearly $\pi_I > \pi_o$. Thus a sufficiently large deterioration in profitability, for example, due to an overvaluation of the real exchange rate, may lead to profits falling below the critical level π_o and the firm leaving the market. However, it will only reenter if profitability recovers sufficiently to ensure that profitability exceeds the level π_I. If profitability was originally in the range $\pi_o < \pi < \pi_I$, a temporary deterioration in profitability will have a permanent effect. Thus a large temporary undervaluation may be necessary to restore the position ab initio.

A very similar story with essentially the same outcome as above could be told invoking the role of investment by incumbents in deterring entry (Dixit, 1980). Yet another argument for hysteresis effects on the supply side comes from the presence of technical progress through "learning-by-doing" (Kaldor 1966; Van Wijnbergen 1984). If the level of total factor productivity depends on past levels of output, then a fall in output today, due to, say, a loss in competitiveness, will lower productivity in the future and reduce supply for any given level of factor prices.

Baldwin and Krugman go on to consider how their argument is affected if there are many industries with different fixed entry costs and profitability and argue that aggregation will not eliminate or smooth away the discrete trigger feature of the model. Evaluating this model econometrically is not an easy matter, however, especially in the absence of data on entry costs. In order to capture the spirit, if not the letter, of this idea, I have therefore estimated a model of supply behavior in export markets in which producers incur adjustment costs in changing the level of exports, and these adjustment costs may be different according to whether exports are increasing or decreasing. Specifically, suppose a representative exporting firm solves the following problem:

$$\text{(8)} \quad \underset{\{X_s,K_s\}}{\text{Max}} \; E\left[\sum_{s=t}^{\infty} \delta^{s-t}\{P(X_s)X_s - c(X_s,W_s,P_s^M,K_{s-1}) - P_s^K\Delta K_s - g(\Delta X_s)\} | \Omega_t\right]$$

where W is the wage, P^M is the price of raw materials, and P^K is the price of capital. $c(.)$ is a restricted cost function (excluding any adjustment costs) with the usual properties, while $g(.)$ is an adjustment cost function. Ω_t is the information set available to the firm. Then the associated Euler equation for X between t and $t + 1$ is simply (omitting t subscripts):

$$\text{(9)} \quad P(1 - 1/\sigma) = c' + g' - \delta E g'_{+1}$$

where σ is the absolute value of the price elasticity of demand (which will be assumed constant).

To render (9) operational econometrically, we need to parameterize the two components of the cost function. As far as marginal costs are concerned, I assume a Leontief technology in value-added and raw materials, while the value-added function is Cobb-Douglas[6] in labor, L, and capital, in which case:

$$\text{(10)} \quad c' = \alpha(WL/X) + \beta P^M$$

For the adjustment cost function I assume the following form:

$$\text{(11)} \quad g(\Delta X) = \begin{cases} P^*[\gamma^+\Delta X + (\epsilon^+/2)(\Delta X)^2] & \text{if } \Delta X > 0 \\ P^*[\gamma^-\Delta X + (\epsilon^-/2)(\Delta X)^2] & \text{if } \Delta X < 0 \end{cases}$$

where $\gamma^+ > \gamma^-$ and $\epsilon^+ > \epsilon^-$ captures the idea that producers may face higher costs in entering new markets or expanding in existing ones than in exiting or contracting. It is natural to assume that such costs are incurred as expenditure abroad, and hence I have written them as proportional to P^* (which also serves to eliminate heteroscedasticity from the final estimating equation).

Finally, I assume that the real interest rate is small so that $\delta \approx 1$ to give:

$$\text{(12)} \quad \begin{aligned} P/P^* = {} & \mu\alpha(WL/P^*X) + \mu\beta(P^M/P^*) \\ & - \mu\gamma E(\Delta D_{+1}) - \mu\epsilon E[\Delta(D_{+1}\Delta X_{+1})] \\ & - \mu\epsilon^- E(\Delta^2 X_{+1}) \end{aligned}$$

where $\mu = \sigma/(\sigma - 1)$, $\gamma = \gamma^{+} - \gamma^{-}$, $\epsilon = \epsilon^{+} - \epsilon^{-}$ and D is an indicator variable such that $D = 1$ if $\Delta X > 0$ and $D = 0$ otherwise.

The presence of the indicator variable complicates estimation a little, and I have adopted the following reasonable, but somewhat ad hoc, estimation strategy. First, suppose $\gamma = \epsilon = 0$. Then (12) can be estimated with standard instrumental variable techniques replacing $E(\Delta^2 X_{+1})$ by its realization $\Delta^2 X_{+1}$ and using elements of the information set Ω_t as instruments (e.g., McCallum 1976 and Wickens 1982). However, the projections of ΔD_{+1} and $\Delta(D_{+1}\Delta X_{+1})$ on Ω_t are nonlinear and in particular have the character of a switching regression model. On the basis that the asymmetric adjustment costs probably have second-order effects on the evolution of X, at least in the region of the null $\gamma = \epsilon = 0$, I have therefore constructed instruments for these terms as follows. First I projected ΔX_{+1} and ΔX on the information set to obtain $\widehat{\Delta X}_{+1}$ and $\widehat{\Delta X}$. I then constructed proxy indicator variables $\hat{D}_{+1}$ and $\hat{D}$ such that $\hat{D}_{+1} = 1$ if $\widehat{\Delta X}_{+1} > 0$ and 0 otherwise, and $\hat{D} = 1$ if $\widehat{\Delta X} > 0$ and 0 otherwise. Finally, $(\hat{D}_{+1} - \hat{D})$ and $(\hat{D}_{+1}\widehat{\Delta X}_{+1} - \hat{D}\widehat{\Delta X})$ were added to the instrument set.

I have not included the dummies added to the demand equation in either the regressor or instrument sets, on the grounds that the occurrence of strikes, wars, and so forth, is largely unpredictable, but in any case it makes little difference to the results. The measure of wages, W, is an earnings series relating to males in manufacturing, converted to dollars. However, since productivity in export (for which read manufacturing) industries (X/L) is unavailable for the full sample, I have proxied it by economywide productivity. Because current productivity may not be weakly exogenous in (12), I have also instrumented the current labor cost term (a full list of instruments appears in the table). The raw material price variable, P^M, is a series relating to worldwide primary product prices. (P/P^*), (WL/P^*X), and (P^M/P^*) have all been normalized to unity in 1980 to aid interpretation.

Equation (1) of table 2.9 presents estimates of the basic model. Since there is strong evidence of serial correlation, and the instruments are unlikely to be strongly exogenous, I have used the forward-filtering technique of Hayashi and Sims (1983), rather then conventional methods, to produce corrected estimates. Of course this serial correlation could be symptomatic of a variety of possible misspecifications, but it is rather difficult to relax the dynamic specification yet still retain the interpretability offered by the theoretical model.

Both ΔD_{+1} and $\Delta(D_{+1}\Delta X_{+1})$ have the a priori expected signs, although only the former borders on significance. There is thus some weak support for the idea of asymmetric adjustment costs. The coefficients on labor and raw material costs both seem plausible, but the equation diagnostics are only barely satisfactory.

Table 2.9 Estimates of Export Supply Equation (Dependent variable: (P/P*))

Sample period: 1901–12, 1922–37, 1949–84.

	Equation (1)	Equation (2)
$(WL/P^*X)\dagger$	.937	0.212
	(23.61)	(1.36)
(P^M/P^*)	0.076	0.011
	(4.38)	(0.64)
$\Delta D_{+1}\dagger$	−0.031	−0.037
	(1.73)	(1.33)
$\Delta(D_{+1}\Delta X_{+1})\dagger$	−0.002	−0.005
	(0.60)	(0.61)
$\Delta^2 X_{+1}\dagger$	0.003	0.008
	(0.70)	(0.92)
$(P_{+1}X_{+1}/X)\dagger$		0.761
		(4.91)
Standard error (%)	3.99	7.44
Durbin-Watson	1.38	1.89
Instrument validity $\chi^2(m)$	22.32 (m = 13)	7.08 (m = 12)
Serial correlation $\chi^2(2)$	–	5.47

Notes: t-statistics in parentheses. A dagger denotes an instrumented variable. Additional instruments are constant, trend, (W/P^*) × (government spending plus investment/labor force), $(WL/PX)_{-1}$, $(P^M/P^*)_{-1}$, X^*_{-1}, X^*, X^*_{-1}, S, S_{-1}, Z, Z_{-1}, $(\hat{D}_{+1} - \hat{D})$, $(\hat{D}_{+1}\widehat{\Delta X}_{+1} - \hat{D}\widehat{\Delta X})$. Equation (1) is estimated using the Hayashi-Sims (1983) forward-filtering technique with serial correlation parameter of 0.623.

This version of the model does, however, ignore the sort of hysteresis effects investigated in section 2.3.1. If firms realize that a loss of market share now will result in a lower level of demand, at given prices, in the future, then they presumably will take this into account in their current pricing behavior. In particular, suppose demand is given by equation (3). In that case, if the firm disregards any effect of its own actions on competitors' prices and output, the Euler equation (9) becomes:

$$(9') \qquad P(1 - 1/\sigma) + \delta\theta\, E(P_{+1}X_{+1}/X) = c' + g' - \delta E g'_{+1}$$

yielding:

$$(12') \qquad P/P^* = \mu\alpha(WL/P^*X) + \mu\beta(P^M/P^*) - \mu\gamma E(\Delta D_{+1}) - \mu\epsilon E[\Delta(D_{+1}\Delta X_{+1})] - \mu\epsilon E(\Delta^2 X_{+1}) - \mu\theta E(P_{+1}X_{+1}/X)$$

Equation (2) of table 2.9 therefore augments the basic model with a term in $(P_{+1}X_{+1}/X)$. This has the merit of eliminating the serial correlation, but unfortunately the new term turns out to have a (significant) positive rather than a negative sign. Clearly this casts some doubt on the validity of the theoretical model. However, the other coefficients remain generally consistent with the view that it is more costly to increase exports than to reduce them. Nevertheless, more work is required to provide convincing evidence of such effects.

2.3.3 Policy Implications

The models of sections 2.3.1 and 2.3.2 are somewhat different in their implications, in that the model of 2.3.1 can produce truly permanent effects from a transitory displacement of the real exchange rate (when $\sigma\theta = 1$). By contrast, the stationary long-run equilibrium in the model of 2.3.2 is independent of the form of the adjustment costs, which only affect the transition path, with adjustment being slower in an upward direction than in a downward direction. In that sense the implications are rather different from those of Baldwin and Krugman. However, whether transitory shocks really do have permanent, or just long-lived, effects seems largely immaterial in practice.

The welfare implications are harder to draw out, however, because they require some knowledge of the causes of the fluctuation in the real exchange rate. If it is the consequence of a bubble, say, or money wage rigidity coupled with a contractionary monetary policy, then state dependence in foreign trade merely perpetuates and accentuates the welfare losses due to the original market distortion. On the other hand, the moral is less clear if the fluctuations are due to changes in real fundamentals, such as the discovery of North Sea oil. For if private agents correctly perceive the future implications of current actions (and the quote by Vickers in the Introduction suggests they may do) then there is apparently no need for any special action by governments.

North Sea oil actually provides a very interesting example, since it in fact represents a temporary rather than permanent change in the United Kingdom's industrial structure. An obvious, and increasingly relevant, question is: What happens when the oil runs out some time early in the next century? Hysteresis effects may mean that the restoration of the status quo ante is not a viable option. This seems to suggest that subsidization of the nonoil tradables sector or a policy of encouraging a weak exchange rate is desirable. But if firms are aware of the problem and correctly internalize the costs of reentering foreign markets, the benefits of learning-by-doing, and so forth, there is no role for government intervention during the interregnum whilst the oil is extracted.

This is, I would argue, too sanguine a view, since it ignores market imperfections elsewhere in the economy. In particular, consumption-smoothing arguments dictate that the benefits of oil be shared with future generations, yet the available evidence does not seem to support such ultrarational behavior by households. As a result, the level of private consumption and the current real appreciation are likely to be excessive,[7] and net investment of the proceeds from oil by the government, either directly in real public or private sector capital or indirectly through a lower budget deficit, would seem to be called for. This would automatically limit the extent of any current real appreciation and the contraction in the nonoil tradables sector.

I conclude, therefore, that hysteresis effects in trade may be a cause for concern, not only when there are temporary misalignments due to irrational speculative behavior or sluggish adjustment of nominal wages, but also when the economy is subject to temporary real disturbances. The models and estimates of this section are admittedly crude in the extreme, but the results seem sufficiently promising (if that is the right word) to suggest that further empirical work, most probably at an industrial level, would be fruitful.

Notes

1. This slightly overstates the importance of oil, because extraction costs have not been deducted. However, since marginal operating costs in 1985 were around 25% of the output price, the bias is not that significant.

2. The subsequent depreciation can, of course, be attributed to the fall in real oil prices since 1980.

3. However, Branson (1983) in his comments points out that the force of this objection is much reduced if one treats the acceleration in inflation over 1979–80 as largely unanticipated.

4. Of course contractionary fiscal policy may have raised unemployment. I have carried out a simulation of the 1979 budget (a three-point cut in the standard rate of income tax, and an increase in VAT [value added tax] from 8.5 to 15% coupled with a 1% reduction in government expenditure in the first year and 2% thereafter). The consequence is a fall of 0.5 to 0.75% in employment, but concentrated entirely in services, and a real appreciation of 4%.

5. There is obviously a certain amount of irrationality about this, but I believe it is probably more realistic than the alternative of assuming that that consumer takes into account the effect of current purchases on his future tastes.

6. I have also experimented with CES technologies, but Cobb-Douglas seems to work as well as anything.

7. If households were ultrarational then they would increase current savings out of the windfall income from oil in order to finance higher consumption in

the future. This would automatically tend to limit the current appreciation of the real exchange rate and so eliminate any reentry problems.

References

Alford, R. F. G., et al. 1971. *The British economy key statistics, 1900–1970.* London and Cambridge Economic Service.

Baldwin, R., and P. R. Krugman. 1986. Persistent trade effects of large exchange rate shocks. National Bureau of Economic Research, Working Paper no. 2017.

Bean, C. R. 1987. The macroeconomic consequences of North Sea oil. In R. Dornbusch and R. Layard, eds., *The performance of the British economy. Oxford: Oxford University Press.*

Bean, C. R., E. Dinenis, and C. Probyn. 1985. A small macroeconomic model. London School of Economics, Centre for Labour Economics, Working Paper no. 794.

Blanchard, O. J. 1981. Output, the stock market, and interest rates. *American Economic Review* 71: 132–43.

Blanchard, O. J., and C. H. Kahn. 1980. The solution of linear difference models under rational expectations. *Econometrica* 48: 1305–11.

Blanchard, O. J., and L. H. Summers. 1986. Hysteresis and the European unemployment problem. In Stanley Fischer, ed., *NBER Macroeconomics Annual,* 15–90. Cambridge, Mass.: MIT Press.

Branson, W. 1983. Comment on Buiter and Miller. *Brookings Papers on Economic Activity,* 2: 372–8.

Branson, W., and J. Rotemberg. 1980. International adjustment with wage rigidities. *European Economic Review* 13: 309–32.

Breusch, T. S., and L. G. Godfrey. 1982. A review of recent work on testing for autocorrelation in dynamic linear models. In D. Currie, R. Nobay, and D. Peel, eds., *Macroeconomic analysis.* London: Croom Helm.

Buiter, W. H., and R. Dunn. 1982. A program for solving and simulating discrete time linear rational expectations models. London School of Economics, Centre for Labour Economics, Discussion Paper no. 127.

Buiter, W. H., and M. H. Miller. 1981a. Monetary policy and international competitiveness: The problem of adjustment. In W. A. Eltis and P. J. N. Sinclair, eds., *The money supply and the exchange rate.* Oxford: Oxford University Press.

———. 1981b. The Thatcher experiment: The first two years. *Brookings Papers on Economic Activity,* 2: 315–67.

———. 1983. Changing the rules: Economic consequences of the Thatcher regime. *Brookings Papers on Economic Activity,* 2: 305–65.

Dickey, D. A., and W. A. Fuller. 1981. The likelihood ratio statistic for autoregressive time series with a unit root. *Econometrica* 49: 1057–72.

Dinenis, E. 1985. Adjustment Costs, Q, Taxation, and Investment in the U.K. London School of Economics, Centre for Labour Economics, Discussion Paper no. 235.

Dixit, A. 1980. The role of investment in entry deterrence. *Economic Journal* 90: 95–106.

Dornbusch, R. 1976. Expectations and exchange rate dynamics. *Journal of Political Economy* 84: 1161–76.

Eastwood, R. K., and A. J. Venables. 1982. The macroeconomic implications of a resource discovery in an open economy. *Economic Journal* 92: 285–99.

Engle, R. G., and C. W. J. Granger. 1987. Co-integration and error correction: Representation, estimation, and testing. *Econometrica* 55: 251–76.

Evans, G. W. 1986. A test for speculative bubbles and the sterling-dollar exchange rate 1981–84. *American Economic Review* 76: 621–36.

Fama, E. 1984. Forward and spot exchange rates. *Journal of Monetary Economics* 14: 319–38.

Forsyth, P. J., and J. A. Kay. 1980. The economic implications of North Sea oil revenues. *Fiscal Studies* 1(3): 1–28.

Frankel, J. A., and K. Froot. 1985. The dollar as an irrational speculative bubble: A tale of fundamentalists and chartists. Mimeo, University of California at Berkeley.

Gregory, R. G. 1986. Wages policy and unemployment in Australia. *Economica,* Supplement, 53: S53–74.

Grubb, D., R. Jackman, and P. R. G. Layard. 1983. Wage rigidity and unemployment in OECD countries. *European Economic Review* 21: 11–39.

Hayashi, F., and C. Sims. 1983. Nearly efficient estimation of time series models with predetermined, but not exogenous instruments. *Econometrica* 51: 783–98.

Jackman, R., and J. Sutton. 1982. Imperfect capital markets and the monetarist black box: Liquidity constraints, inflation, and the asymmetric effects of interest rate policy. *Economic Journal* 92: 108–28.

Kaldor, N. 1966. *Causes of the slow rate of growth of the United Kingdom.* Cambridge: Cambridge University Press.

Klemperer, P. D. 1987. Entry deterrence in markets with consumer switching costs. *Economic Journal,* Supplement, 97: 99–117.

Layard, P. R. G., and S. J. Nickell. 1986. Unemployment in Britain. *Economica,* Supplement, 53: S121–70.

Lindbeck, A., and D. Snower. 1986. Wage-setting, unemployment, and insider-outsider relations. *American Economic Review* (Papers and Proceedings) 76: 235–39.

McCallum, B. T. 1976. Rational expectations and the estimation of econometric models: An alternative procedure. *International Economic Review* 17: 484–90.

Matthews, K., and P. Minford. 1987. Mrs. Thatcher's economic policies 1979–1986. *Economic Policy.* Forthcoming.

Meese, R. A. 1986. Testing for bubbles in exchange markets: A case of sparkling rates? *Journal of Political Economy* 94: 345–73.

Meese, R. A., and K. Rogoff. 1983. Empirical exchange rate models of the seventies: Do they fit out of sample? *Journal of International Economics* 14: 3–24.

Newell, A., and J. S. V. Symons. 1986. The Phillips curve is a real wage equation. London School of Economics, Centre for Labour Economics, Discussion Paper no. 246.

Sargan, J. D. 1964. Wages and prices in the United Kingdom: A study in econometric methodology. In P. E. Hart, G. Mills, and J. K. Whitaker, eds., *Econometric analysis for economic planning.* London: Butterworths.

Schmalensee, R. 1978. Entry deterrence in the ready-to-eat breakfast cereal industry. *Bell Journal of Economics* 9: 305–27.

———. 1982. Product differentiation advantages of pioneering brands. *American Economic Review* 72: 349–65.

Van Wijnbergen, S. 1984. The "Dutch Disease": A Disease After All? *Economic Journal* 94: 41–55.

Wickens, M. R. 1982. The efficient estimation of econometric models with rational expectations. *Review of Economic Studies* 49: 55–67.

Appendix
Listing of the Macroeconomic Model

The equations of the log-linearized model are:

(1a) $pm = 0.19pe + 0.08pn + 0.73(wm + ty) + 0.17(ym - km_{-1})$.

(1b) $pn = 0.12pe + 0.6pm + 0.28(wn + ty) + 0.27(yn - kn_{-1})$.

(2a) $ym = 0.57c + 0.2g + 0.83(km - km_{-1}) + 2.06(kn - kn_{-1}) + 0.295(p^* + e - pm)_{-1} - 0.133sm_{-1}$.

(2b) $yn = 0.664c + 0.232g + 0.962(km - km_{-1}) + 2.38(kn - kn_{-1}) + 0.133(p^* + e - pm) + 0.376(pm - pn) - 0.072sn_{-1}$.

(3a) $(lm - ym) = 0.19pe + 0.08pn - 0.27(wm + ty) + 0.17(ym - km_{-1})$.

(3b) $(ln - yn) = 0.06pe + 0.32pm - 0.38(wn + ty) + 0.14(yn - kn_{-1})$.

(4a) $km = km_{-1} + 0.018E_{-1}qm$.

(4b) $kn = kn_{-1} + 0.0122qn + 0.0125E_{-1}qn$.

(5a) $sm = 0.974ym + 0.394sm_{-1}$.

(5b) $sn = 0.543yn + 0.667sn_{-1}$.

(6a) $\mathrm{E}qm_{+1} = i + pc - pc_{+1} + 1.05\,qm - 0.2ym + km - 0.929km_{-1}$.

(6b) $\mathrm{E}qn_{+1} = i + pc - pc_{+1} + 1.05qn - 0.374yn + kn - 0.925kn_{-1}$.

(7a) $wm = 0.73wm_{-1} - 0.21wm_{-2} + 0.79pc - 0.31pc_{-1} + 1.4l$.

(7b) $wn = 1.1wn_{-1} - 0.5wn_{-2} + 0.5pc - 0.1pc_{-1} + 1.2l$.

(8) $c = 0.94yp + 0.06a_{-1} - 0.45i$.

(9) $a = a_{-1} + 0.7i_{-1} - (pc - pc_{-1}) + 0.21(yp - c) + 0.09(qm - qm_{-1}) + 0.21(qn - qn_{-1}) - 0.7(i^L - i^L_{-1})$.

(10) $ws = 0.58ws_{-1} + 0.3(wm - pc) + 0.7(wn - pc) - 0.174(wm - pc)_{-1} - 0.406(wn - pc)_{-1} + 0.42l_{-1}.$

(11) $cg = 0.087(wm - pc) + 0.203(wn - pc) + 0.29rr - 0.94l.$

(12) $yp = 0.82ws + 0.18cg + \eta(xo + e - pc).$

(13) $Ee_{+1} = e + i - i^{*}.$

(14) $Ei^{L}_{+1} = 1.1i^{L} - 0.1i.$

(15) $m - pc = 0.24y + 0.48(m - pc)_{-1} - 1.3i.$

(16) $y = 0.3ym + 0.7yn.$

(17) $l = 0.3lm + 0.7ln.$

(18) $pe = 0.32(pr + e) + 0.16(po + e) + 0.16pm + 0.36pn.$

(19) $pc = 0.35pm + 0.55pn + 0.1(p^{*} + e) + tx.$

An *m* after a letter denotes a manufacturing variable while an *n* after a variable denotes a nonmanufacturing variable. The variables are:

a = real private wealth at end of period.
c = real private consumption.
cg = real current grants.
e = nominal dollar exchange rate (price of foreign currency).
g = real government spending.
i = nominal short-term interest rate.
i^{L} = nominal long-term interest rate.
ki = capital stock at end of period (i = m, n).
li = employment ($i = m, n$).
l = total employment.
m = nominal money stock.
pi = price of output ($i = m, n$).
p^{*} = price of foreign manufactures (dollars).
po = price of oil (dollars).
pr = price of nonoil raw materials (dollars).
pe = price of material inputs.
pc = consumer price index.
qi = Tobin's Q ($i = m, n$).
rr = replacement ratio.
si = stock of inventories at end of period ($i = m, n$).
tx = expenditure tax rate.
ty = income tax rate (including employers contributions).
wi = post-tax nominal wage ($i = m, n$).
ws = real post-tax wages and salaries.
xo = value of oil rents (dollars).

yi = output ($i = m, n$).
y = total (nonoil) output.
yp = private post-tax nonproperty income.

Equations (1), (2), (3), (4), and (5) determine prices, output, employment, the capital stock, and inventories in each sector. Equations (6) are arbitrage relationships determining stock prices, while equations (7) determine wages. Equation (8) is the consumption function, and equation (9) determines the level of real wealth as a function of stock prices, interest rates, and savings. Equations (10), (11), and (12) determine wages and salaries, current grants, and hence personal disposable income. The coefficient $\eta = 0.037$ when the United Kingdom is considered to be an oil producer and $\eta = 0$ when the United Kingdom is considered not to be an oil producer. Equation (13) is the uncovered interest parity condition, (14) is the arbitrage condition for long bonds, and (15) is a conventional demand for money function. Equations (16) to (19) are quasi-identities determining total output and employment and the price of inputs and consumer prices. All variables are in logarithms except the interest rates and Tobin's Q.

Comment Willem H. Buiter

This is a very interesting paper which opens up a range of important theoretical, empirical, and policy issues. In my comment I can only hope to explore the tip of this rather large iceberg.

The paper falls into two parts that are connected fairly loosely. In the first part, the linearized version of a small econometric model of the U.K. economy, specified and estimated by the author, is used to evaluate the contributions of monetary policy, the discovery and exploitation of North Sea oil, and a number of adverse supply shocks to U.K. economic performance over the period of 1978–81, with special reference to the real exchange rate. The second part is a theoretical and empirical exploration of the significance of hysteresis, or path dependence, in various dimensions of U.K. economic behavior, that is, of the phenomenon that temporary shocks may have permanent consequences. Weaker interpretations of this concept characterize as hysteretic any high degree of persistence of shocks to the demand for and supply of U.K. output, to equilibrium output, to the trade balance, and so forth. I discuss these two main sections of the paper in turn, after some brief comments on the econometric model.

Willem H. Buiter is professor of economics at Yale University and a research associate at the National Bureau of Economic Research.

The Model

The econometric model is a IS-LM, aggregate demand–aggregate supply model with rational expectations in the (efficient) financial asset markets, some real and financial asset dynamics, and a rather rich supply side. The three-sector model of production distinguishes a manufacturing sector, a nonmanufacturing sector, and an oil sector. The manufacturing-nonmanufacturing split corresponds to the traditional traded-nontraded goods distinction. Oil production is exogenous. Apart from the familiar caveat that many of Britain's services are highly traded (financial, shipping and other international transportation, tourism, education, etc.) this sectoral disaggregation is appropriate and important for understanding the recent behavior of the U.K. economy.

The government budget identity is not considered explicitly. This can be justified on the grounds that, in the model, the U.K. economy is specified as a small open economy on the financial side. Capital mobility is perfect, interest-bearing financial claims at home and abroad (including government debt) are perfect substitutes, and the world rate of interest is taken to be parametric. These assumptions are appropriate, however, only if the U.K. government is, and is perceived to be, solvent. If current and prospective future deficits imply some risk of partial or complete repudiation or default, the assumption of a perfectly elastic world supply of funds schedule will cease to be correct. It should therefore be checked, in the simulations, that the behavior implied for public debt and deficits is indeed consistent with solvency. Cuts in tax rates that are never (expected to be) reversed or balanced by future spending cuts or increases in future seigniorage are, for example, likely to be inconsistent with solvency (pace the Laffer curve and/or "fiscal increasing returns").

The Sterling Real Exchange Rate 1979–81

Between 1978 and 1981, sterling's real exchange rate (as measured by relative producer prices) appreciated by 23%. Using different price or cost indices, the real appreciation (and the subsequent real depreciation) can be made to look even more dramatic, reaching over 40% for the IMF's series for normalized relative unit wage costs in manufacturing.

Four possible causes of this appreciation can be distinguished: monetary policy shocks, fiscal policy shocks, oil, and adverse supply shocks.

In spite of the erratic and high growth rates of the U.K. government's initial monetary target, sterling M3, there can be little doubt that money became tight in Britain shortly after the new Conservative administration assumed office in 1979. The degree of tightening, actual and expected, remains hidden in the entrails of the behavior of the narrow monetary aggregates (M_0 and M_1), nominal and real interest rates, and so forth. It would of course be improper to infer the degree of monetary tightness from the behavior of the exchange rate if our aim is to assess the effect of tight money on the exchange rate. Tight money should only have first-order real effects, including effects on the real exchange rate, if there is nominal inertia or stickiness in the wage-price mechanism. Empirical evidence suggesting that the degree of nominal inertia in the United Kingdom (and in most other European economies) is very limited would, if it were convincing, weaken or even undermine completely the monetary interpretation of the real appreciation. On the other hand, the fact that the real appreciation was temporary and has by now been reversed to a large extent is consistent with a monetary interpretation.

Fiscal policy works the wrong way, at any rate with regard to the behavior of the real exchange rate. With a floating exchange rate and a high degree of international capital mobility, tight fiscal policy causes a real (and a nominal) depreciation. The real depreciation will in this case be permanent unless the fiscal contraction is reversed. The fiscal contraction in the United Kingdom during 1980–81 was indeed reversed after 1982. While fiscal policy can help explain the depth of the 1979–81 recession in the United Kingdom (and the subsequent recovery) it renders more difficult the explanation of the behavior of sterling.

Bean's model (correctly in my view) ignores any direct supply-side effects of the oil discovery and of the coming-on-stream of oil production. The oil industry certainly faced a perfectly elastic supply schedule of foreign capital and had a very small impact on the demand for nonproduced domestic resources such as labor and land.

Modeling the oil shocks is difficult. Bean's specification seems as reasonable as any: the volume of reserves and production were correctly evaluated but assumed zero prior to the first OPEC oil price shock. Each of the two oil price shocks is viewed as unanticipated, immediate, and permanent. The fiscal aspects of oil are important, since the government appropriated an increasing share of the rents during the period under consideration. This share has reached 80 or 90% by now. In the oil shock simulations, real government spending and tax rates are kept constant. Given the backward-looking nature of the consumption function, anticipated future oil revenues would have influenced consumption today only through their effect on forward-looking financial asset prices. Since only the deficit and the debt are assumed to be affected by the oil revenues, even this financial transmission channel will be inoperative under the assumption of perfect capital mobility. Alternative current and anticipated future responses of spending and/or tax rates could have produced quite different simulation results.

The contractionary effects attributed to oil discoveries or oil price increases (in the case of a next exporter) come either through lags in spending (Eastwood and Venables 1982) or through a wealth effect on the demand for money (Buiter and Purvis 1983). Wealth effects on money demand seem unlikely with Bean's narrow monetary aggregate. Spending lags are more likely, given a backward-looking consumption function, absence of debt neutrality, and a fiscal policy that did not, in the early years of the Thatcher regime, reduce taxes or raise public spending by the annuity value of the increase in oil wealth.

The adverse-supply-shock view of the causes of the real depreciation summarizes the winter of discontent (1978–79) and its aftermath by a 2-percentage-point increase in the natural rate of unemployment. The sign of the effect obviously goes in the right direction (with regard to both the real exchange rate and real output), but it seems sufficiently ad hoc to warrant being treated with caution. Surely by now these temporary effects have worn off after eight successive winters of content and significant legislative initiatives curbing union power. The real exchange rate indeed has come down again, but unemployment and activity have not recovered.

Bean's reminder that the greater portion of the 1979–80 sterling appreciation may have been due to a speculative bubble rather than to a movement of fundamentals is appropriate. A definitive decomposition of the "Thatcher wiggle" in the real exchange rate remains to be done.

Permanent Effects From Temporary Misalignments

The second half of the paper concerns the continuing saga of the unit root, the infestation of martingales and random walks that after affecting observables like the stock market, the nominal and real exchange rates, and consumption, now touches unobservables like the natural rate of unemployment.

Bean investigates whether there is hysteresis, or path dependence, in British trade performance, that is, whether temporary shocks (e.g., to competitiveness) have permanent consequences for British exports, X, relative to world imports X^*. P is the price of British exports, P^* the appropriate foreign price index, and both are measured in terms of a common currency. The (demand) equation that is tested in given in (1).

$$(1) \qquad \Delta(X - X^*)_t = j_0 + j_1(P^* - P)_t + j_2(X - X^*)_{t-1}.$$

If the restriction $j_2 = 0$ is accepted, there is hysteresis in British export demand as there is a unit root in the $X - X^*$ process. The hysteresis issue is then approached by considering whether X and X^* are cointegrated. If $P - P^*$ is strongly exogenous and stationary and if $j_2 = 0$, then X and X^* cannot be cointegrated. Finding that the null hypothesis that X and X^* are not cointegrated cannot be rejected (i.e., that X and X^* are cointegrated) therefore implies (if $P - P^*$ is a strongly exogenous stationary process) that $j_2 \neq 0$. However, John Huizinga (1987) finds that his real exchange rate measure for the United Kingdom (which is similar but not identical to Bean's $P - P^*$ measure) is nonstationary (the univariate representation of his real exchange rate process has a unit root). Doubts must also exist with regard to the strong exogeneity of $P - P^*$. Strong exogeneity of $P - P^*$ is weak exogeneity plus Granger noncausality (i.e., the nonpredictability of $P - P^*$ from past values of the other variable(s), once the predictive content of past values of $P - P^*$ has been allowed for). Granger noncausality can in principle always be tested, (although no tests were reported in the paper), but the assertion that $P - P^*$ is weakly exogenous always relies on a priori assumptions, that is, it can only be tested together with other restrictions on the model. Let $\bar{Z}$ and $\bar{Y}$ be matrices of observations on Z and Y. The joint likelihood function can be written as L $(\lambda_1, \lambda_2; \bar{Z}, \bar{Y})$, where λ_1 contains the parameters of interest and λ_2 the nuisance parameters. $\bar{Z}$ is weakly exogenous if $L(\lambda_1,\lambda_2;\bar{Z}, \bar{Y}) = L_1(\lambda_1;\bar{Y}/\bar{Z})L_2(\lambda_2;\bar{Z})$. In that case the parameters of interest are confined to the likelihood in Y conditional on Z. In a simultaneous demand-supply equilibrium model, weak exogeneity of price with respect to quantity seems unlikely (although this will of course depend on what the parameters of interest are).

If X and X^* are cointegrated, then a linear combination of the two is stationary and the behavior of each of them can be described by an error-correction mechanism.

More precisely, let $I(i)i = 0,1,2 \ldots$ denote the order of integration of a stochastic process. $f(I(i))_t$ denotes a stochastic process integrated of order i. A set of variables, each of them $I(1)$ is cointegrated if a linear combination of them is $I(0)$. Let X and X^* both be $I(1)$. They are cointegrated if

$$X_t = a_0 + a_1 X_t^* + f(I(0))_t. \tag{2}$$

In that case there exist error-correction mechanisms

$$\Delta X_t = b_1 f(I(0))_{t-1} + \tilde{f}(I(0))_t \tag{3}$$

and

$$\Delta X^*_t = b_2 f(I(0)_{t-1} + \tilde{\tilde{f}}(I(0))_t \tag{4}$$

where $|b_1| + |b_2| \neq 0$.

This decomposition into error correction and short-run dynamics does not seem to be unique, however. If X_t and X^*_t are cointegrated, for example, so are X_t and X^*_{t-1}, since (2) can be written as

$$X_t = a_0 + a_1 X^*_{t-1} + a_1(X^*_t - X^*_{t-1}) + f(I(0))_t.$$

$X^*_t - X^*_{t-1}$ is $I(0)$ and $a_1(X^*_t - X^*_{t-1}) + f(I(0))_t = \hat{f}(I(0))_t$ is therefore also $I(0)$, as it is the sum of two stationary stochastic processes. The error-correction mechanisms in (3) and (4) therefore can be rewritten as

$$\Delta X_t = b'_1 \hat{f}(I(0))_{t-1} + \hat{\hat{f}}(I(0))_t$$

and

$$\Delta X''_t = \mathrm{b}'_2 \hat{f}(I(0))_{t-1} + \hat{\hat{\hat{f}}}(I(0))_t.$$

The decomposition of the ΔX and ΔX^* dynamics into a long-run error-correction component and a short-run disequilibrium-adjustment component therefore seems not uniquely identified, limiting the usefulness of these exercises. More generally, if X_t and X^*_t are cointegrated, so are X_t and X^*_{t-j} for any finite j.

Bean considers equation (1) to be a representation of the demand side of the U.K. export market. The paper also contains a specification and estimate of a supply equation. His discussion in section 2.3.1 shows clearly that hysteresis in the demand side need not imply hysteresis in the equilibrium quantities. It isn't quite clear to me whether we should be interested primarily in demand-side hysteresis, in supply-side hysteresis, or in hysteresis in the equilibrium quantities.

The discussion of the economic mechanisms that might generate hysteresis at times seems to take us far from the narrow or strict definition of hysteresis. A strictly hysteretic dynamic system is one for which the steady-state or long-run values (distributions) of the endogenous variables depend not only on the steady-state values (distributions) of the exogenous variables but also on the initial conditions of the state variables and on the values of the exogenous variables during the adjustment process: how you get there determines where you get to. In discrete time, linear dynamic systems hysteresis is present when there are one or more unit roots. Adjustment costs do not in general imply hysteresis. Irreversibilities may well imply hysteretic behavior, but this is unlikely to show up in the form of a linear process with unit roots. Nonlinearities (such as kinked oligopolistic demand curves) may generate local hysteresis, but not the global hysteresis of linear systems with unit roots. In the end, the paper tries to identify a weaker (and perhaps more relevant) form of hysteresis, that is, long lags and a high (but not perfect) degree of persistence in the behavior of important economic variables.

If we detect hysteresis (even perfect hysteresis), should we worry about the working of the economic system? A priori, the presence of hysteresis in equilibrium prices or quantities is not a cause for alarm and does not indicate a malfunctioning of the economy. Consumption may follow a random walk in economic systems in which the invisible hand is doing a marvellous job. In an economy in which uncovered nominal interest parity holds, the real exchange rate will follow a random walk if the authorities pursue a policy of equalizing ex ante real interest rates at home and abroad. This will be true when the economy is a neoclassical wonderland or a sticky-price, Keynesian unemployment world in which, under a different policy regime (such as a random walk for the level or growth rate of the nominal money stock) overshooting of nominal and/or real exchange rates could occur.

In conclusion, this very interesting paper points towards a range of unresolved theoretical and empirical issues concerning hysteresis: (1) the distinction between strict hysteresis and weaker notions of a high degree of persistence; (2) the distinction between hysteresis in particular decision rules (e.g., demand or supply) (or structural-form hysteresis) and hysteresis in equilibrium variables (or reduced-form hysteresis); (3) the distinction between deep hysteresis (such as the hysteresis in the natural rate of unemployment that may come out of human capital or insider-outsider mechanisms) and shallow hysteresis, such as the hysteresis of the real exchange rate reflecting a particular monetary or fiscal policy; (4) the need for a careful welfare economics of hysteretic behavior. The presence of hysteresis is not prima facie evidence of an externality.

References

Buiter, W. H., and D. Purvis. 1983. Oil, disinflation, and export competitiveness: A model of the Dutch disease. In J. S. Bhandari and B. H. Putnam, eds., *Economic interdependence and flexible exchange rates*, pp. 221–47. Cambridge: MIT Press.

Eastwood, R. K., and A. J. Venables. 1982. The macroeconomic implications of a resource discovery in an open economy. *Economic Journal* 92:285–99.

Huizinga, J. 1987. An empirical investigation of the long-run behavior of real exchange rates. Mimeo.

3 Exchange Rate Variability, Misalignment, and the European Monetary System

Paul De Grauwe and Guy Verfaille

3.1 Introduction

The European Monetary System (EMS) was launched in March 1979. It came as a reaction to the large fluctuations of the dollar and was stimulated by the belief of policy makers that the intra-European exchange rate uncertainty was detrimental to trade and investment in Europe. The primary purpose of the founders of the EMS was therefore to create a zone of relative exchange rate stability which, if successful, could contribute to better prospects for growth of income and trade in Europe. Moreover, it was hoped that the workings of the EMS would facilitate the convergence of the economies of the EEC. By doing so, it would create the necessary conditions for further economic and political integration in Western Europe.

In this paper we first analyze to what extent the EMS has been successful in stabilizing the exchange rates among its member currencies (section 3.2) and in avoiding the misalignments of exchange rates which have been prevalent outside the system (section 3.3). In section 3.4 the salient features of the growth of trade between EMS countries and a group of non-EMS countries are presented. This section leaves us with a puzzle. Despite the relative success in stabilizing exchange rates, the EMS zone is faced with a slow growth of its internal trade.

The rest of the paper is an attempt at explaining this puzzle. In order to do so, we specify an econometric model (section 3.6) and use it to

Paul De Grauwe is a professor of economics at the University of Leuven, Belgium. Guy Verfaille is a research associate at the University of Leuven, Belgium.

The authors are grateful to Jacques Melitz and to the participants of the conference for many useful suggestions.

quantify the contribution of several factors in the explanation of the slowdown of intra-EMS trade.

3.2 The EMS and Exchange Rate Stability

How successful has the EMS been in reducing exchange rate variability within the system? This question has been discussed in great detail in recent studies (see, e.g., Ungerer 1983, 1986, EC Commission 1984, Rogoff 1985). The general conclusion to be drawn from these studies is that the EMS indeed contributed to a relative stability of the intra-EMS exchange rates.

Some additional evidence on the variability of real exchange rates is provided here. The way we proceed is to compare measures of exchange rate variability of the EMS countries before and after 1979 and inside and outside the system.

Table 3.1 presents the standard deviations of the monthly changes in the real effective exchange rates of the EMS during 1973–78 and 1979–86. Tables 3.2 and 3.3 do the same for the quarterly and yearly changes, respectively, in the real effective exchange rates. These effective exchange rates were computed for each EMS country relative to the rest of the EMS and relative to a control group of countries consisting of the eight major industrial countries outside the EMS (Austria, Canada, Japan, Norway, Sweden, Switzerland, the United States, and the United Kingdom). This allows us to compare the exchange rate variability of EMS currencies inside and outside the system.

The results of table 3.1 (monthly changes) suggest the following interpretation. First, the intra-EMS effective exchange rates generally tend to become significantly less variable after 1979. This decline in intra-EMS exchange rate variability is most pronounced for the newcomers in the EMS (i.e., those countries that prior to 1979 did not participate in an exchange rate arrangement) and for Germany. The latter can be explained by the fact that a significant part of the German trade is with France and Italy, two countries that joined the EMS arrangement.

Second, the variability of the exchange rates of the EMS countries with the industrialized countries outside the EMS does not change significantly after 1979. The exception here is Ireland, which uncoupled its currency from the pound sterling when entering the EMS. Third, we observe that the variability of the EMS exchange rates with the currencies outside the EMS is for all countries significantly higher than the intra-EMS variability.

This broad picture of the short-term (monthly) exchange rate variability can also be found in table 3.2, which presents evidence concerning quarterly exchange rate variability. There is a difference,

Table 3.1 **Standard Deviation of the Monthly Changes of the Real Effective Exchange Rates (%)**

	Intra-EMS		Extra-EMS[a]	
	1973–79[b] (1)	1979–86[b] (2)	1973–79 (3)	1979–86 (4)
Belgium	0.82	0.86	1.56	1.72
Denmark	1.25	0.87	1.62	1.48
Netherlands	0.99	0.73	1.83	1.81
Ireland	2.33	1.10	1.19	1.85
France	1.43	1.06	1.74	1.80
Germany	1.22	0.66	1.71	1.42
Italy	2.09	0.92	1.57	1.40
	F-tests on the Columns[c]			
	(1) – (2)	(3) – (4)	(1) – (3)	(2) – (4)
Belgium	1.10	1.21	3.64*	3.97*
Denmark	2.08*	1.20	1.69*	2.93*
Netherlands	1.82*	1.02	3.42*	6.11*
Ireland	4.50*	2.41*	3.80*	2.86*
France	1.80*	1.07	1.48	2.87*
Germany	3.38*	1.45	1.98*	4.60*
Italy	5.13*	1.24	1.79*	2.31*

Source: International Monetary Fund, International Financial Statistics.

[a]The Extra-EMS group of countries consists of Austria, Canada, Japan, Norway, Sweden, Switzerland, the United States, and the United Kingdom.

[b]The first subperiod goes from January 1973 to February 1979, and the second from March 1979 to October 1986.

[c]The F-statistics reported test for the significance of the variances between the two columns indicated.

$^*p < .05$.

however. The decline in intra-EMS variability of the French franc and the Danish krone after 1979 seems to be insignificant on a quarterly basis.

When looking at the standard deviation of yearly changes of the real effective exchange rates in table 3.3, we even observe an increase in the intra-EMS variability after 1979 for the Belgian franc, the Danish krone and the deutsche mark (DM). The limited degrees of freedom however, prevent formal F-tests on the significance of these increases.

A comparison of the monthly,,quarterly, and yearly changes in the real effective rates suggests that the decline in intra-EMS variability has been somewhat more significant at the short end. It is nevertheless fair to conclude that the EMS has succeeded in creating a zone of relative exchange rate stability in Europe.[1]

Table 3.2 **Standard Deviation of the Quarterly Changes of the Real Effective Exchange Rates (%)**

	Intra-EMS		Extra-EMS[a]	
	1973–78[b] (1)	1979–86[b] (2)	1973–78 (3)	1979–86 (4)
Belgium	1.25	1.24	2.87	3.11
Denmark	1.61	1.28	2.27	2.60
Netherlands	1.68	1.20	3.02	3.48
Ireland	4.21	1.84	2.40	3.63
France	2.40	2.03	2.63	3.04
Germany	2.20	1.17	3.06	2.73
Italy	3.51	1.47	2.61	2.56
	F-tests on the Columns[c]			
	(1) – (2)	(3) – (4)	(1) – (3)	(2) – (4)
Belgium	0.99	1.17	5.29*	6.25*
Denmark	1.58	1.31	1.99	4.12*
Netherlands	1.96*	1.32	3.25*	8.41*
Ireland	5.23*	2.29*	3.08*	3.89*
France	1.40	1.34	1.20	2.25*
Germany	3.51*	1.25	1.94	5.44*
Italy	5.73*	1.04	1.81	3.06*

Source: International Monetary Fund, International Financial Statistics.

[a]See note *a* of table 3.1.

[b]The first subperiod goes from 1973:II to 1978:IV, and the second from 1979:I to 1986:III.

[c]See note *c* of table 3.1.

3.3 The EMS and Misalignment

Another way to evaluate the performance of the EMS in stabilizing exchange rates is to compare measures of misalignment within and outside the EMS. This is done in this section. At first, however, the equilibrium rate that will be used as a reference for the calculations of misalignment needs to be defined. There are several possible ways to calculate an equilibrium exchange rate. One has been made popular in recent years by Williamson.[2] In this view the "fundamental equilibrium exchange rate" is the real exchange rate leading (over the cycle) to a current account balance which is sustainable given the long-run equilibrium capital movements. An alternative and computationally easier way is to calculate purchasing power parity (PPP) rates and correct them for productivity differences between countries.[3] Here we used the latter approach. As derived more formally in appendix A, we can write the measure of misalignment M as:

Table 3.3 **Standard Deviation of the Yearly Changes of the Real Effective Exchange Rates (%)**

	Intra-EMS		Extra-EMS[a]	
	1974–78[b] (1)[c]	1980–86[b] (2)[c]	1974–78 (3)[c]	1980–86 (4)[c]
Belgium	2.58	3.66	5.24	7.61
Denmark	2.77	3.47	3.25	4.80
Netherlands	3.63	2.84	4.91	8.88
Ireland	7.63	3.28	4.34	7.09
France	5.02	4.78	5.06	6.52
Germany	3.01	3.46	4.31	7.70
Italy	5.14	2.84	5.02	6.53

Source: International Monetary Fund, International Financial Statistics.

[a]See note *a* of table 3.1.

[b]The first subperiod goes from January 1974 to February 1979, and the second from March 1980 to October 1986. These subperiods were chosen since monthly observations of 12-month changes are considered and we didn't want to mix periods with different exchange rate regimes.

[c]The limited number of independent observations did not allow us to perform the same kind of F-tests as in tables 3.1 and 3.2.

$$M = S + P_c^* - P_c + (1 - a)(q - q^*)$$

where M = misalignment of the exchange rate (%)
S = log of the nominal exchange rate
P_c = log of the general price index
q = log of the productivity level in the tradables sector
a = share of traded goods in the consumption basket
* refers to a variable of the foreign country.

A common problem with PPP-based calculations like these is the proper choice of the base period. To minimize distortions from choosing a particular year, we have taken the average over 1974–85 as constituting the equilibrium value.

In figures 3.1 to 3.7 we present the misalignment of a number of currencies against non-EMS currencies and against EMS currencies. These misalignments are calculated using measures of effective exchange rates. To take an example: figure 3.1 indicates that in 1985 the DM was overvalued (on average) against the other EMS currencies and undervalued against the group of non-EMS currencies.

On the whole, the evidence indicates that although misalignments were also present among the EMS currencies, they seem to have been smaller than those between currencies which were not explicitly linked through an exchange-rate agreement. More evidence is shown in table 3.4. This table concentrates on the period in which the EMS was in

Table 3.4 **Maximum Misalignment (in Either Direction) during the Period 1979–85 (%)**

	vs. EMS Currencies	vs. Non-EMS Currencies
Belgian franc	19.00	30.20
Danish krone	8.17	13.98
Guilder	11.38	16.74
French franc	8.64	21.51
Deutsche mark	8.91	12.77
Italian lira	11.47	15.83
Pound sterling	27.21	24.50
U.S. dollar	39.37	18.06
Yen	18.69	23.39

effect. It presents the maximum misalignment of the effective rates during 1979–85. We observe that the EMS currencies always recorded the highest misalignment with respect to the group of non-EMS currencies.

3.4 The EMS and Trade

One of the striking phenomena concerning the growth of trade within the EMS is its sluggishness since 1979. The evidence is summarized in figure 3.8. It shows the average yearly growth of intra-EMS trade during 1973–78 and 1979–85 and compares this with the growth of trade (export + import) of the EMS countries with the non-EMS industrialized countries during the same two periods.

Two observations can be made from the evidence of figure 3.8. First, the yearly growth of the intra-EMS trade declined on average from 4.44% in 1973–78 to 2.74% in 1979–85. The trade of the EMS countries with the non-EMS industrial countries does not seem to have been subjected to the same deceleration. As this trade might have been affected by the large movements of the dollar, we also show the growth rates of the trade of the EMS with the non-EMS group, excluding the United States. Although we observe a somewhat larger deceleration, it is nevertheless a less pronounced slowdown than the one observed within the EMS.[4]

Second, during both the pre-EMS and the post-EMS periods, the average growth of the intra-EMS trade was substantially lower than the average growth of the trade of the EMS countries with the non-EMS industrialized countries. Thus, the intra-EMS trade flows continued to grow at about half the rate of the trade between EMS and non-EMS countries, despite a significantly greater exchange rate stability

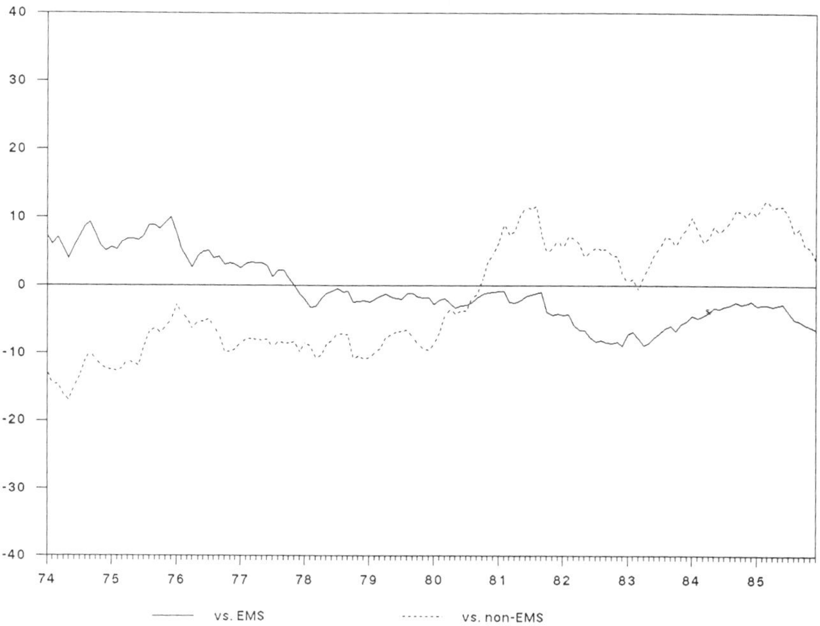

Fig. 3.1 Misalignment of the DM versus EMS and non-EMS currencies (+ = undervaluation of the DM).

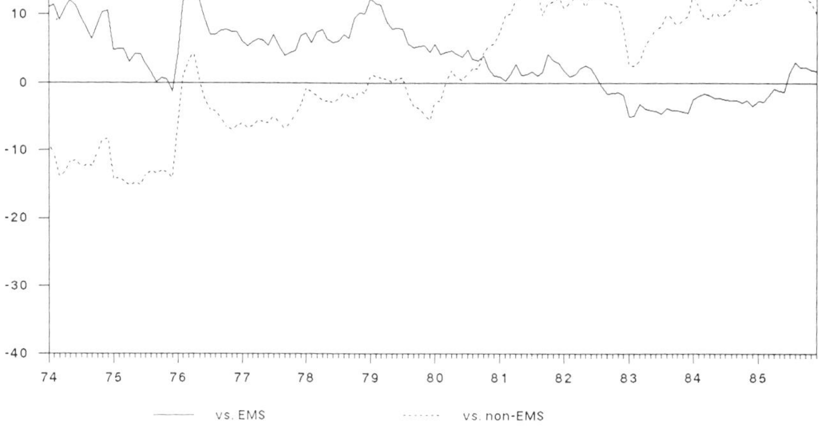

Fig. 3.2 Misalignment of the lira versus EMS and non-EMS currencies (+ = undervaluation of the lira).

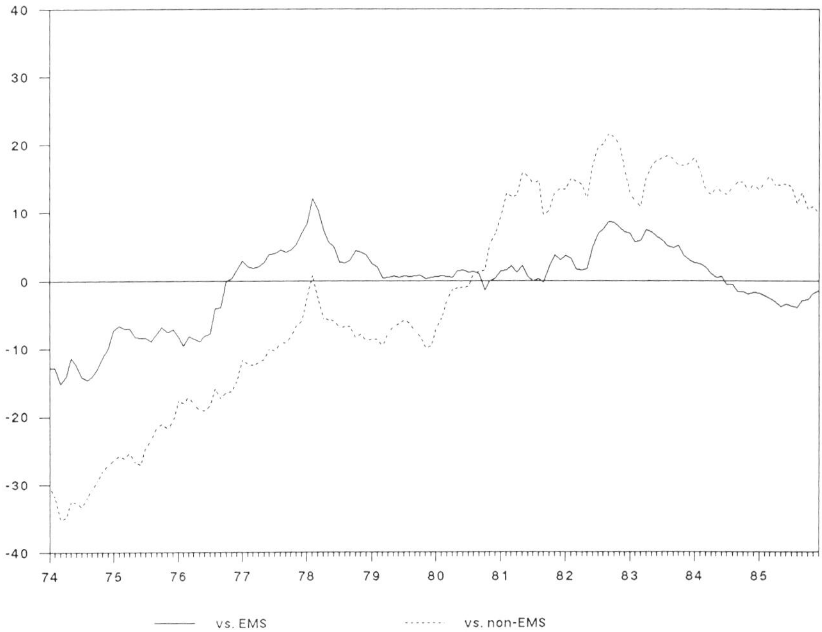

Fig. 3.3 Misalignment of the French franc versus EMS and non-EMS currencies (+ = undervaluation of the French franc).

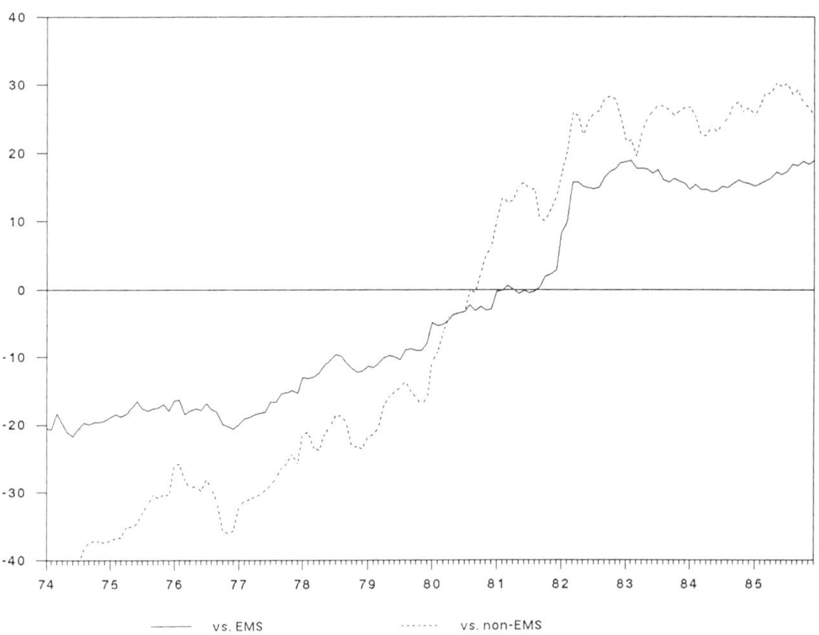

Fig. 3.4 Misalignment of the Belgian franc versus EMS and non-EMS currencies (+ = undervaluation of the Belgian franc).

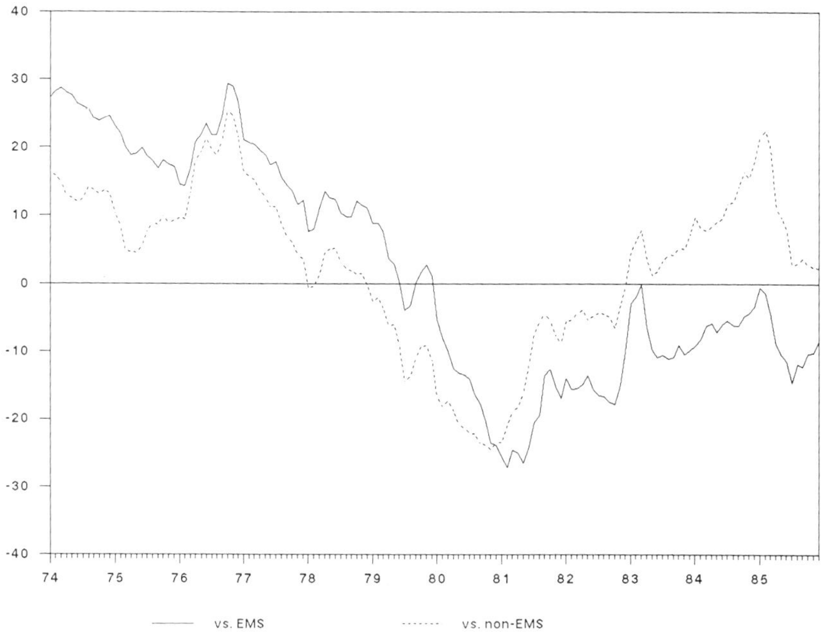

Fig. 3.5 Misalignment of the pound sterling versus EMS and non-EMS currencies (+ = undervaluation of the pound).

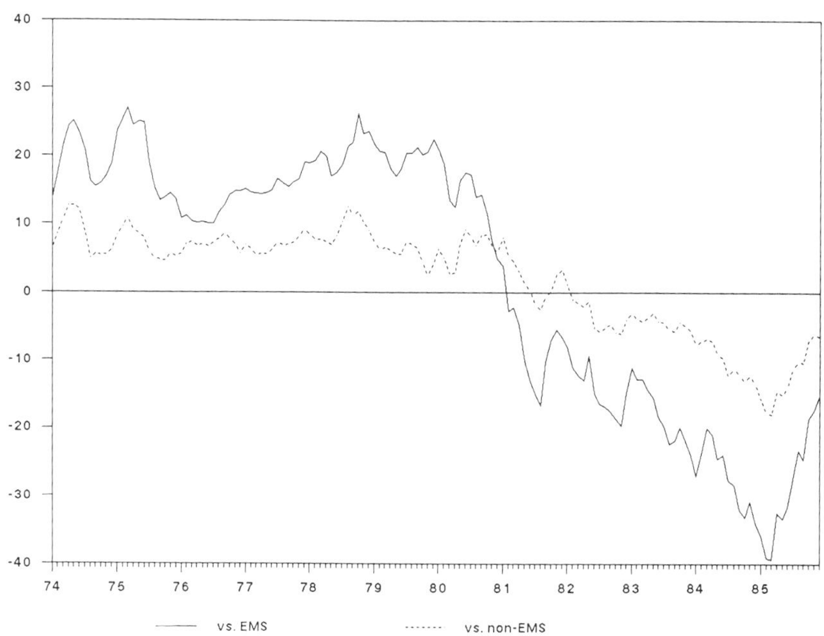

Fig. 3.6 Misalignment of the U.S. dollar versus EMS and non-EMS currencies (+ = undervaluation of the dollar).

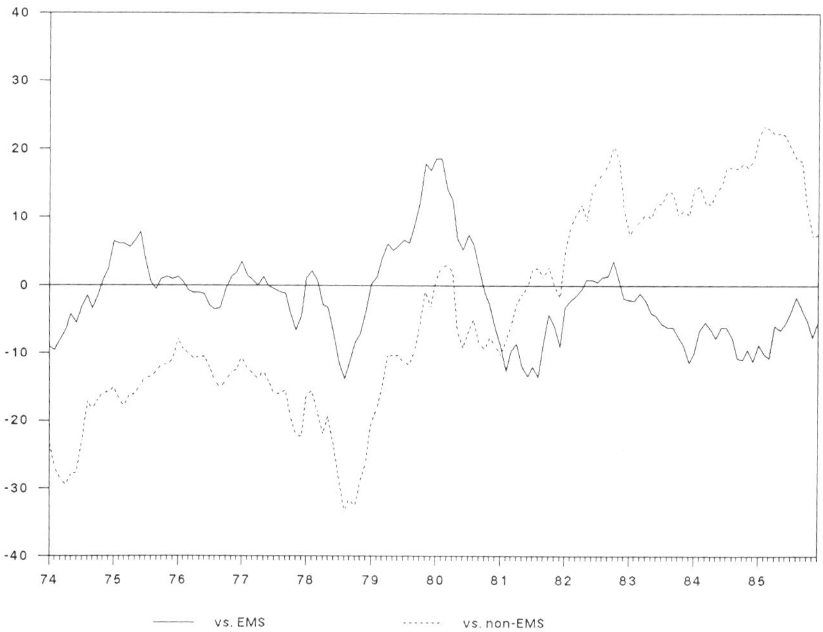

Fig. 3.7 Misalignment of the yen versus EMS and non-EMS currencies (+ = undervaluation of the yen).

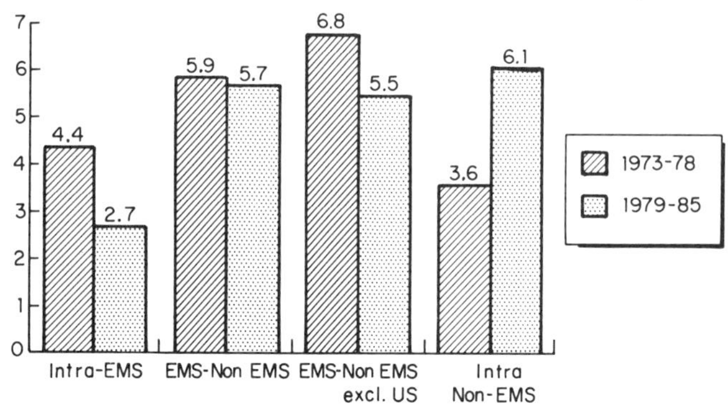

Fig. 3.8 Average yearly growth of trade (export + import) in constant prices (in percentages). *Source:* IMF, Direction of Trade; IMF, International Financial Statistics. *Notes:* 1. The group of non-EMS industrialized countries consists of Austria, Canada, Japan, Norway, Sweden, Switzerland, the U.K., and the U.S. 2. The export figures of each country were deflated by the index of export unit values of the same country; in order to obtain import figures in constant prices we used export unit values of the different countries of origin of these imports and weighted these indices using the share of each exporting country in the total imports. The trade figures are the sum of exports and imports.

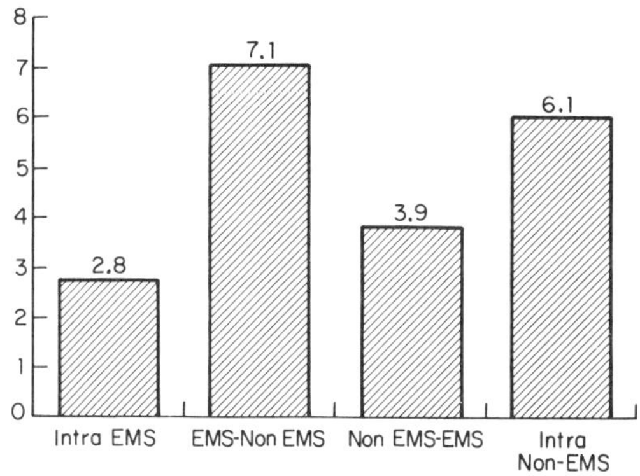

Fig. 3.9 Average yearly growth of exports in constant prices (in percentages) 1979–85. *Source:* IMF, Direction of Trade; IMF, International Financial Statistics. *Notes:* 1. The group of non-EMS countries consists of Austria, Canada, Japan, Norway, Sweden, Switzerland, the U.S., and the U.K. 2. The export figures of each country were deflated by the index of export unit values of the same country.

inside the EMS. Figure 3.9 presents some additional evidence about these trade flows in the post-1979 period. Whereas the intra-EMS exports grew at an annual rate of 2.79%, the exports from the EMS to the rest of the industrial countries and the exports between the non-EMS countries grew at more than twice this rate. Even the exports from the non-EMS to the EMS grew substantially faster than the intra-EMS exports. This is surprising, since these export flows also include the exports of the United States to the EMS, which were hampered by the significant appreciation of the dollar during the period.

It is clear that there is a puzzle to explain. On the one hand, the EMS has been successful in avoiding the high variability of exchange rates observed outside the system. On the other hand, it has not only experienced a slowdown of its internal trade, but the intra-EMS trade now grows at a substantially slower pace than that in the rest of the industrialized world. These phenomena raise a number of issues. First, there is the question of how exchange rate variability affects international trade flows. Second, if it can be established that exchange rate stability fosters trade, how important is this effect? The evidence of the EMS indicates that if exchange rate stability has a positive effect, it must have been swamped by other variables which negatively affected intra-EMS trade. What are these variables? And how important have they been? These are some of the questions we intend to answer in the following sections. As we are primarily interested in the possible effects of the EMS arrangement on trade among its members, we limit the empirical work to the period 1979–85. This of course prevents us from analyzing why intra-EMS trade has decelerated after 1979, but allows us to focus on the difference in trade growth during the period in which the EMS was in effect.[5]

3.5 Exchange Rate Variability and International Trade

Exchange rate variability can affect the growth rate of international trade in several ways. One has to do with the effects of exchange risk on international trade. The other could be labeled the political economy of misaligned exchange rates.

According to the traditional analysis of behavior under risk, an increase in risk will lead risk-averse individuals to reduce their efforts in the risky activity and to concentrate their energies in less risky endeavors (given an unchanged return). This theory has led many to conclude that by increasing the risk of international trade activities, the exchange rate volatility must in principle have a negative effect on trade. In this view, exchange rate volatility leads economic agents to a retrenchment into domestic activities.[6] The empirical evidence of the models based on this theory has up until now not been very convincing about the significance of the negative effects of exchange rate risk on international trade.

There is another strand of literature which analyzes the effects of exchange rate variability on international trade and which appears to come to more clear-cut results about this relationship. One can call this literature the "political economy of exchange rate variability."

Although this literature is far removed from the level of formalization which is found in the pure theory of risk, it is important to look at the problem from the political economy perspective. We can summarize the main ideas as follows. Exchange rate changes which wander away from purchasing power parities (or more generally from their equilibrium values) lead to adjustment problems and "real" effects on the economy. These misalignments lead to a boom in the traded goods sectors of the countries whose currency has become undervalued. In the countries with overvalued currencies as a result of these swings in the real exchange rate, the traded goods sector is squeezed. This leads to a loss of output and employment which is not easily absorbed in the short run by the other sectors in the economy.

The political economy part of this story is set in motion when, as a result of output and employment losses, individuals hurt by these developments organize themselves to pass protectionist legislation. These protectionist measures can take a variety of forms; from import tariffs and quantitative restrictions to very subtle ways of subsidizing exporting and import-competing industries.[7] As a result, markets become more protected, such that international trade is negatively affected.

This hypothesis only makes sense if there is some asymmetry in the protectionist tendencies. It must be that the protectionist legislation passed when the currency tended to be overvalued is not easily scrapped when the currency is in the undervaluation cycle. If such asymmetries are present, then the swings in the real exchange rates will lead to a trendlike increase in protectionism and will negatively affect international trade. Thus, this theory predicts that the volatility of real exchange rates over periods exceeding a few months or quarters is likely to lead to a reduction in the growth of international trade.

The political economy theory of the effects of misalignment also suggests a way in which in the empirical work a distinction can be made between the effect of changes in competitiveness and the effects of misalignment. The influence of misalignment can be introduced into the model through the inclusion of an indicator of "protectionist pressure stemming from misalignment."

In section 3.6 we present an econometric model which aims at quantifying the effects of exchange risk and misalignment. In addition, the model will allow us to separate these effects from the effects of other variables like the growth of income and relative price changes. The empirical results will enable us to shed some light on the puzzle of why intra-EMS trade was growing more slowly than other trade flows after 1979.

3.6 The Econometric Model

In order to specify the empirical model, we rely on what standard trade theory tells us about the determinants of international trade flows. Let us start from the following general equation:

$$X_{ij} = f(Y_j, Y_i, R_{ij}, T_{ij}, S_{ij}, M_{ij}). \tag{1}$$

The growth of exports of country i to country j (X_{ij}) is a positive function of the growth of demand in country j as measured by the real income of that country (Y_j). It is a positive function of the growth of the supply possibilities of the exporting country. This is measured by the growth rate of output of country i (Y_i). The growth of the exports of country i to country j is a positive function of the change in the bilateral real exchange rate (R_{ij}). A real depreciation of the currency of the exporting country i will increase its exports to country j.

The growth of trade between countries i and j is also influenced by the nature of the trade arrangements between the two countries (T_{ij}). In particular, if countries i and j form a customs union, this should increase their bilateral trade flows relative to the trade with third countries. We will use this variable to measure the effect of the trade arrangements between the EEC countries in the sample. In the empirical analysis we will further isolate the trade flows among the original EEC members (Belgium, France, Germany, Italy, and the Netherlands) from the other intra-EEC flows. In this way we can catch differences in the phases of the integration process.

In equation (1) we also include a measure of exchange rate variability (S_{ij}). We expect that this variable negatively affects trade flows between countries *i* and *j*. In contrast to most of the empirical literature on the effect of exchange rate volatility on international trade, we will use a measure of long-term (yearly) variability of the real exchange rate.

Finally, we add the variable M_{ij}. This is our indicator of protectionist pressure in country *j* (induced by a sustained overvaluation of the currency of country *j*) against imports from country *i*. Thus this variable measures the negative effect of past and current misalignments on bilateral exports. It is calculated as the cumulative percentage overvaluation of the currency of the importing country relative to the productivity-adjusted bilateral real exchange rate (for more details see appendix A). One way to interpret this variable is as follows: misalignments (overvaluations of the currency) which have occurred in the past affect today's trade flows by the protectionist measures they have set in motion.

3.7 The Empirical Results

A cross-section analysis was performed on the average yearly change of the volume of exports during the period 1979–85. The sample included the bilateral exports of 15 industrial countries which together constitute more than 90% of trade among industrial countries.[8] In total we thus have a sample of 210 bilateral export flows. A detailed description of the data can be found in appendix B. Two further remarks should be made here. The first concerns the way the variable M_{ij} is calculated. It is calculated over the whole floating-rate period 1974–85 and not over the period 1979–85 as the other variables are. The reason is that we assume that protectionist pressure built up before 1979 will still influence trade flows during 1979–85. The second remark deals with the way the effects of trade arrangements between countries (T_{ij}) are introduced. Integration effects are assumed to work through higher income elasticities on the import side. The same increase in the income of the importing country belonging to a trade arrangement such as the EEC is expected to have a greater effect on the exports of the partners than those of other countries.[9] The results of the estimation of equation (1) are shown in table 3.5.

These empirical results suggest the following interpretation. First, the demand and supply variables as measured by the changes in the income of the importing and the exporting country have the expected

Table 3.5 **Estimation Results, with Average Real Change in Exports, 1979–85, as Dependent Variable (in Millions of 1980 Dollars)**

	Eq. (la)	Eq. (lb)	Eq. (lc)
c	94.71**	39.21	124.68**
	(2.22)	(0.86)	(2.55)
Y_i	0.008**	0.005**	0.008**
	(4.62)	(2.65)	(4.28)
Y_j	0.012**	0.010**	0.013**
	(6.80)	(5.59)	(6.91)
Y_j*OLD	0.013	0.023**	0.012
	(1.23)	(2.17)	(1.17)
Y_j*NEW	0.022**	0.027**	0.024**
	(2.10)	(2.54)	(2.30)
R_{ij}	1413.43*	807.35	1066.45
	(1.70)	(0.89)	(1.22)
S_{ij}	−3.010**		−2.829**
	(4.33)		(3.99)
M_{ij}		−0.081**	−0.049
		(2.03)	(1.24)
SER	322.97	334.16	322.54
F	13.10**	10.01**	11.48**
Adj. R^2	.26	.21	.26
$F_{S,M}$	18.82**	4.14**	10.21**

Note: Y_i = average yearly change in income exporting country; Y_j = average yearly change in income importing country; OLD = dummy which takes the value of 1 for flows among the 5 original members of the EEC in the sample; NEW = dummy which takes the value of 1 for intra-EEC flows involving the U.K., Ireland, and Denmark; R_{ij} = average annual rate of real depreciation of the exporting country's currency; S_{ij} = real exchange rate variability, measured as the variance of the annual changes of the real exchange rate; M_{ij} = indicator of protectionist pressure created by exchange rate misalignment. t-statistics in parentheses. $*p < .05$. $**p < .01$.

positive and significant effect on bilateral export flows. Second, integration effects are positive and significant. They are more pronounced for the EMS trade with the new members of the EEC. The variable measuring the integration effects among the old EEC countries is less pronounced and often insignificant. This suggests that for the trade among these old EEC members some saturation effect is present. Third, changes in relative prices have the expected positive effect, that is, a real depreciation of currency i leads to an increase of the exports of country i. This effect, however, is usually not significant (except in equation 1a in table 3.5).

When the exchange rate variability (S_{ij}) and the indicator of protectionist pressure created by misalignment (M_{ij}) are entered separately into the equation (eqs. 1a and 1b in table 3.5), they show up with a significant negative coefficient. When entered simultaneously into the equation, the misalignment variable looses its significance (eq. 1c in table 3.5). The *F*-statistics reported at the bottom of table 3.5 indicate that variability and/or misalignment contribute significantly to the explanation of the change in bilateral exports.

Our finding that exchange rate variability has a significant negative effect on exports contradicts earlier findings by Hooper and Kohlhagen (1978), Gotur (1985), Bailey et al. (1986), and IMF (1984). It is, however, consistent with the results of Cushman (1983, 1986), Abrams (1980), and Thursby and Thursby (1985). The evidence on the effect of misalignment is not that clear-cut. Table 3.5 would suggest that the misalignment variable is overshadowed by the variable measuring yearly variability of exchange rates when entered simultaneously. This lack of precision of the misalignment variable may be due to the high correlation with the variable measuring exchange rate variability.

We have observed in this section that exchange rate variability and misalignment have a negative effect on international trade. The question remains, however, whether this effect is also economically important. We analyze this question in section 3.8.

3.8 Real Growth of Exports

In figures 3.8 and 3.9 it was illustrated that after 1979 trade flows among the EMS members were growing much more slowly compared with other trade flows. In this section we use the empirical results of section 3.7 to quantify the contribution of different variables in the explanation of this phenomenon.

The calculations were made using the estimated coefficients of equation (1c) in table 3.5. Using the average values of the independent variables for each group of countries, we calculated their contribution to the actual growth rate of exports. The results are presented in table 3.6.

Table 3.6 Contribution to the Real Growth Rate of Exports (1979–85)

	Exports			
	EMS to EMS	EMS to Non-EMS	Non-EMS to EMS	Non-EMS to Non-EMS
Income	2.28	10.60	10.67	11.83
Misalignment	−0.50	−2.21	−2.16	−1.53
Variability	−0.68	−8.05	−10.34	−9.18
Relative prices	0.0	1.11	−1.43	0.0
Other	1.69	5.61	7.20	5.02
Total	2.79	7.06	3.94	6.14

The totals of the columns of table 3.6 give the observed real growth rate of exports between the groups of countries during 1979–85. These figures correspond to the ones in figure 3.8. The entries in table 3.6 give the effects of the different explanatory variables on the growth rate of exports. They should be interpreted as follows. Changes in the income of the EMS countries were responsible for 2.28% of the 2.79% growth in intra-EMS exports. (Note that this includes the effect of the higher income sensitivity of intra-EMS trade, due to the higher level of trade integration.) Protectionist pressure as a result of misalignment slowed the growth of intra-EMS trade by 0.50%, while exchange rate variability reduced that growth rate by another 0.68%.

We can conclude from table 3.6 that income and exchange rate variability are certainly the most important factors in explaining the growth of exports. Misalignment and changes in relative prices seem to play a secondary role. The question remains now to what extent divergent evolutions of these variables can account for the difference in growth rate after 1979 between intra-EMS exports and other export flows. In order to answer this question, we performed some simulation experiments.

3.9 Some Simulation Results

In this section we report the results of thrce simulation experiments. The purpose is to write an "anti-histoire" of what would have happened to intra-EMS exports if conditions had been different. The results of the simulations are summarized in table 3.7. The base line is the actual real growth rate of exports between the groups of countries.

Case 1

In this simulation experiment we assumed that the average real growth rate of income in the EMS was the same as the one observed for the group of countries outside the EMS.[10] The growth of intra-EMS exports increases by 1.44% relative to the observed value. Thus if the EMS countries had managed to grow at the (higher) rate observed outside

Table 3.7 Simulation Results: Real Growth of Exports (1979–85) (%)

	Exports			
	EMS to EMS	EMS to Non-EMS	Non-EMS to EMS	Non-EMS to Non-EMS
Base	2.79	7.06	3.94	6.14
Case 1	4.23	8.10	9.00	6.14
Case 2	0.38	7.06	3.94	6.14
Case 3	2.02	7.83	4.79	6.19

the EMS, their trade would have grown on average by 4.23% per year instead of only 2.79%. In addition, the growth rate of their imports from the non-EMS area would have been more than twice as high as in the base value. Thus, it appears that the slow growth of GDP observed within the EMS is an important variable in the explanation of the low intra-EMS growth of trade. It is, however, insufficient to explain the full extent of the sluggish intra-EMS trade. Even when we assume, as we do in this simulation, that the EMS GDP would have grown at the higher (non-EMS) rate, the resulting growth of trade within the EMS falls short of the one we observe outside the EMS.

Case 2

In order to have an idea of the beneficial effects of the EMS as a stabilizer of the bilateral exchange rates, we performed the following experiment. We calculated the growth rate of exports assuming that inside the EMS we would have had the same degree of exchange rate variability and misalignment as among the non-EMS countries. The results in table 3.7 indicate that intra-EMS export growth would have dropped by 2.41%, from 2.79% to 0.38%. This 2.41% growth of exports can be interpreted as the beneficial effect of the exchange rate arrangement of the EMS on the trade flows among its members. This experiment suggests that through the exchange rate stability it provided, the EMS was successful in preventing an even more unfavorable evolution in its internal trade than the one we observed.

It should be stressed that these experiments are somewhat artificial. We cannot exclude, for example, that the low growth of GDP and the low variability of exchange rates are correlated. If this is the case, one could also argue that the EMS contributed to both low growth and low exchange rate variability. The present partial equilibrium exercise does not allow us to resolve this issue.

Case 3

In this third experiment we calculate what would have happened if the variability of the real exchange rates during the period 1979–85 had been the same as during the period 1974–78. The growth rate of intra-EMS exports would have been somewhat lower, while the other trade flows would have grown faster. The difference however, is not very large. These results reflect the fact that after 1979, long-term exchange rate variability has on average slightly decreased among EMS members, while it has increased somewhat outside the EMS when compared to the period 1974–78.

From the preceding experiments we can conclude that the low growth of GDP within the EMS explains a substantial part of the low growth of trade within the EMS since 1979. However, this negative growth effect was completely offset by a favorable effect resulting from the relative exchange rate stability within the EMS. We are back at square one. Where does the observed decline in the growth rate of intra-EMS trade come from?

The answer must be sought in the slowdown of the trade integration process within the old EEC countries, which comprise the EMS countries. To illustrate this, we calculated the implied income elasticities of export demand (using the results of equation [1c] in table 3.5). For the trade among the original members of the EEC, this elasticity is 0.91. This is much lower than the one for the intra-EEC trade involving the United Kingdom, Denmark, and Ireland (4.10) and the one for all trade flows involving countries outside the EEC (2.31). These figures indicate that the trade integration process within the group of original EEC members has leveled off. Outside this old EEC zone, however, there is still a substantial trade integration momentum. The latter has been operating strongly enough to overcome the negative effects of exchange rate variability.

This evidence about new trade integration patterns has also been documented in the more disaggregated studies of Jacquemin and Sapir (1986, 1987).[11] In these studies it was found that the EEC countries' trade with non-EEC countries has been expanding much faster than the intra-EEC trade since the early eighties. These new trade integration processes are the result of the internationalization of European industries on a worldwide scale. They also explain a slowdown of the growth rates of traditional intra-EEC trade.

3.10 Conclusion

One of the objectives of the EMS was to create a zone of monetary stability in Europe. If we measure monetary stability by the variability of the exchange rates, it can certainly be said that the EMS was a success. In general, the intra-EMS exchange rates tended to be less variable and less prone to large misalignments than the exchange rates of currencies outside the system.

Despite the relative stability of intra-EMS exchange rates, the intra-EMS trade grew at a substantially lower pace than in the rest of the industrialized world. In addition, the EMS trade (both exports and imports) with the rest of the industrialized world increased significantly faster than the intra-EMS trade. This is certainly a puzzling phenomenon. The founding fathers of the EMS expected that a low exchange rate variability would boost internal EMS trade.

In this paper we have tried to explain this phenomenon. Our main findings are that the slowdown of the growth of GDP in the EMS, which was much larger than in the rest of the industrialized world, is an important explanatory variable. However, we also found that the low growth of GDP explains less than half of the slow intra-EMS trade.

The other unexplained part was interpreted as reflecting the slowdown in the trade integration process of the EMS countries, which all (except Ireland and Denmark) belong to the original EEC.

Our second main finding is that the low exchange rate variability contributed positively towards the intra-EMS trade. In other words, in a different (more variable) exchange rate regime, the EMS countries would probably have experienced an even larger slowdown of their internal trade than the one observed during the 1979–85 period. This positive effect of the relative stability of exchange rates within the EMS, however, has not been strong enough to overcome the combined negative growth effect and the negative effect coming from the slowdown of the trade integration process in the EEC countries.

One unresolved issue of this empirical analysis has to do with the question whether the EMS arrangement might have induced both low exchange rate variability and low growth of output. The latter may have occurred if the EMS arrangement forced the participating countries to follow a more deflationary demand policy than in a different exchange rate arrangement. If this is the case, the success of the EMS is less obvious.

Notes

1. It should be stressed here that we have looked only at measures of ex post (unconditional) variability. Better measures of risk involve the computation of ex ante (conditional) variability. The evidence using measures of unconditional variability, however, leads to conclusions similar to the ones arrived at here (see Rogoff 1985).

2. See Williamson (1985).

3. There is a large literature on this topic. See Balassa (1964), Kravis and Lipsey (1986), and Marston (1986).

4. It should be noted that the appreciation of the dollar during the first part of the eighties stimulated export flows from the EMS to the United States, but discouraged export flows from the United States to the EMS. The two effects tend to cancel out in the data presented in figure 3.8.

5. For an analysis of the factors which explain the slowdown of the intra-EMS trade since 1979, see P. De Grauwe (1987b).

6. A representative study is Hooper and Kohlhagen (1978). It should be stressed here, however, that the negative effect of exchange risk on trade is derived by making relatively restrictive assumptions about the utility function. In a more general setup with less restrictive assumptions about the shape of the utility function, it is generally not possible to derive such a clear-cut conclusion about the effect of risk on trade. See Newbery and Stiglitz (1981); see also De Grauwe (1987a).

7. These subsidies can take a more direct form of employment subsidies, cheap loans, or government participation or can be much more disguised as safety regulations, technical standards, and so on.

8. The group of 15 countries comprises the 7 members participating in the exchange rate mechanism of the EMS (Belgium, Denmark, France, Germany, Ireland, Italy, and the Netherlands) and the same group of 8 countries outside the exchange rate agreement as in section 3.2 (Austria, Canada, Japan, Norway, Sweden, Switzerland, the United Kingdom, and the United States).

9. In earlier experiments we also allowed for different income elasticities for trade among members of the EFTA in the sample (Austria, Norway, and Sweden). Since no significant difference was found, however, we dropped this complication.

10. The actual average growth rate of GDP in the EMS during that period was 1.51% as opposed to 2.50% in the group of non-EMS countries.

11. See also P. De Grauwe (1987b) and P. De Grauwe and B. de Bellefroid (1987).

References

Abrams, R. K. 1980. International trade flows under flexible exchange rates. Federal Reserve Bank of Kansas City Economic Review, vol. 65(3): 3–10.

Bailey, M. J., G. S. Tavlas and M. Ulan. 1986. Exchange rate variability and trade performance: Evidence for the big 7 industrial countries. *Weltwirtschaftliches Archiv* 122: 466–77.

Balassa, B. 1964. The purchasing power parity doctrine: A reappraisal. *Journal of Political Economy* 72: 584–96.

Cushman, D. O. 1983. The effects of real exchange risk on international trade. *Journal of International Economics* 15: 45–63.

Cushman, D. O. 1986. Has exchange risk depressed international trade? The impact of third-country exchange risk. *Journal of International Money and Finance* 5: 361–79.

De Grauwe, P. 1987a. Exchange rate variability and the slowdown in growth of international trade. Unpublished manuscript, International Monetary Fund Working Paper /87/38.

———. 1987b. International trade and economic growth in the European Monetary System. *European Economic Review* 31: 389–98.

De Grauwe, P., and B. de Bellefroid. 1987. Long-run exchange rate variability and international trade. In S. Arndt and J. D. Richardson, eds., *Real-financial linkages among open economies*. Cambridge: MIT Press.

EC Commission. 1984. Cinq ans de cooperation monetaire en Europe. Mimeo, March.

Gotur, P. 1985. Effects of exchange rate volatility on trade: Some further evidence. IMF Staff Papers, vol. 32, no. 3, pp. 475–512.

Hooper, P., and S. W. Kohlhagen. 1978. The effect of exchange rate uncertainty on the prices and the volume of international trade. *Journal of International Trade* 8: 483–511.

IMF. 1984. Exchange rate volatility and world trade. IMF Occasional Paper no. 28, July.

Jacquemin, A., and A. Sapir, 1986. Intra-EC trade: A sectoral analysis. CEPS Working Documents, October.

———. 1987. European integration or world integration? Mimeo, February.

Kravis, I. B., and R. E. Lipsey. 1986. The assessment of national price levels. NBER Working Paper no. 1912, May.

Marston, R. C. 1986. Real exchange rates and productivity growth in the United States and Japan. NBER Working Paper no. 1922, May.
Newbery, D. M. G.,and J. E. Stiglitz. 1981. *The theory of commodity price stabilization: A study in the economics of risk.* Oxford: Clarendon Press.
Rogoff, K. 1985. Can exchange rate predictability be achieved without monetary convergence? Evidence from the EMS. *European Economic Review*, vol. 28, no. 1–2, pp. 93–115.
Thursby, M., and J. G. Thursby. 1985. The uncertainty effect of floating exchange rates: Empirical evidence on international trade flows. In S. Arndt, R. J. Sweeney, and T. D. Willett, eds., *Exchange rates, trade, and the United States economy*. Cambridge, Mass.: Ballinger.
Ungerer, H., et al. 1983. The European Monetary System 1979–82. IMF Occasional Paper no. 19, May.
Ungerer, H., et al. 1986. The European Monetary System: Recent developments. IMF Occasional Paper no. 48, December.
Williamson, J. 1985. *The exchange rate system.* Institute for International Economics, Washington, D.C.

Appendix A

Measures of Misalignment

1. Calculating the Equilibrium Rate

The general price index P_c of the home country can be written (in logs) as :

$$P_c = aP_t + (1 - a)P_n \tag{1}$$

where P_t = price index of traded goods
P_n = price index of nontraded goods
a = share of traded goods in the consumption basket.

Analogously, we have for the foreign country:

$$P_c^* = a^*P_t^* + (1 - a^*)P_n^*. \tag{2}$$

Assuming we can write prices as a function of wages and productivity in the tradables and nontradables sector, we have:

$$\begin{aligned} P_t &= w - q \qquad & P_n &= w - v \\ P_t^* &= w^* - q^* \qquad & P_n^* &= w^* - v^* \end{aligned} \tag{3}$$

where w, w^* = the general wage index in the domestic and the foreign country, respectively
q, q^* = the (log of the) productivity levels in the tradables sector in the two countries
v, v^* = the (log of the) productivity levels in the nontradables sector in the two countries.

Substituting eq. (3) into (1) and (2) yields, after rearranging:

$$(4) \qquad P_c = aP_t + (1 - a)(P_t + q - v)$$
$$P_c^* = a^*P_t^* + (1 - a^*)(P_t^* + q^* - v^*).$$

If PPP holds for the tradable goods, we have:

$$(5) \qquad P_t = S^{PPP} + P_t^*$$

where S^{PPP} is the spot exchange rate when *PPP* holds.

If we furthermore assume that consumption patterns are the same in both countries ($a = a^*$) and productivity in the nontradables sector is the same ($v = v^*$), we can write

$$(6) \qquad P_c - P_c^* = aS^{PPP} + (1 - a)(S^{PPP} + q - q^*).$$

Solving for S^{PPP}, the productivity-adjusted *PPP* rate can be written as:

$$(7) \qquad S^{PPP} = (P_c - P_c^*) - (1 - a)(q - q^*).$$

2. Calculating Misalignment

Misalignment is equal to the difference between the log of the actual spot rate and S^{PPP}. The share of traded goods in the consumption basket a, was set equal to 0.7. Productivity in the traded goods sector q was proxied by the real value added per person employed in the manufacturing sector (Source: OECD). Wholesale prices are used as the general price index. All series are on the basis average 1974–85 = 100.

3. Comparison with Williamson (1985)

It is interesting to compare our estimates of misalignment for selected dollar exchange rates with the estimates of Williamson (1985).

	Authors' (%)			Williamson (%)	
	March 83	Dec. 84	Dec. 85	1983:I	1984:IV
DM	7.8	32.5	10.8	18	50
Yen	11.0	22.7	9.1	15	24
PS	13.7	31.4	7.4	3	25
FF	18.8	33.3	15.2	17	44

Though the estimates are not equal, they tend to go in the same direction.

4. Measure of Protectionist Pressure

Our measure of protectionist pressure M_{ij} used in the empirical analysis is equal to the cumulative sum of the monthly percentage overvaluation of the currency of the importing country with respect to that of the exporter. Because of the asymmetry referred to in the text, the observations where the currency of the importer is undervalued were set to zero. The larger the overvaluation of the importer's currency and the longer the overvaluation lasts, the larger M_{ij} will be.

Appendix B

Data Sources

Y_i = Average yearly change in GDP of country i during the period 1979–85 (in millions of 1980 dollars).
Source: OECD Main Economic Indicators.

X_{ij} = Average yearly change in the exports of country i to country j. Deflated by export unit values (IFS, line 74d).
Source: IMF, Direction of Trade Statistics.

R_{ij} = Average yearly percentage change in the real exchange rate. R_{ij} is positive when the exporter's currency depreciates in real terms with respect to the currency of the importing country. It is calculated as $\log E_t - \log E_{t-12}$, where the real exchange rate E is calculated using monthly data on wholesale prices and nominal exchange rates from IFS, lines RF and 63.

S_{ij} = Variance of R_{ij} during the period 1979–85.

Comment Jacques Melitz

Much of the recent analysis of the European Monetary System (EMS) has concerned the strategic implications of the system in modifying the macroeconomic policy choices of the participating members. De Grauwe and Verfaille do us a service by reminding us that, quite apart from the latter sorts of considerations, the system was also intended to promote trade. From this last perspective, the performance of the system has been uneven, as the two point out. The EMS has indeed succeeded in stabilizing the terms of trade. But to all appearances, the system has not promoted trade. Growth of internal trade within the EMS in 1979–86 slipped significantly below 1974–78 levels. In addition, the growth of trade between the members was far lower than that of their trade with nonmembers in the OECD (Organization for Economic Cooperation and Development) in 1979–86. The authors offer some

Jacques Melitz is a research economist at the Institut National de la Statistique et des Etudes Economiques, Paris, France, and Professor at the Institut des Etudes Politiques, Paris, France.

answers to this puzzle, though they do not pretend their answers are complete.

They indicate that the stability of the terms of trade has indeed promoted trade. However, slower economic growth of the EMS members as compared to the other major industrialized countries in the West worked toward a slowdown of the growth of trade. This lower growth has also seemingly damaged internal trade between the members more than external trade with the rest. Additionally, the authors suggest that the trade-integration effects of membership in the European Community (EC) diminished in 1979–85. This would also account for a reduction in the growth of trade between the members, since the only member who is also a newcomer to the EC is Ireland.

This general reconciliation of the evidence, it may be noted, would seem to place the EMS in a favorable light. This bears emphasis, since in the past De Grauwe has been one of the EMS's staunchest critics.[1] He may wish to remind us, though, that the EMS could be largely responsible for its own lower economic growth, as he also argues in the paper. This view would be based on the sort of strategic considerations to which I alluded at the beginning. That is, membership could have led to more anti-inflationary policies because of a tendency to follow the German example of a strong preoccupation with inflation. This would mean, naturally, that the EMS has not been as advantageous to the non-German members than it might otherwise seem, or more precisely, that the advantages to the others would depend on their sharing of the German anti-inflationary priorities.

However, as for the empirical work, I believe that three sorts of improvements could be made. First, the authors might abandon their measure of the annual volatility of the terms of trade in favor of either their monthly or their quarterly measure. Their annual measure is faulted by the use of overlapping observations. It is based on consecutive monthly observations of annual changes. Obviously this use of monthly data multiplies the data, but without adding any independent observations. Thus, it cannot serve to measure annual volatility properly. The authors recognize this implicitly when they acknowledge that the F-statistic can tell them nothing about the reliability of their annual volatility measure. But by the same token, they should have recognized that the measure should be scrapped as insignificant, whereas they use it to test in their econometric work. It is impossible to find the annual volatility of anything over two years simply by multiplying the number of annual observations within the same two-year stretch.

1. See Paul De Grauwe, Should the United Kingdom join the EMS? In House of Commons, Treasury and Civil Service Committee, *The financial and economic consequences of UK membership of the European Communities, Memoranda on the European Monetary System*. London: HMSO (1985), pp. 5–11.

The second problem is that the authors improperly limit their statistical analysis to the period 1979 to 1985, while they should have begun earlier, in 1974, since their empirical discussion calls for it. By limiting themselves to 1979–85, they cannot really explain the puzzling reduction in the growth of internal trade in the EMS from 1974–78 to 1979–85 to which they call our attention. This they recognize. But there is a similar problem hounding their efforts to explain the stronger reduction in the growth of internal than external trade in the EMS based on the diminution of the trade-integrating effects of the EC. How can we be sure that the trade-integrating effects of membership even fell off in 1979–85 if we do not look at the earlier period? De Grauwe and Verfaille attempt to answer this objection by referring to independent evidence from Jacquemin and Sapir that trade integration has fallen off since the beginning of the EC. But surely this will not do in the context of an effort to provide a quantitative assessment of the significance of different factors. The only indication of a drop in the trade-integrating effects of EC membership that emerges in their own work, as such, is the estimate that the output elasticity of the demand for EMS exports by the newer EC members—the United Kingdom, Ireland, and Denmark—was higher in 1979–85 than this elasticity of demand by the older members. This is admittedly suggestive, but it is quite consistent with the same elasticities of demand for EMS-country exports by the older members of the EC in 1979–85 as in the preceding years 1974–78.

The third problem concerns the issue of misalignment. De Grauwe and Verfaille sensibly argue that the benefits of stable terms of trade come partly from the avoidance of misalignment. But they focus exclusively on the benefits coming through political channels. Their measure of misalignment in their econometric work is even tailor-made to fit their political hypothesis. Whereas in their general discussion of misalignment in section 3.3 (and the accompanying figures 3.1 through 3.7), misalignment refers to productivity-adjusted movements away from PPP, in their econometric work they use the term to refer to the cumulative value of the previous sorts of movements in one particular direction—the one pointing toward a loss of competitivity. The idea is that periods of low competitiveness (relative to average) produce protectionist actions that are never canceled during times of higher-than-average competitiveness. I have some misgivings about the application of this political hypothesis to the trade relations between the members of the EC in the same way as to their trade relations with outsiders. This would seem to deny the importance of the free-trade rules in the EC and the trade-integrating effects of these rules, to which the authors otherwise give weight. But mostly I wish to emphasize the authors' neglect of the possibility of other effects of misalignment, such as those suggested in some of the other contributions to this conference volume, like the Baldwin-Krugman argument about fixed costs of entry in a foreign market. These other effects would tend to say that a misalignment damages exports in one direction while encouraging them in the opposite one, contrary to De Grauwe and Verfaille's argument that misalignment hurts exports in every direction. This is important since it could mean that De Grauwe and Verfaille's neglect of other effects interfered with finding the ones they were looking for. In any event, the authors take too limited a view of the possible effects of misalignment.

The paper would gain considerable interest, in my opinion, if these problems were repaired or at least given proper attention. The simulations would benefit too—quite independently of the test significance of the estimated parameters, which could remain a problem. But even as the paper now stands, it provides a lot of food for thought about the effects of the EMS.

4 Realignment of the Yen-Dollar Exchange Rate: Aspects of the Adjustment Process in Japan

Bonnie Loopesko and Robert A. Johnson

The 50% appreciation of the yen-dollar exchange rate in the last two years (or the 90% appreciation when expressed in dollar-yen terms) appears dramatic even when compared to the frequent sizable swings in exchange rates that have characterized the floating rate period. For Japan, this is the largest unidirectional movement of its exchange rate since the advent of floating. (See Manuel Johnson and Bonnie Loopesko 1987 for an overview of the yen-dollar relationship during the floating exchange rate period.) In light of Japan's record external surpluses, it is widely agreed that the yen was substantially undervalued in early 1985 when it began its steep ascent. The only source of debate has been just how high the yen needs to go.

Faced with an unprecedented shift in its exchange rate and mounting domestic and international pressure to restructure its economy away from export-oriented growth, Japan has embarked on what may turn out to be a major transformation of its industrial structure. If the strong yen—termed *endaka* in Japanese—persists (and most analysts believe that it will), then steps already taken towards outsourcing of production and shifting of investment away from the manufacturing sector will be

Bonnie Loopesko is a staff economist at the Federal Reserve Board, principally responsible for analyzing Japanese economic and financial developments. Robert A. Johnson is Chief Economist for the United States Senate Committee on Banking, Housing, and Urban Affairs.

The authors would like to thank Bill Helkie for invaluable assistance in modeling the Japanese trade sector, Karen Johnson, Sean Craig, Richard Marston, Jacob Frenkel, and other participants at the NBER Conference and an IMF Research Department seminar for helpful comments, and Joerg Dittmer for excellent research assistance. This paper represents the views of the authors and should not be interpreted as reflecting those of the Board of Governors of the Federal Reserve System or of other members of its staff.

accelerated in the future. This adjustment process could be the most profound in Japanese postwar history.

As this process gets under way, the costs of adjustment are already apparent throughout the Japanese economy. Unemployment, while still low by international standards, has touched a record 3% level in recent months and is expected to continue to rise this year. In addition to the rise in unemployment, there is more subtle evidence of a slackening of labor market conditions. A recent survey by the Keidanren (Keizai Koho Center 1987), the Japanese equivalent of the Business Roundtable, indicates that nearly 60% of companies surveyed have instituted tighter control on overtime, and a third have reduced bonuses and cut back employment of part-time employees. A quarter of companies have increased transfers of employees to subsidiaries and begun training for reassignment. On the production side, 40% of firms reported they had reduced production, while one-third reported increases in their imports of parts. Outsourcing of production is also under way: the Keidanren survey indicates that a quarter of companies surveyed have already expanded offshore production facilities and another 20% have plans to do so. Thus important changes appear to be under way in Japan, and this paper examines several aspects of the adjustment process to endaka.

The next section provides a brief review of recent calculations of the appropriate level of the yen-dollar exchange rate. Evidence is then presented on the degree of trade balance adjustment that has occurred to date. The following section examines what econometric models of Japanese trade reveal about the traditional channels of trade adjustment, the income and relative price elasticities. The forecasting performance of the trade equations presented suggests that, while the model fits reasonably well over the floating rate sample period through 1984, it predicts stonger adjustment in Japanese trade than has actually occurred in the past two years. The next sections look at possible reasons why Japanese trade is adjusting more slowly to the yen's recent sharp rise than would be indicated by historical experience. Evidence on pass-through of the yen's appreciation to export and consumer prices suggests two possible explanations. Next, a model is presented to highlight the spillover effects of a recession in the export sector (resulting from the yen's sharp appreciation) to the entire economy. The danger of an economywide recession in Japan and its implications for trade adjustment are addressed. Finally, the role of fiscal policy in fostering external adjustment is explored. Evidence from the Federal Reserve Board staff's Multi-Country Model indicates that Japanese fiscal expansion would make a smaller contribution than U.S. fiscal contraction to the reduction of external imbalances between the two countries, but that potentially important third-country effects should not be ignored.

4.1 Purchasing Power Parity Calculations

The relative version of purchasing power parity (PPP) states that the movement in the exchange rate from some base period is determined by the inflation differential over the same period. There is a long history of debate over which price index is appropriate for PPP calculations (see Frenkel 1978, pp. 3–4), although most recent calculations are based on prices of homogeneous and internationally traded goods expressed in a common currency. The base year (or weighted average of years) is usually chosen to represent a period of approximate external balance. Despite the many well-recognized problems with PPP as a notion of the equilibrium exchange rate, calculations of the deviation from PPP are often cited in discussions of exchange rate misalignment.

Table 4.1 shows several recent PPP calculations for the yen-dollar exchange rate. While the differing calculation methods (e.g., selection of base year, type of price index used, other adjustments) yield quantitatively different PPP estimates, all of the simple (unadjusted) PPP calculations show the yen-dollar rate to be substantially overvalued at its recent level of about 140.

One important difficulty with the calculations shown in table 4.1 is that, except for Krugman's (1986b) calculation, they do not take account of possible changes in the long-run equilibrium exchange rate. Particularly for the case of the yen-dollar exchange rate, the assumption that the long-run equilibrium exchange rate is constant appears implausible. Marston (1986) has shown that productivity in the traded goods sector in Japan has exceeded that in the nontraded services

Table 4.1 **Purchasing Power Parity Calculations for the Yen-Dollar Exchange Rate**

Morrison and Hale	203
McKinnon and Ohno	215
Krugman	
adjusting for estimated divergence between manufacturing price and CPI	140

Notes: Morrison and Hale (1987): PPP calculations adjusted for "tradability." Deflators for disaggregated GDP components (provided in OECD, 1987) are weighted by trade shares to obtain a PPP rate for 1980. Then movements since 1980 in relative producer prices for manufacturing goods are used to update the calculation. McKinnon and Ohno (1987): estimated by the "price pressure method," incorporating the effect of exchange rate misalignment (deviations from PPP) on prices. The resulting PPP is that exchange rate which exerts no upward or downward pressure on domestic prices relative to those abroad. Krugman (1986b): taking the geometric average manufacturing real exchange rate over 1973–79 as the base period, he assumes that the manufacturing PPP rate has continued to fall relative to the ratio of CPIs at the same rate as during the 1973–83 period, i.e., 4.4% per year, and extrapolates using actual CPI inflation.

sector by a substantial margin, so that PPP comparisons of prices that include services will misrepresent the gains in competitiveness. Krugman's calculation attempts to adjust for Japan's relatively rapid productivity growth in the traded goods sector, and this adjustment alone suggests that the yen-dollar rate would have to appreciate to 140.

A more general problem with the PPP calculations is that, in theory, PPP provides a guide to the appropriate level of the exchange rate only if all disturbances since the base period are monetary in nature. In light of the sizable real disturbances that have characterized the past 15 years (e.g., oil price changes and changes in government net saving), PPP calculations provide a poor guide to the appropriate level of the exchange rate. If changes in real economic factors alter the equilibrium exchange rate after the base period, the PPP exchange rate may imply large and perhaps growing current account imbalances. In this case, there is nothing in PPP calculations to ensure that the current account imbalances associated with a given PPP exchange rate would be sustainable in terms of the accompanying capital flows required to finance the imbalances.

4.2 Sustainability Calculations

An alternative to PPP as an indication of the appropriate level of the exchange rate is the "underlying balance," or "sustainability," approach. An early formulation of this framework may be found in Nurkse (1945). In the 1970s, the International Monetary Fund (IMF) further developed the approach (see Frenkel and Goldstein 1986 for a description of the IMF framework).

A recent contribution to this tradition was provided by Williamson (1983) who asked the following question: "What set of exchange rates would have been needed in a specific period . . . to induce a set of current account balances that matched 'underlying capital flows'?" (p. 22). The concept of underlying capital flows is meant to capture the notion that the equilibrium exchange rate will change in line with shifts in propensities to save and invest. For example, a country with a high savings rate may save in excess of its domestic investment opportunities and hence tend to export capital. Thus differential rates of savings and investment across countries are reflected in underlying capital flows and associated current account imbalances.

Williamson calculated the exchange rates consistent with underlying capital flows in 1976–77, extrapolated forward based on differential inflation (a PPP approach), and finally adjusted the calculation for substantial changes in real factors that have affected the equilibrium exchange rate since the base period. The most recent calculation based on the Williamson approach, reported in Bergsten and Cline (1987), suggests an equilibrium yen-dollar rate of about 150 by the end of 1986 and of 140–45 in 1987.

Krugman (1985, 1987) developed a simple model to address a related but slightly different question: what exchange rate is consistent with a sustainable current account imbalance? In essence, Krugman looks at the change in the exchange rate implied by the current interest rate differential and asks whether that change would suffice to eliminate the noninterest current account imbalance and thus stabilize the level of foreign debt relative to GNP. If the exchange rate change implied by the current interest differential would lead to an accelerating rise in the debt-to-GNP ratio, then the current exchange rate is judged to be unsustainable.

In September 1985, Krugman calculated that the dollar would have to decline 26% to restore U.S. current account balance. If the dollar declined equally against all currencies, this would imply a yen-dollar rate of about 175. He also calculated that if the dollar declined as slowly as the interest differential indicated at that time (1.6% per year), the U.S. debt-to-GNP ratio would rise for the next 30 years to a level of over 50%. This would bring U.S. external indebtedness to a level comparable to that of Brazil and Mexico, which, Krugman notes, few people would find feasible. In 1987, Krugman revisited the sustainability issue and concluded that if the dollar were to depreciate at the rate implied by the interest differential, external debt as a percent of GNP would rise to 38.8% after 10 years, again a level he thought unsustainable.

Morrison and Hale (1987) used Krugman's methodology and asked how much further the dollar would need to decline if the entire remaining U.S. noninterest current account deficit were to be eliminated within 10 years by exchange rate changes alone. On the assumption that the dollar declines equally against all currencies, they calculate that a sustainable yen-dollar rate would be about 135.

Laurence Krause (1986) took a similar approach: what dollar exchange rate is consistent with a balanced U.S. current account by 1990 or 1991, and what is the implied value of the yen? This is a stronger condition than that imposed by Krugman or Morrison and Hale, so it is not surprising that Krause finds that more yen appreciation—to 100 yen/dollar—is required.

The underlying capital flows–sustainability approach has the virtue of taking explicit account of the dynamic consistency of the implied exchange rate path. It also recognizes that some degree of persistent current account imbalance may be implied by differences in savings and investment propensities across countries. One limitation of this approach is that it requires as input a number of parameter values that are difficult to specify with confidence. For example, one parameter in

Table 4.2 Sustainable Yen-Dollar Exchange Rates

Williamson, as quoted in Bergsten and Cline (1987)	150 in 1986 140–45 in 1987
Krugman (September 1985)	26% dollar depreciation (a yen-dollar rate of about 175)
Morrison and Hale (1987)	135 yen-dollar
Krause (1986)	100 yen-dollar

Note: See text for descriptions of each calculation.

Krugman's calculations (assumed to be a constant) represents all factors other than the exchange rate change upon which the current account depends. Also, it is difficult to render concrete the notion of underlying capital flows in the IMF-Williamson approach.

A comparison of tables 4.1 and 4.2 shows that the estimates of the "equilibrium" yen-dollar rate from PPP calculations tend to indicate that the yen is currently overvalued, while the estimates derived from the sustainability–underlying capital flow approach often indicate a need for further yen appreciation. This divergence occurs despite the fact that both approaches incorporate some notion of external balance as the anchor for the calculations. The most likely explanation for the discrepancy is the earlier-noted failure of the PPP calculations to take account of real factors that have shifted the equilibrium exchange rate since the base period. The sizable shifts in fiscal policy in Japan and the United States are one likely important factor. Also, as noted above, the difference in productivity growth between traded and nontraded goods sectors was substantial in the 1970s. If productivity in the nontraded goods sector has changed little, then the fact that productivity growth in the Japanese manufacturing sector has slowed markedly in recent years—as can be seen in table 4.3—suggests that this factor may not continue to be an important source of secular appreciation of the yen. It is worth noting that the productivity differential between the United States and Japan in the manufacturing sector has narrowed in the 1980s, as can also be seen in table 4.3.

4.2.1 Capital Account Considerations

The sustainability approach applied to the current U.S. situation asks whether a decline of the dollar at the rate implied by the interest differential would produce a sustainable path for U.S. net external indebtedness. Even if the debt-to-GNP ratio does not rise at an accelerating rate, it may still increase to very high levels in the medium term. The question then becomes, would foreign investors be willing to finance the implied path of current account imbalances? This turns attention to the capital account side of the balance of payments.

Table 4.3 **Productivity Growth in the United States and Japan (Annual Percentage Growth In Output per Hour in Manufacturing)**

Period	Japan	United States
1950–59	11.4	2.1
1960–69	14.8	3.0
1970–79	7.7	2.5
1980–85	5.1	3.3

Source: Bureau of Labor Statistics (1986).

Table 4.4 **U.S. Treasury Bonds and Notes: Foreign Transactions (Millions of Dollars)**

	1984	1985	1986	1986			1987
Purchaser				Oct.	Nov.	Dec.	Jan.
All foreign	16,496	28,768	25,210	2,778	−270	−543	353
Foreign official institutions	505	8,135	14,277	3,506	138	240	1,488
Other foreign	15,992	20,631	10,936	−727	−408	−783	−1,135
Japan	6,289	17,909	3,916	−453	186	−2,086	−76

Source: Federal Reserve Bulletin, April 1987, table 3.25.

Some recent developments may shed light on this issue. Japanese and other foreign investors appeared to be adjusting their investment portfolios in response to large perceived dollar exchange risk in late 1986 and early 1987. This may have indicated that some investors believed the yen-dollar exchange rate to be unsustainable (i.e., that the dollar must decline faster than the small decline implied by the interest differential). This shift in beliefs would be reflected in changes in interest rates and exchange rates.

One important implication of this portfolio reshuffling by Japanese and other foreign investors is that it became more difficult for the United States to finance its fiscal deficit by private capital inflows at unchanged interest rates and exchange rates. Indeed, interest rates on U.S. Treasury bonds rose in late March 1987, accompanied by renewed downward pressure on the dollar. Data from the *Federal Reserve Bulletin,* shown in table 4.4, indicate that for 1986 as a whole, Japanese purchases of Treasury notes and bonds fell 79%. Foreign purchases in 1986 were sustained by a 76% rise in purchases of Treasury securities by foreign official institutions, while "other foreign" purchases fell 46%. Since November 1986, total foreign purchases of Treasury securities have been negative (the total would have been even more negative if official purchases had not been positive).

Problems with this data, produced by the U.S. Treasury, are discussed by Drexler (1987) and Sargen and Schoenholtz (1987). The main difficulty is that data are gathered according to the geographic location of the investor rather than his nationality. Thus, purchases by Nomura Securities in London for eventual resale to Japanese residents would appear as a sale to the United Kingdom (the eventual sale back to Japan would not be tracked by the U.S. data).

Still, these data on Treasury securities may be indicative of a general trend whereby official purchases of dollar securities are substituting for private purchases. However, if official purchases do not continue higher U.S. interest rates and a lower dollar may result. A change in policy stance in either Japan or the United States could reverse this process and draw Japanese and other foreign money back into the U.S. Treasury securities market. For example, a substantial shift towards fiscal ease in Japan or fiscal restraint in the United States would affect both PPP and sustainability calculations.

4.3 Adjusting to Endaka

The sustainability calculations of the appropriate yen-dollar exchange rate cited in section 4.2 suggest that the current rate is either close to a sustainable level or that some further appreciation is required. These calculations thus indicate that the yen was dramatically undervalued prior to the appreciation that started in February 1985, and that the strong yen is likely to persist. This exchange rate adjustment will induce substantial trade balance adjustment and necessitate fundamental changes in the structure of industry in Japan.

The magnitude of the adjustment currently required of the Japanese economy is one powerful example of the costs of misalignment. To undo the substantial undervaluation of the yen that accumulated prior to 1985, the yen-dollar exchange rate has appreciated by 47% (or 90% in terms of the dollar-yen exchange rate) in the space of just two years. As can be seen in figure 4.1, this is the largest unidirectional percentage change of the yen-dollar rate since the advent of floating rates, although the sharp appreciation in 1976–78 was close to the same magnitude (42% in yen-dollar terms). Figure 4.1 shows that the trade weighted-average yen has also appreciated, but by a smaller amount. (Similar time paths are evident in the real yen exchange rate—see Manual Johnson and Loopesko 1987.) This section will look at the adjustment process currently under way in Japan and discuss how the dynamics of adjustment are influenced by structural features of the Japanese economy.

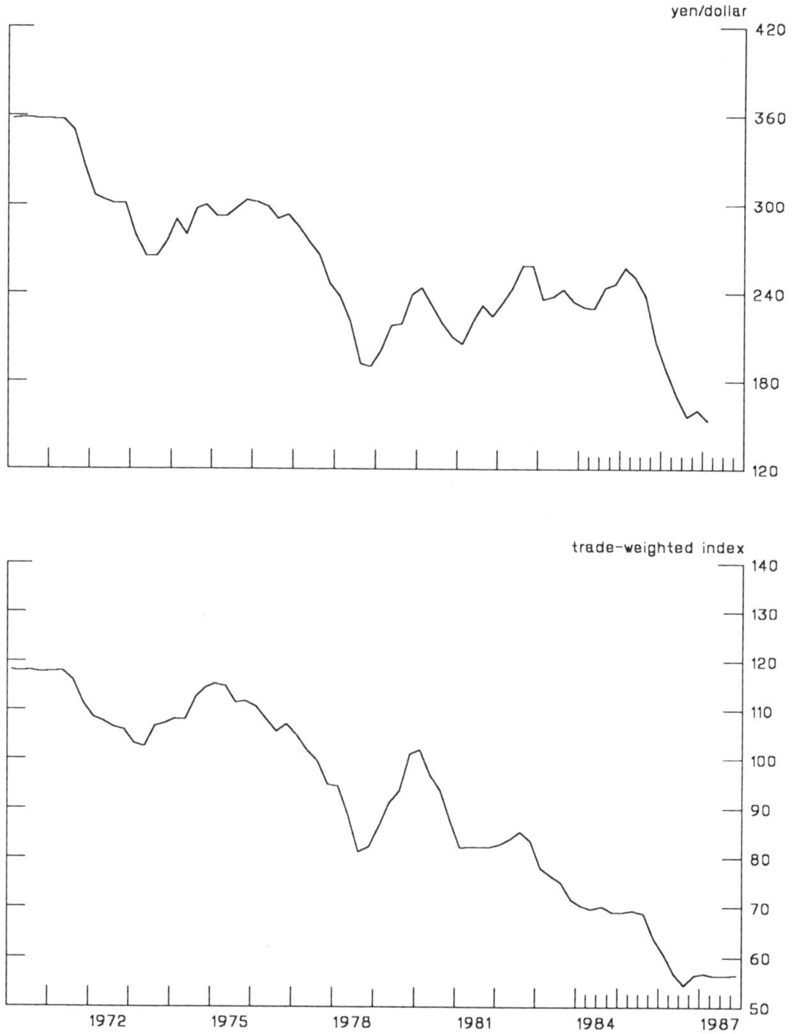

Fig. 4.1 Yen exchange rates. Source: Board of Governors. Note: The top panel plots the monthly average value of the yen-dollar exchange rate. The bottom panel plots a weighted-average yen exchange rate index based on bilateral exchange rates for 16 major trading partners, i.e., the 10 major industrial economies plus South Korea, the Philippines, Taiwan, Hong Kong, Singapore, and Malaysia. The weights are based on average multilateral trade in 1978–83.

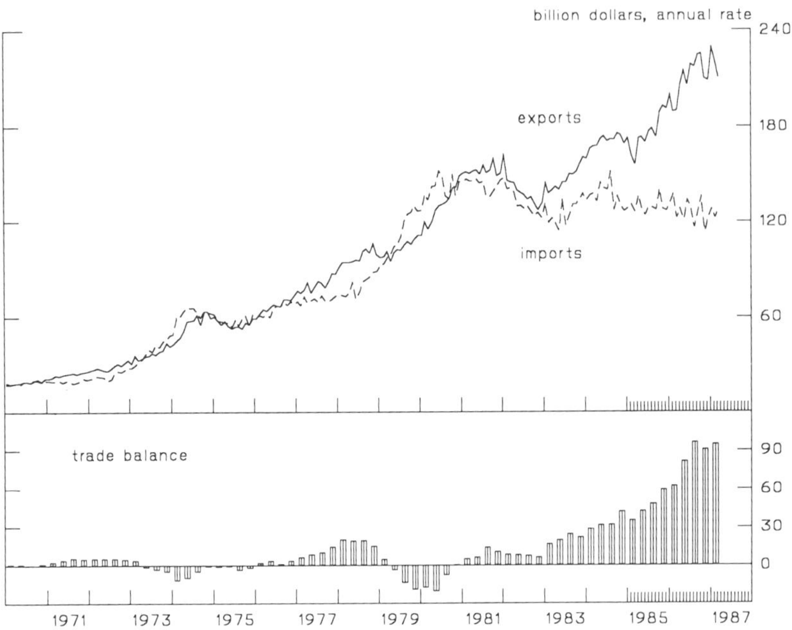

Fig. 4.2 Japanese trade (in dollars). Source: Board of Governors database. Note: Based on customs-basis trade data.

4.3.1 Recent Adjustment of Japanese Trade

The Japanese trade balance has already started to adjust to the sharp rise of the yen, as can be seen in figures 4.2 through 4.4. In both dollar and yen terms, shown in figures 4.2 and 4.3, the Japanese surplus has started to decline slightly. The decline is even more evident when the trade balance is expressed in real terms, shown in figure 4.4. Nonetheless, a record surplus remains (in 1986, the trade surplus reached \$82.5 billion), and the arithmetic of adjustment of the trade imbalance implies that, over time, imports would have to grow about 80% faster than exports to attain balance (since exports are presently about 80% greater than imports).

Figure 4.5 highlights the growing importance of the bilateral trading relationship between Japan and the United States in Japan's overall trade pattern. Both Japanese exports to the United States and imports from the United States have grown in the 1980s. In 1986, the United States purchased 39% of Japan's exports and provided 23% of its imports.

Japan's trade imbalance vis-à-vis the United States measured in dollars, shown in table 4.5, may have started to decline in 1987. The surplus for the first quarter of 1987 fell to \$11 billion dollars, compared to \$14.4

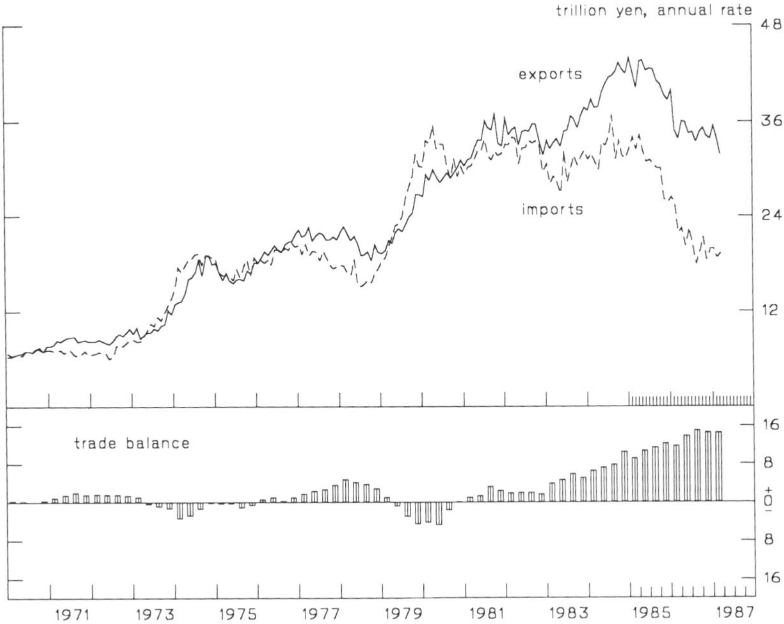

Fig. 4.3 Japanese trade (in yen). Source: Board of Governors database. Note: Based on customs-basis trade data.

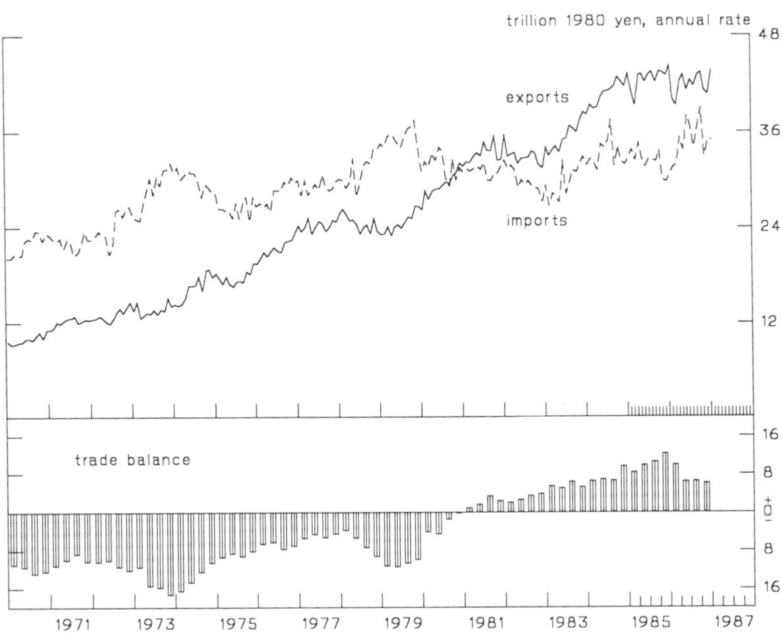

Fig. 4.4 Japanese real trade (in 1980 yen). Source: Board of Governors database and Bank of Japan. Note: Customs-basis data on nominal exports and imports in current yen were deflated by export and import price indices that are reported in the Bank of Japan, *Economic Statistics Monthly*, table 120.

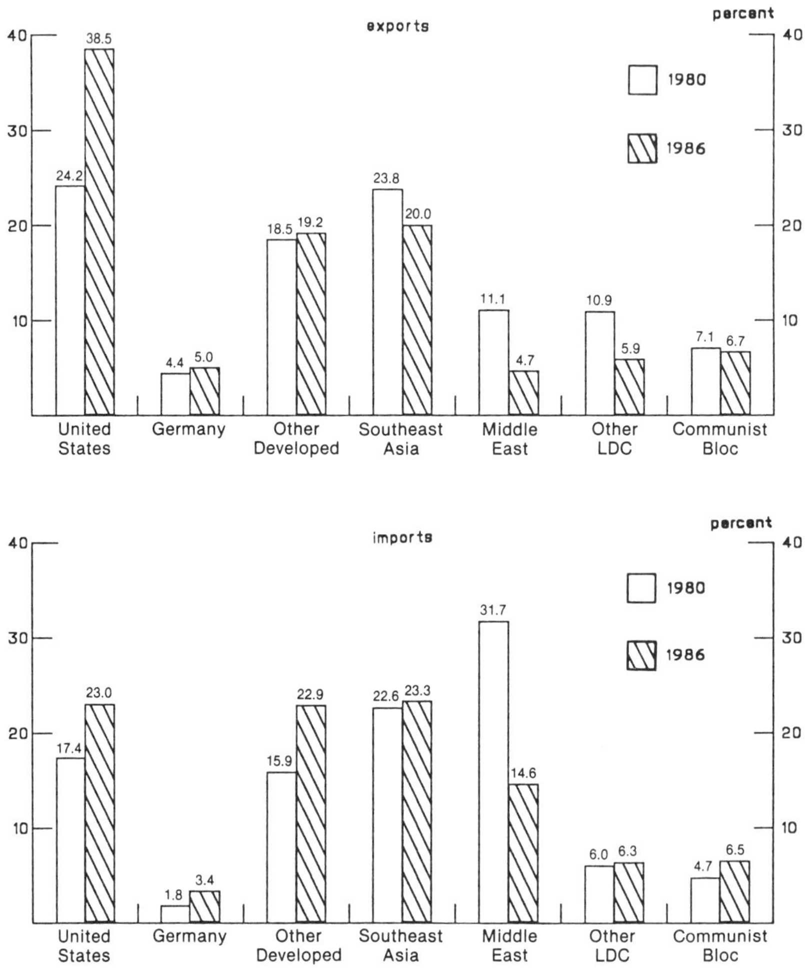

Fig. 4.5 Direction of Japanese trade, 1980 and 1986. Source: Japan Tariff Association, *The Summary Report on Trade of Japan.*

billion in the fourth quarter. However, since these data are reported on a seasonally unadjusted basis, and declines in the first quarter are common, it is too early to determine if the turning point has been reached. Calculations by the Bank of Japan of the real trade balance between the United States and Japan, shown in figure 4.6, indicate that the decline in the real bilateral trade surplus started early in 1986. The Bank of Japan calculations also show declines in Japan's real surplus vis-à-vis Asia and the European Community.

Table 4.5 **Japan-U.S. Trade (in Billions of Dollars)**

	Exports (F.O.B.)	Imports (C.I.F.)	Trade Balance
1982	$36,330	$24,179	$12,151
1983	42,829	24,648	18,181
1984	59,937	26,862	33,075
1985	65,278	25,793	39,485
1986	80,462	28,984	51,478
1986:I	16,706	6,275	10,431
1986:II	20,923	8,272	12,651
1986:III	21,281	7,518	13,764
1986:IV	21,552	6,920	14,632
1987:I	17,979	6,948	11,031

Source: Japan Tariff Association, *Summary Report of Trade*.

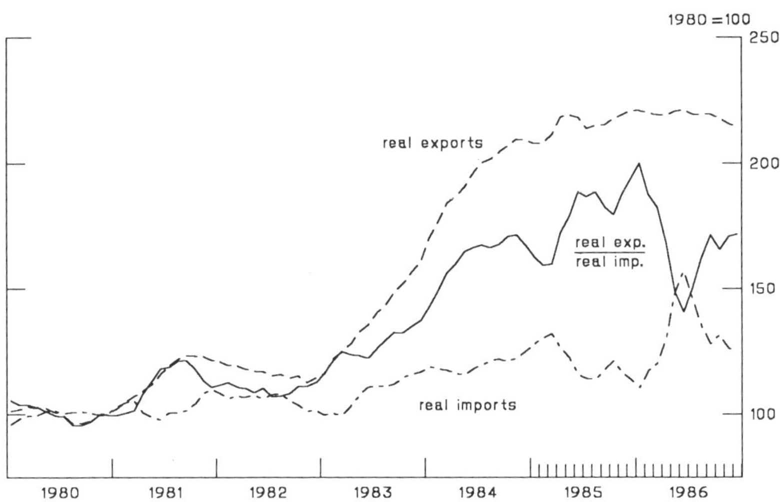

Fig. 4.6 The U.S.-Japan real trade balance (in 1980 yen). Source: Bank of Japan. Note: Real exports and imports vis-à-vis the United States have been estimated on the basis of the commodity composition of exports and imports between the United States and Japan.

4.4 Traditional Channels of Trade Balance Adjustment

It is interesting to investigate the channels through which this trade balance adjustment can be expected to occur in Japan. Much of the empirical literature on trade balance adjustment focuses on income and price elasticities in export and import demand equations. This section first reviews some of the estimates of Japanese trade equations provided

Table 4.6 Elasticity Estimates for U.S.-Japan Trade

	Relative Price Elasticity	Income Elasticity
Bergsten and Cline (1987)		
1960–84 (annual data)		
Japanese exports	−2.12[a]	1.62[b]
Japanese imports	−1.16	1.81[c]
Craig (1986)		
1961:III–1985:IV		
Japanese exports	−1.14	3.57
Japanese imports	0.66	0.75

[a]Constrained to equal 2.12, which is the elasticity estimated by Peter A. Petri (1984).
[b]Ratio of U.S. actual to trend GNP.
[c]Ratio of Japanese actual to trend GNP.

by earlier research and then presents some new estimates. The review proceeds from the most partial of partial equilibrium frameworks, equations for bilateral trade between Japan and the United States, to equations for Japanese multilateral trade. Because it is impossible to evaluate the role of policy in fostering trade adjustment in these partial equilibrium frameworks, section 4.8 provides some empirical evidence based on simulations of the Federal Reserve Board staff's Multi-Country Model (MCM).

4.4.1 Bilateral Trade Equations

Trade between the United States and Japan has been modeled recently by Bergsten and Cline (1987). Their elasticity estimates are summarized in table 4.6. In the equation for Japanese exports to the United States, they estimate two income elasticities, one for the ratio of actual GNP to trend GNP to capture the cyclical position of the economy and another for real U.S. GNP. The cyclical income elasticities are reported in the table (the other income elasticity is 0.7 for Japanese exports—but it is not statistically significant—and 0.8 for Japanese imports). While the elasticity estimates reported in table 4.6 suggest a substantial responsiveness of Japanese exports and imports to fluctuations in both relative prices and cyclical fluctuations in real income, there appear to be some technical problems with the estimates. In particular, the income elasticity of U.S. demand for Japanese exports is arrived at using an unusual estimation procedure. The authors take as given the relative price elasticity (using the elasticity estimated in a study by Petri 1984) and then estimate the remainder of the equation. Clearly, by construction, the Petri elasticity is an estimate that is conditional on the other variables included in his equation and cannot simply be transplanted into another equation with a different functional form.

Because of these problems, table 4.6 also reports estimates by Craig (1986) which are derived from very simple equations incorporating a lagged dependent variable, a contemporaneous activity variable, and a contemporaneous relative price term. These estimates suggest that the income and price elasticities of U.S. demand for Japanese exports are of a typical magnitude for a major industrial economy, but that those for Japanese demand for imports from the United States are quite low. Very substantial increases in Japanese real income would then be required to induce a significant change in Japanese imports.

Both sets of equations suggest that changes in relative prices are an important influence on Japanese exports to the United States. It is important to note, however, that in both sets of estimates the relative price terms are not constructed to isolate the relative prices of goods traded between the United States and Japan. Instead, aggregate price indices are used which may be heavily influenced by prices of goods that are not involved in U.S.-Japanese trade. For this reason, the price estimates should be interpreted with caution.

Table 4.7 reports the full set of Japanese bilateral trade elasticities estimated by Craig. It is interesting to note that while Japanese income elasticities of demand for imports from all of the major industrial countries studied are quite low, the income elasticity is largest for imports from the developing countries. Japanese imports from industrial countries other than the United States are moderately price elastic, while Japanese exports to the industrial countries are quite responsive to changes in foreign real economic activity. Taken together, these estimates suggest that quite different geographic patterns of bilateral trade

Table 4.7 Japanese Bilateral Trade Elasticities (1961:III–1985:IV)

	Japanese Imports		Japanese Exports	
	Price	Income	Price	Income
United States	−0.66	0.75	−1.14	3.57
	(0.06)	(0.05)	(0.10)	(0.31)
Canada	−1.12	0.61	−1.39	2.19
	(0.09)	(0.05)	(0.19)	(0.20)
United Kingdom	−1.14	0.78	−1.06	5.90
	(0.18)	(0.10)	(0.09)	(0.34)
Germany	−1.00	0.71	−0.50	4.80
	(0.08)	(0.06)	(0.15)	(0.28)
Other OECD	−1.08	0.92	−1.09	2.45
	(0.10)	(0.10)	(0.08)	(0.20)
Developing countries	−0.20	1.39	−0.71	0.74
	(0.08)	(0.14)	(0.07)	(0.07)

Source: Sean Craig (1986).
Note: Standard errors in parentheses.

Table 4.8 **Survey of Estimates of Japanese and U.S. Long-Run Income and Price Elasticities: Average and Range of Estimates**

	Exports		Imports	
	Japan	U.S.	Japan	U.S.
Long-run price elasticity	−1.4 (−3.0 to −0.5)	−1.2 (−2.3 to .03)	−1.0 (−1.2 to −0.7)	−1.3 (−1.7 to −1.0)
Long-run income elasticity	2.6 (1.5 to 4.2)	1.4 (0.9 to 2.2)	1.2 (0.8 to 1.7)	1.9 (0.8 to 4.0)

Note: From Goldstein and Khan (1985), who report representative estimates of income and price elasticities from recent studies. The entries in this table are the average of the estimates reported, and the range of estimates is in parentheses.

adjustment would result from changes in relative prices versus changes in real economic activity.

4.4.2 Multilateral Trade Equations

Table 4.8 reports the average and the range of the elasticity estimates from recent studies of U.S. and Japanese multilateral trade equations surveyed in Goldstein and Khan (1985). As in the bilateral equations estimated by Craig, there appear to be some asymmetries between the Japanese and U.S. elasticity estimates. Both the average estimates and range of estimates for the Japanese import elasticities appear lower than those for the U.S. equations. In contrast, the average estimates and range of estimates for the Japanese export elasticities appear larger than those for the United States. This would suggest that efforts to stimulate the domestic economy in Japan would result in less trade adjustment than either changes in relative prices or a slowdown in domestic demand in the United States. The MCM simulations reported in section 4.8 confirm this impression.

Table 4.9 takes another look at Japanese and U.S. trade equations. These estimates are from work with Bill Helkie at the Federal Reserve Board. Japan's aggregate import elasticities again appear relatively low, but these aggregate elasticities mask substantial differences in the elasticities of the components of imports, shown in the bottom panel. The disaggregated Japanese import equations indicate that fuel and raw materials have quite low income and price elasticities. Table 4.10 shows that fuel and raw materials accounted for about 43% of Japanese imports in 1986 but only 28% of U.S. imports, so that these low elasticity components are more important as a percentage of total imports for Japan. Japanese manufacturing imports, about 42% of total imports, are more responsive to income and relative price movements. In fact,

Japan's elasticities for manufacturing imports look more like the typical elasticities of major industrial economies. This evidence suggests that the differences in elasticities between the United States and Japan may derive in part from the different commodity composition of trade of the two countries.

Table 4.9 Estimates of Japanese and U.S. Multilateral Trade Elasticities

	Income Elasticities		Price Elasticities	
	Japan	U.S.	Japan	U.S.
Aggregate trade equations				
Exports	1.60	2.19	−1.14	−0.83
1970:I–1986:I	(9.10)	(5.46)	(−3.57)	(−6.11)
Imports	1.07	2.11	−0.44	−1.15
1968:I–1986:IV	(14.03)	(5.30)	(−4.69)	(−10.03)
Disaggregated import equations				
Manufacturing	1.86		−0.90	
1975:I–1986:IV	(9.13)		(−9.21)	
Fuel	1.00[a]		−0.17	
1974:I–1986:IV			(−5.06)	
Raw materials	0.97		−0.50	
1974:I–1986:IV	(3.40)		(−7.24)	

Notes: For the United States, the table reports Helkie and Hooper's (1987) estimates for nonagricultural exports and nonoil imports. The estimates for Japan are based on work with William Helkie at the Federal Reserve Board. The dates refer to the estimation period for the Japanese equations. The U.S. equations were estimated over 1969:I to 1984:IV.

[a]Constrained to be unity.

Table 4.10 Commodity Composition of Trade for the United States and Japan, 1986 (Percentage Shares)

	U.S.	Japan
	Exports	
Agricultural products	12	1
Raw materials	25	1
Manufactured goods	63	98
	Imports	
Food and beverages	6	15
Raw materials, excluding fuel	20	14
Fuel	8	29
Manufactured goods	67	42

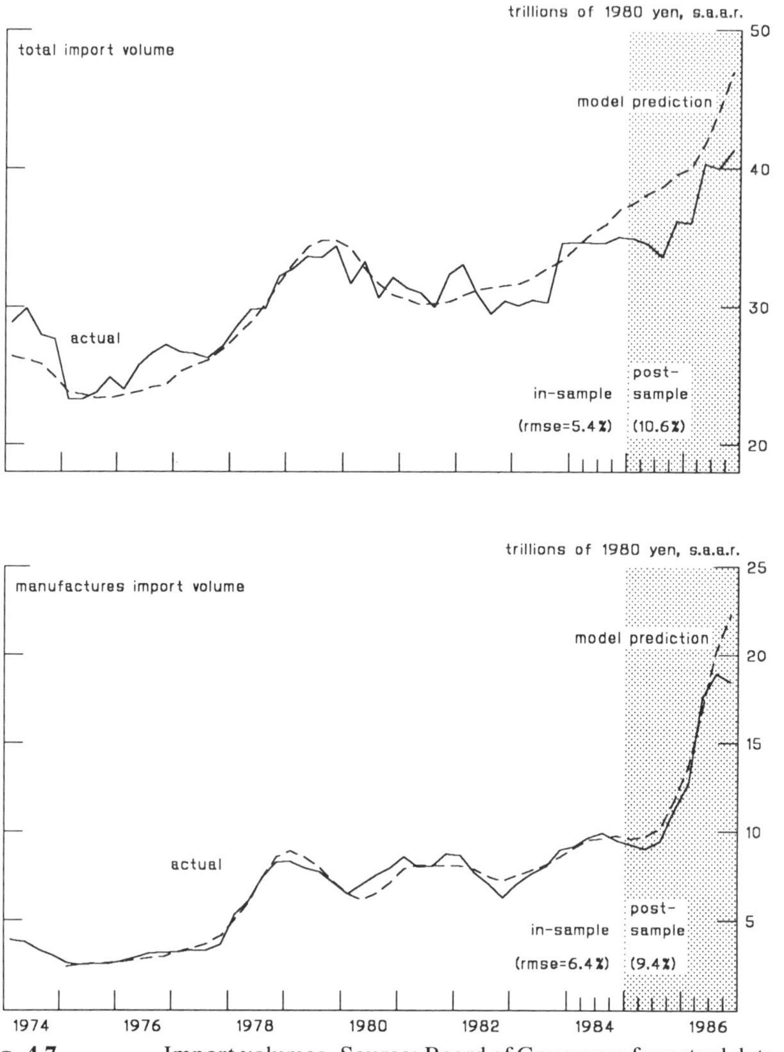

Fig. 4.7 Import volumes. Source: Board of Governors for actual data. Note: Detailed descriptions of the trade equations underlying the model prediction are available from the authors by request.

The forecasting performance of these Japanese trade equations, shown in figures 4.7 to 4.9, suggests that the current process of trade balance adjustment for Japan differs from that of recent historical experience. The total import volume equation tracks moderately well in sample, but predicts a more substantial rise in imports in 1985 and 1986 than actually materialized. This overprediction of Japanese imports is a feature of all of the disaggregated import equations, although the root-

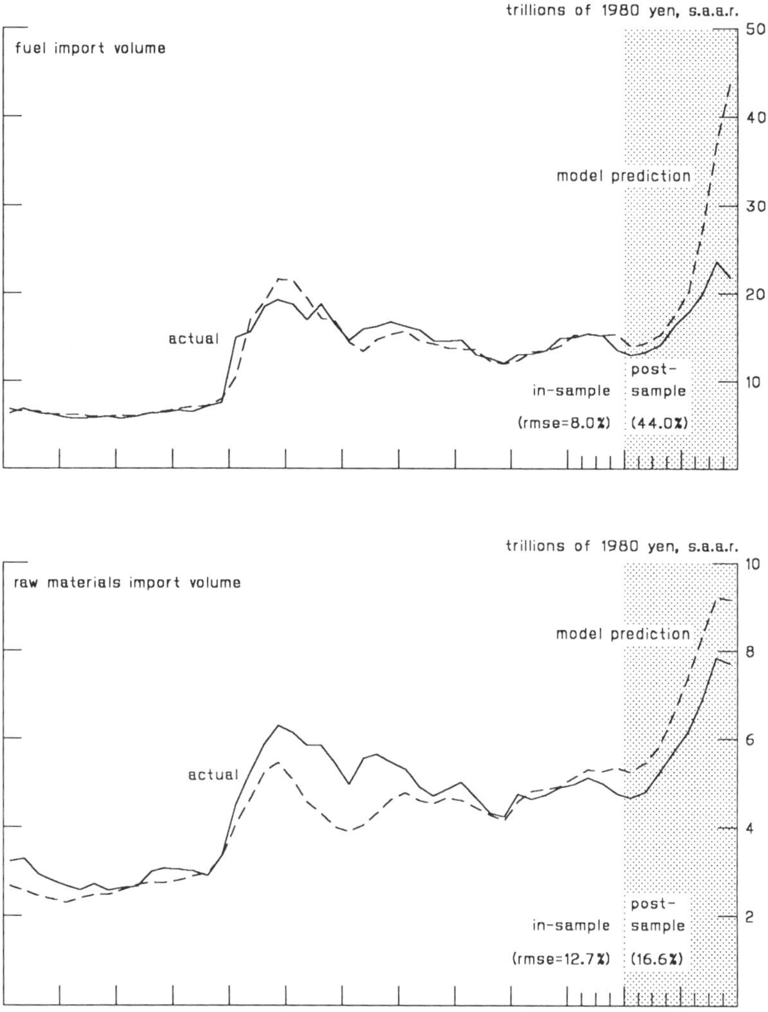

Fig. 4.8 Import volumes. Source: See fig. 4.7. Note: See fig. 4.7.

mean-squared error of the postsample forecast is largest for fuel. For aggregate Japanese exports, the equation again fits moderately well in sample, but predicts a more substantial decline in exports than has in fact occurred.

Based on these estimates, it would appear that Japanese trade has been less responsive to changes in income and relative prices in the last two years than would have been predicted based on recent historical experience. Section 4.5 explores some possible explanations for this slow adjustment of Japanese trade.

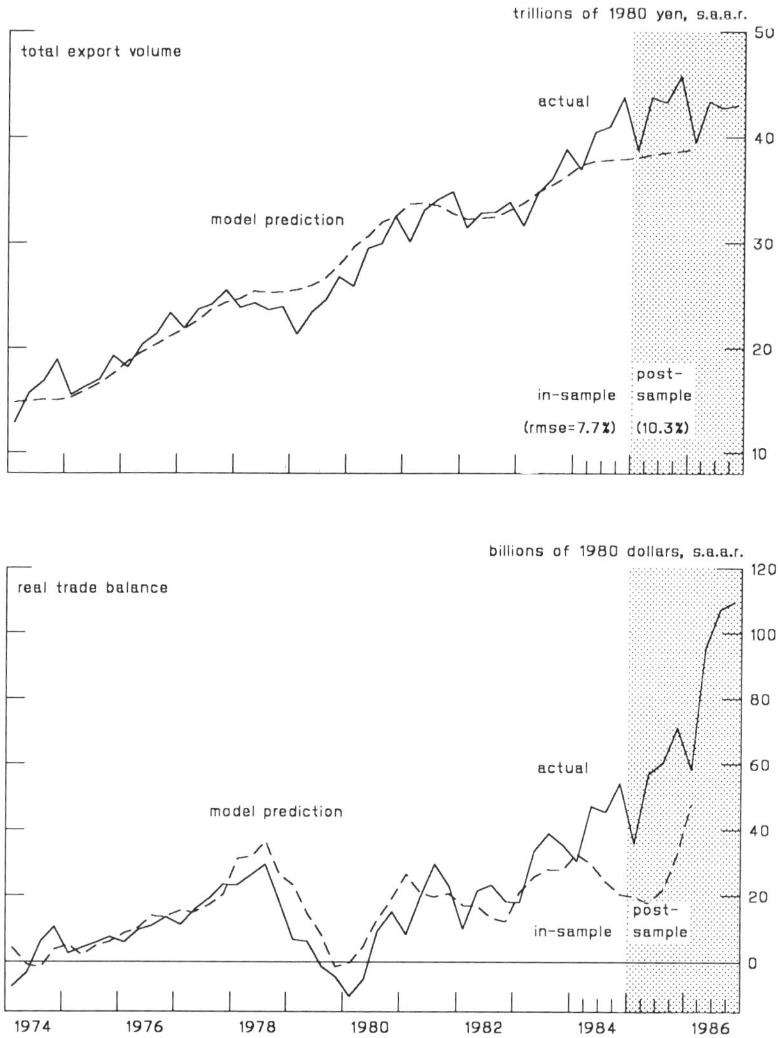

Fig. 4.9 Export volume and real trade balance. Source: See fig. 4.7. Note: See fig. 4.7.

4.5 The Slow Adjustment of Japan's Trade Surplus

4.5.1 Slow Pass-through

One factor that has contributed to the sluggish adjustment of Japanese exports is slow pass-through of the yen's appreciation to export prices in foreign currency terms. Failure to adjust foreign-currency prices of exports by the amount of an exchange rate change may correspond to an attempt to maintain market share. The resulting squeeze

Table 4.11 Pass-Through of the Yen's Appreciation to Export Prices, November 1976 to November 1985 and February 1985 to February 1987 (%)

Export Industry	Nov. '76–Nov. '78	Feb. '85–Feb. '87
Total exports	65.8	47.6
Chemicals	−25.4	9.5
Textiles	98.0	51.4
Metals and related products	50.8	20.0
General machinery and precision instruments	105.1	66.1
Electrical machinery	93.4	46.8
Transportation equipment	61.6	64.2

Sources: Bank of Japan, *Economic Statistics Monthly* (export prices) and Japan Tariff Association, *The Summary Report of Trade* (conversion exchange rate for custom-cleared exports).

on Japanese exporters' profit margins has been documented by Mann (1986) and Jones (1987). Recent theoretical explanations of pass-through and profit margin phenomena are provided by Dornbusch (1985) and Krugman (1986a). Fisher (1987) explores the dependence of the degree of pass-through on domestic and foreign market structures and the exchange rate regime.

Recent evidence on pass-through is presented in table 4.11, which presents pass-through estimates for various categories of Japanese exports for the period since the start of the yen's rise in February 1985. The percentage of pass-through is calculated by comparing the actual yen export price to the yen export price that roughly corresponds to full pass-through of the yen's appreciation. Zero pass-through implies that yen export prices would fall by the amount of the yen's appreciation against the dollar in order to keep dollar prices constant, while full pass-through implies that yen export prices would remain constant. Under the assumption that the change in the yen's value was the only influence on the yen export price since February 1985, the export price in February 1985 provides a rough approximation of the full-pass-through export price in February 1987 (i.e., no change should have occurred in yen terms if profit margins were not being reduced in response to the yen's appreciation). Thus, the calculations in table 4.11 compare the difference between the actual yen export prices in February 1987 and February 1985 to the exchange rate change over that period.

The calculated rate of pass-through of the 41% appreciation of the yen-dollar exchange rate over that period (calculated from the conversion exchange rate used for customs-cleared exports) is 47.6% for total exports. This is low in comparison to the 66% average pass-through of a roughly comparable (37%) yen appreciation that occurred in November 1976–November 1978.

Lower pass-through in the recent period may reflect a number of factors. One important change since the mid-seventies is the greater degree of competition for Japanese exporters from the Asian NICs (Hong Kong, Singapore, Korea, and Taiwan). The most rapid rates of pass-through in the recent period occurred in industries such as general machinery and precision instruments and transportation equipment, whereas the lowest rates of pass-through occurred in competitive industrial materials industries such as metals and chemicals. In the former areas, Japanese exporters now have a well-established reputation for high quality, so that the new competition poses a less immediate threat to market share. It is interesting that the rate of pass-through is actually slightly more rapid in the recent period for the transportation industry, suggesting that the quality factor may have been particularly strong in this sector. In the latter (industrial materials) areas, international competition has been strong for many years, and even in the second half of the seventies these sectors had relatively low rates of pass-through.

Another factor differentiating the recent period from the mid-seventies is that the most recent episode of yen appreciation coincided with a period of sharply declining commodity prices, including a steep fall in the price of oil (petroleum product imports account for more than one-third of Japanese imports). This decline in costs of imported intermediate inputs to production has permitted Japanese producers to reduce production costs, thereby limiting the extent to which prices of their exports in foreign-currency terms need to be increased with the yen's appreciation.

A final factor that may have influenced the rates of pass-through in the two periods is the state of profit margins at the start of the yen's appreciation. It is frequently alleged that profit margins of Japanese exporters were unusually large in early 1985 when the yen started its prolonged ascent, thereby providing a considerable cushion before prices in foreign currency terms had to be raised. It would be an interesting topic for further research to explore the importance of this factor in pricing behavior.

Several Japanese government agencies have recently done some pass-through calculations, although unfortunately this work is only reported in Japanese-language sources. A few highlights of this work are reported below.

The Economic Planning Agency (EPA) has done calculations comparing rates of pass-through for various time periods. In particular, the EPA reports pass-through rates for November 1977–October 1978 and for September 1985–January 1987. They find that the rate of pass-through has declined from 64% in the earlier period to 43% in the most recent period. They report pass-through rates by industry for only the most recent period. The EPA finds pass-through to be lowest in the chemical industry (35%) and metal industries (15%), but also (unlike in table 4.11) in the textile industry (31%). The EPA also finds high rates of pass-through in the electrical machinery industry (74%) and in general machinery industries (55%). Most of these EPA findings are qualitatively quite similar to the results in table 4.11.

The Japanese Ministry of International Trade and Industry (MITI) has also done some research on pass-through by industry for roughly the same time periods. MITI compares pass-through rates by industry for the June 1977–November 1978 and September 1985–February 1987 periods. The MITI findings again broadly support those in table 4.11. (Approximate figures are reported below, since only a chart, and not data, was readily available.) For all industries, the rate of pass-through slowed from about 65% in the earlier period to about 55% in the recent period. The decline was most dramatic in the iron and steel industries (from 55% to 10%), where international competition has become particularly intense. The MITI results also show that pass-through was quite high in the recent period in those industries where Japan has a well-established reputation for high-quality products (60% for passenger cars, 80% for photocopying machines, and 65% for machine tools).

MITI also has done some interesting calculations of the rates of pass-through adjusted for declines in raw materials costs for certain industries. As was noted above, the decline in prices of imported intermediate inputs to production has permitted lower pass-through rates in the recent period. After this adjustment is made, the overall pass-through rate for the two time periods appears to be quite similar (about 70% in both time periods). However, in the iron and steel and the passenger car industries, where international competition has been increasing, there was a sharp fall in even these adjusted rates of pass-through between the two time periods. Thus it would appear that the increase in international competition is a key factor explaining slower pass-through in a few industries, but in most industries the slower pass-through is more strongly related to the recent sharp declines in raw-material import costs.

The fact that pass-through has been slower in the past two years (for any of the above reasons) than in recent historical experience can help explain why adjustment of export volume has been slower than predicted. The out-of-sample predicted value for export volume in figure 4.9 is generated using predicted yen export prices, and the predicted yen export price has fallen less than the actual yen export price because of this weaker pass-through. Thus slow pass-through provides one explanation for the gap between the actual and predicted export volume.

The above evidence compares the response of Japanese export prices during two periods of yen appreciation. It is also interesting to ask whether an asymmetry exists in the adjustment process of Japanese export prices to yen appreciations and yen depreciations. Such an asymmetry might occur if, as is often alleged, Japanese exporters use strategic pricing in order to maintain market share. In this case, they might attempt to keep the dollar price of exports constant in the face of a yen appreciation (i.e., reduce yen export prices), but would allow some decline in dollar export prices with yen depreciations (i.e., not increase yen export prices).

The Appendix reports a test of the particular strategic pricing hypothesis that yen export prices respond asymmetrically to a strengthening and weakening of the yen. The exchange rate enters a typical yen export price equation through its impact on the yen value of competitors' export prices. Thus the question of interest is whether Japan's export price responds differently to a rise in competitors' export prices (expressed in yen) than to a decline. More specifically, Japanese exporters are concerned about movements in competitors' export prices relative to their own export prices, so that the precise hypothesis test is in terms of the significance of a dummy variable, $a6$, that is unity when Japan's export price rises relative to competitors' export prices and zero otherwise. Competitors' export prices in yen terms may fall relative to the Japanese export price because of a decline in competitors' export prices in foreign currency terms or because of an appreciation of the yen. In either case, a Japanese exporter may choose to match declines in competitors' prices, but not increases, in order to maintain export share. The test is a simple variation on the profit margin theme.

Dummy variables that isolate appreciations and depreciations are entered multiplicatively with the competitors' export price variable. The null hypothesis that the coefficient on the appreciation dummy is equal to the coefficient on the depreciation dummy (or the equivalent test that the coefficient $a6 = 0$) is rejected at the 2% confidence level. This is further evidence of strategic pricing on the part of Japanese exporters.

4.5.2 Distributor and Dealer Margins

Another factor that may help explain the deviation between actual and predicted values for imports and exports is the behavior of Japanese retail distributors of imported goods and foreign dealers for Japanese exports. It is very difficult to obtain data to document these phenomena, but anecdotal evidence abounds. For example, it is widely recognized in Japan that Japanese retail distributors of imported goods have not been passing on fully the benefits of the yen's appreciation to consumers in Japan. Indeed, the issue has attracted the attention of Japanese policymakers, and recent demand-stimulus packages have all included promises to promote greater pass-through to consumers of terms-of-trade gains. Thus, even though precise data on the pass-through of exchange rate changes to consumers is difficult to obtain, the authorities clearly acknowledge that the pass-through has been slow.

One institutional factor is worth noting in this regard. In Japan, the same trading companies generally handle both exports and imports. Thus, if Japanese trading companies' profit margins are being compressed to maintain export market shares, it is possible that some offset may be sought by slowing the pass-through of the yen's appreciation to domestic prices of imported goods. Again, it is not possible to find data to document whether this is in fact occurring, but numerous Japanese officials acknowledge that it is a reasonable hypothesis.

Most of the evidence of slow pass-through to consumer prices remains anecdotal, but it is reflected in the very modest decline in consumer prices relative to the sharp appreciation of the yen, shown in figure 4.10. In the 12 months through March 1987 when the yen appreciated about 20%, the CPI declined just 0.3%, while import prices fell 16%. The failure of consumer prices to fall further reduces the terms-of-trade gains to the consumer associated with the yen's appreciation (and with the recent decline in the price of oil as well).

The EPA has done some interesting work (again only available in Japanese) attempting to discern why consumer prices have declined less in the recent period than their model would have predicted. The model would have predicted a 4.2% fall in consumer prices between September 1985 and September 1986, whereas a 0.2% increase actually occurred. They show that sluggish adjustment of administered prices

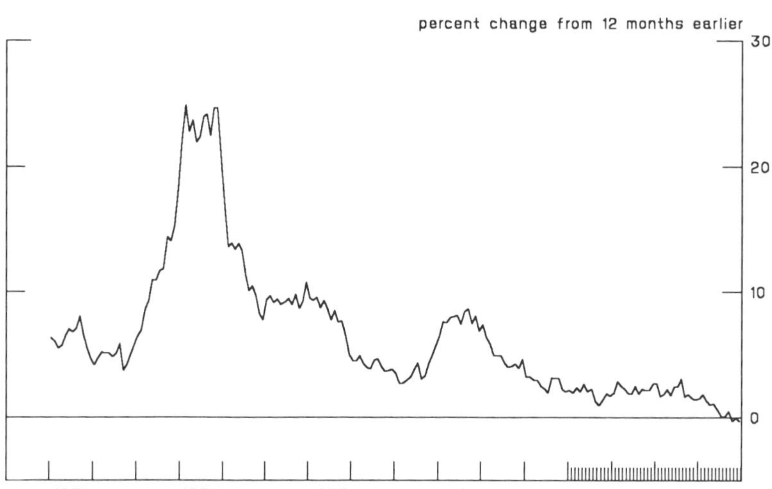

Fig. 4.10 Consumer prices. Source: Board of Governors database.

(such as those of public utilities and state corporations) was one key factor inhibiting consumer price adjustment. Their results also suggest that factors relating to the distribution network between the wholesale and retail levels and perhaps supply-and-demand conditions in particular markets may have contributed to the sluggishness of retail price adjustment following the yen's recent rise.

On the export side, dealer margins may have affected the adjustment of Japanese exports. For example, in the United States many consumers who purchased a Toyota or other popular Japanese cars prior to the yen's appreciation had to pay a dealer markup over the list price reflecting excess demand. In the Washington, D.C., area, these markups often were on the order of $1,000 to $2,000. More recently, as Toyota's import price has risen and demand has accordingly waned, dealer markups have generally been reduced or eliminated.

Thus, even though the dollar export price may rise, a concurrent decline in dealer markups means that the effective price facing the U.S. consumer has not changed by the full amount of the yen's rise. As a result, the relative export price in the export demand equation does not fully capture the movements in prices facing consumers. Since these dealer markups are a fairly recent phenomenon, they would not be captured in a stable manner by the coefficient on relative export prices in the reported equation. If such markups were common for a wide variety of Japanese exports, they might be one source of the less-than-predicted decline in exports in the postsample period. This could be a topic for further research.

4.6 A Model of the Adjustment Process in Japan

Beyond the issue of explaining the prediction errors in our forecasting equations, there is the broader question of whether an overreliance on exchange rate movements to correct external imbalance can actually turn out to be counterproductive. As the dollar has fallen relative to the yen, some observers have suggested that the rapid depreciation of the dollar may actually worsen the U.S. trade balance. They emphasize that the sharp rise of the yen will induce a recession in Japan and therefore reduce the demand for U.S. exports in the short-to-medium term. In essence they claim that the recession-induced income effects will dominate the substitution effects associated with the change in the exchange rate. Those advocating this point of view do not necessarily argue that the dollar has overshot its equilibrium position. Rather they emphasize that the speed of the yen's appreciation has been too rapid to allow Japan to adjust without experiencing a sharp deceleration of economic activity.

It is difficult to believe that the induced income effects would dominate the substitution effects, given the small income elasticity of Japanese demand for U.S. exports of about 0.75 (see table 4.7). The induced recession effect on the bilateral trade balance between the United States and Japan is probably quite small even when Japan experiences a severe contraction of economic activity. Thus, one may desire to slow the descent of the dollar to alleviate the burden of adjustment on Japan or for other reasons, but if reducing the U.S. trade balance is the primary objective, a fall in the dollar will almost assuredly bring about an improvement in the bilateral balance of trade.

There may be considerations other than the U.S.-Japan bilateral trade balance that could influence policymakers to try to reduce the adjustment costs borne by the Japanese economy. Quite simply, trade is multilateral and the evidence in table 4.9 indicates that the Japanese multilateral income elasticity is not particularly small. As is shown in table 4.7, the Japanese income elasticity of demand for imports from developing countries is the largest of the bilateral income elasticities, so that Japanese income growth may bear heavily upon the ability of debt-burdened developing countries to service their external debt. A recession in Japan, given their dependence on imported raw materials, would increase the strain on some of these countries. This could occur despite the fact that the appreciation of the yen has made these inputs to production cheaper in Japan, which may have helped raw-materials exporters.

In light of these broader multilateral considerations, it seems fruitful to investigate the impact of a large exchange rate change on the Japanese domestic economy. This section will present a stylized model of the Japanese economy in the short run and analyze the impact of an exchange rate appreciation on output, employment, and the trade balance. The model emphasizes the interaction between the tradable and nontraded goods sectors of the economy and also examines the influence of intermediate imports on sectoral adjustment and the trade balance when wages are rigid. We employ a slightly modified version of a model by Dornbusch (1980) as the workhorse, but perform some different exercises with the model which are particularly relevant to the recent Japanese experience. In this framework, one can illuminate some of the forces within the Japanese economy that might lead to a deceleration of economic activity in the short run as well as those elements of economic structure that would help mitigate the difficulties of adjustment to an exchange rate change.

We begin with a model that has two sectors, tradable and nontraded goods. Each sector utilizes two inputs to production: labor and an imported factor of production. Each sector's production technology exhibits constant returns to scale. Therefore prices can be related to factor prices as follows:

(1) $$P_T = a_T * w + b_T * (e * p_r).$$

(2) $$P_N = a_N * w + b_N * (e * p_r)$$

where P_T = price of tradable good
P_N = price of nontraded good
a_i = input of labor per unit of output in sector i
b_i = input of imported factor per unit of output in sector i
e = exchange rate (yen per unit of foreign currency)
p_r = world price of imported factor of production.

Taking the total differential of equations (1) and (2) yields

(3) $$\hat{P}_T = \Theta_{LT} * \hat{w} + (1 - \Theta_{LT}) * (\hat{e} + \hat{p}_r).$$

(4) $$\hat{P}_N = \Theta_{LN} * \hat{w} + (1 - \Theta_{LN}) * (\hat{e} + \hat{p}_r)$$

where Θ_{ij} = factor i's share in sector j ($\Theta_{Lj} = a_j * w/P_j$)
"$\hat{x}$" denotes a percentage change of x.

The demand structure of the model consists of three components. The first two, the domestic demand for tradable goods, D_T, and the domestic demand for nontraded goods, D_N, are both functions of real income, Y, and the relative price of tradable and nontraded goods, P_{TN}.

(5) $$D_T = D_T(Y, P_{TN}).$$

(6) $$D_N = D_N(Y, P_{TN})$$

where $P_{TN} = P_T/P_N$.

The third component of demand is the foreign demand for the home country's exportable goods, M^*:

(7) $$M^* = M^* (P_{TW}, Y^*)$$

where Y^* = exogenous foreign income
$P_{TW} = P_T/(e * P_w)$
P_w = the world price of exportable goods.

Define real income as

(8) $$Y = (w * L)/Q$$

where $Q = P_T^{\delta} * P_N^{(1-\delta)}$, the weighted-average consumer price index, and δ = the share of tradable goods in domestic consumption.

A change in real income can be expressed as

(9) $$\hat{Y} = \hat{w} + \hat{L} - \delta * \hat{P}_T - (1 - \delta) * \hat{P}_N.$$

Combining equations (3) and (4) and substituting into (9) yields

(10) $$\hat{Y} = \hat{L} - \Omega * (\hat{e} + \hat{p}_r) - \alpha * \hat{w}$$

where $\Omega = \delta * \Theta_{MT} + (1 - \delta) * \Theta_{MN}$
$\alpha = 1 - (1 - \delta) * \Theta_{LN} - \delta * \Theta_{LT}.$

To solve equation (10) for income or employment, one must utilize another equilibrium condition. The derived demand for labor used in the production of both tradable and nontraded goods can be expressed as

(11) $$L^d = a_T * [D_T + M^*] + a_N * D_N.$$

When wages are fixed in the short run, employment is demand determined. Fixed wages in conjunction with the explicit incorporation of the effects of labor income on product demand implies a multiplier effect on demand. A fall in demand implies layoffs which reduce income and further reduce demand.

Taking the total differential of (11) and substituting in (10), one can produce an expression for $\hat{L}$:

(12) $$\begin{aligned}\hat{L} = {} & 1/(1 - \tau) * (\lambda_{LM} * \epsilon_M^{Y^*}) * \hat{Y}^* + 1/(1 - \tau) * [\lambda_{LM} * \epsilon_M^P] \\ & * \hat{P}_W - 1/(1 - \tau) * [\lambda_{LM} * \epsilon_M^P * (1 - \Theta_{LT}) - \phi + \tau\Omega] \\ & * \hat{p}_r + 1/(1 - \tau) * [\tau\alpha + \phi - \lambda_{LM} * \epsilon_M^P * \theta_{LT}] \\ & * \hat{w} + 1/(1 - \tau) * [\lambda_{LM} * \epsilon_M^P * \Theta_{LT} + \phi - \tau\Omega] * \hat{e}.\end{aligned}$$

where $\phi = (A/wL) * \epsilon_T^P * \delta * [\Theta_{LT} - \Theta_{LN}]^2$,

λ_{Li} = the proportion of total labor employed producing good i and $\lambda_{LM} + \lambda_{LT} + \lambda_{LN} = 1$.

Θ_{ij} = the income share of factor i in sector j

γ_i = the marginal propensity to consume good i

δ = the expenditure share of the traded good

$\tau = \Theta_{LT} * \gamma_T + \Theta_{LN} * \gamma_N$

$\alpha = 1 - (1 - \delta) * \Theta_{LN} - \delta * \Theta_{LT}$

ϵ_j^i = the elasticity of demand for j with respect to argument i. (Defined as a positive quantity. For instance, if dD/dP is negative, then the elasticity is defined as $-dD/dP * (P/D)$.)

The expression for $\hat{L}$ can be introduced into equation (9) to solve for the changes in real income in terms of the change in the various exogenous variables. We now turn to the model's implications when the only exogenous change is an appreciation of the exchange rate.

4.7 Effects of a Currency Appreciation

An exchange rate appreciation, holding wages, foreign income, and the world price of both factors and goods constant in the short run, will transmit through the economy along several channels. The rise in the exchange rate will alter the domestic relative prices of tradable and nontraded goods if the relative factor intensities of the two sectors differ. If the tradable goods sector is less labor intensive (more imported factor intensive) than the nontraded sector, as is likely to be the case in Japan, the fall in the price of the imported factor will lead to a fall in the relative price of the tradable goods. This can be seen by subtracting equation (4) from equation (3), while holding wages constant:

$$(13) \qquad \hat{P}_T - \hat{P}_N = (\Theta_{LN} - \Theta_{LT}) * \hat{e}.$$

The implications of an appreciation for output and employment are somewhat more difficult to ascertain. The expression shown in equation (12) can serve as a guide to these effects. Equation (12) can be rewritten when the only shift in the exogenous variables is a change in the exchange rate:

$$(12') \qquad \hat{L} = 1/(1 - \tau) * [\lambda_{LM} * \epsilon_M^P * \Theta_{LT} + \phi - \tau\Omega] * \hat{e}$$
$$\text{where } \phi = (A/WL) * \epsilon_T^P * \delta * [\Theta_{LT} - \Theta_{LN}]^2$$
$$A = (P_T * D_T + P_N * D_N).$$

The first term in parentheses reflects the influence of the exchange rate on employment resulting from the change in foreign demand for the exportable good. An appreciation increases the price of exportables relative to the world price, because of the increase in the labor costs in terms of foreign currency. This term implies a reduction in employment when the exchange rate appreciates.

The second term in parentheses represents the employment effects of demand substitution between tradable and nontraded goods by domestic consumers. An exchange rate appreciation reduces the relative price of the import-intensive sector, which induces a demand shift toward the sector that is less labor intensive. Employment declines are sharper when the relative price elasticity of tradable goods demand is high, when the share of labor in the two sectors is greatly different, and when the trade surplus is small, or equivalently, when domestic absorption, A, is large in relation to domestic income.

The third term in parentheses represents the stimulus to demand in both sectors resulting from the increase in real income created by the appreciation of the currency. That appreciation will lower prices and raise the real consumption wage. The stimulus to income will increase employment in both sectors. Overall, the combined effect of the three terms is ambiguous, so that the effect of an exchange rate change on employment will depend on the relative magnitudes of the three terms.

From equations (10) and (12′) one can also assess the impact of the appreciation on real income:

$$(10') \qquad \hat{Y} = [1/(1 - \tau) * [\lambda_{LM} * \epsilon_M^P * \Theta_{LT} + \phi - \tau\Omega] - \Omega] * \hat{e}.$$

Here the income-effect terms enter twice, once because prices fall and raise income when the currency appreciates and a second time because that same effect raises employment and demand. Overall, however, the result is still ambiguous, although an appreciation will always increase real income by a greater percentage than the percentage increase in employment (or decrease it by a lesser percentage).

Also of interest is the impact of an exchange rate change on the trade balance. For simplicity in this model, the trade balance consists of manufactured exports and intermediate imports.

$$T = P_T * M^* - p_r * [b_T * (D_T + M^*) + b_N * D_N]. \tag{14}$$

The change in the trade balance as a fraction of total earnings in response to an exchange rate change can be expressed as follows:

$$dT/wL = (1 - \rho) * \hat{Y} + \Delta * \hat{e} \tag{15}$$

where $\Delta = [\delta * (1 - \Theta_{LN}) + (1 - \delta) * (1 - \Theta_{LT})] * (T * Q)/Y.$

Note that when trade is in balance this equation reduces to $dT/wL = (1 - \rho) * \hat{Y}$, which is the result of Dornbusch (1980).

Using equations (10′) and (15), one can derive an expression for the change in the trade balance as a function of the exchange rate change.

$$dT/wL = ((1 - \rho) * [1/(1 - \tau) * [\lambda_{LM} * \epsilon_M^P * \Theta_{LT} + \phi - \tau\Omega] - \Omega] + \Delta) * \hat{e}. \tag{16}$$

Alternatively, one can look at imports and exports separately:

$$dX = X * [(1 - \Theta_{LT}) + \epsilon_M^{P^*} * \Theta_{LT}] * \hat{e}. \tag{17}$$

$$dM = M * [\lambda_{rT} * \epsilon_T^Y + \lambda_{rN} * \epsilon_N^Y] * \pi * \hat{e} + M * [1 - (\Theta_{LN} - \Theta_{LT})^2 * \epsilon_{DT}^P * \delta * M/(W * L) + \lambda_{tM}{}^* * \epsilon_M^{P*} \Theta_{LT} + \phi - \tau\Omega] - \Omega] \tag{18}$$

where $\tau + [1/(1 - \tau) * [\lambda_{LM} * \epsilon_M^{P*} \Theta_{LT} + \phi - \tau\Omega] - \Omega]$

X = exports
M = imports
λ_{ri} = the proportion of total imported materials used in sector i
ϵ_i^Y = the income elasticity of demand in sector i
ϵ_i^P = the relative price elasticity of demand in sector i.

The effect of an appreciation on exports is negative. First, the rise in the exchange rate lowers the domestic currency price of exports because the lower price of raw materials is passed through to goods prices. Second, volume falls as exports become more expensive to foreigners because domestic labor costs do not fall along with materials costs as a result of the change in the exchange rate. An increase in the foreign relative price elasticity will increase the decline in exports associated with an appreciation. Also, if the export sector reduces its labor intensity, the effects will be offsetting. The greater pass-through of the exchange rate change into prices will reduce prices by more but volume by less. The net effect will depend upon whether the magnitude of the foreign price elasticity is greater or less than one.

Equation (18) shows the expression for the change in intermediate imports. The first term represents the change in volume because of the change in derived demand resulting from the effects of the exchange rate on real income. If real income falls when the exchange rate appreciates, $\pi > 0$, then demand will decline and factor imports will fall.

The second bracketed term represents three effects. First, the value of imports falls directly because of the appreciation. Second, an appreciation will reduce the relative price of the sector that uses the imported factor most intensively. That will shift demand toward that sector and increase the volume of imports. Finally, the third term represents the decline in imports resulting from foreign consumers substituting away from domestic exports when the exchange change does not entirely pass through into prices because of the rigidity of wages in the short run.

Overall, the implications of an exchange rate change for the Japanese economy in the model above is ambiguous. The model predicts that (1) exports will decline both in value and in volume terms; (2) if real income falls, imports of the intermediate input will also decline in both value and volume terms; (3) employment will decline on net if the propensity to consume is low and/or the share of intermediate imports in production is small; and (4) if real income falls, the trade balance will worsen if the income elasticity of demand for imports is large.

From this discussion it is clear that the effect of the yen's appreciation on real income and the Japanese trade balance is ambiguous. However, as noted earlier, even if real income declines in Japan, this would probably translate into a relatively small increase in imports from the United States given the small Japanese income elasticity of demand for U.S. imports. Thus it is unlikely that even a strong yen appreciation would have a recessionary impact large enough to actually cause a widening of Japan's trade surplus with the United States.

While this model captures many of the structural links affecting the Japanese economy, it does not address some of the other elements of economic structure that would affect performance in the short-to-medium run. First of all, it does not include an imported final good. An appreciation would lower the price of a final-good import and provide another channel for terms-of-trade gains to reach consumers.

Second, capital accumulation is neglected. A model such as the one presented by Mussa (1974), which emphasizes the role of sector-specific capital in the adjustment process, would further illuminate the impact of an exchange rate change on economic activity in Japan. (The Krugman contribution to this volume incorporates a model of this nature.) Such a specification would highlight the idea that the appreciation of the yen would reduce capital in the traded goods sector while either stimulating or retarding investment demand in the nontraded sector in the short run. The compression of profits in the export part of the tradable goods sector would also constitute a source of income deterioration that would reduce domestic demand for both tradable and nontraded goods.

A third element not addressed in the model is the role of consumer imports and pass-through of exchange rate changes into imported final goods prices. The pass-through, or lack thereof, would influence real income, demand, and employment growth.

Finally, there is no attempt to incorporate the effects of policy into this framework. If domestic demand stagnation and unemployment resulted from exchange rate appreciation, then domestic macroeconomic stimulus could alleviate some of the costs of transition. To explore the role of policy in the adjustment process, section 4.8 employs the Federal Reserve Board staff's MCM to evaluate the impact of fiscal policy on the trade adjustment process.

4.8 Asymmetries in the Impact of U.S. and Japanese Fiscal Policy on External Adjustment

The spillover effects described in the theoretical model above highlight the danger of a recession in Japan from the effects of the yen's appreciation. Japanese growth has already slowed dramatically, with real GNP increasing only 2% in 1986 on a fourth-quarter-over-fourth-quarter basis. As a result, domestic and international pressure has been mounting on Japan to relax fiscal policy. The Japanese government (the Ministry of Finance in particular) has been reluctant to abandon its policy of fiscal restraint adopted in 1979 to reverse the sharp rise in the debt-to-GNP ratio. The authorities have repeatedly expressed concern over the unfunded liabilities of the social security system in Japan in light of the rapid aging of the population. Nonetheless, temporary fiscal stimulus is currently being instituted through the so-called "Emergency Economic Measures" entailing about 6 trillion yen (about 1.8% of GNP) of supplementary government spending and tax measures for fiscal year 1987 (ending 31 March 1988).

There are at least three issues in the debate over the effectiveness of temporary fiscal stimulus in Japan: the ability of Japanese fiscal policy to offset the deflationary impact on the domestic economy of the yen's rise, the potential for Japanese fiscal policy to offset the recessionary impact on the world economy of the withdrawal of stimulus implied by the (even partial implementation of the) Gramm-Rudman-Hollings Act in the United States, and the ability of Japanese fiscal actions to foster a reduction in Japan's trade surplus. The first two issues are the least controversial, while the third issue is disputed. For example, U.S. authorities have strongly urged Japanese fiscal stimulus as an antidote to trade imbalances, while some Japanese authorities including Masaru Yoshitomi (1987), using the OECD (Organization for Economic Cooperation and Development) Interlink model, have argued that Japanese fiscal policy can have little impact on Japan's trade imbalance.

These issues are evaluated below in the context of the Federal Reserve Board staff's MCM. Table 4.12 reports the results of simulations on the MCM of the impact of a permanent standardized fiscal shock equal to 1% of GNP for the United States and Japan (about 3 trillion yen for Japan and $40 billion for the United States). The complete set of simulation results is analyzed in Craig and Loopesko (1986) (which also reports similar results for Germany). The baseline for the simulations is derived from a recent OECD forecast. Exchange rates are flexible and monetary policy is assumed to be nonaccomodative in the sense that the path for the targeted monetary aggregate is unchanged.

Table 4.12 Asymmetries in the Effects of U.S. and Japanese Fiscal Policy

	Japanese Fiscal Expansion		U.S. Fiscal Contraction	
Impact on:	After 1 Year	After 5 Years	After 1 Year	After 5 Years
U.S. current account[a]	2.0	0.9	13.7	41.9
Japanese current account[a]	−3.1	−5.9	−2.0	−10.7
U.S.-Japan bilateral imbalance[b]	0.2	0.1	1.7	2.9
U.S. real GNP	0.1	0.0	−1.9	−0.5
Japanese real GNP	1.3	1.1	−0.7	−1.3
Foreign real GNP[c]	0.4	0.3	−0.4	−0.5

Source: Craig and Loopesko (1986)

Note: The U.S. fiscal contraction equals 1% of U.S. real GNP and the Japanese fiscal expansion equals 1% of Japanese real GNP. Both shocks are permanent.

[a]Absolute deviations from baseline.

[b]A positive entry indicates an improvement for the United States.

[c]Defined as a weighted average of the four other MCM countries (the MCM includes the United States, Japan, Germany, the United Kingdom, and Canada).

A Japanese fiscal expansion causes the Japanese current account to worsen as expected, but by a relatively small amount ($5.9 billion after 5 years). The U.S. current account improves by a smaller amount ($0.9 billion after 5 years). The U.S.-Japan bilateral trade balance improves by yet a smaller amount, indicating that other foreign economies benefit more. Thus Japanese fiscal stimulus does little to foster a reduction in the U.S. current account or in the U.S.-Japan bilateral trade imbalance.

It has a more powerful impact, however, on domestic and foreign (defined as the four other industrialized economies included in the MCM) growth. Japanese real GNP rises by more than 1% over the forecast horizon, and although the impact on U.S. GNP is negligible, that on foreign GNP is just under 0.5%.

A U.S. fiscal contraction has a much more powerful impact on external imbalances, causing a $41.9 billion improvement in the U.S. current account after five years and a $10.7 billion narrowing in the Japanese current account surplus over the same time period. The U.S. fiscal contraction initially has a strong deflationary impact on the domestic economy (U.S. real GNP falls by almost 2%), but that effect declines over the forecast horizon. The associated decline in the U.S. demand for imports translates into a sharp decline in real activity in Japan and other foreign economies as well.

These simulations suggest that an asymmetry exists between the effects of U.S. and Japanese fiscal policy on external imbalances. A U.S. fiscal contraction makes an important contribution to the reduction of U.S. and Japanese current account imbalances, while a Japanese fiscal expansion fosters less external adjustment. Similarly, while Japanese fiscal policy has little impact on the U.S. current account, U.S. fiscal policy exerts a powerful influence on Japan's current account.

The effects of fiscal policy on income are the primary source of the differences between the two policy experiments. There are three facets of the income transmission channel of fiscal impulses which contribute to the asymmetry. First, in the MCM the income elasticity of Japanese demand for imports from the United States (0.8) is less than half that of U.S. demand for imports from Japan (1.8). Second, Japan's exports are substantially greater than its imports, while the opposite is true for the United States. For both of these reasons, the policy experiment that has the greatest impact on U.S. income (i.e., a U.S. fiscal contraction) has the greatest impact on the U.S. and Japanese current accounts. Finally, the dollar value of the impact of the two shocks on the current account is influenced by the absolute size of the two shocks: the standardized shocks are each 1% of the country's real GNP, but the mean level of U.S. GNP is approximately twice that of Japan's over the baseline forecast horizon. Taken together, these three influences on the magnitude of the income effects of fiscal policy account for most of the observed asymmetry.

Even though Japanese fiscal policy does not provide a strong impetus towards external balance in the MCM simulations, it still has substantial effects both on domestic growth and on growth abroad. Although the MCM explicitly models only five major industrialized economies (the United States, Japan, Germany, the United Kingdom, and Canada), growth in the developing world is generally thought to be quite sensitive to growth in the industrialized economies. Thus the positive impact of Japanese fiscal stimulus on these industrialized economies implies that a Japanese fiscal expansion could provide an important impetus to growth in the developing world. Moreover, the evidence in table 4.7 showing that the income elasticity of Japanese demand for imports from the developing countries is the largest of the bilateral elasticities reported suggests the potential for Japanese fiscal stimulus to help growth prospects in the developing world. Thus Japanese fiscal stimulus could be particularly valuable as an offset to the deflationary impact of a U.S. fiscal contraction on the developing countries.

4.9 Concluding Remarks

Calculations of the appropriate yen-dollar exchange rate based on the sustainability of the implied path of the noninterest current account indicate that the substantial appreciation of the yen that has occurred to date is warranted, and that even further appreciation may be required. Some of the difficulties associated with the perception of an unsustainable yen-dollar rate may have been evident recently in the U.S. Treasury bill market, when foreign private purchases declined (particularly Japanese private purchases) and foreign official purchases rose. The latter may prove to be temporary, however, and a reduction in foreign official purchases could cause higher bond yields and a lower dollar. The recent rise of interest rates in the United States in conjunction with the lowering of interest rates in Japan may help prevent this in the near term at least.

In Japan, a major restructuring of production away from export-oriented growth is currently under way in response to the yen's rise. This paper has examined several aspects of this adjustment process, focusing particularly on factors affecting Japan's record external surplus. Evidence is provided that, at least in real terms, the Japanese trade surplus has started to decline, both on a multilateral basis and on a bilateral basis vis-à-vis the United States.

We find that an econometric model of Japanese trade that tracks moderately well through 1984 veers substantially off track in forecasting both exports and imports over the 1985–86 period. In particular, actual adjustments in both export and import volumes are less than what is predicted by the model. Possible reasons for this slower-than-predicted adjustment in trade volumes were examined. Evidence that the pass-through of the effects of the yen's appreciation to export prices is slower than in the past provides one explanation. Also, we find econometric evidence supporting the notion that Japanese export prices in yen respond asymmetrically to yen appreciations and depreciations. This is consistent with the hypothesis that Japanese exporters have been squeezing their profit margins during the yen's recent appreciation in order to preserve market share. On the import side, the slow pass-through of the fall in import prices to consumer prices may be a factor.

A theoretical model of the adjustment process in Japan is used to examine the claim frequently made by policymakers both here and abroad that a very sharp rise in the yen can induce a recession in Japan that, in turn, can frustrate the process of trade adjustment. While this is shown to be a theoretical possibility, it is argued that this is unlikely for an economy with Japan's structure.

Finally, evidence from the Federal Reserve Board Staff's MCM suggests that a fiscal expansion in Japan will have little impact on the U.S. current account, but that it can have a greater impact on domestic demand in Japan and on growth and trade in the developing economies. This in itself may justify a Japanese fiscal expansion, particularly in light of the recessionary impact on the world economy of the U.S. fiscal contraction implied by the Gramm-Rudman-Hollings Act.

Appendix

A Test of Strategic Pricing by Japanese Exporters

The following equation was estimated over the period 1974:I–1986:I:

$$\log(PXY/PXY_{-1}) = a1 + a2 * \log(PXY_{-1}/PXY_{-2}) + a3 * \log(JWPI/JWPI_{-1}) + a4 * \log(PCOM/PCOM_{-1}) + a5 * \log(PXCOMP/PXCOMP_{-1}) + a6 * DUM * \log(RPXCOMP/RPXCOMP_{-1})$$

where PXY = yen Japanese export price index

JWPI = Japanese wholesale price index for manufactures

PCOM = yen commodity price index

PXCOMP = weighted-average competitors' export price index (expressed in yen)

RPXCOMP = PXY/PXCOMP

DUM = 1 when Japan's export prices rise relative to competitors' export prices and 0 otherwise.

The estimated coefficients are (t-ratios in parentheses):

$$\begin{aligned} a1 &= -0.01\ (-2.14) \\ a2 &= -0.16\ (-2.28) \\ a3 &= 0.82\ \ (4.42) \\ a4 &= 0.05\ \ (1.44) \\ a5 &= 0.45\ \ (5.95) \\ a6 &= -0.25\ (-2.51) \\ R_2 &= 0.76\ \ \mathrm{DW} = 1.89. \end{aligned}$$

Note: The hypothesis of strategic pricing—that Japanese exporters respond asymmetrically to increases and decreases in competitors' export prices expressed in yen (relative to Japanese export prices)—is a simple t-test of the null hypothesis that the coefficient $a6 = 0$. This is because it is equivalent to estimating an equation with two dummy variables multiplying the competitors' relative price variable: one isolating increases in Japanese export prices relative to competitors' prices and one isolating decreases. If the coefficients on the two dummy variables are $b1$ and $b2$, then it can be shown that the coefficient $a6$ in the equation above is equivalent to $(b1 - b2)$. Thus the null hypothesis $a6 = 0$ is equivalent to the hypothesis $b1 = b2$ (i.e., that increases and decreases in Japanese export prices relative to competitors' prices have the same impact on yen export prices). The null hypothesis is rejected at the 2% confidence level.

References

Bank of Japan. 1987. Adjustment of the Japanese economy under the strong yen. Research and Statistics Department, Special Paper no. 149. Tokyo.

Bergsten, C. Fred, and William R. Cline. 1987. The United States–Japan economic problem. *Policy Analyses in International Economics* no. 13. Washington, D.C.: Institute for International Economics. Revised from 1985

Bureau of Labor Statistics. 1986. International trends in productivity and unit labor costs in manufacturing. *Monthly Labor Review,* December. Washington, D.C.: Bureau of Labor Statistics.

Craig, Sean. 1986. Japanese bilateral trade elasticities. Memorandum, Division of International Finance, Federal Reserve Board. Washington, D.C.

Craig, Sean, and Bonnie Loopesko. 1986. Asymmetries in the effects of U.S., Japanese, and German fiscal policy. Memorandum, Division of International Finance, Federal Reserve Board. Washington, D.C.

Dornbusch, Rudiger. 1980. *Open economy macroeconomics,* pp. 82–116. New York: Basic Books.

———. 1985. Exchange rates and prices. Manuscript, Massachusetts Institute of Technology.

Drexler, Paul H. 1987. Japanese capital: The growing role of U.S. financial markets. *International Comment,* January 28. New York: Brown Brothers Harriman.

Fisher, Eric O'N. 1987. A model of exchange rate pass-through. International Finance Discussion Papers no. 302. Federal Reserve Board. Washington, D.C.

Frenkel, Jacob A. 1978. A monetary approach to the exchange rate: Doctrinal aspects and empirical evidence. In *The economics of exchange rates,* ed. Jacob A. Frenkel and Harry J. Johnson, pp. 1–25. Reading, Mass.: Addison-Wesley.

Frenkel, Jacob A., and Morris Goldstein. 1986. A guide to target zones. *International Monetary Fund Staff Papers* 33:633–73. Washington, D.C.

Goldstein, Morris, and Mohsin S. Khan. 1985. Income and price effects in foreign trade. In *Handbook of international economics,* Vol. 2, ed. R. W. Jones and P. B. Kenen, pp. 1041–1105. Amsterdam: Elsevier Science.

Helkie, William L., and Peter Hooper. 1987. The U.S. external deficit in the 1980s: An empirical analysis. International Finance Discussion Papers no. 304, Federal Reserve Board. Washington, D.C.

Johnson, Manuel H., and Bonnie E. Loopesko. 1987. The yen-dollar relationship: A recent historical perspective. In *Japan and the United States today: Exchange rates, macroeconomic policies, and financial market innovations,* ed. Hugh Patrick and Ryuichiro Tachi, pp. 95–116. New York: Columbia University Center on Japanese Economy and Business.

Jones, Randall. 1987. Yen appreciation taking effect. In *Japan Economic Survey,* April. Washington, D.C.: Japan Economic Institute.

Keizai Koho Center. 1986. Struggling with Endaka: Japanese business grapples with the high yen. *KKC Brief,* no. 37, November. Tokyo: Keidanren (Japan Federation of Economic Organizations).

Krause, Lawrence B. 1986. Does a yen valued at 100 per dollar make any sense? Manuscript. Washington, D.C.: Brookings Institution.

Krugman, Paul. 1985. Is the strong dollar sustainable? In *The U.S. dollar: Prospects and policy options,* Federal Reserve Bank of Kansas City.

———. 1986a. Pricing to market when the exchange rate changes. Manuscript, Massachusetts Institute of Technology.

———. 1986b. Is the Japan problem over? Manuscript. Conference on Trade Frictions, NYU Center for Japan-U.S. Business and Economic Studies, April.

———. 1987. Has the dollar fallen enough? Manuscript. Brookings Workshop on the U.S. Current Account Deficit. Washington, D.C.

McKinnon, Ronald I., and Kenichi Ohno. 1987. Getting the exchange rate right: Insular versus open economies. Manuscript, Conference on U.S.-Canadian Trade and Investment Relations with Japan, University of Michigan, April.

Mann, Catherine L. 1986. Prices, profit margins, and exchange rates. *Federal Reserve Bulletin* (June): 366–79. Washington, D.C.: Federal Reserve Board.

Marston, Richard C. 1986. Real exchange rates and productivity growth in the United States and Japan. Manuscript, American Enterprise Institute Conference on Real-Financial Linkages, January.

Morrison, David, and Jeremy Hale. 1987. *The search for equilibrium exchange rates.* New York: Goldman, Sachs.

Mussa, Michael. 1974. Tariffs and the distribution of income: The importance of factor specificity, substitutability, and intensity in the short and long run. *Journal of Political Economy,* vol. 82, no. 6, pp. 1191–1203.

Nurkse, Ragnar. 1945. *Conditions of International Monetary Equilibrium.* Essays in International Finance no. 4. Princeton: Princeton University Press.

Petri, Peter A. 1984. *Modeling Japanese-American trade: A study of asymmetric interdependence,* 52–71. Cambridge: Harvard University Press.
Organization for Economic Cooperation and Development 1987. Purchasing power parities and international comparisons of price levels and real per capita GDP in OECD countries. Paris, France: OECD.
Sargen, Nicholas, and Kermit L. Schoenholtz. 1987. Are Japanese investors diversifying? Salomon Brothers Bond Market Research, February. New York: Salomon Brothers.
Williamson, John. 1983. *The exchange rate system.* Policy Analyses in International Economics, No. 5. Washington, D.C.: Institute for International Economics.
Yoshitomi, Masaru. 1987. Growth gaps, exchange rates and asymmetry: Is it possible to unwind current account imbalances without fiscal expansion in Japan? In *Japan and the United States today: Exchange rates, macroeconomic policies, and financial market innovations,* edited by Hugh Patrick and Ryuichiro Tachi, 18–29. New York: Columbia University Center on Japanese Economy and Business.

Comment Richard C. Marston

Loopesko and Johnson have provided us with a wide-ranging investigation of Japan's adjustment to the yen's appreciation. The paper raises a host of interesting issues about this adjustment process, including, for example, the extent of currency pass-through, the price sensitivity of Japanese trade, and the effects of fiscal policies on income and the trade account. I will divide my comments along the lines of three questions about Japanese adjustment: (1) has the yen appreciated enough (or has the dollar fallen enough)? (2) have Japanese prices changed enough to reflect the appreciation of the yen? and (3) is the Japanese trade balance likely to respond to the appreciation of the yen?

To make sense of the first question, I would like to distinguish three possible approaches to measuring the yen's equilibrium value.

Purchasing Power Parity

Many recent estimates of the yen-dollar equilibrium exchange rate, several of which have been cited by Loopesko and Johnson, rely on a purchasing power parity (PPP) calculation. As is well known, PPP estimates which are based on general price series like the consumer price index can be seriously misleading as measures of international competitiveness, because they reflect the prices of nontraded goods and services as well as traded goods. In the case of comparisons be-

Richard C. Marston is the James R. F. Guy Professor of Finance and Economics in the Wharton School of the University of Pennsylvania and a research associate of the National Bureau of Economic Research.

between the yen and other currencies, the distortion introduced by using broad-based indexes is particularly large. That is because productivity growth is so much greater in the traded sector of Japan than in its nontraded sector (over 70% greater during the 1973–83 period), so prices in the traded sector fall relative to those in the nontraded sector (by almost 60% over this same 11-year period). In Marston (1986), I show that bilateral PPP calculations between the yen and dollar based on the consumer price index mistakenly indicate that the yen had appreciated in real terms between 1973 and 1983, rather than depreciated. In contrast, estimates based on prices in the traded sector show a depreciation of from 25 to 35%, depending on the price series used.

Real Exchange Rates in Traded Sectors

More reliable as a measure of competitiveness are estimates of the yen's equilibrium value based on prices in the traded sectors of Japan and its trading partners. One common approach is to measure changes in the real exchange rate based on traded goods prices relative to some base year. A real exchange rate series can provide a measure of changes in competitiveness relative to this base year, although as Williamson (1983) has emphasized, investigators must be careful to adjust such series for real changes in the economy, such as the oil price shocks, which alter the competitiveness of a country's traded sector. In the study cited above, I used real exchange rate series based on traded goods prices adjusted for changes in the prices of imported inputs to measure how much the yen had depreciated relative to the dollar over the period from 1973 to 1983. Loopesko and Johnson cite Krugman's recent estimate of ¥140/$ for the equilibrium value for the yen-dollar rate based on a similar type of calculation.

Current Account Estimates

Measures of an equilibrium exchange rate based on trade competitiveness alone may be misleading if interest payments or other elements of the service account change dramatically. In the case of the U.S. service account, the accumulation of debt which will occur before the current account deficit is reversed is likely to lead to sizable interest payments which must either be financed or paid for by trade surpluses. How the United States services this debt will make considerable difference to the bilateral exchange rate between the yen and the dollar (as well as other key bilateral rates). At one extreme, the United States might be able to continue running current account deficits indefinitely as long as it stabilizes its debt-GNP ratio. This is the suggestion made by Paul Krugman in his paper for this volume. Whether this is feasible depends on whether foreign investors are willing to continue to maintain

U.S. dollar holdings at present levels (in relation to GNP), which are much higher than in the early 1980s. (In fact, investors would have to hold even higher levels than at present, since it will take several years to stabilize the debt-GNP ratio even under the most optimistic scenarios.) Loopesko and Johnson present evidence in table 4.4 which suggests that the Japanese private sector has already cut back drastically on its purchases of U.S. securities.

At the other extreme, it could be argued that the United States must stop generating new debt by achieving equilibrium in its current account.[1] The U.S. trade surplus would then have to be large enough to pay interest on its newly acquired debt. For the trade surplus to be that large, the dollar would have to fall substantially further than to date. Loopesko and Johnson cite Lawrence Krause's estimate of an exchange rate for the yen of ¥100/$, a number which two years ago would have been regarded by many economists as implausible.

The preceding discussion presumed that the adjustment process can proceed without a hitch. As long as the correct exchange rate is achieved, the trade account will adjust accordingly. But in the case of the yen, additional questions about the adjustment process have been raised. Loopesko and Johnson ask whether the appreciation of the yen has been "passed through" to final goods prices. Table 4.11 indicates that pass-throughs have varied widely, from 9.5% in chemicals to over 60% in machinery and transport equipment.

I would have liked to see the paper sketch out a theoretical model of pass-through in order to suggest what patterns are to be expected in different industries. For example, how does pass-through vary depending on the nature of competition in the industry? To what extent is actual price discrimination involved? Is a low degree of pass-through a temporary phenomenon, and will greater pass-through be observed once firms become convinced that the yen's appreciation is more than a temporary shock?

The paper presents very intriguing evidence indicating that pass-through behavior in Japan may be asymmetric. In the Appendix, Loopesko and Johnson report estimates of a pricing equation with significantly different pass-through coefficients for periods of yen appreciation than for periods of yen depreciation. They interpret these differences as reflecting strategic pricing behavior by Japanese export firms. According to the estimates, Japanese firms lower the prices of exports (in yen terms) when the yen appreciates more readily than they raise prices of exports when the yen depreciates. By lowering yen prices

1. Actually, there is an even more extreme case where the United States must pay back its debt, returning dollar holdings to their 1980 levels. This would require an even lower yen-dollar rate.

when the yen is appreciating, Japanese firms attempt to maintain shares in foreign markets. The equation that is estimated is based on aggregate price data. I would have liked to see the same equation estimated with disaggregated data to see if pass-through behavior varies systematically across industries depending on the degree of competition in each industry.

The final piece of the puzzle about Japanese adjustment concerns the trade balance itself. Why hasn't the bilateral balance between the United States and Japan, or the Japanese trade balance as a whole, responded more sharply to the yen's appreciation? Loopesko and Johnson paint a somewhat grim picture of the prospects for trade adjustment. They point out that with such a large trade imbalance, Japanese imports must increase much more than exports to reduce the surplus significantly. The price responsiveness of Japanese imports, moreover, is unlikely to be very high, since imports are so heavily weighted towards price-inelastic commodities.

The variety of evidence which they present concerning price elasticities is somewhat confusing. For bilateral trade between the United States and Japan, they show in table 4.6 that Bergsten and Cline (1987) have reported much higher price elasticities than Craig (1986). For multilateral trade, they show that Goldstein and Khan (1985) have reported price elasticities greater than one for Japan as well as the United States, whereas table 4.9 (based on work at the Federal Reserve) reports elasticities for Japanese imports much lower than one. Yet the estimates based on disaggregated data reported in table 4.9 do follow a discernible pattern. The price elasticity of Japanese imports of manufactured goods is almost one, while those of fuel and raw materials are much lower. Given the low percentage of manufactured goods in Japanese imports, these elasticities suggest only limited scope for improving the trade imbalance through the expansion of Japanese imports.

My own view is that trade adjustment will occur mostly on the export side and not primarily through a reduction of exports to the United States (unless there is a recession here). Instead, the main benefits of the yen's appreciation and the dollar's depreciation will be found in third markets, where until recently U.S. firms were effectively priced out of the market by the dollar's misalignment. With the sizable changes in relative prices which have already occurred, U.S. firms should begin to make inroads in third markets and Japanese firms will have to surrender some market share to firms from the United States as well as from the newly industrializing countries of Asia.

In figures 4.7–9, the authors present some interesting simulations of the Board's disaggregated trade equations over the recent period. Not only do actual exports exceed predicted exports, but actual imports also fall short of predicted imports. This suggests that recent trade adjustment has been less extensive than even historical experience would suggest. The limited pass-through of the yen's appreciation to export and import prices may explain part of this pattern, but the failure of the Japanese and U.S. trade accounts to adjust more rapidly remains in part a mystery.

Although various questions remain unresolved, Loopesko and Johnson succeed admirably in clarifying many of the issues involving Japanese trade adjustment. I have not discussed other interesting sections of the paper, which are recommended to the reader. These include an analysis of trade adjustment in a model with only imported inputs to demonstrate the role of such imports in the adjustment process and simulations of the Federal Reserve Board's MCM model to investigate the effects of fiscal policy changes in Japan and the United States.

References

Bergsten, C. Fred, and William R. Cline. 1987 (revised from 1985). The United States-Japan economic problem. *Policy Analyses in International Economics,* no. 13. Washington, D.C.: Institute for International Economics.

Craig, Sean. 1986. Japanese bilateral trade elasticities. Memorandum, Division of International Finance, Federal Reserve Board. Washington, D.C.

Goldstein, Morris, and Mohsin S. Khan. 1985. Income and price effects in foreign trade. In *Handbook of international economics,* 2, edited by R. W. Jones and P. B. Kenen, 1041–1105. Amsterdam: Elsevier Science Publishers B.V.

Marston, Richard C. 1986. Real exchange rates and productivity growth in the United States and Japan. Manuscript, American Enterprise Institute Conference on Real-Financial Linkages, January.

Williamson, John. 1983. *The exchange rate system.* Policy Analyses in International Economics, no. 5. Washington, D.C.: Institute for International Economics.

5 Roundtable on Exchange Rate Policy

Stanley W. Black, Dale W. Henderson, and John Williamson

Remarks Stanley W. Black

Since 1973, players in international financial markets have been operating with floating exchange rates among major currencies, such as the U.S. dollar, the West German mark, and the Japanese yen. Initially, most experts in international finance were very supportive of these arrangements. Our views were based on one of several types of asset market theories of exchange rate determination with rational expectations, usually either a monetary theory or a portfolio theory. These theories seemed to explain reasonably well the functioning of the markets as we observed them.

Time passed, and exchange rates fluctuated, indeed rather more than expected. So did inflation and unemployment and the growth of world trade. Many of us have become much more skeptical of our initial predictions, which were based on partial equilibrium models that assumed domestic prices, outputs, and/or monetary policies were given. Subsequent analysis of the relationship between exchange rate behavior and monetary and fiscal policies in industrial countries has identified several major problems with floating exchange rates (see Crockett and Goldstein 1987; Obstfeld 1985; and Black 1977).

First, the increased short-run exchange rate risk associated with floating may have affected international flows of trade and investment. Second, wide medium-run exchange rate fluctuations may represent misalignment of exchange rates induced by some combination of inefficient or risk-averse market participants and/or divergent monetary

Stanley W. Black is Georges Lurcy Professor of Economics and chairman of the department of economics at the University of North Carolina, Chapel Hill.

and fiscal policies in major industrial countries. Third, large swings in global credit creation have caused serious problems for both borrowing and lending countries. Fourth, the market-oriented system of floating exchange rates appears to have caused serious management problems for a number of countries with relatively weak fiscal and monetary institutions. Fifth, major industrial countries may have overcontracted in response to common inflationary shocks in the mid and late seventies.

Exchange Risk

Let us now examine these problems as they are reflected in the events of the last few years. To begin with, the evidence clearly shows that short-run exchange rate risk in both nominal and real terms has increased sharply by comparison with the period of pegged rates of the sixties (see International Monetary Fund [IMF] 1984). The effects of this increased variability on trade and investment have, however, been disputed. The IMF's study found no appreciable effects on trade flows. More recently, Cushman (1986) has found significant negative effects of risk on bilateral trade flows among industrial countries, while Kenen and Rodrik (1986) have found significant negative effects on aggregate trade flows. The magnitude of these effects is of the order of 5% of U.S. exports. Striking confirmation of these results based on a time series approach comes from De Grauwe and Verfaille's paper for this conference using a cross-section approach.

Misalignment

The second major problem raised above is misalignment. If we focus on the U.S. dollar, the Federal Reserve Board's index of the dollar vis-à-vis the currencies of ten industrial countries rose 80% between 1980 and February of 1985—75% in real terms after allowing for relative domestic and foreign inflation. Since February 1985, the dollar has fallen about 40% relative to the currencies of the ten industrial countries in nominal terms, and about 30% in real terms.

Whether these movements reflect misalignment or not depends on their causes, which are not always easy to agree on. Nevertheless, a representative list of the causes of the rise of the dollar would include the sharp relative decline in inflation in the United States after 1981 and our high real interest rates compared to other countries. The relative increase in U.S. real interest rates is attributable to the difference between the U.S. mix of tight monetary policy and loose fiscal policy and the tighter fiscal policies in other industrial countries discussed in Bill Branson's paper for this conference. Additional causes that have been suggested include capital inflows induced by tax cuts, efforts to invest inside a protectionist quota wall, and capital flight from disturbed regions elsewhere. Finally, a speculative bubble at the peak in February 1985 has been suggested.

Relatively permanent factors affecting the dollar exchange rate, such as lower inflation, lower tax rates, and a safer business environment, could not be described as causing the exchange rate to deviate from a sustainable long-run equilibrium level. On the other hand, an unsustainable fiscal policy or a speculative bubble would lead to misalignment, in the sense that the exchange rate deviates from its sustainable equilibrium level.

The decline in the dollar since early 1985 has coincided with a decline in real interest rates and an expectation of increased fiscal restraint in the United States after the passage of the Gramm-Rudman-Hollings bill discussed by Branson. This movement, based as it seems clearly to have been on the evident unsustainability of the previous path of U.S. fiscal policy, reinforces the designation of the high dollar as a misalignment. A related factor was the shift in Administration policy on exchange market intervention embodied in the Plaza Agreement of September 1985. In this case it was the political unsustainability of the current account deficit that led to the shift in exchange rate policy in response to protectionist pressures in Congress.

The effects of the large misalignment of the dollar in the eighties have been penetrating and pervasive. The $150 billion trade deficit, amounting to 4% of GNP, has devastated major sectors of the economy, including agriculture, textiles, machinery, and electronics. The protectionist trade legislation even now passing the Congress is directly attributable to the misalignment. I understand from my Congressman, who voted for it, that the bill is mainly for political posturing, and that the Gephardt Amendment against bilateral trade imbalances only passed because Congressman Gephardt is running for President.

The Global Credit Cycle

During the seventies and eighties there have been two complete cycles of credit expansion and contraction. The first expansion coincided with the breakdown of the Bretton Woods system of pegged exchange rates from 1970 to 1973 and was fueled by the purchase of dollars by foreign central banks to prevent their currencies from rising. It also coincided with a period of relatively low real interest rates in the United States and elsewhere. It concluded with a sharp rise in oil prices and the global recession of 1974–76. The second major expansion during the period 1977–80 featured monetary and fiscal stimulus from the United States and again low real interest rates. It concluded with the second rise in oil prices, a sharp tightening of monetary policy, and the recession of 1980–84. These cycles in real interest rates and credit expansion have been a major factor in creating the environment for the debt crisis of the eighties.

Global Policy Conflict

The final problem raised above was that of overrestrictive national policy responses to global inflationary shocks. Following the analysis of Hamada, Canzoneri and Gray (1985) developed the argument that two countries responding to a common inflationary shock in a noncooperative fashion with a floating exchange rate may overcontract. Acting separately, each country seeks to export inflation to the other via restrictive monetary policy that would, in isolation, appreciate its exchange rate. The negative external effect on the other country results in an overrestrictive response, as the two countries compete with each other in deflation. This analysis appears relevant to the recessions of 1974–76 and 1980–82.

Reforming the System

The discussion above suggests that the most important failing of the current system of floating rates is the wide divergence it has allowed in monetary and fiscal policies, both between governments and over time. The issue of more discipline over macroeconomic policies has been widely discussed (Crockett and Goldstein 1987; Obstfeld 1985), although agreement on the need for it and the most likely way to get it is lacking. In my opinion, the need for greater discipline rests strongly on the arguments made above. If less divergence of monetary and fiscal policies could be obtained, there should be fewer and smaller misalignments, smaller global credit cycles (if the United States is more constrained in its cyclical fluctuations), less-widespread debt problems, and fewer policy conflicts. These gains should also reduce short-term exchange rate risk.

It can be argued that the "target zone" approach (Williamson 1983) offers the most appropriate way forward. The basic argument in favor of an exchange rate target is that it is an indirect method of requiring coordination of monetary and fiscal policies. The target zone is a form of managed floating that requires aiming at, but not necessarily enforcing, moveable exchange rate targets, with a wide band around them. Monetary and fiscal policies would have to be more or less consistent with such external targets, as well as with internal targets.

The indirect form of policy coordination, which also underlay the Bretton Woods system, is surely imperfect and would not solve all problems. However, we have to recognize that direct policy coordination also has perhaps even more serious drawbacks. Different governments often do not agree on objectives. In many cases it appears that they do not agree even on the models which should be used for analysis of macroeconomic problems. One reason that might be so is that the true models differ for countries with different economic structure and institutions. Under these circumstances, it is not surprising that international discussions of policy coordination now are focused on so-called "objective indicators" (Crockett and Goldstein 1987). This amounts to discussion of the outcomes for various targets and instruments in each country, which falls considerably short of true policy coordination. As a friend once remarked, "The secret of success is to aim low."

The target zone approach, while designed to avoid some of the problems of the Bretton Woods system such as reluctant adjustment of parities, asymmetric adjustment responsibilities, and destabilizing capital flows, would clearly retain some others. For example, nothing would prevent global inflation, if several major countries agreed to joint expansion, as happened in the last years of the Bretton Woods system. An international monetary growth rule of the McKinnon type could contain this problem. However, both monetary growth rules and exchange rate targets create problems when there are shifts in the demand for money, the equilibrium terms of trade, or other factors influencing long-run equilibrium. Thus both proposals require a flexible interpretation.

How Can Economic Policy Affect Exchange Rates?

The desirability of an exchange rate policy is of little relevance in the absence of evidence concerning its feasibility. The available tools are monetary policy, fiscal policy, capital controls, and sterilized exchange market intervention. There is little doubt that monetary policy, by affecting current and expected future inflation, interest rates, and output, can affect both the nominal and the (short-run) real exchange rate. As Bill Branson's paper shows, fiscal policy can also have powerful effects on real and nominal exchange rates, although in most industrial countries it is likely to be focused mainly on internal targets. Capital controls act as a tax on the ownership of domestic or foreign assets, and the threat of their future imposition affects the political risk premium on foreign assets.

Sterilized exchange market intervention is the only policy that is explicitly oriented to the exchange market. Therefore it is a bit surprising that it is so controversial. Perhaps that is because under the Bretton Woods system and occasionally under floating rates it has not infrequently been used to avoid following a monetary policy that is consistent with an exchange rate target. Such misuse should not blind one to the potential, if limited, usefulness of intervention that is in support of a consistent monetary policy (Kenen 1987).

Let me provide a specific model to illustrate the effectiveness of sterilized intervention in support of an equilibrium exchange rate. This model is adapted from Black (1985), but the diagrammatic analysis is new. Define the (logarithm of the) real exchange rate as $q = e + p^* - p$, where p and p^* are the given domestic and foreign price levels and e is the nominal exchange rate. The given real interest rates at home and abroad are r and r^*. I assume the accumulation of private foreign assets Δf occurs through the current account and sterilized intervention to support a target rate $\bar{e} = p - p^*$, which is equivalent to $\bar{q} = 0$. $\Delta f = \mu q + \theta(e - \bar{e}) + u = (\mu + \theta)q + u$. Here μ is the semielasticity of the current account with respect to the real exchange rate, θ is the intervention parameter, and u is a random disturbance. Secondly, the exchange risk premium is proportional to the stock of foreign assets with proportionality factor $\rho = \phi\sigma^2$, where ϕ is the coefficient of risk aversion and σ^2 is the conditional variance of the one-period-ahead exchange rate. $E\Delta q + r^* - r = \rho f$. In this simple model, the equilibrium real exchange rate is $\bar{q} = 0$ and the equilibrium stock of foreign assets is $\bar{f} = (r^* - r)/\rho$. The phase diagram has a saddle path with slope equal to

$$-\frac{1}{.5(\mu + \theta)\,(1 + \sqrt{4/\rho(\mu + \theta)})}.$$

An increase in the intervention parameter θ from zero will reduce the slope of the saddle path from SS to $S'S'$ in the diagram. If the stock of foreign assets varies from A to B, the exchange rate will fluctuate

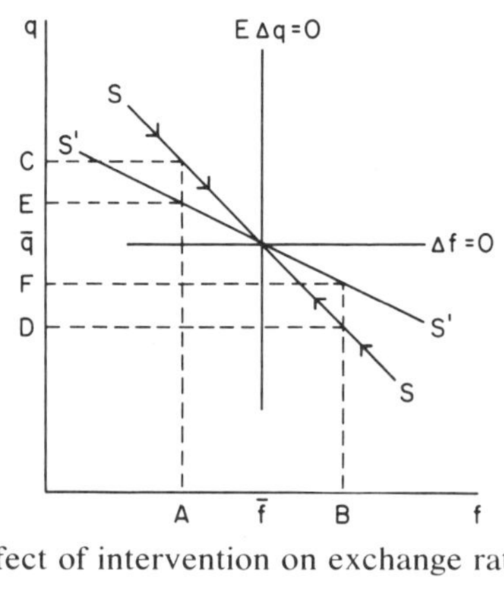

Fig. 5.1 Effect of intervention on exchange rate.

between C and D without intervention and between E and F with intervention. The reduction in σ^2 lowers the risk premium ρ and leads to a further flattening of the saddle path.

In an effort to test for the empirical significance of this effect, Michael Salemi and I (Black and Salemi 1986) have estimated such a model for the dollar value of the deutsche mark over the pegged and floating rate periods. We find evidence for such an effect, if it is assumed that the monetary processes driving relative interest rates and price levels shifted between the two periods.

Needless to say, the effectiveness of the intervention policy discussed above is absolutely dependent upon the choice of a consistent target rate $\bar{e} = p - p^*$.

Conclusion

A system with more international restraints over national policies is likely to perform better than current arrangements. But we are not likely to have such a reform in the absence of a major shock to the system. Therefore we should promote the evolution of the IMF's methods of surveillance in the direction of a target zone system.

References

Black, Stanley W. 1977. *Floating exchange rates and national economic policy.* New Haven: Yale University Press.

______. 1985. The effect of alternative intervention policies on the variability of exchange rates: The Harrod effect. In *Exchange rate management under uncertainty,* ed. J. S. Bhandari. Cambridge: MIT Press.

Black, Stanley W., and Michael K. Salemi. 1986. Risk aversion, risk premia, and the market for foreign assets. Processed. Chapel Hill, N.C.: Department of Economics, University of North Carolina.

Canzoneri, Matthew B., and Joanna A. Gray. 1985. Monetary policy games and the consequences of non-cooperative behavior. *International Economic Review* 26:547–64.

Crockett, Andrew, and Morris Goldstein. 1987. Strengthening the international monetary system: Exchange rates, surveillance, and objective indicators. Occasional Paper no. 50. Washington, D.C.: International Monetary Fund.

Cushman, David O. 1986. Has exchange risk depressed international trade? The impact of third-country exchange risk. *Journal of International Money and Finance* 5:361–79.

International Monetary Fund. 1984. Exchange rate volatility and world trade. Occasional Paper no. 28. Washington, D.C.: International Monetary Fund.

Kenen, Peter B. 1987. Exchange rate management: What role for intervention? *American Economic Review Papers and Proceedings* 77:194–99.

Kenen, Peter B., and Dani Rodrik. 1986. Measuring and analyzing the effects of short-term volatility in real exchange rates. *Review of Economics and Statistics* 58:311–15.

Obstfeld, Maurice. 1985. Floating exchange rates: Experience and prospects. *Brookings Papers on Economic Activity* pp. 369–464.
Williamson, John. 1983. *The exchange rate system*. Washington, D.C.: Institute for International Economics.

Remarks Dale W. Henderson

Overview

During the 1970s the Poole (1970) analysis of stabilization policy was extended to include exchange rate policy. In this type of analysis, stabilization problems are caused by exogenous shocks. The policymaker's objective is stabilizing employment, which in the absence of productivity shocks is the same thing as stabilizing output. The usual approach is to assume that stabilization policy must be carried out with the instruments of financial policy; the instruments of fiscal policy are presumed to be too inflexible. There are two main conclusions. First, for some shocks the interest rate and exchange rate should be allowed to vary, and for others they should be fixed. Second, interest rate and exchange rate movements can be used to make inferences about the sources of shocks.

In the first half of the 1980s, the world economy was subjected to a major shock originated by policymakers—fiscal expansion in the United States accompanied by fiscal contraction in other major industrial countries. Taking this shock as given, it seems clear that allowing interest rates and exchange rates to vary was a better policy than trying to keep them fixed. However, it might be argued that if the major industrial countries had been committed to exchange rate targets, the shock would never have occurred.

Recently, the relationship between the exchange rate regime and the control of inflation has been explored using game-theoretic approaches. On the one hand, Canzoneri and Gray (1985) have shown that when policymakers are combating a symmetric inflationary shock, a kind of fixed-exchange-rate regime can lead to better outcomes than Nash noncooperative policymaking. On the other hand, Rogoff (1985) has demonstrated that when policymakers face the inflation bias problem of

Dale Henderson is professor of economics at Georgetown University, research associate of the National Bureau of Economic Research, and consultant at the Board of Governors of the Federal Reserve System.

Kydland and Prescott (1977) and Barro and Gordon (1983), a fixed-exchange-rate regime can lead to higher world inflation.

Financial Policy in the Open Economy

Analysts of financial policy in the open economy have made two different assumptions about the degree of substitutability between home (currency) bonds and foreign (currency) bonds. Some authors assume that home and foreign bonds are imperfect substitutes. In this case there are two instruments of financial policy: monetary operations, defined as trades of home money for home bonds, and intervention operations, defined as trades of home bonds for foreign bonds. Intervention operations affect the exchange rate and can be used to stabilize it in the face of shocks. Other authors assume that home and foreign bonds are perfect substitutes. In this case there is only one instrument of financial policy—monetary operations. Monetary policy and exchange rate policy are one and the same. Here, as in Henderson (1984), I focus on the more general imperfect substitutes case.

1. Financial Policy When the Source of the Shock is Known

If the policymaker knows the source of the shock, the correct financial policy response is usually clear. I consider four possible shocks: a shift in demand toward home goods away from foreign goods, a shift in demand toward home money away from home bonds, a shift in demand away from home bonds toward foreign bonds, and an increase in expected inflation. For each shock I consider an aggregates-constant policy, defined as undertaking no monetary operations or intervention operations, and a rates-constant policy, defined as using monetary operations and intervention operations to keep the interest rate and the exchange rate fixed.

A shift in demand toward home goods away from foreign goods increases home output. Suppose the financial policymaker pursues an aggregates-constant policy. The increase in home output raises money demand, pushing up the interest rate and causing the home currency to appreciate. The movements in both the interest rate and the exchange rate tend to reduce the demand for home goods, dampening the increase in output. If instead the policymaker pursued a rates-constant policy, output would expand by the full amount of the initial increase in demand. For shifts in demand between goods, an aggregates-constant policy is better.

Now consider a shift in asset demands toward home money away from home bonds. If the policymaker responds with an aggregates-constant policy, the interest rate must rise and the home currency must appreciate. These movements in rates tend to reduce home output. The policymaker is better off keeping rates constant by using monetary operations to offset the shift in asset demands. By acting in this way, he completely insulates output from the financial shock.

Another kind of financial shock is a shift in asset demands away from home bonds toward foreign bonds. With aggregates constant, the home currency must depreciate. Actual depreciation raises demand for home bonds by reducing expected depreciation and raising the home currency value of world wealth. Output rises, stimulating money demand and pushing up the interest rate. A better policy is to keep the exchange rate constant by using intervention operations to offset the shift in asset demands. This policy forestalls any change in output and the interest rate. Thus, for both kinds of financial shocks a rates-constant policy is better.

The final shock is an increase in expected inflation. Suppose that there are simultaneous and equal increases in the expected future price level and the expected future exchange rate. At the initial nominal interest rate, price level, and exchange rate, there is an increase in aggregate demand because of the drop in the real interest rate, and there is a decrease in the demand for home bonds since foreign bonds are now relatively more attractive. With aggregates constant, output rises and the home currency depreciates. The rise in output pushes up the nominal interest rate. With rates constant, output rises. The increase in output may be greater or less with aggregates constant. The depreciation of the home currency tends to make it greater, but the increase in the nominal interest rate tends to make it less.

2. Financial Variables as Information Variables

The source of a shock to the economy is often not known. Data on financial variables become available before data on output. Financial data contain information about the disturbances that are affecting the economy. It has been recognized that more information can be obtained if movements in a number of financial variables are analyzed simultaneously.

The policymaker extracts information from financial variables and then acts on it. I will outline the procedure using an example. First, the policymaker selects a desired value for his ultimate target variable, say output; the actual value of output is not observable in the current period. The policymaker then chooses some financial variables, say financial aggregates, as policy instruments. He regards another group of financial variables, say the interest rate and the exchange rate, as information variables. He selects values for the financial aggregates that are consistent with desired output if there are no disturbances and makes forecasts of the interest rate and the exchange rate. Unanticipated movements in the interest rate and the exchange rate are used to make inferences about the disturbances that are affecting the economy and therefore about thc value of output that is likely to emerge if the financial aggregates remain unchanged. On the basis of these inferences, the values of the financial aggregates are changed to increase the likelihood that the desired value of output will be attained.

All four of the disturbances considered above cause increases in the nominal interest rate. However, the first two disturbances (the shift toward home goods away from foreign goods and the shift toward home money away from home bonds) lead to appreciation of the home currency, while the second two disturbances (the shift away from home bonds toward foreign bonds and the increase in expected inflation) lead to depreciation of the home currency. Thus, the information contained in exchange rate movements makes it possible to distinguish between the two pairs of disturbances. Unfortunately, the policymaker cannot distinguish between the two disturbances in each pair on the basis of interest rate and exchange rate movements. Other information must be brought to bear before the policymaker can decide how to change the financial aggregates.

Exchange rate movements have been used to distinguish between possible explanations for interest rate movements. For about two years after October 1979, the Federal Reserve was targeting M1 quite closely. During this period, if announced M1 was higher than a widely distributed private forecast, the Federal Funds rate rose. Some argued that the interest rate rose because market participants were anticipating a reduction in nonborrowed reserves designed to get M1 back on track. Others argued that the interest rate rose because market participants believed that the Federal Reserve had given up on its M1 target and therefore expected an increase in nonborrowed reserves and higher inflation. The fact that the dollar appreciated when the interest rate rose convinced most observers that the first group was right.

Exchange Rate Targets as a Constraint on Economic Policy

In the first half of the 1980s, the world economy was hit by a large shock originated by policymakers. There was a fiscal expansion in the United States accompanied by a fiscal contraction in other major industrialized countries. The nature of the shock was clear. World demand was shifted toward U.S. goods away from foreign goods. Furthermore, those in control of fiscal policy both in the United States and abroad chose not to reverse the changes in fiscal policy.

According to the analysis above, the appropriate financial policy response to a shift in demand between goods is an aggregates-constant policy. Interest rates rise in the expanding country and fall in the contracting country, and the currency of the expanding country appreciates. These movements in financial variables cause changes in aggregate demands that reduce the output and inflation effects of the demand shift.

U.S. financial policy conformed fairly closely to the aggregates-constant prescription. Financial policy in the other major industrial countries is more difficult to interpret. It is clear that most of these countries took actions to insure that their nominal interest rates would rise somewhat in order to prevent even more dollar appreciation.

It seems clear that an attempt to fix the exchange rate would have been a disaster. According to the best available evidence, intervention operations have little or no effect on exchange rates. Therefore, monetary operations would have to have been used to fix the exchange rate. The required U.S. monetary expansion would have made it possible for the increase in demand to be translated into increases in both output and the price level. Much of what had been gained on the inflation front would have been lost.

Most economists agree that given the shift in fiscal policies, allowing the exchange rate to vary was the right thing to do. However, it might be argued that if the United States and other major industrial countries had been parties to an agreement to keep exchange rates near target levels, say the average levels for the 1973–79 period, the shift in fiscal policies would never have occurred. Those in control of fiscal policy would have recognized that, given the likely response of financial policy, in particular U.S. financial policy, their plans would lead to exchange rates far from the target levels, and they would not have executed them.

This argument is not very convincing. The Reagan administration seemed determined to try to force a drastic cut in nondefense government spending by cutting taxes, increasing defense spending, and then insisting that the resulting government deficit must be eliminated. Those in control of fiscal policy in the other major industrial countries appeared to be convinced that they must try to reduce their government deficits at almost any cost. Most would agree that exchange rate targets would place some constraints on sovereign policymakers. However, it seems unlikely that an administration would let an exchange rate target keep it from pursuing one of its major objectives.

Exchange Rate Regimes and Inflation Control

Suppose that a world economy with two symmetric countries is hit by a negative productivity shock that raises inflation everywhere. Nash noncooperative behavior leads to too much monetary contraction in this case. Both policymakers have an incentive to contract, accepting some unemployment in order to reduce inflation. Each policymaker thinks that by contracting he can reduce inflation not only by reducing the price of his own output but also by causing his country's currency to appreciate. However, when both policymakers contract, neither gains through exchange rate appreciation. The exchange rate ends up remaining fixed, but both money supplies are too low in the sense that both policymakers would be better off if both money supplies were higher.

Canzoneri and Gray (1985) show that what they call fixed-exchange-rate leadership can lead to a better outcome than Nash noncooperative behavior in this case. The fixed-exchange-rate follower commits himself to vary his money supply to keep the exchange rate fixed. The fixed-exchange-rate leader minimizes his loss subject to this constraint and commits himself to deliver the resulting money supply. In this regime the leader knows that contraction will not lead to an appreciation of his country's currency. Therefore he contracts less, the follower contracts less, and they are both better off.

Unfortunately, the fixed-exchange-rate leadership equilibrium lacks credibility. It is not clear who the third party is who enforces the commitments. If the commitments are not enforced, each policymaker has an incentive to break his commitment. If one policymaker thinks the other will deliver the fixed-exchange-rate money supply, he has an incentive to contract in order to reap the gains from exchange rate appreciation.

Now suppose that the policymakers face the inflation bias problem of Kydland and Prescott (1977) and Barro and Gordon (1983). That is, suppose that the policymakers have target levels of employment that are higher than the natural levels of employment for some reason and that they dislike inflation. In this situation, wage setters know that if wage inflation is zero, each policymaker has an incentive to create positive price inflation in order to increase employment above its natural level. Thus, in order to keep employment at its natural level, they choose a rate of wage inflation high enough that the policymaker has no incentive to create a higher rate of price inflation. The losses generated directly by higher price inflation would just offset the gains from stimulating employment.

Rogoff (1985) explains why Nash noncooperative behavior may lead to lower inflation in these circumstances. A Nash policymaker thinks that if he expands his money supply, inflation will go up, not only because the price of home output will rise but also because his country's currency will depreciate. In contrast, a fixed-exchange-rate leader thinks that if he expands his money supply, inflation will go up only because the price of home output will rise. Therefore the fixed-exchange-rate leader will choose to expand more. Wage setters know the incentives of the policymakers in the two regimes and will choose a higher rate of wage inflation in the fixed-exchange-rate leadership regime.

The point is that a fixed-exchange-rate regime may or may not be helpful to policymakers who are trying to control inflation. The answer depends on what is causing the inflation.

References

Barro, Robert J., and David B. Gordon. 1983. Rules, discretion, and reputation in a model of monetary policy. *Journal of Monetary Economics* 12:101–21.

Canzoneri, Matthew B., and Jo Anna Gray. 1985. Monetary policy games and the consequences of noncooperative behavior. *International Economic Review* 26:547–64.

Henderson, Dale W. 1984. Exchange market intervention operations: Their role in financial policy and their effects. In John F. O. Bilson and Richard C. Marston, eds., *Exchange rate theory and practice*. Chicago: University of Chicago Press.

Kydland, Finn E., and Edward C. Prescott. 1977. Rules rather than discretion: The inconsistency of optimal plans. *Journal of Political Economy* 85:473–92.

Poole, William. 1970. Optimal choice of monetary policy instruments in a simple stochastic macro model. *Quarterly Journal of Economics* 84:197–216.

Rogoff, Kenneth S. 1985. Can international monetary policy cooperation be counterproductive? *Journal of International Economics* 18:199–217.

Remarks John Williamson

The purpose of this conference is to assess the effects of exchange rate misalignments. I hope it will succeed in this aim, since I have long been convinced that misalignments are indeed costly, even though the case has not been well documented.

At least the U.S. Congress seems to believe this to be true. The Competitive Exchange Rate Act of 1987, which was incorporated into the trade bill (HR 3) approved by the House of Representatives in April 1987, includes the following (Section 402):

> The Congress hereby finds that—
>
> . . . .
>
> (3) an important factor contributing to our current trade crisis has been the United States dollar, the rise in which over earlier years contributed substantially to our current trade deficit;
>
> . . . .

John Williamson is a senior fellow at the Institute for International Economics in Washington, D.C.

> (5) a sudden and severe drop in the dollar would reignite inflation and increase interest rates;
> (6) fundamental misalignments and erratic fluctuations in exchange rates frustrate business and government planning;
> (7) a relatively stable exchange rate for the dollar at competitive levels is desirable and should be encouraged.

If misalignments are indeed costly, it is natural to infer that policy should in future seek to limit them, rather than treating the exchange rate as the residual in the process of policy determination, as is the essence of a system of floating exchange rates. The Congress again appears to agree, since the Competitive Exchange Rate Act also contains the following language.

> (10) the actual exchange rate of the dollar cannot be brought into alignment with its competitive exchange rate unless—
> A. the Federal budget deficit is reduced;
> B. some modification is made in the existing international exchange rate system; and
> C. the macroeconomic policies of the major industrialized nations are well coordinated.
>
> SEC. 403. INTERNATIONAL NEGOTIATIONS ON EXCHANGE RATE REFORM.
> (a) Policy.—A priority of the United States in international economic negotiations shall be the achievement of a competitive exchange rate for the dollar.
> (b) International Negotiations on Exchange Rates.—The President shall seek to confer and negotiate with other countries on the exchange rate system. . . .
> (2) to develop a program for modification of that system to provide for long-term exchange rate stability and an agenda for implementing such program; and
> (3) to recommend proposals to achieve—
> (A) better coordination of macroeconomic policies of the major industrialized nations; and
> (B) greater stability in trade and current account balances and in the exchange rates of the dollar and other currencies.

It seems to me that these words represent a challenge to the economics profession.

If policy is to be directed in part to limiting misalignments, a prerequisite is obviously a body of analysis devoted to the identification of a correct set of exchange rate alignments. My own analysis of this question leads me to fear that the dollar may be beginning to overshoot (the key rates were ¥138 and DM 1.78 to the dollar when this judgment was offered), although any such overshooting would seem too modest as yet to justify policy action to support the dollar. The arithmetic that leads me to this view is as follows (all figures in billions of dollars).

1986 current account deficit	140
Estimate of net unrecorded service receipts (U.S. share of world current account discrepancy)	20
Adjustment in the pipeline from past dollar correction and deficit reduction	60
Effect of desirable additional fiscal measures in U.S., Europe, and Japan	40
Additional interest payments on increment in U.S. foreign debt	30
Maximum sustainable current account deficit c. 1990	50

(The last line assumes U.S. foreign debt of $700 billion in 1990 and a growth in nominal income of 7% per year, so that debt can grow up to $50 billion per year without the debt/income ratio rising, as explained in Paul Krugman's paper for this conference.)

Thus I see no reason to abandon my earlier estimates of where exchange rates need to be in order to facilitate a return to a sustainable pattern of payment imbalances in the medium term, provided that fiscal policies are indeed modified. Conversely, without those modifications present policies will not lead to a sustainable payments outcome. But I do not conclude that the absence of assurance that those policy modifications are in train (to phrase the matter delicately) implies that the dollar should decline more, for any further fall unaccompanied by fiscal retrenchment will threaten to undo the inflation stabilization of the early 1980s. I cannot understand how economists who objected to using monetary policy to limit the rise in the dollar in 1983 on the ground that this would have jeopardized the assault on inflation (Dornbusch 1986, p. 12) or that the trade deficit was a second-best response to the budget deficit (Feldstein 1983) can now call for a further 20% or 30% decline in the dollar.

My calculations make no allowance for the possibility of hysteresis. But I am reluctant to make such an allowance in advance of firm evidence that it is necessary, since the existence of hysteresis would imply that it is critically important to prevent other currencies from following the dollar into a period of gross overvaluation.

The disregard of other countries' interests implicit in the Dornbusch-Feldstein call for an undervalued dollar is fortunately not replicated in Congress, which calls in the passage quoted above for a process of international negotiation. It is indeed evident that if exchange rate management directed to limiting misalignments is to do more good than harm, then it will be essential to ensure that the various countries are pursuing consistent targets. This presupposes an international mechanism by which target exchange rates can be negotiated.

Once exchange rate targets have been agreed upon, their pursuit will require a willingness to take the exchange rate into account in formulating monetary policy. One reason for suggesting that exchange rate targets be surrounded by wide zones (± 10 %) is to enable countries to continue to use monetary policy for domestic stabilization. But the pursuit of an exchange rate target does imply a willingness to override the domestically preferred monetary policy by a concern for the exchange rate: since monetary policy is what really can influence exchange rates, it is fatuous to suggest that one can have an exchange rate policy that does not ultimately drive monetary policy. Conversely, once the market is convinced that in the last analysis monetary policy will be driven by a concern for the exchange rate, then I find it reasonable to suppose that sterilized intervention can be helpful in widening the bounds within which monetary policy can be diverted toward domestic ends without pushing the exchange rate to unacceptable levels.

If monetary policy is to be directed in substantial part toward managing the exchange rate, then it will be important to ensure that fiscal policy is consistent with satisfactory domestic performance. This was already made clear in my first discussion of the target zone proposal (Williamson 1983, p. 33):

> One has to conclude that it would be quite wrong to accept macroeconomic follies like the U.S. budget deficit as exogenous, and accommodate them without further question. . . . On the contrary, a principal purpose of seeking a more structured exchange rate system is precisely to expose such examples of myopic and internationally inconsistent national decision making. If the administration had to explain that its budgetary policy required approval of an appreciation of the dollar's FEER, which Congress could recognize would threaten a large number of tradable goods industries, it is surely likely that political forces to restore fiscal discipline would be strengthened.

However, last year two associates and I (Edison, Miller, and Williamson 1987) were led to spell out more explicitly the characteristics of the rule for fiscal policy that would be needed to complement the target zone proposal. We were induced to do this by two considerations. One was the apparent continuing belief of some academic economists that no fiscal coordination was implied, so that target zones might under certain circumstances be a recipe for inflation. The other was the apparent willingness of the Tokyo Summit to contemplate a more ambitious scheme of policy coordination covering fiscal as well as monetary policy.

Our study involved a search for a set of robust policy rules that could be expected to lead to satisfactory outcomes for the world as a whole and each of the major participating countries individually under a wide range of circumstances. We deliberately sought relatively simple feedback rules rather than attempting to seek optimal rules out of a belief that feedback rules are more robust and that robustness—the assurance that the rules will behave satisfactorily under a wide range of circumstances—is a critically important quality in the context of guidelines for international economic policy coordination.

We suggested that each country should pursue two intermediate targets, related respectively to "internal balance" and "external balance." Dale Henderson argued that because recent shocks have emanated primarily from policy aberrations, it would be better to target policy variables directly rather than intermediate targets. I am unconvinced, because I doubt whether we can rely on a continuing absence of exogenous shocks.

The internal balance target would take the form of a target rate of growth of nominal income, which is of course a simple compromise between promotion of real growth and control of inflation. Our simulations suggested that it would be helpful to endogenize this target according to the formula:

$$(1) \qquad \hat{y}^* = g + \alpha \hat{p}_{t-1} + \beta d$$

where $\hat{y}^*$ = target rate of growth of nominal income

g = estimated rate of growth of productive potential

$\hat{p}^*_{t-1}$ = inherited rate of inflation

d = deflationary gap.

The other intermediate target would be a target for the (real effective) exchange rate, where the target would be set at a level estimated to reconcile internal and external balance in the medium term (what I have previously termed the fundamental equilibrium exchange rate, or FEER). It would be inappropriate to adopt a current balance target directly as the intermediate target, because the lags of trade flows behind exchange rates are so long.

The assignment rules that we suggest to achieve these intermediate targets are the following:

1. The average level of world real interest rates should be revised up (down) if aggregate growth of nominal income is threatening to exceed (fall short of) the sum of the target growth of nominal income for the participating countries.
2. Differences in interest rates among countries should be revised when necessary to limit the deviations of currencies from their target levels.
3. National fiscal policies should be revised with a view to achieving national target rates of growth of nominal income.

Rule (1) deals with the $(n - 1)$ problem in a McKinnonesque way (McKinnon without the monetarism). Rule (2) embodies the essence of the target zone system. Rulc (3) endorses Keynesian fiscal policy.

Practical implementation of policy coordination would doubtless be less stark than this summary might suggest. In particular, the guidance to expectations provided by credible target zones plus exchange market intervention plus the wide band will allow significant scope for interest rate differentials to fluctuate with regard to the needs of domestic stabilization. Hence rule (3), which suggests that fiscal policy be used as the residual instrument of anticyclical policy, need not necessarily imply the reinstatement of fine tuning: avoidance of gross mistuning plus the automatic fiscal stabilizers may well suffice. But there is no point in pretending that the world economy can perform satisfactorily irrespective of the fiscal policies pursued by the major powers. Neither can markets be expected to achieve sensibly aligned and reasonably stable exchange rates without the official sector explicitly asking itself what those rates are and being willing to adjust monetary policy to achieve them.

I hope that the economics profession will ask whether the above set of guidelines might not provide an appropriate response to the challenge that the Congress has issued to us.

References

Dornbusch, Rudiger. 1986. *Dollars, debts, and deficits*. Cambridge: MIT Press.

Edison, Hali J., Marcus Miller, John Williamson. 1987. On evaluating and extending the target zone proposal. *Journal of Policy Modeling* 9, no. 1, 199–224.

Feldstein, Martin. 1983. The world economy today. *The Economist* 287, no. 7293 (11 June) pp. 43–48.

Williamson, John. 1983. *The exchange rate system*. Washington: Institute for International Economics. First edition.

6 Monopolistic Competition and Labor Market Adjustment in the Open Economy

Joshua Aizenman

6.1 Introduction and Summary

The volatility of the real exchange rate exhibited in recent years has led to a growing concern regarding the need for labor market adjustment in the presence of misalignment. It is important to recognize that the potential role of policies stems not from the volatility per se but from the consequences of unanticipated shocks in the presence of an institutional structure that limits the flexibility of adjustment. In the absence of rigidities and with complete markets, volatility should not concern the policymaker. Thus, an assessment of the role of policies can be conducted after we specify a framework that allows for the presence of rigidities.

The purpose of this paper is to address the nature of adjustment and the role of policies in an economy characterized by labor contracts that limit the flexibility of wage adjustment. Specifically, I postulate a stochastic monopolistic competitive economy, where wage negotiations are carried out every several periods because of the presence of transaction costs.[1] These costs can reflect the expenses of collecting and processing information, as well as direct output losses associated with a time-consuming negotiation process. The wage negotiation periods are assumed to be distributed uniformly over time. This distribution results in wage and price paths that differ across firms according to the

Joshua Aizenman in an associate professor of business economics at the University of Chicago and research associate of the National Bureau of Economic Research.

The research reported here is part of the NBER's research program in international studies. Any opinions expressed are those of the author and not those of the National Bureau of Economic Research. The author would like to thank Stephen Turnovsky and Maurice Obstfeld for useful suggestions. Any errors, however, are his.

timing of their most recent pricing decision. Following the construction of the building blocks of the economy, we derive the optimal wage presetting rule. Such a rule is characterized by two elements. First, for a given frequency of wage negotiation, we derive the optimal path of wages to be preset at the beginning of each contract cycle. Second, we solve for the optimal frequency of wage negotiation.

Armed with the optimal wage presetting rule, I analyze the evolution of goods prices and the implication of the wage presetting rule for the aggregate economy. Specifically, I investigate the adjustment of output, exchange rate, prices, employment, and wages to nominal and real shocks. The discussion focuses on the dependency of the adjustment on the market power enjoyed by each producer. The analysis shows that unexpected monetary shocks can generate persistent aggregate output and relative price shocks whose nature is determined by the degree of substitutability between domestic and foreign goods. Greater substitutability induces a greater output and employment effects and smaller price effects in the short and the intermediate run. On the other hand, greater substitutability is shown to reduce the persistency and duration of the adjustment. These results follow from the observation that a larger substitutability is associated with shorter wage contracts. Thus, a greater degree of substitutability has two opposing effects—it raises the magnitude but reduces the duration of the output and employment shocks resulting from a given monetary innovation.

The details of the adjustment to real shocks are more involved, being determined by the magnitude of the income elasticity of the demand for money and the substitutability between domestic and foreign goods. If the income elasticity of the demand for money is less than unity (as is suggested by empirical studies) the presence of nominal wage contracts tends to magnify the responsiveness of the economy to real shocks, and a larger degree of substitutability will magnify the short-run and the intermediate-run adjustment of prices and output to real shocks and will reduce the needed adjustment of relative prices. The direction of the nominal exchange rate adjustment induced by real shocks is shown to be determined by the size of the income elasticity of the demand for money and by the substitutability between domestic and foreign goods. Large (small) elasticities are associated with a nominal appreciation (depreciation) in the presence of expansionary real shocks. An important feature of our staggered framework is that the speed of adjustment to real and nominal shocks accelerates during the adjustment. It is noteworthy that the result regarding the accelerated speed of adjustment differs from the one obtained applying linear models, where typically the speed of adjustment drops during the cycle.

Section 6.6 evaluates the potential role of labor market policies in the presence of misalignment. I distinguish between two sources of misalignment. The first is due to a large realization of the nominal or real shocks. The second is due to structural shocks that change the underlying parameters, like a change in the substitutability between various goods, a change in the share of labor in the GNP, changes in the covariance structure of the shocks, and so forth. The analysis demonstrates that a wage rule that will index the wage to nominal income will stabilize employment in the presence of the first type of shocks. Such a rule, however, will not stabilize employment in the presence of the second type of shocks: accommodation to structural shocks will necessitate wage renegotiation and a change in the frequency of wage adjustment.

Section 6.2 describes the model by formulating the goods, the money, and the labor market. Section 6.3 derives the long-run equilibrium where all prices and wages are flexible. Section 6.4 studies the dynamics of adjustment to monetary and real shocks. Section 6.5 discusses the factors determining contract length, and section 6.6 evaluates the role of labor market policies in the presence of misalignment. Section 6.7 closes the paper with concluding remarks.

6.2 The Model

In this section I outline the building blocks of the model. I start with the goods market specification and conclude with the labor and the money market.

6.2.1 The Goods Market

Consider an economy characterized by producers organized in a monopolistic competitive manner. There are two classes of goods—domestic and foreign. All domestic producers are facing the same demand function and share the same technology. Demand facing producer k is given by

$$(1) \qquad D_k = (\bar{P}/P_k)^{\beta} (EP^*/P_k)^{\alpha}, \ \alpha + \beta > 1,$$

where $\bar{P}$ is the average price of domestic goods, E is the exchange rate, P^* is the average price of foreign goods (in units of the foreign currency), and P_k is the price of good K.[2] I assume a large number of domestic producers (denoted by h), such that each of them treats $\bar{P}$ as given.[3] I denote by β the demand elasticity with respect to the competing domestic goods. The substitutability between domestic and foreign goods is measured by α, and for simplicity of exposition I invoke the law of one price for foreign goods.[4]

The production function of each domestic producer is characterized by

$$(2) \qquad X_k = Q(L_k)^{\gamma},$$

where L_k is the labor employed in the production of good k, and Q stands for labor productivity. Aggregate output is denoted by $\bar{X}$, where

(3) $$\bar{X} = \Sigma\, P_k X_k / \bar{P}.$$

Suppose we start from an initial equilibrium. Let us use lowercase letters for the logarithm of the uppercase variable. Thus, for a variable Z, $z = \log Z$. For example, applying equations (1) and (3) yields that the (percentage) change in output is proportional to the change in the terms of trade:

(4) $$\Delta \bar{x} = \alpha \Delta (e - \bar{p}).$$

6.2.2 The Labor and the Money Markets

For the purpose of my analysis I will distinguish between two types of labor markets. In the first case, I will consider a flexible prices economy where the labor market always clears. This corresponds to the case where wages are fully flexible and where the labor market is cleared in an auction manner. The usefulness of this environment stems from providing the benchmark economy for my subsequent discussion, where I will allow for the presence of nominal contracts in the labor market. In this benchmark economy money is neutral, because all prices are flexible to adjust fully to the state of liquidity. Thus, the benchmark economy serves to define the long-run equilibrium. The presence of nominal contracts will introduce a distinction between the long, the intermediate, and the short run. Among other topics, my analysis will study the factors determining the effective duration of the short and the intermediate run.

Consider the case where labor is employed subject to nominal contracts that preset the wage path for several periods, where within the contract duration employment is demand determined. To simplify notation I normalize the labor force to h (the number of firms) and assume an inelastic long-run supply of labor.[5] The presetting rule is governed by the notion that wages are preset at a level that is expected to clear the labor market facing the producer. Let W denote the money wage rate. Application of equations (1) and (2) yields the dependency of the price charged by producer k on the money wage:

(5) $$p_k = a_1 (p^* + e) + a_2 \bar{p} + a_3 w + \theta(c - \tilde{\gamma}\, q)$$

where
$$\tilde{\gamma} = 1/\gamma$$
$$\theta = 1/[1 + (\tilde{\gamma} - 1)(\alpha + \beta)]$$
$$c = \log\{\tilde{\gamma}(\alpha + \beta)/(\alpha + \beta - 1)\}$$
$$a_1 = \alpha(\tilde{\gamma} - 1)\theta$$
$$a_2 = \beta(\tilde{\gamma} - 1)\theta \text{ and}$$
$$a_3 = \theta.$$

Note that the sum of the elasticities of P_k with respect to foreign prices (a_1), the wage (a_2), and domestic competitors' prices (a_3) adds up to one: $a_1 + a_2 + a_3 = 1$. This is a reflection of the homogeneity postulate, implying that an equiproportional rise in all prices will not affect the real equilibrium. The relative importance of foreign prices in the determination of the domestic price P_k is characterized by the substitutability of domestic and foreign goods. As we approach perfect substitutability (i.e., as $\alpha \rightarrow \infty$), we approach an absolute purchasing power parity (PPP) pricing rule, where $p = p^* + e$.[6]

I conclude this section with the specification of the money market. Let us denote by M the supply of money and consider a simple money demand function:

$$m = \bar{p} + \xi\bar{x} \tag{6}$$

where ξ is the income elasticity of the demand for money.[7] We turn now to the characterization of the long-run, flexible price equilibrium.

6.3 The Long-Run Equilibrium

The long-run equilibrium is characterized by flexibility of wages and prices. In such an economy all domestic producers are facing the same demand and supply conditions. As a result, in this equilibrium all producers will employ $L = 1$ and will charge the same price ($p_k = \bar{p}$). Applying equations (1) and (2) yields that the long-run PPP ratio is equal to:

$$e + p^* - \bar{p} = q/\alpha. \tag{7}$$

The PPP ratio is determined by two factors—the measure of the efficiency of production (Q) and the substitutability between domestic and foreign goods (α). A rise in domestic efficiency ($d\,q > 0$) or a drop in the substitutability between domestic and foreign goods is associated with a deterioration in the terms of trade. As one might expect, the long-run equilibrium is independent of monetary considerations. Applying (7) to (5) we infer that the producer's real wage is

$$w - p = q - c. \tag{8}$$

The term c represents the markup pricing rule, where the price is a markup of wages. From the definition of c (see [5]), it follows that the markup rate drops with $\alpha + \beta$, which corresponds to the degree of substitutability. It can be also shown that as $\alpha + \beta \rightarrow \infty$ we approach the competitive outcome, where the labor bill share approaches γ. We turn now to an analysis of the short and the intermediate run.

6.4 The Short and the Intermediate Run

The purpose of this section is to design a framework that will allow assessment of the short- and intermediate-run adjustment to unanticipated monetary and real shocks and the evaluation of economic factors determining the effective duration of the intermediate run. I introduce nominal rigidities by assuming that pricing decisions in the labor market are carried out every several periods because of the presence of transaction costs associated with frequent wage negotiation.[8] I consider the case where labor is employed subject to contracts that preset the wage path for n periods, where within the contract duration, employment is demand determined. At the beginning of each contract cycle, the contract sets the wage path for the next n periods. I start this section with the assumption that n is exogenously given and conclude with an analysis of the endogenous determination of n.[9]

The wage in period d that was preset h periods ago is denoted by $W_{d,h}$, and the price charged by the producer who employs labor that is paid $W_{d,h}$ is denoted by $P_{d,h}$. For example, a producer who starts a contract cycle in t should negotiate at period t the path of ($W_{t,0}$, $w_{t+1,1}$, . . .; $W_{t+n-1,n-1}$). Figure 6.1 describes the prices and wages prevailing in our economy. At time t we observe n prices and a corresponding n wages, as described by the vertical vector. A producer charging $p_{t,0}$ at period t is also presetting wages for the next $n - 1$ periods, as is described by the horizontal vector. The presetting rule is governed by the notion that wages are preset at a level that is expected to clear the labor market facing the producer. In doing so, labor and management are using all the information regarding the wages that have already been set, the expected path of the exchange rate and foreign prices, and the prices that other competitors are expected to set in the future.[10] Wages are set at time t for period $t + k$ such that the goods market at time $t + k$ is expected to clear at the full employment output ($L = 1$). Thus, applying equations (1), (2), we get:

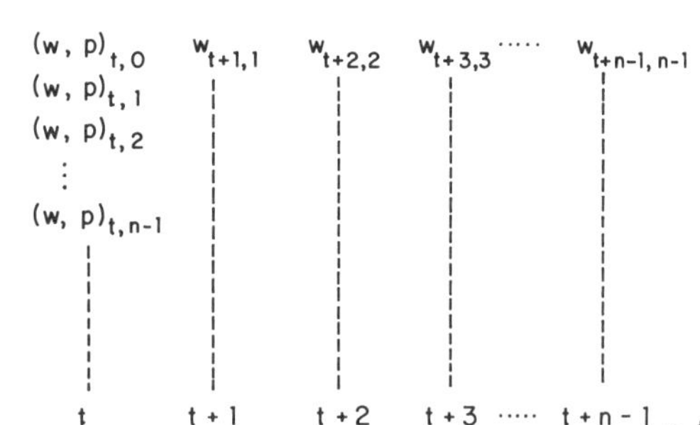

Fig. 6.1 Temporal arrangement of wages (W) and prices (P).

$$(9) \quad E_t(q_{t+k}) = \beta\, E_t(\bar{p}_{t+k} - p_{t+k,k}) + \alpha\, E_t(e_{t+k} + p^*_{t+k} - p_{t+k,k})$$

where E_t denotes the conditional expectation operator, when expectations are conditional on the information at time t. Applying (9) to (5) we obtain

$$(10) \qquad w_{t+k,k} = E_t(p_{t+k} + q_{t+k} - c).$$

We assume a stable stochastic structure, and unsynchronized price setting—that is, that the contracts decision periods are distributed uniformly over time. Within this assumption the complexity of the problem is reduced significantly. This assumption breaks the symmetry of all domestic producers that is observed in the flexible pricing equilibrium, while at the same time it imposes enough structure to allow a tractable solution. Within each period a fraction $1/n$ of the producers determines the time path of prices. The result is pricing decisions for each period that differ across firms, according to the timing of their most recent wage contract negotiation. Consequently, the domestic price level is given by

$$(11) \qquad \bar{p}_t = \sum_{i=1}^{n} (p_{t,n-i}/n).$$

Consider the case where we start at time zero in the long-run equilibrium, with contracts that are fully adjusted to all the past shocks. I would now like to study adjustment to real and nominal shocks. To simplify notation I assume that by the choice of units, all prices and aggregate output in the initial equilibrium are one (or zero in logarithmic terms). My subsequent analysis will focus on deriving the changes in all variables relative to this benchmark. Consequently, I will use the logarithmic notation to denote the percentage changes relative to this benchmark. I allow for two stochastic shocks: a monetary (m) and a real shock (q). Applying equations (4), (5), (6), (10), and (11) yields

$$(12) \qquad p_{t,n-k} = \theta[\, E_{t-(n-k)}p_{t,n-k} + q_{t-k} - \bar{\gamma}q_t + (\bar{\gamma} - 1)(\alpha + \beta - 1/\xi)\bar{p}_t + (\bar{\gamma} - 1)m_t/\xi].$$

Equation (12) describes the actual price at time t charged by a producer that negotiated the labor contract $n - k$ periods ago. This price is a function of three types of variables: the expected producer price at the time of the wage negotiation, the price level at time t, and the realization of the nominal and the real shocks.

To gain further insight it is useful to impose restrictions on the stochastic structure in order to allow a reduced-form solution of the time path of the key variables. For example, consider the case where both liquidity m and productivity q follow a random walk:

$$(13) \qquad m_t = m_{t-1} + \eta_t.$$

$$q_t = q_{t-1} + \epsilon_t. \tag{14}$$

To simplify exposition I proceed by analyzing two polar cases. I start with an economy where all shocks are nominal, and continue with an economy where all shocks are real. The general case where both types of shocks are present is obtained as a linear combination of these two polar cases.

6.4.1 Short-Run Adjustment to Monetary Shocks

I start my analysis by providing the general solution for prices and quantities and proceed by studying the dynamics of adjustment to a nominal shock starting from a long-run equilibrium.

Following some tedious steps, I can show that the wage setting rule and the corresponding prices are given by

$$w_{t,n-k} = \sum_{j=1}^{k} A_j \eta_{t-(n-j)} + \{m_{t-n} - (\xi - 1)q_{t-n} - c\}. \tag{15}$$

$$p_{t,n-k} = \sum_{j=1}^{k} A_j \eta_{t-(n-j)} + \sum_{j=k+1}^{n} B_j \eta_{t-(n-j)} + \{m_{t-n} - (\xi - 1)q_{t-n} - c\} \tag{16}$$

$$\text{where } A_j = \frac{1 + (\bar{\gamma} - 1)(\beta + \alpha)}{(n - j + 1)/n + (\bar{\gamma} - 1)(\beta + \alpha) + (j - 1)(\beta + \alpha)\xi/n}$$

and

$$\text{where } B_j = \frac{(\bar{\gamma} - 1)(\beta + \alpha)}{(n - j + 1)/n + (\bar{\gamma} - 1)(\beta + \alpha) + (j - 1)(\beta + \alpha)\xi/n}.$$

Note that A_j equals the elasticity of the wage for period t that was set at period $t - (n - k)$ with respect to innovations at period $t - (n - j)$ for $j = 1, \ldots, k$. Thus, smaller values of j are associated with older innovations. From (15) it follows that innovations that took place in or before period $t - (n - 1)$ affect the wage with a unitary elasticity. The logic of this result stems from the observation that equations (6), (7), and (8) imply that the long-run wage is given by $m - (\xi - 1)q - c$. Because in our economy there are staggered contracts whose duration is n, it takes $n - 1$ periods to accomplish the adjustment to a given innovation. Once the adjustment is accomplished, it affects nominal wages with a unitary elasticity.

To gain further insight it is useful to consider the adjustment path to shocks starting from a long-run equilibrium at time $t - 1$. For example, suppose that at time t, $\eta_t = 1$. With the exception of the producers that negotiate at period t ($1/n$ of all producers), all the other producers do not adjust wages to reflect η_t. Applying (15) and (16) yields that

(17) $$w_{t,0} = p_{t,0} = \frac{1 + (\bar{\gamma} - 1)(\beta + \alpha)}{1/n + (\bar{\gamma} - 1)(\beta + \alpha) + (n - 1)(\beta + \alpha)\xi/n}$$ and

(18) $$p_{t,1} = p_{t,2} = \ldots = p_{t,n-1}$$

$$= \frac{(\bar{\gamma} - 1)(\beta + \alpha)}{1/n + (\bar{\gamma} - 1)(\beta + \alpha) + (n - 1)(\beta + \alpha)\xi/n}.$$

(19) $$\bar{p}_t = \frac{(\bar{\gamma} - 1)(\beta + \alpha) + 1/n}{1/n + (\bar{\gamma} - 1)(\beta + \alpha) + (n - 1)(\beta + \alpha)\xi/n} < 1.$$

The result of the increase in liquidity is to raise all prices. Note that if all domestic prices rise at the same rate we will obtain an excess supply of goods produced by producers that preset wages for time t in the past, because they enjoy a cost advantage relative to the producers that set their wage at time t. Thus, the presetters will increase prices by less than the producers that are setting wages at time t(i.e., $p_{t,1} < p_{t,0}$). The overall effect of the presetting of wages is that the aggregate price level rises by less than the implied long-run adjustment (i.e., $\bar{p}_t < 1$). Note also that if $(\beta + \alpha)\xi < 1$, the price and the wage of producers that negotiate the contract at time t will overshoot the long-run adjustment (i.e., $w_{t,0} = p_{t,0} > 1$). Applying (4) and (6) we infer that

(20) $$e_t = \bar{p}_t + (1 - \bar{p}_t) / (\alpha\xi) = 1 + (1 - \bar{p}_t)(1 - \alpha\xi)/(\alpha\xi).$$

Applying (19) and (20), we infer that the exchange rate depreciation exceeds the aggregate price adjustment, implying that the monetary shock induces real depreciation in the short run at a rate of

(21) $$e_t - \bar{p}_t = \frac{(n - 1)(\beta + \alpha)/n}{\alpha[1/n + (\bar{\gamma} - 1)(\beta + \alpha) + (n - 1)(\beta + \alpha)\xi/n]}.$$

Another implication of equation (20) is that exchange-rate overshooting will occur if $1 > \alpha\xi$. Note that (4) and (6) imply that the elasticity of the demand for money with respect to the exchange rate is $\alpha\xi$, and overshooting will occur if this elasticity falls short of unity.[11] We turn now to an assessment of the short-run output effect of the monetary innovation. Note that (1) implies that for any producer k

(22) $$x_k = \alpha(e - \bar{p}) + (\alpha + \beta)(\bar{p} - p_k).$$

The first term reflects the common effect due to the real depreciation, whereas the second term reflects the producer-specific effect due to deviations of his prices from the economy's average price. As my analysis indicates, the common effect implies that output will rise. The producer-specific effect works towards output contraction for "flexible" producers (i.e., producers that are setting wages at time t). In fact, because of the inelastic supply of labor we obtain that the two effects cancel each other for the flexible producers and that $x_{t,0} = 0$. On the other hand, the producer-specific effect works towards output expansion for the producers that preset wages before period t. Direct application of (17)–(20) reveals that

(23) $$x_{t,o} = 0.$$

(24) $$x_{t,1} = \ldots = x_{t,n-1} = (\alpha + \beta)/[1/n + (\bar{\gamma} - 1)(\beta + \alpha) + (n - 1)(\beta + \alpha)\xi/n].$$

(25) $$\bar{x}_t = (n - 1)(\alpha + \beta)/[1 + n(\bar{\gamma} - 1)(\beta + \alpha) + (n - 1)(\beta + \alpha)\xi].$$

(25′) $\bar{l}_t = \bar{\gamma}\,\bar{x}_t$ where $\bar{l}_t$ is the change in aggregate employment.

Figure 6.2 plots the dependency of prices and output on the substitutability between domestic and foreign goods (α). Notice that greater substitutability induces greater output and employment effects and smaller price effects. Similar results apply for the variances of the variables plotted in figure 6.2 for the case where only monetary shocks are affecting the economy. Direct calculation reveals that the degree of staggering (i.e., the contract length n) affects the adjustment in the following way

(26) $$\frac{\partial \bar{x}_t}{\partial n} > 0$$

$$\frac{\partial (e_t - \bar{p}_t)}{\partial n} > 0$$

$$\frac{\partial e_t}{\partial n} > 0$$

$$\frac{\partial \bar{p}_t}{\partial n} < 0$$

$$\frac{\partial \bar{l}_t}{\partial n} > 0.$$

Longer contracts magnify the exchange rate, the output, and the relative price effects induced by monetary shocks in the short run, while they dampen the price level adjustment.

6.4.2 Intermediate-Run Adjustment to Monetary Shocks

We turn now to the adjustment observed in the intermediate run. Over time, more wage contracts are renegotiated to reflect the liquidity shock. Because the impact effect of the shock is to cause output ex-

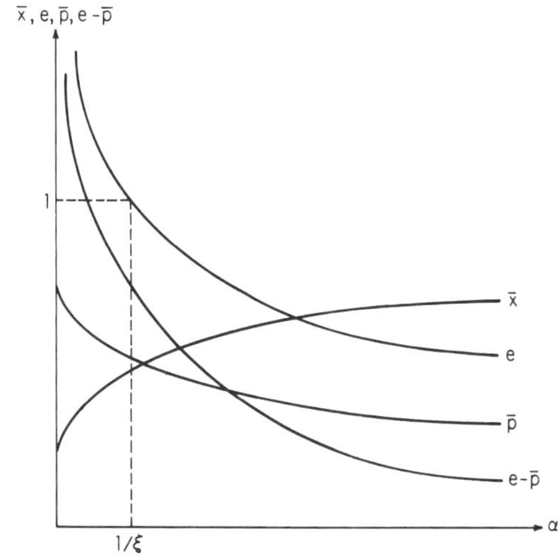

Fig. 6.2 Substitutability (α) and the adjustment of prices ($\bar{p}$), output ($\bar{x}$), nominal and real exchange rates (e and $e - \bar{p}$) to a monetary shock.

pansion at the previously preset wages, forces of excess demand in the labor market will raise wages in the renegotiated contracts at a rate that will reduce output and employment to the preshock level. This in turn will enable other producers to raise prices. Thus, over time aggregate prices will rise, while aggregate output will drop. This adjustment in turn will reduce the real depreciation implied by the initial shock. More formally, applying equations (4), (6), (15), and (16), we obtain that after k periods the monetary shock $\eta_t = 1$ will result in:

$$(19') \quad \bar{p}_{t+k} = \frac{(\bar{\gamma} - 1)(\beta + \alpha) + (k + 1)/n}{(1 + k)/n + (\bar{\gamma} - 1)(\beta + \alpha) + (n - (k + 1))(\beta + \alpha)\xi/n} < 1.$$

$$(20') \quad e_{t+k} = \bar{p}_{t+k} + (1 - \bar{p}_{t+k})/(\alpha\xi)$$

$$= 1 + \frac{(1 - \alpha\xi)(n - (k + 1))(\beta + \alpha)\xi/[n\alpha\xi]}{(1 + k)/n + (\bar{\gamma} - 1)(\beta + \alpha) + (n - (k + 1))(\beta + \alpha)\xi/n}$$

$$(21') \quad e_{t+k} - \bar{p}_{t+k} = \frac{(n - (k + 1))(\beta + \alpha)/n}{\alpha[(1 + k)/n + (\bar{\gamma} - 1)(\beta + \alpha) + (n - (k + 1))(\beta + \alpha)\xi/n]}.$$

$$(25'') \quad \bar{x}_{t+k} = \frac{(n - (k + 1))(\beta + \alpha)/n}{(1 + k)/n + (\bar{\gamma} - 1)(\beta + \alpha) + (n - (k + 1))(\beta + \alpha)\xi/n}.$$

Note that the condition generating short-run overshooting (i.e., $1 > \alpha\xi$) implies also intermediate-run overshooting, where over time we will observe nominal appreciation. Applying the above equations we obtain that the dynamics of intermediate-run adjustment are characterized by

$$\begin{aligned}
(27)\qquad & \Delta\bar{p}_{t+k}/\Delta k > 0 \\
& \Delta^2\bar{p}_{t+k}/\Delta k^2 > 0 \\
& \bar{p}_{t+n-1} = 1 \\
& \Delta\bar{x}_{t+k}/\Delta k < 0 \\
& \Delta^2\bar{x}_{t+k}/\Delta k^2 < 0 \\
& \bar{x}_{t+n-1} = 0 \\
& \Delta(\bar{e}_{t+k} - \bar{p}_{t+k})/\Delta k < 0 \\
& \Delta^2(\bar{e}_{t+k} - \bar{p}_{t+k})/\Delta k^2 < 0 \\
& \Delta\bar{e}_{t+k}/\Delta k < 0 \\
& \Delta^2 e_{t+k}/\Delta k^2 < 0 \text{ if } 1 > \alpha\xi \text{ and} \\
& \Delta\bar{e}_{t+k}/\Delta k > 0 \\
& \Delta^2 e_{t+k}/\Delta k^2 > 0 \text{ if } 1 < \alpha\xi.
\end{aligned}$$

Figure 6.3 summarizes the dynamics of adjustment of aggregate prices and output.[12] An important feature of my staggered framework is that

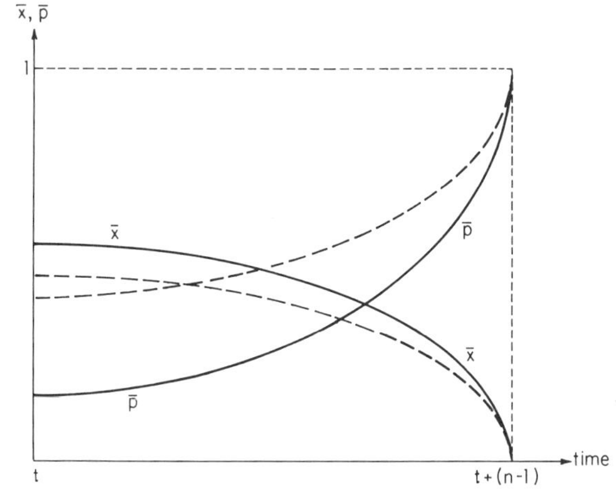

Fig. 6.3 The dynamics of price ($\bar{p}$) and output ($\bar{x}$) adjustment to a monetary shock.

the speed of adjustment accelerates during the adjustment. Following the shock at time t, the monetary shock triggers persistent relative price and output shocks. Over time the shocks to relative prices and output will die down at an accelerated rate, and the rise in liquidity is absorbed via accelerated aggregate price adjustment. It can be shown that smaller substitutability α will raise the curvature of the adjustment path. This in turn implies greater persistency of prices and output during the first phase of the adjustment and a more abrupt adjustment towards the end of the adjustment cycle. In terms of figure 6.3 we will observe that a drop in α is associated with adjustment on the dotted (instead of on the solid) curves. It is noteworthy that the result regarding the accelerated speed of adjustment differs from the one obtained applying linear models, where typically the speed of adjustment drops during the cycle.[13]

6.4.3 Adjustment to Real Shocks

We turn now to the case of productivity shocks. We follow a procedure similar to our analysis of nominal shocks. Suppose that we start in a long-run equilibrium in period $t - 1$ and consider the adjustment to a productivity shock at time t, given by $\epsilon_t = 1$. Applying the characteristics of a long-run equilibrium and the corresponding money market equilibrium (equations [2], [4], and [6]) we obtain that the long-run effects of the productivity shock are

$$(28) \qquad \begin{aligned} \Delta\bar{x} &= 1 \\ \Delta\bar{p} &= -\xi \\ \Delta e &= (1 - \xi\alpha)/\alpha \\ \Delta(e - \bar{p}) &= 1/\alpha \\ \Delta w &= 1 - \xi. \end{aligned}$$

The productivity shock implies a rise in output and a corresponding drop in prices. To clear the induced excess supply of domestic goods we need a real depreciation. There is ambiguity regarding the induced exchange rate and wage adjustment. Notice that low substitutability (α) or low output elasticity of demand for money tends to be associated with nominal depreciation, and low income elasticity of the demand for money (i.e., $\xi < 1$) implies that money wages will go up.[14]

Following some tedious steps, it can be shown that the wage-setting rule and the corresponding prices are given by

$$(15') \qquad w_{t,n-k} = \sum_{j=1}^{k} F_j \eta_{t-(n-j)} + \{m_{t-n} - (\xi - 1)\, q_{t-n} - c\}.$$

$$(16') \quad p_{t,n-k} = \sum_{j=1}^{k} F_j \epsilon_{t-(n-j)} + \sum_{j=k+1}^{n} G_j \epsilon_{t-(n-j)} + \{m_{t-n} - (\xi - 1)\, q_{t-n} - c\}$$

where F_j

$$= -\xi \frac{1 + (\bar{\gamma} - 1)(\beta + \alpha) + (j - 1)\{\beta + \alpha - 1/\xi\}/n}{1 + (\bar{\gamma} - 1)(\beta + \alpha) + (j - 1)\{(\beta + \alpha)\xi - 1\}/n}$$

and

where $G_j = F_j - (F_j + 1)/\{1 + (\bar{\gamma} - 1)(\beta + \alpha)\}$.

We turn now to the analysis of the short- and intermediate-run adjustment. Formally, the time path of the variables of interest is given by

$$(29) \quad \bar{p}_{t+k} = -\xi - \frac{(1 - \xi)\xi(\alpha + \beta)(n - (k + 1))/n}{1 + (\bar{\gamma} - 1)(\beta + \alpha) + (n - (k + 1))\{(\beta + \alpha)\xi - 1\}/n}$$

$$= -\xi \frac{(k + 1)/n + (\alpha + \beta)(\bar{\gamma} - (k + 1)/n)}{1 + (\bar{\gamma} - 1)(\beta + \alpha) + (n - (k + 1))\{(\beta + \alpha)\xi - 1\}/n} < 0.$$

$$(30) \quad e_{t+k} = \bar{p}_{t+k}(\xi\alpha - 1)/(\xi\alpha).$$

$$(31) \quad e_{t+k} - \bar{p}_{t+k} = -\bar{p}_{t+k}/(\xi\alpha).$$

$$(32) \quad \bar{x}_{t+k} = -\bar{p}_{t+k}/\xi > 0.$$

$$(33) \quad \bar{l}_t = \bar{\gamma}[\bar{x}_{t+k} - 1] = \bar{\gamma}[\alpha(e_{t+k} - \bar{p}_{t+k}) - 1]$$

$$= \frac{(1 - \xi)\bar{\gamma}(n - (k + 1))(\beta + \alpha)/n}{1 + (\bar{\gamma} - 1)(\beta + \alpha) + (n - (k + 1))\{(\beta + \alpha)\xi - 1\}/n}.$$

The impact effect of the gain in productivity is a drop in prices, a rise in output, and real depreciation. This real depreciation is needed to clear the incipient excess supply induced by the rise in productivity. As can be seen from (29)–(33), the dynamics of adjustments to the new long-run equilibrium are determined by the magnitude of the income elasticity of the demand for money (ξ). Note that (29) implies that if that elasticity is smaller than unity, the short-run drop in domestic goods prices will exceed the long-run adjustment. This will also be the case where employment will increase in the short run (see [33]). Henceforth we will assume that this condition is satisfied (i.e., that $\xi < 1$). As is evident from (30), the path of the nominal exchange rate is determined by the sign of $(1 - \alpha\xi)/\alpha$. In general, small elasticities (i.e., $\alpha\xi < 1$) are associated with a nominal depreciation and large elasticities with a nominal appreciation. The relative complexity of the nominal exchange rate adjustment stems from the fact that the nominal exchange rate serves both as a component of the real exchange rate and as a factor determining the price level. The expansion of output calls for appreciation to accommodate the drop in domestic prices that is needed to clear the money market and for a depreciation needed to make domestic goods cheaper in order to clear the domestic goods market. It is the balance of these two forces that determines the path of the nominal exchange rate.

Direct calculation reveals that the degree of staggering (i.e., the contract length n) affects the adjustment according to the relative size of the income elasticity of the demand for money. Specifically, I demonstrated before that if $\xi < 1$, nominal contracts will magnify the response to real shocks (relative to the long-run adjustment). Consequently, we expect that for $\xi < 1$ a longer presetting horizon will increase the short-run impact of the shock on prices, the exchange rate, output, and employment. This can be verified by equation (29), which implies that:

$$\text{sign} \frac{\partial \bar{p}_{t+k}}{\partial n} = \text{sign}\ (\xi - 1). \tag{34}$$

Figure 6.4 summarizes the dynamics of adjustment. It is drawn for the case where $\xi < 1$. As in the previous discussion, the effect of a staggered price path is that we observe an accelerating adjustment to

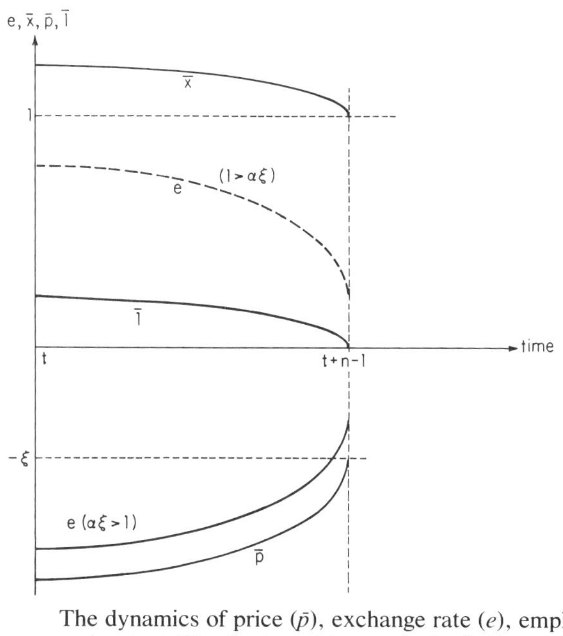

Fig. 6.4 The dynamics of price ($\bar{p}$), exchange rate (e), employment ($\bar{l}$), and output ($\bar{x}$) adjustment to a real shock (drawn for $\xi < 1$).

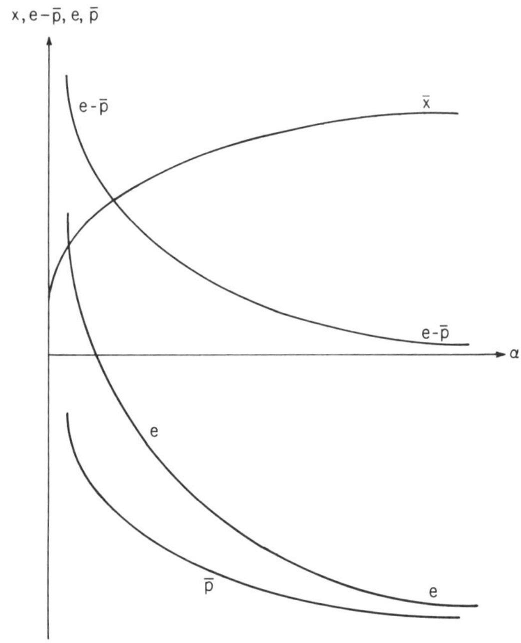

Fig. 6.5 Substitutability (α) and the adjustment of prices ($\bar{p}$), output ($\bar{x}$), nominal and real exchange rates (e and $e - \bar{p}$) to a real shock (drawn for $\xi < 1$).

the new long-run equilibrium. It is noteworthy that for $\xi < 1$, a larger degree of substitutability has the effect of magnifying the short- and intermediate-run adjustment of prices and output to real shocks, reducing the needed adjustment of relative prices.[15] These results are summarized in figure 6.5 (drawn for $\xi < 1$).

6.5 Contract Length

Our previous discussion was conducted for the case where the contract length was exogenously given. We turn now to the analysis of the determinants of contract length.[16] Consider the case where each contract negotiation involves a cost. Negotiating the contract every n periods ($n > 1$) is associated with deadweight losses in the labor market, because the employment subject to the preset wage is suboptimal. More frequent wage negotiation will reduce the net present value of the expected deadweight losses in the labor market, but will raise the net present value of the negotiation costs. The contract length is set to balance these two effects at the margin, such that the rise in the net present value of expected losses resulting from extending the contract by one period equals the drop in the net present value of the negotiation costs.[17] Among the factors determining the contract horizon are the substitutability between goods and the volatility of the shocks affecting the economy. It can be shown that a higher volatility of the shocks and a greater goods substitutability will raise the deadweight losses in the labor market for a given contract length, implying thereby a shortening of the contract horizon.[18] Denoting the optimal n by n^* and the variances of the shocks by V_ϵ, V_η, we can summarize the factors determining n^* by: $n^* = n^*(\alpha, \beta, V_\epsilon, V_\eta)$,

where $\partial n^* / \partial \alpha < 0$; $\partial n^* / \partial \beta < 0$; $\partial n^* / \partial V_\epsilon < 0$; $\partial n^* / \partial V_\eta < 0$.

6.6 Labor Market Adjustment in the Presence of Misalignment

The purpose of this section is to review the role of labor market adjustment in the presence of exchange rate misalignment. We define exchange rate misalignment as a major change in the real exchange rate to a level that is not consistent with full employment in the presence of existing labor contracts. This misalignment can be the result of large shocks. We start our discussion by classifying these shocks into several categories. The first type of shocks is the result of a large realization of the nominal or real shocks specified before. The second type is structural shocks that change the underlying parameters, like a change in the substitutability between various goods, a change in the share of labor in the GNP, changes in the covariance structure of the shocks, and so forth.

Our previous discussion specified a framework that is applicable for an economy where the shocks are small enough to operate with contracts that preset the wage path for several periods. Such a framework can be modified to reduce the welfare consequences of the first type of shocks significantly. Throughout our discussion we have assumed simple noncontingent labor contracts. The implicit rationale for this assumption is that some of this information may be costly or unobservable, or may be adversely affected by the producer. This rationale suggests that priority should be given to contingencies that use public information that is available in a frequency that exceeds the frequency of wage negotiation. A possible candidate that should enhance adjustment to the first type of shocks is wage indexation to the nominal GNP.[19] To verify this point, note that (1) and (5) imply that if we start from a long-run equilibrium, the effect of various shocks is given by:[20]

$$(35) \qquad \Delta l = \Delta(\bar{x} + \bar{p}) - \Delta c - \Delta w.$$

The change in employment can be approximated as the change in nominal GNP (the first term) plus the change in the markup ($-\Delta c$) minus the change in wage. Equation (35) implies that whenever there are no structural shocks affecting the markup rate, a wage rule that will index the wage to nominal income (i.e., $\Delta w = \Delta(\bar{x} + \bar{p})$) will stabilize employment.

Suppose now that the economy is subjected to the second type of shocks, that is, structural shocks that affect the markup. Equation (35) suggests that if these shocks are public information in the short run, wage adjustment at a rate equal to the change in the markup will stabilize employment (i.e., $\Delta w = -\Delta c$). Unlike the case where shocks are of the first type, however, one expects structural shocks to be harder to identify, and indexation to a simple aggregate like nominal GNP will not suffice. In these circumstances, adjustment can be enhanced by changing the frequency of wage negotiation. For example, as analyzed in 6.4.4, a structural shock in the form of a rise in the substitutability between domestic and foreign goods or a rise in the volatility of real and monetary shocks calls for more frequent wage negotiations.

6.7 Concluding Remarks

This paper analyzed dynamics of adjustment in the presence of staggered labor contracts in a monopolistic competitive economy. One of the key assumptions of this paper concerns the timing of contracts decisions. It was assumed that the various producers are distributed uniformly over time, so that at each point in time an equal fraction of the producers ($1/n$) determines the time path of wages. With this assumption, the complexity of the problem was reduced significantly. In practice, however, it is evident that in many industries the pricing decisions are made at specific periods of time that are determined frequently by industry-specific considerations (like the season of the year, the end and the beginning of the school year, and the like). Furthermore, it was assumed that each producer sets wages for precisely n periods. Again, in reality one typically observes that the length of the wage cycle differs across sectors in the economy. Such considerations were not allowed in the present analysis, and their incorporation would constitute a useful extension.

Notes

1. Dixit and Stiglitz (1977) revived the interest in monopolistic competition. A growing body of research has recognized the importance of a limited degree of goods substitutability in explaining transmission of macro shocks. See, for example, Rotemberg (1982), Dornbusch (1985), Flood and Hodrick (1985), Giovannini (1985), Aizenman (1986), Svennson (1986), and Svennson and van Wijnbergen (1986). On monopolistic competition in the context of trade models, see Helpman and Krugman (1985).

2. To simplify exposition we consider here the case where the demand is a function only of relative prices. Our analysis can be extended to the case where income effects are added without affecting the main results.

3. Formally, $\bar{P}$ is defined as $\bar{P} = \sum_{k=1}^{h} [P_k/h]$. To simplify notation we assume that h is large enough to imply that $\partial \bar{P}/ \partial P_k \approx 0$. See Aizenman (1986) for an alternative analysis (though in a different context) that does not impose this assumption.

4. My analysis could be conducted for the symmetric case where the "foreign good" is composed of a large number of differentiated products. See, for example, appendix B in Aizenman (1986).

5. My analysis can be extended to the case where the supply of labor is dependent on real wages without affecting the main results. My analysis applies to economies with limited mobility of labor. In my model, wages are equated across producers only on average, and within each period wages will differ across producers according to the time of the recent wage negotiation.

6. Note that as $\alpha \to \infty$, $a_1 \to 1$, $a_2 \to 0$, $a_3 \to 0$ and $\theta[c - \bar{\gamma} q] \to 0$. For a discussion on the PPP doctrine, see Frenkel (1981).

7. Allowing for a dependency of the demand for money on the interest rate and foreign prices will complicate the reduced-form solutions for all variables, but it will not affect the main results regarding the determinants of contract lengths and the nature of the adjustment to shocks.

8. To highlight the role of wage contracts, we assume that prices in the goods market are flexible. Alternative modeling strategy can focus on price rigidities in the goods market, as in Sheshinski and Weiss (1977), Mussa (1981), Rotemberg (1982), and Aizenman (1986).

9. The present formulation is related to that of Fischer (1977), who studies the determinations of contracts in the presence of two-period staggered contracts. The new aspect of the present discussion is in allowing for endogenous determination of the extent of staggering prices, focusing on the role of substitutability between various goods and the stochastic structure in explaining the nature of the resultant equilibrium. My approach is closer to that of Fischer (1977) than to that of Taylor (1980) and Calvo (1983), who consider a staggered equilibrium that sets one price for the presetting horizon, which is taken to be exogenously given. This paper applies Fischer's formulation because it allows for a more tractable analysis regarding the role of goods substitutability in the determination of wages and final prices.

10. I start my formulation with the case where I do not allow for preset wages contingent on future (presently unavailable) information. At the extreme case, where I would make optimal use of all future information in a contingent wage contract, I would converge on the flexible equilibrium economy described earlier. This paper does not attempt to provide a theoretical justification for noncontingent contracts (for further discussion on this issue see Blanchard 1979). Rather, their existence is taken for granted. In section 6.6 I will allow for limited contingencies by considering wage indexation to nominal income.

11. This condition is similar to the one derived in Dornbusch (1976). It is noteworthy that the condition for overshooting of the wage and the price of the "flexible" producers (i.e., producers that set wages at time t) is more stringent than the condition for exchange rate overshooting.

12. Note that equation (4) implies that the PPP ratio (i.e., $e - \bar{p}$) follows a time path similar to that of output ($\bar{x}$).

13. See, for example, Dornbusch (1976).

14. Formally, depreciation requires that $1 > \alpha\xi$, which is also the condition for exchange rate overshooting to nominal shocks.

15. This follows from the fact that sign $\partial \bar{p}_{t+k}/ \partial \alpha$ = sign $(\xi - 1)$.

16. I sketch here the framework described in Aizenman (1966, appendix A). The analysis there refers to the determination of the desired presetting horizon of goods prices in a staggered equilibrium. For a related analysis see Gray (1978).

17. Note that I assume no coordination among the various producers in their contract negotiation. Thus, in calculating the desired contract length from the point of view of a producer k (denoted by n_k), the producer balances the marginal costs and benefits, assuming that other producers are following a policy of contract length n. In his calculation the producer is using the information regarding the characteristics of the economy in an equilibrium where all producers follow a policy of contract length n. The "equilibrium" n is obtained where the desired n_k for each producer coincides with the "market" n.

18. This is the result of the fact that a higher substitutability magnifies the output effects (and consequently the change in the demand for labor) of a given shock (as can be seen from [25′] and [33]).

19. For a discussion of wage indexation to nominal GNP, see Marston and Turnovsky (1985) and Aizenman and Frenkel (1986).

20. Equation (5) implies that $\bar{\gamma}\,[\alpha(p^* + e - \bar{p}) - q] - \alpha(p^* + e - \bar{p}) + w - \bar{p} + c = 0$. Applying equation (1) to this result, we infer that for small deviations from the initial long-run equilibrium $\bar{\gamma}\,[\Delta\bar{x} - \Delta q] - \Delta\bar{x} + \Delta w - \Delta\bar{p} + \Delta c = 0$. Applying equation (2) to this result we obtain equation (35) for small deviations from the initial long-run equilibrium.

References

Aizenman, Joshua. 1986. Monopolistic competition, relative prices, and output adjustment in the open economy. NBER Working Paper no. 1787, January.

Aizenman, Joshua, and Jacob A. Frenkel. 1986. Supply shocks, wage indexation, and monetary accommodation. *Journal of Money, Credit, and Banking* 18: 304–22.

Blanchard, Olivier J. 1979. Wage indexation rules and the behavior of the economy. *Journal of Political Economy* 87.

Calvo, Guillermo A. 1983. Staggered contracts and exchange rate policy. In Jacob A. Frenkel, ed., *Exchange rates and international macroeconomics*. Chicago: University of Chicago Press.

Dixit, Avinash, and Joseph Stiglitz. 1977. Monopolistic competition and optimal product diversity. *American Economic Review* 67:297–308.

Dornbusch, Rudiger. 1976. Expectations and exchange rate dynamics. *Journal of Political Economy* 84:1161–76.

———. 1985. Exchange rate and prices. NBER Working Paper no. 1769.

Fischer, Stanley. 1977. Wage indexation and macroeconomic stability. In Karl Brunner and Allan H. Meltzer, eds., Stabilization of domestic and international economy. *Carnegie-Rochester Conference on Public Policy, Journal of Monetary Economics*, Suppl. 5, pp. 107–47.

Flood, Robert P., and Robert J. Hodrick. 1985. Optimal price and inventory adjustment in an open economy model of the business cycle. *Quarterly Journal of Economics* 100:887–914.

Frenkel, Jacob A. 1981. The collapse of purchasing power parity during the 1970s. *European Economic Review* 16:145–65.
Giovannini, Alberto. 1985. Exchange rates and traded goods prices. Working paper, Columbia University.
Gray, J. A. 1978. On indexation and contract length. *Journal of Political Economy* 86 (February): 1–18.
Helpman, Elhanan, and Paul Krugman. 1985. *Market structure and foreign trade*. Cambridge: MIT Press.
Marston, Richard C., and Stephen J. Turnovsky. 1985. Imported material prices, wage policy, and macro-economic stabilization. *Canadian Journal of Economics* 18:273–84.
Mussa, Michael. 1981. Sticky prices and disequilibrium adjustment in a rational model of the inflationary process. *American Economic Review* 71:1020–27.
Rotemberg, Julio J. 1982. Sticky prices in the United States. *Journal of Political Economy* 90:1187–1211.
Sheshinski, Eytan, and Yoram Weiss. 1977. Inflation and costs of price adjustment. *Review of Economics Studies* 44:287–304.
Svennson, Lars E. O. 1986. Sticky goods prices, flexible asset prices, monopolistic competition, and monetary policy. *Review of Economic Studies* 53:385–405.
Svennson, Lars E. O., and Sweder van Wijnbergen. 1986. International transmission of monetary policy. Working paper no. 362, University of Stockholm.
Taylor, John B. 1980. Aggregate Dynamics and Staggered Contacts. *Journal of Political Economy* 88:1–23.

Comment Stephen J. Turnovsky

Joshua Aizenman has written a very elegant paper. It is primarily about the impact of shocks on a small open economy. This is a topic which encompasses an extensive literature. Aizenman's analysis enhances this literature by embodying two features:

(1) The determination of wages through multiperiod contracts
(2) The characterization of the output market by monopolistic competition

The introduction of overlapping wage contracts is an extension of Fischer-Taylor type models and is fairly familiar. The introduction of monopolistic competition into international macroeconomics is much less well known, and here the author applies some of his previous work; see Aizenman (forthcoming).

I shall focus my remarks on the following aspects: (1) the structure of the model, (2) some observations on the implications of the model and comparisons with some standards, and (3) some comments on exchange rate misalignment.

Stephen J. Turnovsky is professor of economics at the University of Washington and a research associate of the National Bureau of Economic Research.

Review of Model

The model consists of three markets: the goods market, the labor market, and the money market. The first and third of these are straightforward. Demand and output are specified by Cobb-Douglas type functions, which have well-known advantages of analytical convenience. The specification of the demand for money to depend upon only real output is also a great simplification, and I shall comment further on this aspect below.

The key sector of the model is the labor market, where two situations are considered. The first is a benchmark economy in which prices and wages are perfectly flexible. This yields a long-run full employment equilibrium in which long-run purchasing power parity holds. Specifically, the long-run equilibrium real exchange rate equals the ratio of the productivity of labor to the degree of substitutability between domestic and foreign goods.

By contrast, most of the analysis deals with an economy in which wages are preset for a number of periods. The wage rule is set such that the labor market is expected to clear at each period. This leads to the pricing equation (5), in which the price of the kth producer is determined as a markup on (1) the domestic price of foreign goods, (2) the general price level, and (3) the wage rate. This equation, together with the relationship between the average price level and the prices set by individual producers at different stages of the contract cycle, is the source of the dynamics in the model.

The model also distinguishes between the short run and the intermediate run. A key assumption is that wage contracts are negotiated at each period for n periods ahead, with a fraction $1/n$ of the producers signing a contract at each point of time. Thus at time t, say, we observe a vector of wages and prices:

$$w_t = (w_{t,0}, \ldots, w_{t,n-1})$$
$$p_t = (p_{t,0}, \ldots, p_{t,n-1})$$

where

$w_{t,i}$ = wage paid at time t by a producer who signed his wage contract i periods ago,

$p_{t,i}$ = price set at time t by a producer who signed his wage contract i periods ago.

Aizenman then solves for $p_{t,n-k}$, $w_{t,n-k}$ as a function of the shocks over the life of the contract, under the assumption that expectations are rational. In the short run the average price $\bar{p}_t$ is given and all wages but the current are taken as preset. Over the intermediate run, new wage contracts are signed and the average price level $\bar{p}_t$ changes as more firms reset their prices.

With this setup, Aizenman analyzes the effects of both monetary and real shocks on a number of key macroeconomic variables, including (1) the nominal exchange rate, (2) the price level, (3) the real exchange rate, and (4) output. He then considers how these responses change with the degree of substitutability between domestic and foreign goods, as well as analyzing the time profile of the adjustment over the intermediate run. Since the source of the lags is the contracts which last just n periods, all the dynamics take just n periods to complete.

Some Implications of the Model

I now comment on some of the implications of the model and compare them to more standard models in the literature. The benchmark I shall use is a typical stochastic IS-LM model, in which the supply side is represented either by a Lucas supply function (possibly justified in terms of a Gray (1976) type one-period contract) or by means of a Phillips curve giving rise to sluggish prices.

First, consider the shocks themselves. Aizenman shows how a positive monetary disturbance raises the domestic price level and causes a depreciation of both the nominal and real exchange rate. A positive productivity disturbance is shown to increase output and reduce the price level and causes a real depreciation of the exchange rate. The nominal exchange rate may either depreciate or appreciate, depending on whether the parameter $\alpha\zeta \lesseqgtr 1$. Virtually the identical qualitative responses can be shown to occur, for example, in the stochastic short-run model of Turnovsky (1983). That model also predicts an indeterminacy of the nominal exchange rate to supply shocks, and when one normalizes the two models for certain aspects of their specification (such as deflating the money supply by the CPI in the Turnovsky model), the conditions for the response of the exchange rate are almost the same. Finally, as Aizenman himself notes, the conditions for the overshooting of the exchange rate to monetary shocks is the same as in the Dornbusch model with flexible output. So overall, the qualitative responses of the economy to the two classes of disturbances are not too different from what more conventional macro models would predict.

Aizenman studies in some detail the effects of an increase in the degree of substitutability between domestic and foreign goods. He shows how this raises the responsiveness of output to the monetary shock but lowers the responsiveness of both the real and the nominal exchange rate, as well as the price level. Comparing this to the Turnovsky model, I now find some differences. A higher degree of substitutability has an analogous effect on output, as well as on the nominal and real exchange rates. But it now raises, not lowers, the response of the price level to a monetary shock.

The reason is straightforward. In either economy, as the degree of substitutability α increases, the real exchange rate becomes less flexible. More of the adjustment in the real sector in response to a monetary shock must be borne by output and less by the real exchange rate. But in the Turnovsky model, supply is determined by a Lucas supply function, or in other words, by price surprises. Output is therefore proportional to short-run price movements. Hence any increase in the responsiveness of output must be reflected by an increase in the responsiveness of the price level.

I now turn to the dynamic adjustment. The key feature of the dynamics is that the responses of prices and output to either a monetary or a supply shock accelerate over the n periods of the adjustment, which is determined by the contract length. This is in marked contrast to a conventional sluggish price model such as Dornbusch (1976), in which these responses decelerate over time and take an infinite time to complete. As a further contrast, the Lucas-Gray one-period contract model yields no persistence from such shocks; the adjustment is completed within just one period.

The reason for the dynamics in the Aizenman model stems from the relationship relating the average price at time t to the prices set by the individual producers at that time, namely, $\bar{p}_t = \frac{1}{n}[p_{t,0} + p_{t,1} + \ldots + p_{t,t-n}]$. Over time, an increasing number of firms will renegotiate their contracts. Since their wages rise, they increase their prices by a greater amount than do those producers whose wages are preset by preexisting contracts. The more firms that go through the renegotiating cycle, the larger the increase in the average price level, although this process comes to an abrupt halt after time n, when all firms have renegotiated.

The dynamic time paths illustrated in figures 6.3 and 6.4 of Aizenman's paper are strong predictions of the model, and one may quite naturally ask whether these are likely to be the kind of dynamics one observes in response to a monetary disturbance. While one might doubt that this is the case, it is intriguing to note that the dynamic time path for the average price $\bar{p}_t$ illustrated in figure 6.3 is identical to that encountered in simple models which analyze the effects of "announced" monetary disturbances. More specifically, consider the dynamics of the Cagan model as described in Sargent and Wallace's (1973) well-known paper. As their analysis showed, a monetary expansion announced at time 0, say, to take effect at time $T > 0$, will lead to an adjustment path in the price level identical to that of figure 6.3. There is an initial jump increase in the price level, with steady acceleration until time T, when the announced monetary expansion takes place and the adjustment is completed. The acceleration reflects the fact that during the adjustment phase, the economy is following an unstable dynamic time path. There is a parallel here, since the contract which presets wages over a number of periods serves very much as an announcement.

Aizenman's model is of course based on several simplifying assumptions, and I would like to briefly comment on two. The first is the assumption that the supply of labor is inelastic. If one were to drop this assumption and assume instead that the supply of labor depends upon the expected real wage rate, we would immediately introduce two real wage rates into the model. While producers would evaluate the real wage in terms of the price of their good, workers would base their decisions on the real wage defined in terms of the consumer price index. In the standard Gray-type contract models, this distinction complicates the contract somewhat, and it must surely do so here as well.

Secondly, the demand for money is assumed to be interest inelastic. If instead the demand for money were to depend upon the interest rate, forward-looking behavior would be introduced into price setting. As it stands, the price equation (12) is entirely backward looking.

Misalignment of Exchange Rates

The model presented is a descriptive one. It tells us how the economy responds to the two types of disturbances introduced in the paper. But it is well known from previous work on stochastic macroeconomics that the impact of shocks depends critically upon the policy regimes in operation. In particular, it will depend upon (1) monetary–exchange market policy and (2) labor market–wage indexation policy. This is touched upon briefly in the paper, but it would seem to merit further discussion.

Long-run optimal real exchange rate equilibrium is defined by the flexible price model through the relation $\tilde{s} \equiv \tilde{e} + \tilde{p}^* - \tilde{p} = q/\alpha$, where $\tilde{}$ denotes steady-state levels. One can then view the deviation of the current real exchange rate s from s, $(s - \tilde{s})$ as a measure of real exchange rate misalignment. An important question to address is how wage indexation and monetary rules, based on responding to the misalignment $s - \tilde{s}$ and the shocks this embodies, can be designed to achieve some specified optimality objective. This is a natural extension of previous work by Aizenman and Frenkel (1985) and Turnovsky (1987). These studies emphasize the tradeoffs and interdependence between labor market and monetary policies under different sets of information structures. The existence of multiperiod wage contracts raises the question of the optimal degrees of indexation of different wages at different points in the contract cycle. Aizenman's paper could be extended to examine this issue.

References

Aizenman, J. Forthcoming. Monopolistic competition, relative prices, and output adjustment in the open economy. *American Economic Review*.

Aizenman, J., and J. A. Frenkel. 1985. Optimal wage indexation, foreign exchange market intervention, and monetary policy. *American Economic Review* 75:402–23.

Dornbusch, R. 1976. Expectations and exchange rate dynamics. *Journal of Political Economy* 84:1161–76.

Gray, J. A. 1976. Wage indexation: A macroeconomic approach. *Journal of Monetary Economics* 2:221–35.

Sargent, T. J., and N. Wallace. 1973. The stability of models of money and growth with perfect foresight. *Econometrica* 41:1043–48.

Turnovsky, S. J. 1983. Wage indexation and exchange market intervention in a small open economy. *Canadian Journal of Economics* 16:574–92.

———. 1987. Optimal monetary policy and wage indexation under alternative disturbances and information structures. *Journal of Money, Credit, and Banking* 19:157–80.

7 On the Effectiveness of Discrete Devaluation in Balance of Payments Adjustment

Louka T. Katseli

7.1 Introduction

> The realignment of exchange rates which have been disaligned for a long time can never be a precision job; it is usually a hit-or-miss business based on impressionistic guesses and hunches. . . . Economists who know that delays in adjustment are wasteful and that large adjustments cause unnecessary disruption have for years recommended that exchange rates be realigned without delay and by smaller changes . . . (F. Machlup 1970:69)

Almost twenty years ago, in his Horrowitz lectures, *The Alignment of Foreign Exchange Rates,* F. Machlup identified three important aspects of the process of exchange rate realignment that are still pertinent today: (*a*) that prolonged misalignment of the exchange rate is costly in real terms, that is, in terms of output and employment in an economy; (*b*) that realignment calls for an adjustment whose direction is usually known, but whose magnitude is not; and finally (*c*) that a system of frequent and small adjustments of the exchange rate is preferable to infrequent and large changes that are usually regarded as means of last resort.

The objective of this paper is to address itself to this last point, leaving aside such important methodological issues as the measurement

Louka T. Katseli is professor at the University of Athens, Greece, and a research associate at the Center for Economic Policy Research, London, and the National Bureau of Economic Research, Cambridge.

Partial financial support from the Ford and Sloan Foundations under the research program administered by CEPR on Macroeconomic Interactions and Policy Design in Interdependent Economies is gratefully acknowledged. The author is also grateful for research assistance by S. Zographakis and J. Anastassakou of KEPE, Athens, as well as helpful comments by A. Giovannini and R. Marston.

of exchange rate misalignment in relation to alternative definitions of the equilibrium real exchange rate.

The starting point of my analysis is the fact that most countries at different times in history find themselves in a situation where they would like to pursue an active exchange rate policy, that is, to change through appropriate action their real exchange rate, with a view towards improving their balance-of-payments position.[1] In such cases, either by itself or as part of a broader policy package, nominal exchange rate adjustment is the usual course of action.

A devaluation of the exchange rate is expected to lead to a real exchange rate depreciation and thus to increased trade competitiveness that is sooner or later translated into an improved trade position.

It has long been recognized that under certain conditions, a nominal devaluation (or revaluation) of the exchange rate might be ineffective in changing the real exchange rate, that is, in improving trade competitiveness. Domestic prices might in fact adjust fully to the exchange rate change, leaving relative prices unaffected. This could be due to structural characteristics of the economy, to the presence of intermediate goods, and/or to full wage indexation in the labor markets.[2]

More recently, the second step in the causal relationship between nominal exchange rate adjustment and trade performance has been questioned. In the context of the new strategic trade literature (Krugman 1986), it has been pointed out that in the presence of an oligopolistic market structure and of high fixed costs in entering third markets, increased price competitiveness might not be as powerful a policy instrument as we once thought for improving the balance of trade. In that view, a prolonged misalignment of the real exchange rate can change the industrial and trade structure enough that there will be long lags before a reversal in price competitiveness affects actual trade performance.

On theoretical grounds, therefore, the link between the nominal exchange rate and balance of payments adjustment can be questioned from quite different perspectives. However, the importance of these considerations in evaluating actual policy options is an empirical matter that varies enormously across countries and across time.

This paper presents a new twist to the traditional arguments pertaining to the potential ineffectiveness of nominal exchange rate adjustment on trade competitiveness. The main conclusion can be summarized as follows: Exchange rate management can have real effects. In other words, not only what you do, but how you do it, will affect price behavior of individual firms and thus the real exchange rate of the economy. A discrete devaluation of the exchange rate acts as a signal in the economy, strengthening expectations that not only aggregate demand but also marginal costs will increase. This causes faster price adjustment in the economy than would be the case under a crawling-peg system.

The theoretical justification of the above argument is presented in section 7.2. It is shown that not only structural characteristics of the economy, but market structure itself, alters the price effects of a nominal devaluation. Under oligopolistic competition and price-setting behavior on the part of firms, a discrete devaluation which increases the variance of the exchange rate increases the overall price level. It also increases the markup of prices over costs, which depends not only on the usual considerations but also on the expected variance of other firms' pricing decisions.[3] The analysis of section 7.2 thus extends and provides more rigorous theoretical underpinnings to the main hypothesis that was first presented in an earlier paper (Katseli 1986).

Section 7.3 presents empirical estimates of price adjustment under regime switching, using Greek monthly data for the period 1981:1–1985:12. This period was characterized by two large discrete devaluations on 9 January 1983 and 10 October 1985, while a crawling peg was followed during the rest of the period. It is shown that the variance of exchange rate changes, that is, the variable that captures exchange rate management differences, is an important determinant of price adjustment.

These results seem to validate the main hypothesis that a discrete realignment of the exchange rate, as opposed to a smooth and continuous path of adjustment, can limit the effectiveness of exchange rate policy in improving trade competitiveness.

7.2 Imperfect Competition and the Effectiveness of Discrete Devaluation

Imperfect competition is a pervasive characteristic of modern industrial economies. It is even more so in semiindustrialized and/or developing economies. Different degrees of concentration in product markets, extensive product differentiation, and unionization give rise to price-setting behavior in both commodity and labor markets.

As Okun has noticed, "even firms with minuscule market shares put price tags on their commodities; in the short-run, they are never surprised by the price, and always subject to surprise about the quantities they sell" (Okun 1975, p. 360). Yet most macroeconomic models assume that markets are perfectly competitive. There are some notable recent exceptions that are still mostly limited to a closed-economy framework (Hart 1983; Rotemberg 1982; Sheshinski and Weiss 1983; Aizenman 1984, 1986).

In a recent paper, Dixon (1986) presents a simple closed-economy model of imperfect competition with Walraysian features that can be easily compared with more traditional macromodels. Imperfect competition in the product market is modeled by Dixon using conjectural-variations Cournot equilibrium that captures a wide range of possible market solutions encompassing perfect competition and Cournot and joint profit maximization as special cases.

While maintaining the simplicity of macromodeling provided by Dixon, the framework of imperfect competition adopted here is one of Bertrand competition with differentiated products, thus assuming differentiated prices and price-setting firms.

For each firm i in the market producing commodity i, there is an expected direct demand for output curve which is given by equation (1):

$$Ex_i = 1 - P_i + a E\tilde{P}_j. \tag{1}$$

The expected demand for each firm's output is a negative function of its own price, as well as a positive function of the expected, unobservable aggregate price that would be established in the market for substitute commodity j.

The expectations operator E refers to firm i's ex ante expectations, that is, before it finalizes its pricing decision, and a is the cross-price elasticity of demand, which is positive and smaller that unity ($0 < a \leq 1$) in the case where commodities are substitutes. Firm i forms its expectations about the aggregate market price of competitive output j by observing the pricing decisions of a neighboring firm j.

The overall price that will be determined by firm j, P_j, will depend on a firm-specific disturbance R_j with mean $\bar{R}_j$ and on the aggregate price component $\tilde{P}_j$ with mean $\bar{P}_j$. Thus,

$$P_j = R_j + \tilde{P}_j \text{ where} \tag{2}$$

$$R_j = \bar{R}_j + \epsilon_1 \text{ and}$$

$$\tilde{P}_j = \bar{P}_j + \epsilon_2.$$

Given the above, the expectational probability of other firms' pricing decisions can be expressed as a function of P_j. In other words,

$$E\tilde{P}_j = \vartheta P_j \text{ and} \tag{3a}$$

$$\vartheta = \frac{\sigma^2_{\tilde{P}j}}{\sigma^2_{Rj} + \sigma^2_{\tilde{P}j}}, \text{ where} \tag{3b}$$

ϑ is the ratio of the variance of the aggregate market component to the sum of the variance of the firm-specific and aggregate component. As the variance of the aggregate price component increases, ϑ and $E\tilde{P}_j$ increase, and this leads firm i to expect a positive increase in the demand for its output.

The expected demand for output curve as given by equation (1) relates expected output of firm i to the firm's own price and the expected aggregate price that would be established in the domestic market for substitute commodities. Import prices are not explicitly modeled here, but this can easily be done without changing the qualitative nature of the results. Alternatively, one can assume perfect substitution in demand between the imported good and commodity j and thus identify commodity j with the tradable commodity and commodity i with the nontradable.

The final step in the argument is to relate the variance of the aggregate price index to the variance of the exchange rate. In a previous article (Katseli 1984), I have shown that the two time series usually exhibit quite different time-series properties. Nominal exchange rate variability has been found to exceed domestic price variability, as there is relative sluggishness of domestic price adjustment in commodity markets as opposed to financial markets. However, in cases where the exchange rate is managed, the variability of the price index is apt to be positively correlated to nominal exchange rate variability. Under a crawling-peg regime, the smooth and continuous adjustment of the exchange rate to economic fundamentals eventually becomes fully anticipated by private market participants and is reflected in a gradual adjustment of prices. Alternatively, if large and discrete adjustments of the exchange rate take place, then there is apt to be price recontracting and thus fast adjustment of prices in response to the "information signal" received in the market about future cost and demand conditions (Katseli 1986). Thus, in cases of managed floating it is reasonable to expect a positive relationship between exchange rate and price variability. Hence,

$$\sigma^2_{Pj} = f(\sigma^2_e) \text{ where } f' > 0. \tag{4}$$

Given the above, equation (1) can be rewritten as

$$Ex_i = 1 - P_i + a\vartheta P_j \text{ where} \tag{5}$$

$$\vartheta = g(\sigma^2_e) \qquad \text{and } g' > 0.$$

According to equation (5), an increase in the variance of the exchange rate would give rise to a positive expected shock in demand for firm i's output.

If marginal costs for each firm are given and are equal to C, then under Bertrand-Nash competition the payoff function for each firm is given by (6):

$$\Pi_i(P_i,P_j) = P_i \,.\, Ex_i - Ex_i \,.\, C = Ex_i(P_i - C). \tag{6}$$

Substituting (5) into (6), it follows that

$$\Pi_i(P_i,P_j) = (1 - P_i + a\vartheta P_j)(P_i - C). \tag{7}$$

Profit maximization implies that the price charged by the firms P_i and P_j will depend positively on ϑ. Specifically,

$$(8) \qquad P_i = \frac{1 + a\vartheta P_j + C}{2}.$$

If the two neighboring and competing firms are symmetric, then the Bertrand price is given by (9) and the price-cost margin, μ, by (10):

$$(9) \qquad P^b = \frac{1 + C}{2 - a\vartheta}.$$

$$(10) \qquad \mu = \frac{P^b - C}{P^b} = \frac{1 - C(1 - a\vartheta)}{1 + C}.$$

As ϑ increases, both P^b and μ increase.

The marginal cost structure of each firm can also be uncertain. Thus C_i can be specified to have a local component, W_i, that is, wages, with mean $\bar{W}_i$ and an unobservable aggregate market component, $\tilde{C}_j$. Expectations about that component of marginal costs can be formed as before through observation of the neighboring firm's marginal cost structure. In turn, firm j's marginal costs depend on W_j and the aggregate market component. Thus,

$$(11) \qquad EC_i = W_i + E\tilde{C}_j \text{ and}$$

$$(12) \qquad C_j = W_j + \tilde{C}_j.$$

From (11) and (12), it follows that

$$(13) \qquad E\tilde{C}_j = \varphi C_j, \text{ where as before,}$$

$$\varphi = \frac{\sigma_{\tilde{C}_j}}{\sigma_{\tilde{C}_j} + \sigma_W}.$$

As the variance of the aggregate cost component increases, firm i anticipates an incipient increase in its marginal cost structure. The variance of the aggregate cost component can now be associated with the variance of the exchange rate, either directly through the cost of imported inputs or indirectly through the final price of domestically produced inputs j in an input-output framework. Thus,

$$(14) \qquad \sigma_{\tilde{C}_j} = Z(\sigma_e^2), \text{ where } Z' > 0.$$

As the variance of the exchange rate increases, marginal costs are expected to increase, and this will be reflected in both the Bertrand price and the markup established in the market. Specifically, under a probabilistic distribution of marginal cost changes, equations (9) and (10) will be replaced by (15) and (16):

$$(15) \qquad P^b = \frac{1 + \bar{W} + \varphi\bar{C}}{2 - a\vartheta}$$

$$(16) \qquad \mu = \frac{P^b - E\bar{C}}{P^b} = \frac{1 - (1 - a\Theta)(\bar{W} + \phi\bar{C}}{1 + \bar{W} + \phi\bar{C}}$$

$$\text{where } \bar{W} = \frac{Wi + Wj}{2} \text{ and } \bar{C} = \frac{Ci + Cj}{2}.$$

An increase in the variance of the exchange rate raises both φ and ϑ, and P^b increases unambiguously. The effects on the price-cost margin, however, seem uncertain, since an increase in ϑ raises μ, while an increase in φ reduces it. It is easy to show, however, that for a given change in σ_e^2, $\frac{\partial\mu}{\partial\vartheta}$ will be larger than $\frac{\partial\mu}{\partial\varphi}$ since α, ϑ and φ are all smaller than unity. Thus not only P^b but also the price-cost margin is raised in the economy as the variance of the exchange rate increases.

This implies that in the context of oligopolistic competition and price-setting behavior, a policy of discrete devaluation which increases the variance of exchange rate changes will produce faster domestic price adjustment than a policy of crawling peg.

It will also lead to a higher markup in the economy and thus a shift in the income distribution towards profits. From the point of view of the effectiveness of exchange rate policy in balance-of-payments adjustment, a policy of discrete devaluation, as opposed to that of a crawling peg, will lessen the expected improvement in price competitiveness as a result of the devaluation. This is so because, ceteris paribus, the real exchange rate will not adjust as much to the nominal exchange rate change.

These propositions are tested empirically on Greek monthly data in section 7.3.

7.3 Empirical Evidence

Despite a significant drop in OECD inflation since 1981, inflation in Greece continued to be high during the early eighties. While it was slowly but steadily reduced from about 25% in 1981 to 16.7% in mid-July 1985, it accelerated again in 1985 as inflationary expectations were reversed during the second half of the year.

In a recent paper that analyzes the determinants of consumer price inflation in Greece on annual data spanning the period 1963–84, Alogoskoufis (1986) concludes that in the period 1980–84, the inflation performance can be largely attributed to exchange rate movements. Nominal wage inflation and the productivity slowdown made relatively small contributions to the rate of price adjustment, while excess monetary growth did not prove to be an important determinant of inflationary pressures.

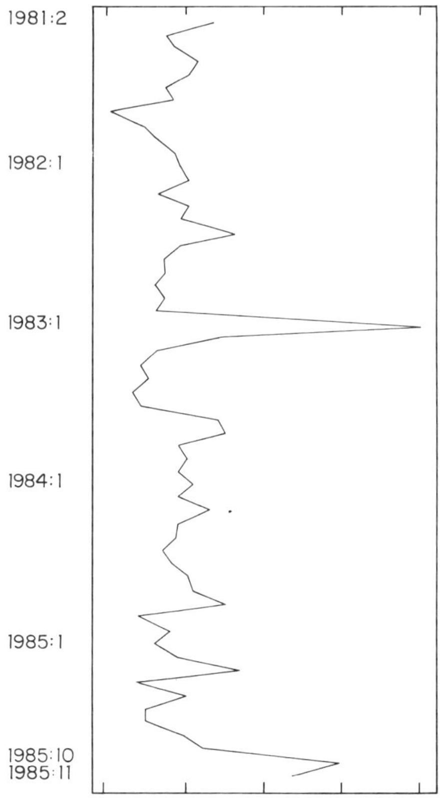

Fig. 7.1 Monthly rate of change of the nominal exchange rate (NNEER), 1981:2–1985:11.

The first part of the 1980s was in fact characterized by two discrete devaluations of the nominal exchange rate. The first took place on 9 January 1983 and the second two-and-a-half years later, that is, on 10 October 1985.

Figures 7.1, 7.2, and 7.3 present (*a*) the monthly rate of change of the nominal effective exchange rate (NNEER) based on the basket of 12 currencies that the Central Bank follows, (*b*) the variance of NNEER over the preceding three-month period (VR3) and (*c*) real exchange rate developments calculated on the basis of the nominal effective exchange rate and the relative consumer price indices of Greece and its main trading partners (REER).

The two episodes of discrete exchange rate adjustment are clearly evident from figures 7.1 and 7.2, while figure 7.3 highlights the reversal of real exchange rate depreciation within the first quarter of 1983 fol-

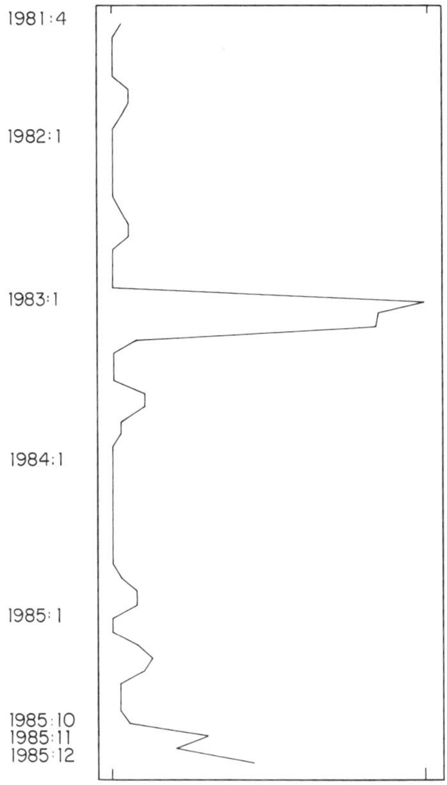

Fig. 7.2 Variance of NNEER over the preceding three-month period (VRT3).

lowing the January devaluation. The same thing actually occurred in the last quarter of 1985.

As can be seen in figures 7.4 and 7.5, what actually took place was a sharp acceleration of inflation as measured not only by the consumer price index (NPGRI) but also the wholesale price index for nontraded goods (NTELPR). The adjustment of prices was almost contemporaneous in 1983 and actually preceded the devaluation in 1985.

In light of this evidence and the theoretical analysis of section 7.2, the objective of the empirical section is to investigate the role of the variance of exchange rate changes in domestic price adjustment.

Following the eclectic approach provided by Alogoskoufis (1986), inflation is considered as both cost-push and structural, as well as demand-pull.

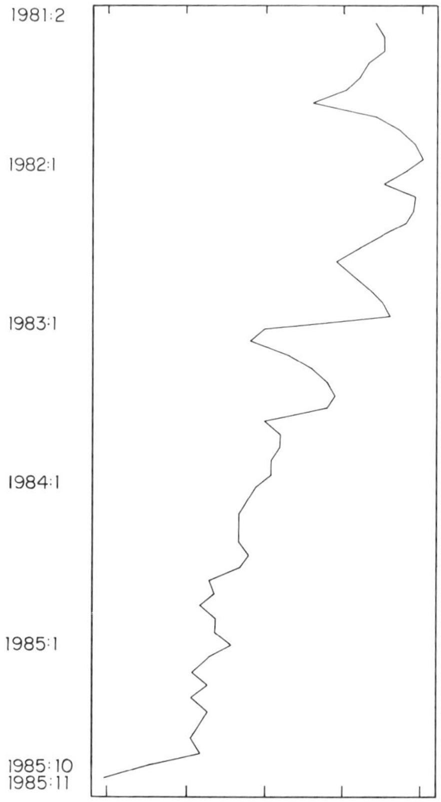

Fig. 7.3 Real exchange rate developments (REER), 1981:2–1985:11.

A cost-push structural interpretation of inflation can be easily modeled along the lines of the so-called Scandinavian model (Aukrust 1977; Edgren, Faxen, and Odhner 1973). As Alogoskoufis (1986) has shown, the underlying model can be extended in a number of ways to yield more general empirical specifications. Tradables can be allowed to be imperfect substitutes, so that their domestic price will depend on both international factors and domestic factors such as domestic labor costs and productivity. According to the structural view, demand factors do not affect domestic price inflation, which is determined solely by world price developments, exchange rate depreciations, wage increases relative to productivity, and changes in indirect taxes. One way to allow for an independent role for monetary influences on inflation is to assume that price increases in both the tradable and nontradable sectors are also due to excess monetary growth (Alogoskoufis 1986). This theoretical extension allows maximum flexibility of specification, and it can

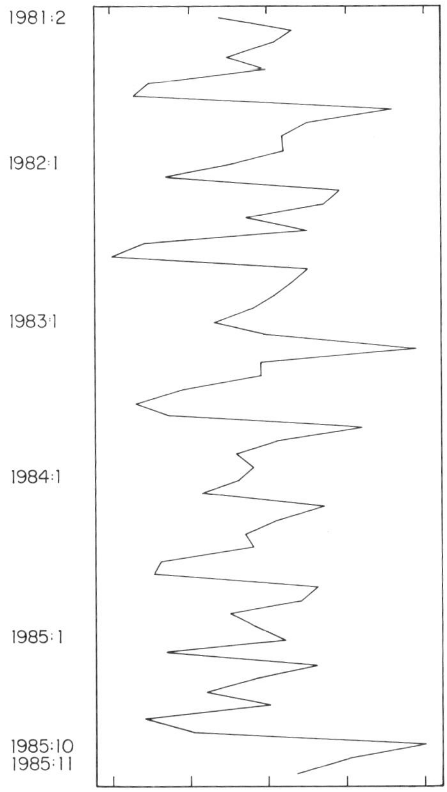

Fig. 7.4 Monthly rate of change of the consumer price index (NPERI), 1981:2–1985:11.

encompass under alternative restrictions not only a cost-push view of inflation but also simple monetary models of the inflationary process in small open economies. Finally, real wage adjustment can be assumed to depend on output market tightness and expectations of future price behavior.

Given the above, and following my analysis in section 7.2, where the variance of exchange rate changes is an important determinant of price adjustment, the following inflation equation was estimated:

$$(17) \quad \hat{P}_t = a_0 + a_1 \hat{W}_{t-i} + a_2 (\hat{P}_w + \hat{e}_t) + a_3 VR3 + a_4 \hat{q}_t + a_5 r_t + a_6 O_t + a_7 \hat{P}_{t-i}$$ where

$\hat{P}_t$ = the rate of change of the consumer price index (NPGRI), or alternatively, of the wholesale price index of nontraded goods (NTELPR) as estimated by the National Statistical Service.

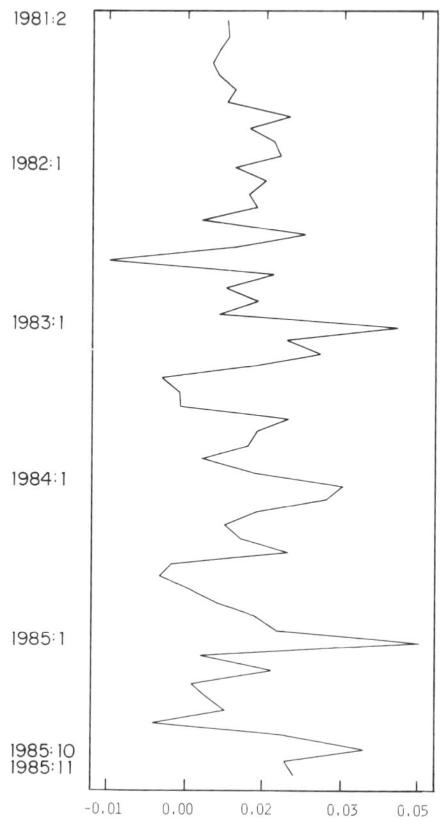

Fig. 7.5 Monthly rate of change of the wholesale price index for non-traded goods (NTELPR).

$\hat{W}_{t-i}$ = the rate of change of the wage rate in the manufacturing sector of the economy under alternative lag specifications.
$\hat{P}_w$ = the world rate of inflation.
$\hat{e}$ = the rate of change of the nominal effective exchange rate (NNEER).
VR3 = the variance of $\hat{e}$ over the past three months (including month t).
$\hat{q}_t$ = the rate of change of average labor productivity measured as industrial output over industrial employment.
r_t = deviations of output from trend calculated as the residual obtained from an estimated equation where industrial production is regressed against a constant and a time trend.
O_t = a proxy of excess monetary growth, that is, the rate of change of the nominal money supply minus the rate of change of long-run money demand as calculated by Alogoskoufis (1986). Specifically, $O = \hat{m} - \hat{y} + 6.57\,\Delta r$, where Δr is the change in the opportunity cost of $M1$.

$\hat{P}_{t-i}$ = the lagged dependent variable.

It should be noted that in equation (17) the variance of the exchange rate is assumed to have an influence on the domestic price separate from the influence of the exchange rate itself.

The main results are presented in table 7.1. All equations were estimated with a constant and monthly seasonal dummies using ordinary least squares.

The results appear markedly better in explaining variations of the consumer price index, as opposed to variations in the price of nontraded goods.

In both cases, contemporaneous wage inflation ($\hat{w}_t$) seems to be an important determinant of price movements. Productivity growth ($\hat{q}_t$) and deviations of output from trend (r_t) have the expected effect on NPGRI, while they do not seem to influence NTELPR. The opposite happens with excess monetary growth (O_t), which exerts a significant inflationary impact as this is measured by NTELPR.

World inflation and/or the contemporaneous change of the nominal effective exchange rate do not appear to be important independent determinants of monthly price adjustments during this period. The effect of these on the dependent variable is probably picked up by the constant term, which appears in all cases statistically significant. Instead, the variance of exchange rate changes over the past three months (VR3) proves to be a significant explanatory variable, as our theory would seem to indicate. The significance of VR3 is maintained even when the rate of change of the exchange rate ($\hat{e}_t$) is introduced as an independent explanatory variable.

As the variance of the exchange rate increased with the shift from a crawling-peg regime to that of a discrete devaluation, prices adjusted fast, as we would have expected. As was explained in section 7.2, the two discrete devaluations strengthened expectations that all prices in the market would be raised accordingly. This led to more rapid price adjustment which could be justified readily to potential customers as they themselves observed the signal. Thus, not only did the process of imperfect competition between firms lead to increased markups for the participants, but this was readily accepted by consumers, who were the net losers in the process.

Explaining monthly deviations of a price index which is highly volatile is not an easy task. Yet the analysis suggests that, traditional factors aside, the variance of exchange rate changes seems to play an important role in explaining price behavior. What this also indicates is that during the period under consideration, expectations about future price developments were the driving force behind price-setting behavior of firms. This is consistent with other evidence regarding speculative movements in the economy, such as hoarding of final consumer goods

Table 7.1 **Estimates of Alternative Specifications of Monthly Price Adjustments in Greece: 1981:1–1985:12**

LHS	$\hat{P}_t$ = NPGRI				$\hat{P}_t$ = NTELPR	
RHS	1.1	1.2	1.3	1.4	2.1	2.2
$\hat{W}_t$	.2284(3.6)	.2305(3.7)	.2182(3.4)	.2198(3.5)	.1684(1.6)	.1853(1.9)
$\hat{W}_{t-1}$			−.0699(1.1)	−.0711(1.1)	−.0919(0.9)	
$\hat{W}_{t-2}$					−.0192(0.2)	
$\hat{P}_w$					.3142(1.4)	.3110(1.6)
$\hat{e}_t$	−0.1338(0.4)		−.0109(0.3)		.0819(1.2)	.0744(1.3)
VR3	2.8920(3.7)	2.7588(4.0)	2.4591(2.9)	2.3478(3.1)	2.1009(1.4)	2.6806(2.2)
$\hat{q}_t$	−.0756(2.7)	−.0751(2.8)	−.0752(2.7)	−.0748(2.7)		
r_t	.0626(2.9)	.0617(2.9)	.0568(2.5)	.0559(2.5)	.0457(1.4)	.0463(1.5)
o_t	.0002(0.3)	.0002(0.3)			.0022(2.0)	.0022(2.1)
$\hat{P}_{t-1}$			.1098(0.8)	.1095(0.8)	.0963(0.7)	
R^2	.902	.902	.905	.905	.639	.6261
DW	1.8	1.8	2.0	2.0	1.9	1.8

Note: t-ratios in parentheses.

and highly volatile import behavior by firms. From a policy perspective, this confirms the view that macroeconomic performance depends not only on economic fundamentals but to a large extent on the psychology of the market. This can be easily upset by careless exchange rate management.

Notes

1. The real exchange rate is equivalent either to the terms of trade in the context of a simple trade model with two countries that completely specialize in production, or to the relative price of traded to nontraded goods in the case of a small-country two-good model.

2. For a review, see Katseli (1983).

3. The type of oligopolistic competition (Cournot vs. Bertrand), the share of each firm in the market, and the cross-price elasticity of substitution are important determinants of the size of the markup.

References

Aizenman, J. 1984. Optimal price adjustment with time-dependent costs. NBER Working Paper no. 1319.

———. 1986. Monopolistic competition, relative prices, and output adjustment in the open economy. NBER Working Paper no. 1787.

Alogoskoufis, G. S. 1986. On the determinants of consumer price inflation in Greece. Birkbeck College Discussion Paper no. 189, (July).

Aukrust, O. 1977. Inflation in the open economy: A Norwegian model. In I. B. Krause and W. S. Salant, eds., *Worldwide inflation*. Washington, D.C.: Brookings Institution.

Dixon, J. 1986. A simple model of imperfect competition with Walraysian features. Birkbeck College Discussion Paper no. 186, (April).

Edgren, G., K. O. Faxen, and C. E. Odhner. 1973. *Wage formation and the economy*. London: Allen and Unwin.

Hart, O. 1983. A model of imperfect competition with Keynesian features. *QJE* 97:109–38.

Katseli, L. 1983. Devaluation: A critical appraisal of IMF'S policy prescriptions. *AER*, May.

———. 1984. Real exchange rates in the 1970s. In J. F. Bilson and R. C. Marston, eds., *Exchange rate theory and practice*. Chicago: University of Chicago Press.

———. 1986. Discrete devaluation as a signal to price setters: Suggested evidence from Greece. In S. Edwards and L. Ahamed, eds., *Economic adjustment and exchange rates in developing countries*. Chicago: University of Chicago Press.

Krugman, P. 1986. New thinking about trade policy. In P. Krugman, ed., *Strategic trade policy and the new international economics*. Cambridge: MIT Press.

Machlup, F. 1972. *The Alignment of Exchange Rates*. New York: Praeqer.
Okun, A. M. 1975. Inflation: Its mechanics and welfare cost. *BPEA:* 351–401.
Rotemberg, J. J. 1982. Sticky prices in the United States. *Journal of Political Economy* 90:1187–1212.
Sheshinski, E., and Y. Weiss. 1983. Optimum pricing policy under stochastic inflation. *Review of Economics Studies* 60:513–29.
Snower, D. 1983. Imperfect competition, under-employment, and crowding out. *Oxford Economic Papers* 35:245–70.

Comment Alberto Giovannini

The paper by Louka Katseli raises the question of the effects of different exchange rate regimes on price dynamics. The paper asserts that a regime with large and infrequent exchange rate changes is suboptimal, since—among other problems—these exchange rate changes are more quickly transferred into domestic prices. In my comments I will not deal with these claims, nor with the details of Katseli's analysis. Rather, I will first concentrate on the empirical data we are offered. Then I will discuss the predictions of alternative models of price setting by firms on the transmission of large and discrete exchange rate changes to domestic prices.

The Evidence

Katseli presents the results of regressions where the CPI inflation rate (or the inflation rate of an index of nontraded goods) is projected on lagged wage inflation, contemporaneous foreign-price inflation measured in drachmas, a variable representing productivity growth, a variable proxying for the business cycle, and a variable representing "excess" money growth (see the paper for a detailed description of these variables).

I view these regressions as an exercise in data description rather than empirical implementations of specific models or frameworks to test hypotheses. Indeed, the choice of the explanatory variables and the lag specification prevent us from interpreting these equations as reduced forms (most of the right-hand side variables are endogenous), while the estimation technique suggests that they should not be viewed as structural equations either.

Katseli's estimates contain an interesting result: a variable which effectively represents a dummy for the five months following the December 1982 devaluation of the drachma has a positive and large coef-

Alberto Giovannini is associate professor at the Graduate School of Business, Columbia University, faculty research fellow at the National Bureau of Economic Research, and Olin Fellow at the National Bureau of Economic Research.

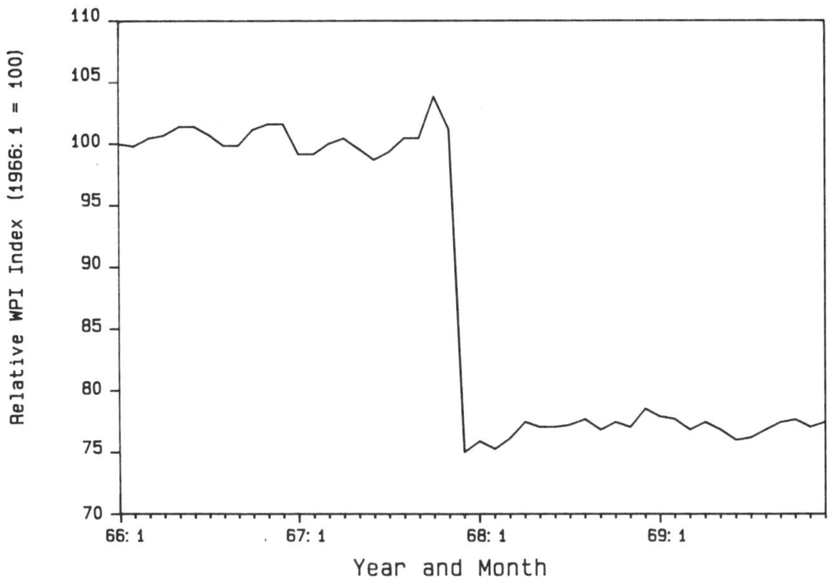

Fig. 7.6 Sterling devaluation in 1967; the U.K. WPI relative to the U.S. WPI.

ficient. In other words, after the 1982 devaluation the inflation rate increased over and above what was predicted by past wage inflation and all the other variables listed above. Figure 7.3 in Katseli's paper further illuminates the nature of the phenomenon described by these regressions. In the second half of 1982 there is a tendency for the real exchange rate to appreciate, a sign of acceleration of the inflation rate in Greece. In the five months following the devaluation, the real exchange rate recovers more than 50% of the initial depreciation, through an acceleration of domestic inflation.

Figure 7.1 reports the experience of the 1967 sterling devaluation. The figure reports an index of the U.K. wholesale price index relative to the U.S. wholesale price index. In correspondence of the devaluation of sterling, the index drops by about 25%. The difference in this case is that the fall in the relative price of domestic output caused by the exchange rate depreciation persists for two years after the devaluation. Both figure 7.6 and Katseli's figure 7.3, however, seem to be suggesting that the nominal exchange rate devaluations have large real effects and suggest that studying these experiences might illuminate the nature of price dynamics in these countries.

The Effects of Nominal Exchange Rate Changes: Nominal Contracts or Imperfect Information?

Can we interpret these experiences as evidence for or against alternative models of price dynamics? Models of price dynamics typically assume some departures from the standard neoclassical hypotheses and can be classified in two families. One family contains the sticky-prices models, stemming from Dornbusch (1976) and Taylor (1980).[1] They typically assume that transactions' imperfections prevent firms from fully adjusting to changes in demand and costs. This happens because firms set prices for more than one period, or because instantaneous price changes are costly. The second family contains the imperfect-information models originated by Lucas (1973) and Phelps (1969). Recent open economy applications of these models include Flood and Hodrick (1986) and Stockman and Koh (1986). The basic idea of these models is that individual agents, using the information at their disposal, cannot accurately tell relative demand fluctuations from aggregate nominal shocks.

These models have sharply different predictions of the channels through which a nominal exchange rate depreciation affects the real exchange rate. Consider the effects of an unanticipated, permanent nominal exchange rate devaluation that is not accompanied by any other exogenous shock. Sticky-prices models would predict a change in the real exchange rate whose size and persistence depends on the specific feature of the transactions' imperfections. In models with overlapping price setting, for example, the dynamics of the response depends on the distribution of the length of price setting across domestic firms.

What are the effects of unanticipated nominal exchange rate changes in imperfect information models? Clearly large nominal exchange rate devaluations are widely publicized events and are accurately perceived by all agents in the economy. Thus, misperceptions cannot justify any direct link between exchange rate realignments and the large observed fluctuations in relative prices. Nominal exchange rate changes, however, affect real wealth and spending by inducing fluctuations in the purchasing power of nominal money balances. In the two-sector model of Dornbusch (1973), for example, the decrease in real balance brought about by an exchange rate devaluation decreases domestic residents' spending. The decrease in total spending decreases the relative price of nontraded goods and thus the real exchange rate. The main channel of nominal exchange rate changes is in this case the real balance effect.

In conclusion, an analysis of large exchange rate devaluations coupled with a careful assessment of the empirical significance of these wealth effects should provide new and possibly illuminating evidence to help discriminate between these competing models of price dynamics.

1. See also the Aizenman paper in this volume.

References

Dornbusch, R. 1973. Devaluation, money, and nontraded goods. *American Economic Review* 63, no. 5 (December), pp. 871–80.

______. 1976. Expectations and exchange-rate dynamics. *Journal of Political Economy.*

Flood, R. P., and R. J. Hodrick. 1986. Money and the open economy business cycle: A flexible price model. NBER Working Paper no. 1967 (June).

Lucas, R. E. 1973. Some international evidence on output-inflation tradeoffs. *American Economic Review* 63:326–34.

Phelps, E. S. 1969. *Microeconomic foundations of employment and inflation theory.* New York: Norton.

Stockman, A., and A. T. Koh. 1986. Open-economy implications of two models of business cycle fluctuations. *Canadian Journal of Economics* (February): 23–34.

Taylor, J. B. 1980. Aggregate dynamics and staggered contracts. *Journal of Political Economy* 88 (February): 1–23.

8 Exchange Rates and U.S. Auto Competitiveness

J. David Richardson

8.1 Introduction and Overview

This paper develops unique disaggregated data to assess how changes in exchange rates, factor costs, and voluntary export restraints have affected recent price competitiveness in the U.S. passenger car market. The changes share a common feature. Each alters the relationship of the auto sector's prices abroad to those at home. This would seem in turn to influence various measures of competitiveness in predictable ways; indeed that is one of the principal purposes of sectoral policies like voluntary export restraints. Such sectoral policies also alter the relationship of the auto sector's prices to prices of other goods.

I find support for several familiar relationships. The support provided by the experience of the late 1970s is straightforward. The dollar's foreign-exchange value fell below its historical trend, in both nominal and cost-adjusted (real) terms, relative to the major suppliers of U.S. auto imports. U.S. price competitiveness tracked U.S. cost competitiveness quite closely, as average prices of U.S. automakers rose more slowly than those of their principal rival firms (all Japanese). Misalignment of the dollar toward weakness by historical norms was reflected

J. David Richardson is a professor of economics at the University of Wisconsin in Madison and a research associate of the National Bureau of Economic Research.

Richard C. Marston has been extremely helpful in criticism, suggestions, and provision of data for this paper. William H. Branson, Koichi Hamada, Takatoshi Ito, Motoshige Itoh, and Robert Z. Lawrence all made helpful comments on an earlier draft of a portion of the paper. Daniel Kaplan, Paul Lally, and James McElroy assisted the author in understanding and obtaining some of the other underlying data. This paper is part of the research program in international studies of the National Bureau of Economic Research, but neither it nor those mentioned above bear any responsibility for opinions expressed within; those are the author's alone.

in competitive relative pricing by U.S. auto firms, again with respect to a historical norm.

The support provided by the experience of the years 1980–85 is more complex and interesting. Relative to major auto suppliers, the effective nominal dollar rose gradually toward its level of the mid-1970s, but the effective real "auto dollar" rose much faster, increasing to a level well above its historical norm by early 1985. U.S. cost competitiveness deteriorated, not so much because of exchange rates, but because unit labor costs in manufacturing rose in the United States relative to those in major auto suppliers. U.S. auto price competitiveness began to deteriorate correspondingly, but soon stopped and instead improved gradually between 1982 and 1985. The Voluntary Restraint Arrangements (VRAs) with Japan, which began in 1981, seem to be the explanation for why the negative effects of exchange rates and costs on U.S. auto price competitiveness were swamped between 1982 and 1985. Average prices of U.S. automakers in fact rose more slowly than those of Japanese rival firms over this period, but they rose faster than other U.S. prices as measured by the consumer price index. In Japan, average prices on auto sales to the United States rose much faster than other Japanese prices.

"Offsetting strong forces" seems the best phrase for summarizing U.S. auto price competitiveness in the early 1980s. Average prices of U.S. automakers were at about the same level relative to Japanese rivals in 1985 as in 1980. Misalignment of the dollar toward strength by historical norms, and deteriorating labor cost competitiveness, which tended to undermine the competitiveness of U.S. auto firms, were offset by the Japanese VRAs, which buttressed it.

To arrive at these conclusions, I compiled a unique data set for effective exchange rates relevant to auto trade and for three U.S. automakers and three Japanese. The data were aggregated in ways suitable to detecting the influence of exchange rates, factor costs, and voluntary export restraints. Existing auto data, although abundant, were unsuitable for my purposes—inadequately disaggregated or inappropriately (even peculiarly) aggregated.

8.2 Inadequacies in Existing Data

Studies of recent U.S. auto trade encounter a number of data problems.[1] Lack of data is not one. There is a veritable car-nucopia of facts and figures. Yet not many are in a format suitable for empirical analysis. There are at least four important difficulties, each of which is addressed in this paper.

8.2.1 Lack of Suitable Exchange-Rate Series

Most researchers are confident that exchange rates have had some important influence on recent U.S. auto trade. Those who have attempted to estimate it have generally employed bilateral rates (e.g., between yen and dollars) or measures of overall effective exchange rates—based on aggregate trade dependence in all products.[2] Over most of the 1970s and 1980s, however, more than 90% of U.S. trade in passenger cars has involved just three trading partners: Canada, Germany, and Japan. An attempt is made below to compute effective exchange rates for these three suppliers and Britain that are appropriate for U.S. passenger car imports. Some surprising insights emerge.

8.2.2 Lack of Suitable Disaggregation

Some of the most readily accessible series on autos lump all domestic suppliers together, and their counterparts for U.S. auto imports lump all foreign suppliers together. This causes difficulties in several ways. First, exchange rates among the various import suppliers have moved quite differently over the past 15 years. Second, during the 1980s U.S. imports from Japan were restrained, and the effects of such discriminatory restraints on aggregate data may be hard to detect if imports from Canada or Europe expanded through trade diversion (see Dinopoulos and Kreinin 1987). Third, the United States and Canada produce virtually identical passenger cars, and intracorporate trade is free of border restraint; for some purposes, it may be better to count net auto imports from Canada as part of the U.S. auto sector rather than as shipments from abroad. Fourth, firm-by-firm competitiveness is interesting in its own right: General Motors (GM) and Honda may be more sheltered than other firms from exchange rates because of their global diversification. Disaggregation along all these lines is begun below, again with some surprising insights.

8.2.3 Inadequate Price Indexes

A number of price indexes for autos exist, yet some of the indexes mix together domestic and imported auto prices, and some mix together new and used car prices. Other indexes are relative newcomers, and many of the indexes are incestuously related to each other.[3] A first-pass attempt is made below to construct several price indexes that would be helpful for empirically assessing the impact of trade policy and exchange rates on the U.S. auto market.

8.2.4 Inadequate Measures of "Real" Variables

Some "real" variables that are available are untrustworthy principally because of the inadequate price indexes.[4] Other real data embody a surprising tolerance for simply adding up numbers of autos produced and imported, as if relative prices of foreign and domestic cars, large and small cars, stripped-down and spruced-up cars were always the same. An attempt is made below to recompute several important real variables for the auto sector as a natural extension of having recomputed the price indexes.

8.3 Effective Exchange Rates for U.S. Passenger Automobiles

Central to any assessment of how exchange rates affect U.S. auto competitiveness are measures of what is meant by "exchange rates" and "competitiveness." This section evaluates alternative measures of effective exchange rates for passenger automobiles in the U.S. market and one measure of U.S. auto cost competitiveness, comparing them to their counterparts for overall trade. Section 8.4 examines alternative measures of the price competitiveness of U.S. automakers and their Canadian affiliates relative to Japanese automakers and their U.S. affiliates and assesses their covariation with the auto exchange rates calculated below.

Figures 8.1 through 8.5 record six alternative measures of effective nominal auto exchange rates for the United States since 1974, computed

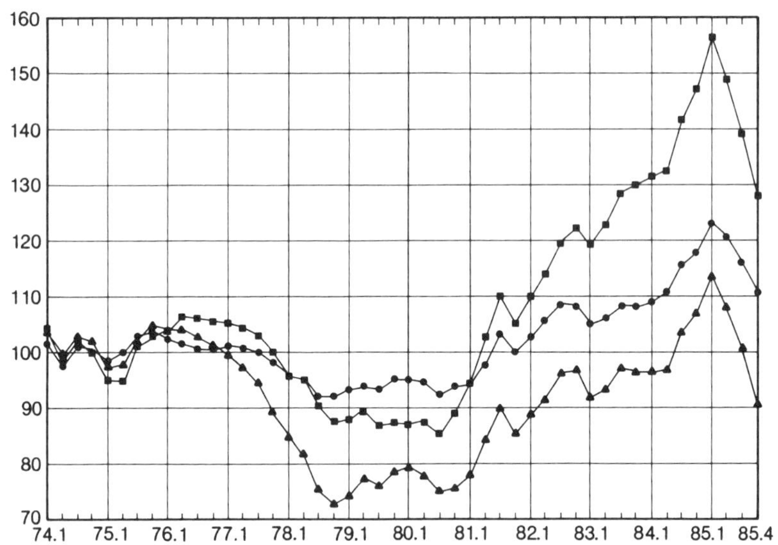

Fig. 8.1 Effective Exchange Value of the U.S. Dollar Overall and Two Measures of the Effective Nominal Auto Dollar: 1972–76 Weighted (Laspeyres) Indexes. ■ = Overall Dollar; ● = Auto Dollar with Canada; ▲ = Auto Dollar without Canada; 100 = March 1973.

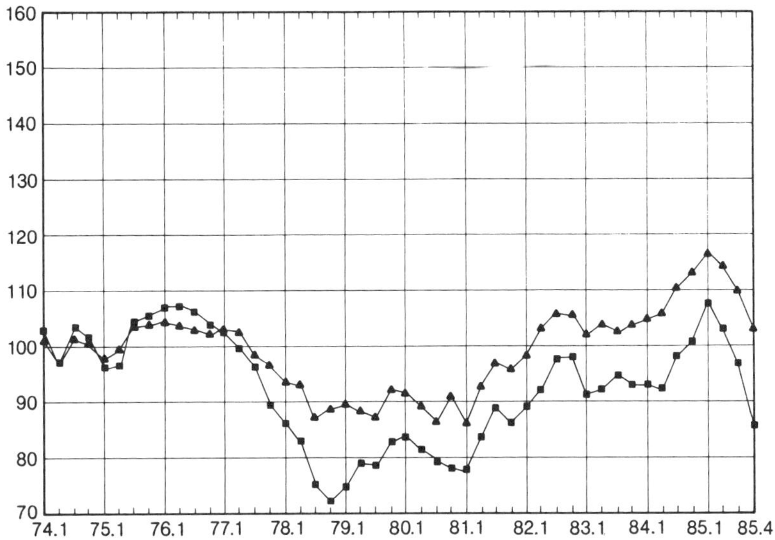

Fig. 8.2 Effective Nominal Auto Dollar with and without Canada: 1980 I, II Weighted (Laspeyres) Indexes. ▲ = Auto Dollar with Canada; ■ = Auto Dollar without Canada; 100 = March, 1973.

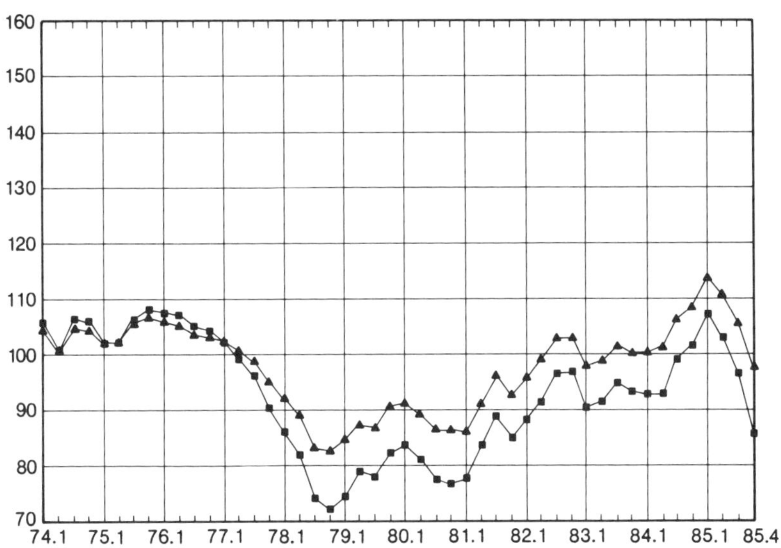

Fig. 8.3 Effective Nominal Auto Dollar with and without Canada: Current-Weight (Paasche) Indexes. ▲ = Auto Dollar with Canada; ■ = Auto Dollar without Canada; 100 = March, 1973.

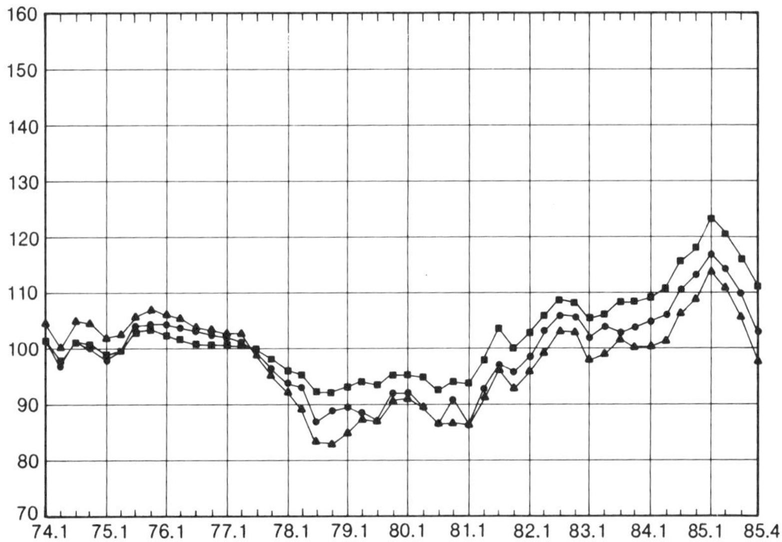

Fig. 8.4 Effective Nominal Auto Dollar with Canada: Alternative Weights. ■ = 1972–76 Weighted (Laspeyres) Indexes; ● = 1980 I, II Weighted (Laspeyres) Indexes; ▲ = Current-Weight (Paasche) Indexes; 100 = March 1973.

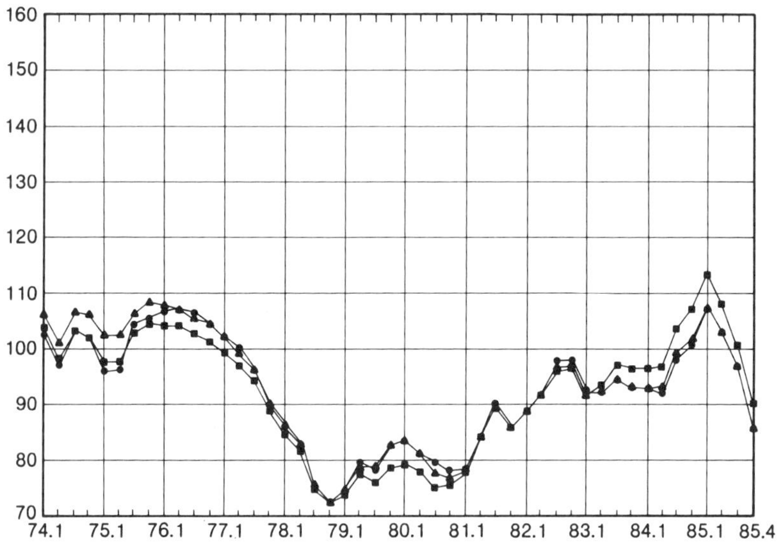

Fig. 8.5 Effective Nominal Auto Dollar without Canada: Alternative Weights. ■ = 1972–76 Weighted (Laspeyres) Indexes; ● = 1980 I, II Weighted (Laspeyres) Indexes; ▲ = Current Weight (Paasche) Indexes; 100 = March 1973.

quarterly. Figure 8.6 compares one of these to a labor-cost-adjusted ("real") measure of auto exchange rates. An "effective" exchange rate is a weighted averagc of bilateral exchange rates, where the weights often reflect trading-partner transaction shares. In all tables the weights are the value shares of total U.S. passenger car imports accounted for by Britain, Germany, and Japan, with and without Canada.[5] Bilateral exchange rates are expressed as index numbers of the strength (price) of the "auto dollar," with March 1973 = 100.

These series for the auto dollar are arguably broader measures of exchange rate pressures on U.S. auto manufacturing than the bilateral exchange rates used in other research. Effective exchange rates like these for other sectors have also been calculated recently by Arndt (1986), Belongia (1986), Clifton (1985), Dutton and Grennes (1985), Hartman (1986), and Marston (1986).

The first important question in calculating a measure of the auto dollar is whether the Canadian dollar should be included or excluded. In principle, the answer depends on the purpose of the calculation. Inclusion seems advisable for purposes of assessing the impact of exchange rates on U.S. geographical variables such as auto employment.

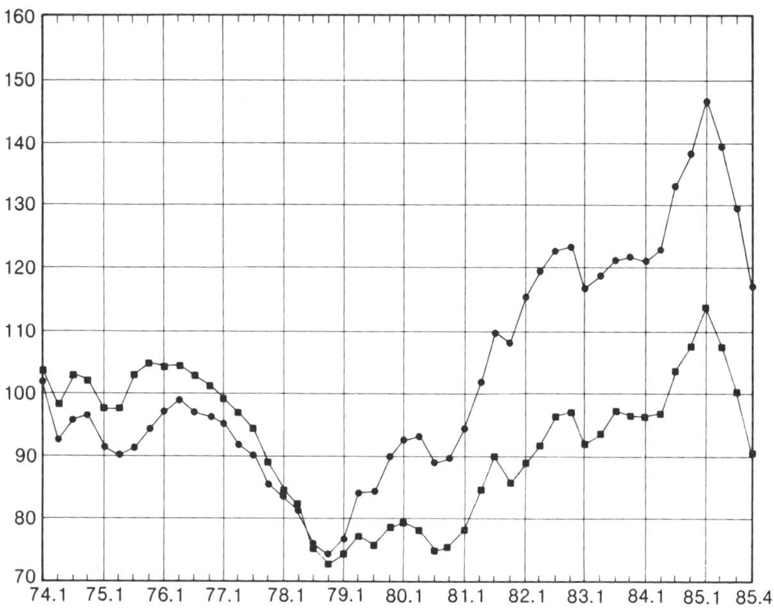

Fig. 8.6 Effective Real and Nominal Auto Dollar without Canada. ▪ = Nominal, 1972–76 Weighted (Laspeyres) Index from Figures 8.1 and 8.5; • = Real = Nominal Index Adjusted for Manufacturing Unit Labor Costs in U.S. and Rival Automaking Countries, Using Same Weights and Base; 100 = March 1973.

Exclusion seems advisable for purposes of assessing the impact of exchange rates on U.S. corporate variables such as Chrysler Corporation market share—Chrysler is free to trade across the U.S.-Canadian border without barriers. Inclusion or exclusion of Canada makes a significant difference in measuring the exchange value of the auto dollar. Two issues that turn out to make much less difference are whether the effective exchange rate index should be fixed weight or current weight, and whether fixed weights should represent trade shares from distant periods or from recent periods.[6]

Figures 8.1, 8.2, and 8.3 reveal the effect of Canada's inclusion or exclusion for alternative weighting schemes. Figures 8.1 and 8.2 differ from figure 8.3 in displaying fixed-weight indexes. One set of fixed weights represents average value shares of U.S. passenger car imports over the period 1972–76. These weights were chosen to make the auto indexes as comparable as possible to the Federal Reserve System's index of the overall weighted-average value of the U.S. dollar, based on 1972–76 global trade of the Group of Ten countries plus Switzerland. This aggregate index is plotted in figure 8.1 for reference, is also equal to 100 in March 1973, and is published monthly in the *Federal Reserve Bulletin*.[7] The other set of fixed weights represents average value shares of U.S. passenger car imports over the first two quarters of 1980. These weights were chosen because the period from late 1979 to late 1980 is often thought to represent a watershed in a number of ways for both auto trade and global economic trends.[8] Figure 8.3 differs from figures 8.1 and 8.2 in displaying current-weight indexes. Each period's set of bilateral exchange rate indexes is weighted by that period's value shares of trade. In general, the choices of weighting system and of base year for the fixed weights make very little difference to the effective value of the auto dollar. This can also be seen in either figure 8.4 or figure 8.5, where the alternative time trajectories for the effective auto dollar are packed tightly together.[9]

Excluding Canada makes a significant difference. The U.S. dollar was much weaker during most of the period in its command over non-Canadian autos than in its command over Canadian autos (which are, of course, usually identical to U.S. manufactured models). This finding arises, naturally, from the general weakening of the Canadian dollar, but its implications for U.S. auto competitiveness need emphasis. The exchange rate between the U.S. and Canadian dollar since the mid-1970s has worked against U.S. geographical competitiveness in auto production. One can interpret the gap between the trajectories in figures 8.2 and 8.3 as one component of a Canadian competitiveness edge in autos, which developed in the late 1970s and which has been more-or-less stable since then. This edge may have little impact on the global competitiveness of integrated U.S. automakers (GM, Ford, Chrysler) but a large impact on where in North America they expand and contract.[10]

A second important question in calculating a measure of the auto dollar is whether the real auto dollar moves differently from the nominal. One familiar way of measuring a real exchange rate is to adjust the nominal exchange rate for relative national factor costs. Indexes of unit labor costs are often employed for this purpose. In focusing on auto competitiveness, the natural choice might seem to be unit labor costs among major producing countries in that sector alone. Yet unit labor costs in all manufacturing, not just the auto sector, give an arguably better indicator of exogenous factor market pressures on auto producers—pressures beyond their ability to influence, in the same way as are exchange rate pressures. I have chosen this method of cost adjustment below. It is a way of detecting how endogenous auto price competitiveness measured in section 8.4 corresponds to (arguably) exogenous cost and exchange rate pressures measured in this section. My inferences are, of course, less meaningful the more insulated or divergent labor cost trends are in each country's auto sector from labor costs in other sectors.

Figure 8.6 reveals the effect of adjusting the nominal auto dollar for manufacturing unit labor costs in the United States relative to manufacturing unit labor costs in rival automaking countries.[11] Fixed weights are used in averaging cost trends across Britain, Germany, and Japan (Canada excluded), for 1972–76 trade shares as described above. The resulting cost-adjusted exchange rate index can be called a measure of the real auto dollar, but it is more revealingly a measure of the cost competitiveness of the U.S. auto sector. Figure 8.6 shows that there is a significant difference between auto cost competitiveness measured by the real auto dollar and the contribution that the nominal auto dollar alone makes to it.

Taken together, figures 8.1 through 8.7 reveal some striking observations on the effective value of the U.S. dollar for purposes of assessing U.S. auto competitiveness.

(1) The nominal auto dollar has been far weaker than the overall nominal dollar ever since 1975, as figure 8.1 reveals. Focusing on nominal rates alone makes it appear that U.S. automakers were protected more by the general weakening of the dollar in the late 1970s than other U.S. producers,[12] and that U.S. automakers were penalized less by the general strengthening of the dollar in the early 1980s than other U.S. producers. Indeed, if exchange rates of the mid-1970s are taken as an alignment norm, figure 8.5 shows that the nominal auto dollar has been weaker than normal from 1977 to date except from early 1984 to early 1985. By this norm, the past 15 years' nominal exchange rates have almost all been procompetitive (or protectionist) for U.S. auto firms, and not just those of the late 1970s.

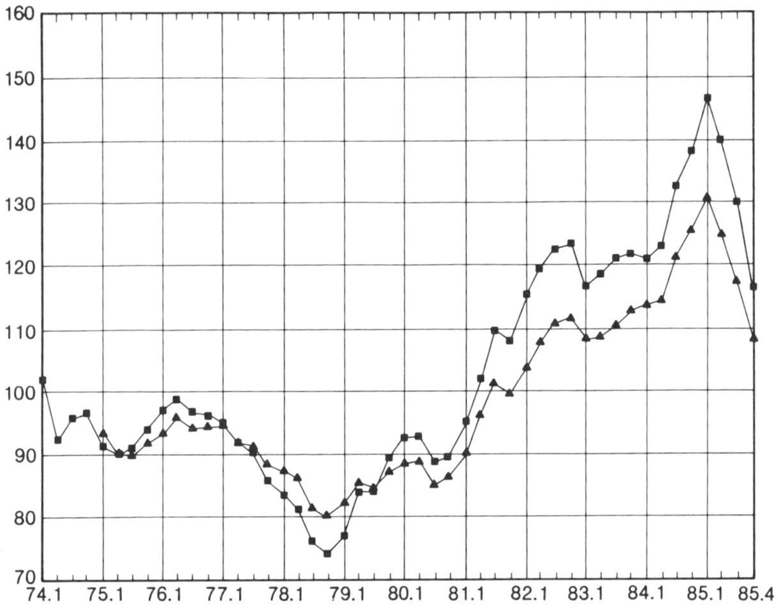

Fig. 8.7 Effective Real Auto Dollar without Canada and Effective Real U.S. Dollar Overall. ■ = Real Auto Dollar from Figure 8.6; ▲ = Effective Nominal Value of U.S. Dollar Overall, from Figure 8.1, adjusted for Manufacturing Unit Labor Costs in U.S. and Rival Trading Countries, Using Same Weights and Base; 100 = March 1973.

(2) But the account is quite different for the real auto dollar. The cost-adjusted auto dollar of figure 8.6 tracks the nominal auto dollar reasonably closely during the 1970s. Adjusting for trends in unit labor costs in the United States and its auto rivals if anything accentuates the procompetitive weakening of the dollar in this period. During the 1980s, however, the parallelism between real and nominal measures vanishes. The real auto dollar becomes progressively stronger than the nominal beginning around 1979. A marked anticompetitive rise in unit labor costs in the United States relative to the (auto-trade-weighted) average of unit labor costs in Britain, Germany, and Japan essentially eclipses the procompetitive sluggishness with which the nominal auto dollar creeps back toward its historical norm.[13] The result is remarkably similar 1980s trajectories for the overall nominal dollar in figure 8.1 and the real auto dollar in figure 8.6. In other words, whatever the advantage was that the U.S. auto sector enjoyed in the 1980s relative to other U.S. producers from confronting rivals whose currencies fell relatively slowly, this advantage was offset by a rapid rise in U.S. unit labor costs relative to these same rivals. In fact, it was perhaps more than offset, as the next paragraph suggests.

(3) The real auto dollar tracks the overall real dollar reasonably closely during the 1970s, as figure 8.7 reveals. During the 1980s, however, the real auto dollar rose progressively more steeply than the overall real dollar. So when exchange rates are adjusted for unit labor costs relative to principal foreign rivals, the U.S. auto sector appears increasingly uncompetitive in world markets relative to other U.S. producers during the 1980s—whereas unadjusted nominal exchange rates suggested exactly the opposite.[14] Trajectories of the 1980s overall dollar and auto dollar have an opposite relation to each other in figure 8.1 (nominal trends) and figure 8.7 (cost-adjusted trends).

Exchange rates and factor costs are obviously some of the most important exogenous contributors to sectoral competitiveness.[15] We turn in section 8.4 to two of its most important indicators, relative product prices and market shares.[16] We see if we can detect any of the expected correlations between relative prices or market shares and exchange rates or factor costs. The indicators of auto competitiveness I calculate are unique, applying to the three largest integrated North American automakers and to their largest three rivals (all Japanese).

8.4 Price Competitiveness for U.S. Passenger Automobiles

To what extent did U.S. auto prices and market shares reflect the international cost and exchange rate pressures described above? To what extent did they reflect other important changes, such as the Japanese VRAs? This section attempts an answer by describing measures of prices and market shares in the U.S. auto market and assessing their covariation with exchange rates, factor costs, and trade policy. Because of inadequacies in existing data aggregates (described in section 8.2), data were collected and constructed for the six firms with largest recent passenger car sales to U.S. buyers. The data were then reaggregated with an eye to detecting the covariations of interest. The six largest suppliers were General Motors (GM), Ford, Chrysler, Toyota, Nissan, and Honda. A data appendix to this paper outlines details for what follows, and is available from the author on request.

8.4.1 Disaggregated Prices by Firm

The U.S. Department of Commerce regularly publishes data on average transaction price per new car, broken down by U.S. domestic sales and imports.[17] Through 1985, the U.S. International Trade Commission regularly published data on maximum and minimum retail list prices by domestic and foreign automaker.[18] Remaining retail prices are, of course, distributed between the maximum and minimum in a way that could be described by a frequency distribution—one for each automaker. By assuming that each automaker has a comparable and symmetric distribution of model list prices between its own unique maximum and minimum, yet around the relevant average transaction price, I have blended the two data sources to obtain a time series of average transactions price per new car for each of the six largest automakers.[19]

These average transaction prices by firm are plotted in figures 8.8 and 8.9, normalized so that 1982's price = 100. Several features are notable. One is that some U.S. firms' average prices turn down after 1983, not only because the component price indexes do (e.g., Chrysler's maximum prices), but also because U.S. automakers' market share of the highest-price models begins to fall off.[20] A second feature is that variation across firms in these price trajectories is quite moderate, and especially slight for the Japanese firms.[21] Third, as a result, there is little indication that exchange rates or other exogenous fundamentals affect different Japanese firms differently or different U.S. firms differently. One might have surmised some such differences due, for example, to different multinationality of production among the firms (GM and Honda having more multinationality than others). In this regard there is only a very slight tendency for GM prices to be more stable over the period than Ford or Chrysler prices.

8.4.2 U.S. and Japanese Auto Price Indexes

These disaggregated average price indexes were then aggregated across firms by nationality to obtain an index of U.S. auto prices and

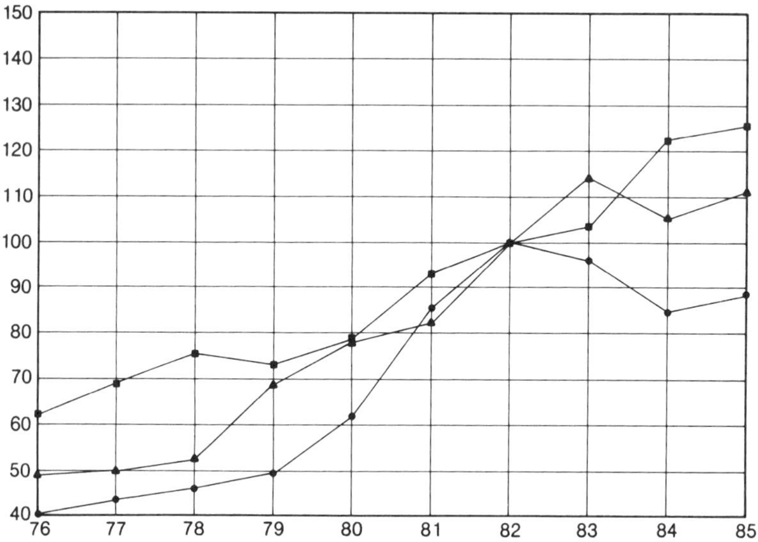

Fig. 8.8 U.S. Firms' Average Normalized Auto Prices. ■ = General Motors; ▲ = Ford; ● = Chrysler; 100 = 1982.

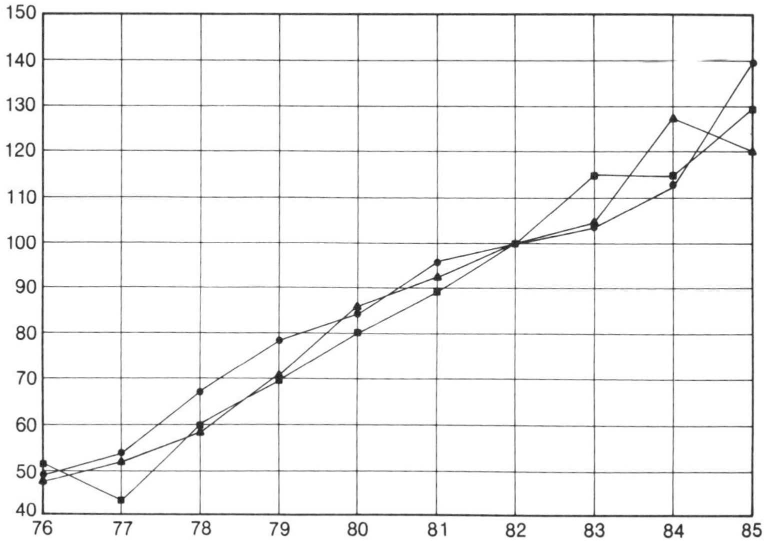

Fig. 8.9 Japanese Firms' Average Normalized Auto Prices. ■ = Toyota; ▲ = Nissan; ● = Honda; 100 = 1982.

an index of Japanese auto prices, both measuring average transaction prices on sales to U.S. buyers. Each index was a current-period weighted average of three firms' average prices, with weights representing each firm's share of real (constant 1982 dollar) U.S. sales of passenger cars.[22]

Figure 8.10 plots the resulting indexes, and figure 8.11 normalizes them by the U.S. Consumer Price Index (CPI) for all items. Table 8.1 records the year-to-year change in the U.S. auto price index relative to that for the Japanese firms. Several observations are notable.

(1) The 1970s feature auto price variation that is consistent in a straightforward way with the trends in the nominal and cost-adjusted exchange rates from figures 8.1–8.7. The relative price of U.S. to Japanese autos falls (U.S. price competitiveness improves) as the auto dollar declines from 1977 through 1979, and by a roughly comparable magnitude.

(2) The 1980s feature auto price variation that is more complex and more interesting. As the nominal and cost-adjusted auto dollar begin rising after 1979, U.S. auto price competitiveness begins to decline (with a slight lag) as expected. But it does not continue to decline as the dollar continues to rise. On the contrary, U.S. auto price competitiveness improves (U.S. auto prices fall relative to Japanese) from 1982 through 1985. This improved price competitiveness is especially striking in contrast to the deterioration in U.S. cost competitiveness suggested by the real exchange rates of figures 8.6 and 8.7. The contrast

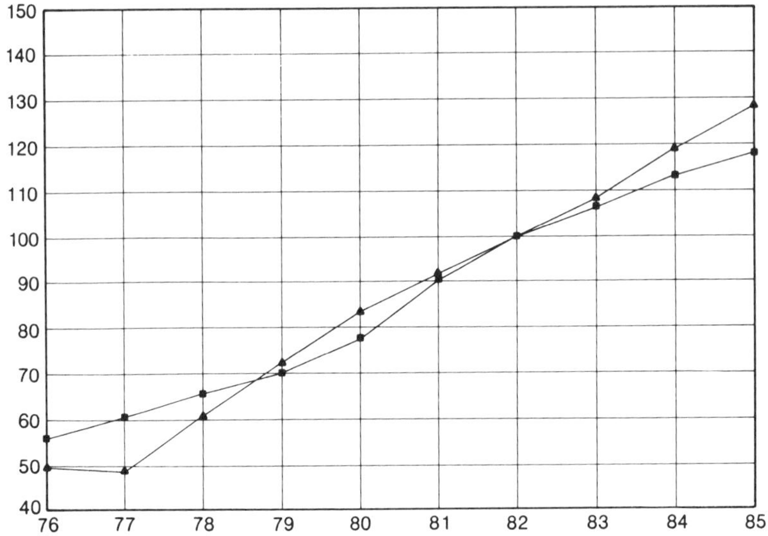

Fig. 8.10 Average Normalized Auto Prices of U.S. Firms and Japanese Firms. ■ = U.S. Firms; ▲ = Japanese Firms; 100 = 1982.

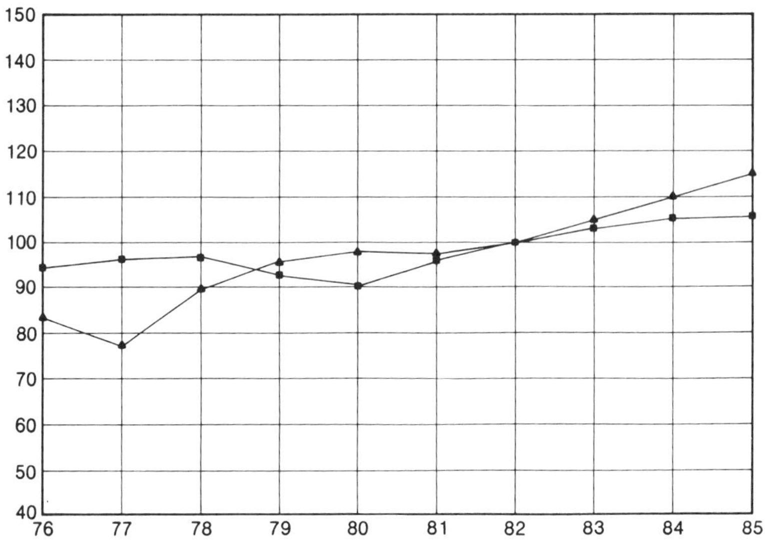

Fig. 8.11 Average Normalized Auto Prices of U.S. Firms and Japanese Firms Relative to U.S. Consumer Price Index. ■ = U.S. Firms; ▲ = Japanese Firms; 100 = 1982.

Table 8.1 **Changes in Big-Three U.S. Auto Prices Relative to Big-Three Japanese Auto Prices (Percentage Change in Aggregate Normalized Price Index)**

Period	Percentage Change
1977 over 1976	10.29
1978 over 1977	−13.12
1979 over 1978	−10.38
1980 over 1979	−4.58
1981 over 1980	6.38
1982 over 1981	1.51
1983 over 1982	−1.73
1984 over 1983	−3.14
1985 over 1984	−3.59

Source: Data underlying figure 8.10 or 8.11.
Notes: U.S. big three are General Motors, Ford, Chrysler. Japanese big three are Toyota, Nissan, Honda.

between price and cost competitiveness hints at either a profit squeeze among U.S. automakers or a profit surge among their foreign rivals on sales in the U.S. market.

(3) The Japanese VRAs and oligopolistic auto market structure are ingredients that give these trends explanation and coherence. Trends in cost competitiveness and price competitiveness need not be parallel when abnormal profits can persist due to entry barriers. Since a VRA pressures Japanese suppliers to raise their prices relative to U.S. automakers, its effects counteract the opposing pressures from the stronger dollar and rising U.S. labor costs. Indeed, U.S. auto price competitiveness begins improving around the time the VRAs are first imposed (spring 1981), and relative U.S.-to-Japanese auto prices end up in 1985 at roughly the same level as in 1980.

(4) Figure 8.11 shows how both auto price indexes begin rising relative to other prices, as measured by the CPI, around the time that the VRAs are imposed. This also is a familiar effect of a sectoral trade barrier, in contrast to exchange rates and labor costs, which should probably not be expected to produce strong effects on auto prices relative to other prices.

(5) Figure 8.12 sheds interesting light on the possible benefits to Japanese automakers of developments in the U.S. auto market, suggestive of surging profits. It converts the dollar price index of Japanese sales in the United States into yen (using the corresponding yen-dollar exchange rate), and compares the implied yen price received to other Japanese prices, measured by their GNP deflator. The yen price of autos exported to the United States rises steeply and continuously from 1978 on, relative to other Japanese goods, signaling either real-

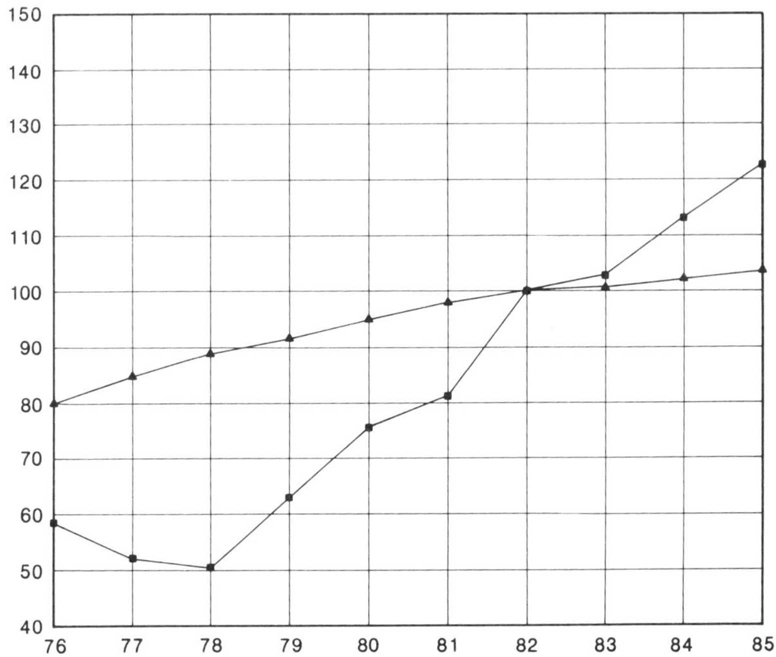

Fig. 8.12 Normalized Yen Prices of Japanese Autos Sold to U.S. and of Other Japanese Goods. ■ = Normalized Auto Price of Japanese Firms, from Figure 8.10, times Index of Yen per Dollar; ▲ = Japanese GNP Deflator; 100 = 1982.

location of production and resources toward U.S. activities in the Japanese auto sector, in a competitive model, or rising profitability if there are entry barriers.

8.4.3 Real Auto Sales and Market Shares

One of the products of the disaggregation described above is an ability to refine aggregate measures of auto sales volume, real market shares, and quantitative indexes. Instead of simply adding together units sold, as is the custom in many tabulations and studies, I weighted each firm's unit sales by its average 1982 price and developed a time series for each firm of real (constant 1982 dollar) sales.[23] These were then aggregated to obtain a measure of real Japanese and U.S. big-three auto sales in the United States, along with corresponding market shares which are often interpreted as ex post indicators of competitiveness.

Figure 8.13 shows how the U.S. market shares of the big-three Japanese suppliers (Toyota, Nissan, Honda) vary over time if measured in units and if measured in real terms. The real market shares lie uniformly below the shares of units, because 1982 prices of Japanese autos were below their U.S. equivalents. The covariation in the series

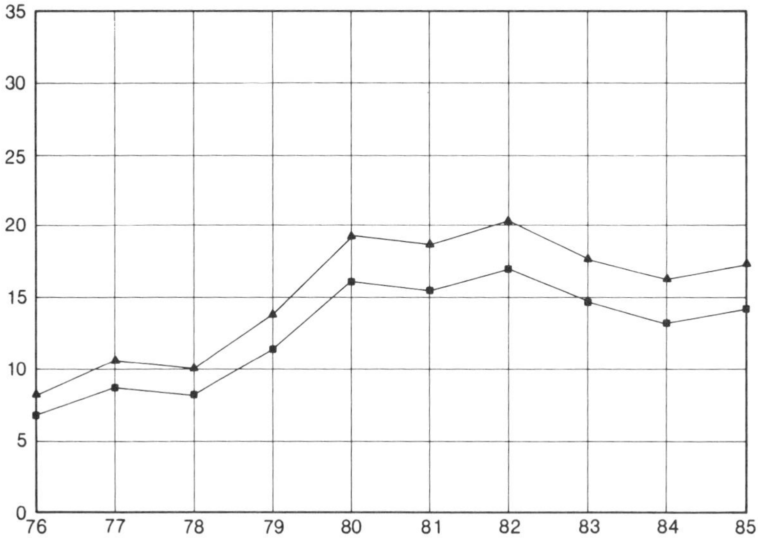

Fig. 8.13 Japanese Firms' Share of Real Auto Sales and Units Sold by Largest Six Firms. ▲ = Share of Units Sold; ■ = Share of Real Sales.

over time, though, is very strong. For this period, indexes of real change and measures of growth are not much affected by choosing simple or more refined aggregation of quantities. If there had been sharper changes in average prices across Japanese firms, there would have been less covariation in the two series in figure 8.13.

Figure 8.14 shows how mild recent variation has been in the real shares of the six principal auto suppliers in their own summed sales.[24] It also suggests only modest covariation with the exchange rate and cost pressures described above. The Japanese incursions of the late 1970s came in spite of adverse trends in exchange rates and at the expense of Ford and Chrysler. Ford's and Chrysler's gradual rebound in the 1980s came at the expense of all other firms except Honda, whose market share continued to rise gradually, as might be expected in light of Honda's 1982 entry into U.S. production facilities that allowed it to avoid the full impact of the Japanese VRAs. Controlling for Honda's unique situation, there is some suggestion of the expected negative covariation between firm-by-firm price competitiveness from figures 8.8 and 8.9 and market shares from figure 8.14.

8.5 Conclusion

Trends in U.S. automakers' competitiveness relative to foreign rivals, especially as measured by relative prices, seem reasonably consistent from 1976 through 1985 with trends in exchange rates, relative

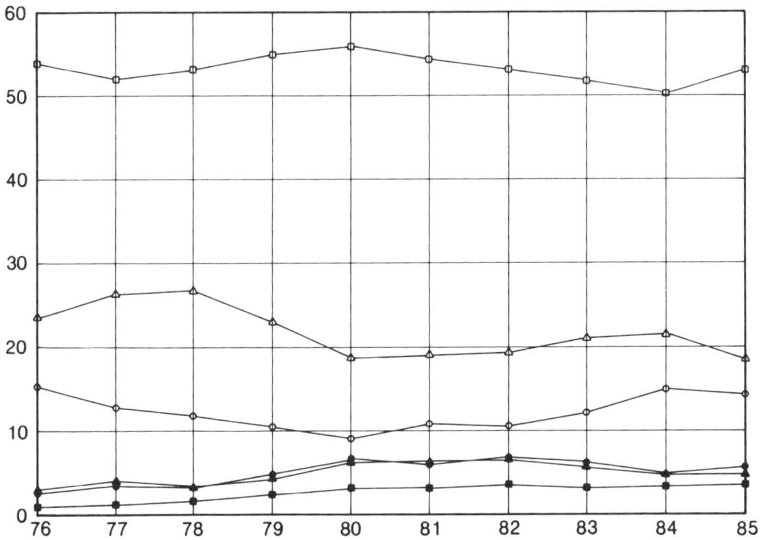

Fig. 8.14 Firm Shares of Real Auto Sales of Largest Six Firms. □ = General Motors; △ = Ford; ○ = Chrysler ▲ = Toyota; ● = Nissan; ■ = Honda.

labor costs, and U.S. trade policy. Table 8.2 summarizes how auto price competitiveness might be very roughly decomposed over this period, as described above. A sensible agenda for ongoing research along these lines would focus on measurement of trends in quality, product mix, and market share, largely ignored above, and on more subtly conditioned covariations and explanations.

Notes

1. Such studies include Bryan and Humpage (1984), Citrin (1985), Collyns and Dunaway (1987), Crandall (1984, 1985, 1987), Dinopoulos and Kreinin (1987), Dixit (1986), Feenstra (1984, 1985a, 1985b, 1986a, 1986b), Gomez-Ibanez and Harrison (1982), Gomez-Ibanez et al. (1983), Hickok (1985), Kaplan (1986), Lambson and Richardson (1987), Levinsohn (1987), Mannering and Winston (1987), Tarr and Morkre (1984), and USITC (1985a).

2. See, for example, Branson and Love (1986), Day (1985), and Schwartz (1985).

3. For example, the imported auto price series from the U.S. Bureau of Labor Statistics (BLS) does not seem to exist in published form prior to 1980. In the U.S. Commerce Department's *Survey of Current Business*, for further example, the price deflator for passenger car imports is calculated to follow the BLS 1980-on series for non-Canadian imports and to follow the U.S. pro-

Table 8.2 Rough Summary of Auto Trends during Sub-periods

	Late 1970s[a]	Early 1980s[b]
Impulses: 1		
Effective nominal auto dollar	Roughly 25% decline	Roughly 25% rise
U.S. unit labor costs relative to auto rivals	Little change	Roughly 25% rise
Residual impulse[c]	Little residual impulse	Roughly 50% offset[d] to above
Competitiveness: 1		
Prices of U.S. automakers relative to Japanese	Roughly 25% decline	Little change

[a]1977–79.

[b]1980–85.

[c]"Residual impulse" denotes pressure on relative auto prices that is unaccounted for by exchange rates and labor costs and is defined by subtracting the first two rows of the table from the last. It includes VRAs, quality, product mix, etc.

[d]That is, impulses that tended to raise prices of Japanese automakers relative to their U.S. rivals.

ducer price index for Canadian imports; and price deflators for purchases of new domestic autos and for purchases of new imports are identical to each other and made to follow the U.S. CPI for new cars.

4. For example, the Commerce Department's constant-dollar auto series in the *Survey of Current Business* come from deflating current-dollar purchases of imports by an index measuring both import prices and domestic prices and from deflating current-dollar domestic purchases by the same mixed-breed index.

5. Weights that are shares of world trade, rather than focus-country trade, are sometimes recommended when there is export competition in third-country markets as well as import competition at home. For illustration, see Feldstein and Bacchetta (1987), Pauls and Helkie (1987), and Pauls (1987). U.S. trade weights are used here because U.S. passenger car exports, except to Canada, are quite small.

6. See Ott (1987) or Hervey and Strauss (1987) for a general discussion of these issues.

7. The 1972–76 weights were (numerators represent shares of total U.S. car imports)

British pound	0.03/0.94
Canadian dollar	0.40/0.94
German mark	0.26/0.94
Japanese yen	0.25/0.94
Sum of four	0.94/0.94.

8. The 1980 I and II weights were

British pound	0.020/0.932
Canadian dollar	0.211/0.932
German mark	0.233/0.932
Japanese yen	0.468/0.932
Sum of four	0.932/0.932.

9. The undulating path of effective exchange rates during this period may help explain the invariance of the trajectories to the choice of fixed and current weights. Fixed-weight (Laspeyre's) indexes overstate inflation but understate deflation; current-weight (Paasche) indexes understate inflation but overstate deflation. Over an undulating price path the biases offset each other within each weighting system.

10. The Canadian share of North American passenger cars (units) produced by GM, Ford, and Chrysler averaged 9.8% in 1976–78 and 11.5% in 1979–85—after the Canadian competitiveness edge developed.

11. I am indebted to Dick Marston for sharing with me the data necessary to do these calculations and, more importantly, the benefits of his insights on what they imply. The unit labor cost series are national-currency indexes of compensation of employees per unit of real output (in the value-added sense) in the manufacturing sector.

12. This seems likely to be true with respect to the weakening of the dollar from 1985 to 1987, too, concentrated as it was on yen and marks.

13. The eclipse would be only partial if the U.S. measure of unit labor costs had been drawn from the auto sector alone, not from overall U.S. manufacturing. Wage givebacks and technological developments of the early 1980s caused unit labor costs in autos to rise somewhat more slowly than in other U.S. manufacturing (Collyns and Dunaway 1987, p. 154). With similar intersectoral divergence in Britain, Germany, and Japan, however, the eclipse would be restored, since nation-to-nation relative unit labor costs would move comparably for autos and overall manufacturing.

14. The measures and weights employed allowed a broader conclusion. Every U.S. sector whose dominant rivals were Germany and/or Japan appeared increasingly uncompetitive in world markets relative to other U.S. sectors during the 1980s. Obviously, though, these conclusions might (or might not) be moderated by employing sectoral unit labor costs, as discussed in note 13.

15. Another factor that plays an important role in section 8.4 is border trade policy, specifically the VRAs with Japan.

16. Quality is a third important contributor to sectoral competitiveness, although it is largely an endogenous choice of automakers. Quality will usually be reflected in price as well as in inherent product characteristics. Disentangling the price influence of trends in relative quality and in relative competitiveness is discussed in more detail by Feenstra (1984) and Collyns and Dunaway (1987), among others.

17. See tabulations of these data in MVMA (1986, p. 38) and Kaplan (1986, table 2).

18. The last and most recent of its compilations is USITC (1986b). The price series have some interest in their own right. For example, the minimum-price series show very little divergence around trend or dispersion across firms, and especially little for the Japanese firms. The maximum-price series, by comparison, show much more divergence and dispersion, especially for the U.S. firms.

19. An obvious objection to this procedure is that percentage discounts on autos with high list prices are probably larger than on autos with low list prices.

20. Calculated Japanese market shares of these highest-price models rise from 1984 to 1985, but European market shares rise even more sharply.

21. This could be due, of course, either to competitive pressures or to implicit price parallelism among oligopolistic firms.

22. The Japanese and U.S. price indexes are implicit price deflators, and the real sales data, compared below to simple aggregates of units sold, record annual sales valued at 1982 prices.

23. Collyns and Dunaway (1987) is a noteworthy, although fairly primitive, exception.

24. In total U.S. market sales, however, real shares of smaller suppliers, both European and Japanese, began rising in 1984.

References

Arndt, Sven W. 1986. Government Policy and the Decline in U.S. Trade Competitiveness. In Phillip Cagan, ed., *Essays in contemporary economic problems, 1986: The impact of the Reagan program*. Washington, D.C.: American Enterprise Institute.

Belongia, Michael T. 1986. Estimating exchange rate effects on exports: A cautionary note. Federal Reserve Bank of St. Louis *Review* 68 (January):5–16.

Branson, William H., and James P. Love. 1986. Dollar appreciation and manufacturing employment and output. National Bureau of Economic Research Working Paper No. 1972, July.

Bryan, Michael F., and Owen F. Humpage. 1984. Voluntary export restraints: The cost of building walls. Federal Reserve Bank of Cleveland, *Economic Review,* Summer, pp. 17–37.

Citrin, Daniel. 1985. Exchange rate changes and exports of selected Japanese industries. International Monetary Fund *Staff Papers* 32 (September), pp. 404–29.

Clifton, Eric V. 1985. Real exchange rates, import penetration, and protectionism in industrial countries. International Monetary Fund *Staff Papers,* 32 (September), pp. 513–36.

Collyns, Charles, and Steven Dunaway. 1987. The cost of trade restraints: The case of Japanese automobile exports to the United States. International Monetary Fund *Staff Papers,* 34 (March), pp. 150–75.

Crandall, Robert W. 1984. Import quotas and the automobile industry: The costs of protection. *The Brookings Review,* Summer, pp. 8–16.

———. 1985. Assessing the impacts of the automobile voluntary export restraints upon U.S. automobile prices. Processed, December 30.

———. 1987. The effects of U.S. trade protection for autos and steel. Processed, April, forthcoming, *Brookings Papers on Economic Activity.*

Day, Alan. 1985. Exchange rate and interest rate effects on Wisconsin employment, 1972 to 1984. Wisconsin Department of Development, Division of Policy Development, Bureau of Research report 85-14, August.

Dinopoulos, Elias, and Mordechai E. Kreinin. 1986. Import quotas and VERs: A comparative analysis in a three-country framework. Processed, July.

———. 1987. Effects of the U.S.-Japan auto VER on European prices and U.S. welfare. Processed, January.

Dixit, Avinash. 1986. Optimal trade and industrial policies for the U.S. automobile industry. Forthcoming, in Robert C. Feenstra, ed., *Empirical methods for international trade*. Cambridge: MIT Press. Proceedings of an April 3–4, 1986, National Bureau of Economic Research Conference on Empirical Methods for International Trade. Processed, March.

Dutton, John, and Thomas Grennes. 1985. Measurement of effective exchange rates appropriate for agricultural trade. Economics Research Report No. 51 of the Department of Economics and Business, North Carolina State University, November.

Feenstra, Robert C. 1984. Voluntary export restraint in U.S. autos, 1980–81: Quality, employment, and welfare effects. In Robert E. Baldwin and Anne O. Krueger, eds., *The structure and evolution of recent U.S. trade policy*. Chicago: University of Chicago Press.

———. 1985a. Automobile prices and protection: The U.S.-Japan trade restraint. *Journal of Policy Modeling* vol. 7, no. 1, pp. 49–68.

———. 1985b. Quality change under trade restraints: Theory and evidence from Japanese autos. Columbia University Department of Economics Working Paper no. 298, August.

———. 1986a. Gains from trade in differentiated products: Japanese compact trucks. Forthcoming, in Robert C. Feenstra, ed., *Empirical methods for international trade*. Cambridge: MIT Press. From a 3–4 April 1986 National Bureau of Economic Research Conference on Empirical Methods for International Trade, processed, March. Also NBER Working Paper no. 1978, July.

———. 1986b. International prices, exchange rates, and trade policy. Processed, 8 August. Presented at a National Bureau of Economic Research/Center for Economic Policy Research Workshop/Mini-Conference on Empirical Studies of Strategic Trade Policy, Cambridge, Massachusetts.

Feldstein, Martin, and Phillipe Bacchetta. 1987. How far has the dollar fallen? National Bureau of Economic Research Working Paper no. 2122, January.

Gomez-Ibanez, Jose A., and David Harrison, Jr. 1982. Imports and the future of the U.S. automobile industry. *American Economic Review* 72 (May 1982): 319–23.

Gomez-Ibanez, Jose A., Robert A. Leone, and Stephen A. O'Connell. 1983. Restraining auto imports: Does anyone win? *Journal of Policy Analysis and Management* vol. 2, no. 2, pp. 196–219.

Hartman, David G. 1986. Focus I: Industry prospects in the world's new competitive environment. DRI (Data Resources Incorporated) *Focus World Outlook,* Summer.

Hervey, Jack L., and William A. Strauss. 1987. The new dollar indexes are no different from the old ones. Federal Reserve Bank of Chicago *Economic Perspectives* 11 (July/August), pp. 3–22.

Hickok, Susan. 1985. The consumer cost of U.S. trade restraints. Federal Reserve Bank of New York *Quarterly Review,* Summer, pp. 1–12.

Kaplan, Daniel. 1986. Automobiles. Chapter 5 of *Has trade protection revitalized domestic industries?* Washington: Congressional Budget Office.

Laffer, Arthur B., Victor A. Canto, Richard V. Eastin, and Charles W. Kadlec. 1985. A high road for the American automobile industry. *The World Economy* 8 (September): 267–86.

Lambson, Val Eugene, and J. David Richardson. 1987. Tacit collusion and voluntary restraint arrangements in the U.S. auto market. Processed, January.

Levinsohn, James. 1987. Empirics of taxes in differentiated products: The case of tariffs in the U.S. automobile industry. Processed January. Presented at a National Bureau of Economic Research Conference on Trade Policy Issues and Empirical Analysis, 13–14 February.

Mannering, Fred, and Clifford Winston. 1987. Economic effects of voluntary export restrictions. In Clifford Winston and Associates, *Blind intersection? Policy and the automobile industry.* Washington, D.C.: Brookings Institution.

Marston, Richard C. 1986. Real exchange rates and productivity growth in the United States and Japan. National Bureau of Economic Research Working Paper no. 1922, May. Forthcoming in Sven W. Arndt and J. David Richardson, eds., *Real-financial linkages among open economies.* Cambridge: MIT Press (1987).

Motor Vehicles Manufacturers Association (MVMA). 1985, 1986. *Facts and Figures.*

Ott, Mack. 1987. The dollar's effective exchange rate: Assessing the impact of alternative weighting schemes. Federal Reserve Bank of St. Louis *Review* 69 (February): 5–14.

Pauls, B. Dianne. 1987. Measuring the foreign-exchange value of the dollar. *Federal Reserve Bulletin* 73 (June): 411–22.

Pauls, B. Dianne, and William L. Helkie. 1987. A reassessment of measures of the dollar's effective exchange value. Board of Governors of the Federal Reserve System, International Finance Discussion Paper no. 306, April.

Salter, Malcolm S., Alan M. Webber, and Davis Dyer. 1985. U.S. competitiveness in global industries: Lessons from the auto industry. In Bruce R. Scott and George C. Lodge, eds., *U.S. Competitiveness in the World Economy.* Boston: Harvard Business School Press.

Schwartz, Elliot. 1985. The dollar in foreign exchange and U.S. industrial production. U.S. Congressional Budget Office Staff Working Paper, December.

Tarr, David G., and Morris E. Morkre. 1984. *Aggregate costs to the United States of tariffs and quotas on imports.* Washington: Federal Trade Commission, Bureau of Economics Staff Report, December.

USITC (United States International Trade Commission). 1980. *Certain motor vehicles and certain chassis therefor.* Publication 1110. Washington, D.C., December.

———. 1985a. *The internationalization of the automobile industry and its effects on the U.S. automobile industry.* Publication 1712, June.

———. 1985b. *Sales, imports, exports, apparent consumption, suggested retail prices, and trade balances for selected countries in motor vehicles, 1964–84.* Publication 1762, October.

White, Lawrence J. n.d. The U.S. automobile industry: A case study of a "de facto" industrial policy. Processed.

Comment Robert Lawrence

Anyone attempting to explain the behavior of the U.S. automobile market in the 1980s is unusually brave. For the eighties have seen major

Robert Lawrence is a senior fellow at the Brookings Institution.

shocks, each of which probably altered the behavioral parameters of the market in a fundamental way. Consumers shifted demand toward Japanese cars, both because they were burned by the second oil shock, which convinced them to shift to smaller cars, and because they perceived Japanese automobiles to be of superior quality. In addition, contributing to the turmoil were voluntary export restraints, currency fluctuations, and toward the end of the period, the arrival of the transplants—Japanese automakers operating assembly plants in the United States. In this paper, David Richardson takes a first cut at trying to understand U.S. auto competitiveness by answering three questions: (1) what is the exchange rate measure relevant for U.S. automotive competitiveness? (2) what is the price series relevant for deflating nominal U.S. automobile aggregates? and (3) what have been the effects of VRAs and exchange rates on price competitiveness?

In my comments, I'd like first to discuss his answers to these questions and then to make a few comments of my own about the effects of VRAs.

Dave argues that conventional multilateral or bilateral exchange rate measures are inappropriate for analyzing U.S. automobile competitiveness. One issue is whether "U.S." includes the profits earned by U.S. firms in their overseas operations or refers only to operations within the geographic boundaries of the United States. He decides that North America is the appropriate focus and proceeds to drop the Canadian dollar from his exchange rate measure. I feel the U.S. domestic industry would be a more pertinent focus, particularly since employment considerations are often a key issue in discussions about competitiveness. But even taking his focus as given, I am not sure he has the correct indicator. If one wants a measure relevant for profitability, why not include consideration of United States-owned corporations in Europe and other parts of the world? The Ford Motor Company, for example, was kept solvent by its European operations during this period. I am also unclear why, given his purpose, Dave uses U.S. import weights and thus neglects to take account of competition between U.S. and foreign automobiles in Canada. Indeed, if the objective is really to capture the impact of exchange rates on profitability, I am not sure that any simple weighting scheme will suffice. It will probably be necessary to obtain weights from a fully specified econometric model of such profit determination (much as the International Monetary Fund uses a trade model in the construction of its multilateral exchange rate measures).

The major finding in the analysis of the automotive exchange rate is that, compared to other U.S. producers, in the 1970s U.S. automakers were helped more, and in the 1980s penalized less, by exchange rate shifts. But surely the real, rather than nominal, exchange rate is relevant for such analysis. Since Japanese and German inflation have been much lower than U.S. inflation, I am not sure this conclusion would hold up.

Dave then turns to construct his own price measures. In general, I agree that the deflators for automobiles are highly questionable. For example, the official data treat government-mandated regulatory changes as if they were improvements in quality. If consumers don't have the same views of these changes, they will be inadequate for explaining behavior. In addition, the measures fail to capture actual transactions prices and the implicit price equivalent of financing.

I am sympathetic to Dave's desire to construct a better price measure, but I have some problems with his. I find it peculiar that he should deliberately construct a quantity measure which is sensitive to shifts in product mix. As Bob Feenstra has shown, VRAs not only led to higher Japanese prices on given models but also influenced the product mix by inducing options loading and shifts towards larger cars. For tracking price competitiveness, I think we need to examine the same products over time.

The analysis of the impact of VRAs and exchange rates does not use an explicit empirical model. Instead, Dave prefers eyeball econometrics. Now I applaud anyone who examines the data closely before using it, but I do not think one can make ceteris paribus statements about cause and effect without controlling for other factors. This is particularly the case when there is strong reason to believe, as I described at the start of these comments, that major influences have not remained constant.

Dave concludes that VRAs had little impact on U.S. relative price competitiveness. First, it should be emphasized that this is not the same as saying they had no effect—domestic and imported auto prices might have risen by the same amount. Second, his analysis leans heavily on the 1982 data. Auto demand was particularly weak when the VRAs were introduced. As the studies of Crandall suggest, their impact might have been more important in subsequent years when demand recovered. But for disentangling such effects, a model is essential. I should note that Dave's conclusion differs from that obtained by others who have used explicit models. More work needs to be done to explain why these findings differ from those in the literature.

Finally, I am not sure that prices are the key issue in auto competitiveness. There could be very important effects from exchange rates, even if prices are similar, if profitability is very different. Indeed, much of the debate about the competitiveness of U.S. autos pertains to the alleged $2,000 difference in production costs between Japan and the United States. A key issue currently is whether, as a result of the recent yen appreciation, that gap has been eliminated. Clifford Winston's work—and the planned increase in Japanese assembly operations in the United States—seem to signal that it has.

I believe that VRAs are particularly counterproductive policies—even when viewed narrowly from the standpoint of protectionists who supported them and other forms of quota protection. Allegedly protection was required to save jobs and permit the industry to restore its competitiveness. Generally when people talk about saving jobs, they mean those of the workers currently employed, and they refer to the competitiveness of the firms currently in the industry. In theory, of course, if a quota enhances domestic monopoly power, it could lead protected firms to so raise prices and thus lower output that on balance jobs could be lost rather than saved. In fact, the work of Winston finds that the VRAs actually cost auto jobs, since the effect, inducing buyers to switch from Japanese to U.S. automobiles, was less than the effect of higher auto prices on sales by U.S.-based firms.

It is also not clear that VRAs had very beneficial effects on the competitiveness of U.S. automobile firms. While VRAs may have enhanced the profitability of U.S. automotive firms, they also raised the profits of their competitors in both Japan and Europe. Moreover, U.S. investment in the auto industry in the early 1980s was below investment in the late 1970s. In addition, as Crandall shows in his recent Brookings paper, compensation in the automobile industry today retains the same relationship to average compensation in manufacturing as it had in the late 1970s.

But in one sense VRAs may have indeed contributed to the competitiveness of firms based in the United States, if not to the U.S.-owned firms themselves. They speeded the introduction of Japanese transplants. One of the issues in this conference has been the degree to which the strong dollar has led to hysteresis. If it has, the dollar may have to depreciate by more than it appreciated to obtain the same current account level. But, partly because of VRAs, the auto industry could be a case on the other side. Our industrial potential in autos may have increased during this period. There is now talk that some of the Japanese transplants, brought here by fears of protection, may actually begin exporting from the United States—perhaps even back to Japan.

9 U.S. Manufacturing and the Real Exchange Rate

William H. Branson and James P. Love

9.1 Introduction and Summary

In the spring of 1981 the U.S. dollar began a four-year period of real appreciation that took it to a peak of more than 50% by first quarter of 1985. The appreciation of the dollar in real terms was part of the adjustment process by which the increase in the structural budget deficit in the United States was financed. By mid-1985, the current account deficit was about \$120 billion at an annual rate, providing a significant source of finance for the \$200 billion Federal budget deficit. The links from the shift in the budget to the appreciation of the dollar are discussed in Branson (1985) and chapter 1 in this volume.

The appreciation of the dollar in real terms reduces the competitiveness of U.S. output in all U.S. industry that is directly or indirectly substitutable for foreign output. It is these effects that are the topic of this paper.

The appreciation of the dollar was a prolonged but temporary phenomenon that is reversible when the structural deficit is reduced or when international investors resist absorption of additional dollar-denominated debt into their portfolios. This reversal began in late 1985. The depression of output and employment in previously competitive U.S. industries may not be completely reversible, however. The protracted period of a high dollar has provided an opportunity for non-U.S. competitors in industries with increasing returns—due to fixed

William H. Branson is professor of economics and international affairs at Princeton University and director of the Program in International Studies and research associate of the National Bureau of Economic Research. James P. Love is lecturer in public affairs and research associate at the Woodrow Wilson School of Public and International Affairs, Princeton University.

costs, learning, or other factors—to establish themselves in the world market. Thus, when the dollar returns to its 1980 level in real terms, U.S. firms will face new international competition that has worked its way down its cost curves while the dollar was high. This is the hysteresis possibility in trade. The estimates provided in this paper of the effects of real appreciation on employment and output do not take this potential asymmetry into account.

In this paper, using time series data through the first quarter of 1986, we use a simple model of supply and demand to estimate the impact of the dollar appreciation on manufacturing employment, disaggregated by industry sectors and by production and non–production workers. These initial results are part of a larger research project to estimate the effects of movements in the real exchange rate on U.S. manufacturing industries.

Section 9.2 of the paper provides a brief theoretical background for the estimation procedure. In section 9.3 we discuss the estimating equation and the data. Section 9.4 presents the basic results at the 2-digit level of manufacturing. These are estimated over three time periods. In section 9.5 the equations are used to decompose changes in employment from 1980 to 1985 into effects due to trend, aggregate unemployment, relative energy prices, and the real exchange rate. We estimate a loss of about 1 million jobs due to the dollar appreciation. Finally, in section 9.6 we present the estimates for non–production and production workers and find that employment of the latter is more sensitive to the real exchange rate, especially in the durable goods sectors. This raises the possibility of hysteresis.

We find significant and substantial effects of the dollar appreciation on employment in U.S. manufacturing. In particular, we find that exchange rate movements have had important effects on the durable goods sector, including primary metals, fabricated metal products, and nonelectrical machinery. Other sectors that suffer large employment losses when the dollar appreciates are stone, clay, and glass products, transportation, instruments, textiles and apparel, chemicals, rubber, and leather goods. We also find especially significant effects on production workers.

9.2 Theoretical Outline

In this section we sketch the theoretical basis for the estimating equations. The discussion is brief, as the basic ideas are well known from trade and computable general equilibrium (CGE) models that distinguish three sectors: exportables X, import-competing goods M, and nontraded goods N. We employ this sectorization for two reasons.

First, to study output and employment effects, we must focus on exportables and import-competing production, rather than on trade in exports and imports. Second, given this focus, we must provide a minimum model of the nontraded sector of the economy to ensure consistency.

The general line of the analysis can be stated simply. In each of the three sectors, demand is sensitive to the relative price of home and foreign goods. In the short run at least, we assume that a change in the nominal exchange rate E moves that relative price, which we interpret as the "real" exchange rate $e \equiv EP^*/P$, where P (P^*) is the relevant home (foreign) price. It is important to note the limiting force of this assumption. If we were to assume that exportables and import-competing goods were perfect substitutes in demand for foreign goods, then a change in the nominal rate E would have no effect on the relative price e, since $P_x = EP^*$ and $P_m = EP^*$, where P^* is the relevant foreign price. Even in this case, in the short run we would see a change in the relative price of nontraded goods when E changes. In the long run, as wages adjust to the change in goods prices, a cost-based model of pricing in the nontraded goods sector would result in the restoration of the original relative price in that sector. The change in $P_{\hat{n}}$ would be equal to the initial change in E, in percentage terms. A rational-expectations model with instantaneous market clearing would collapse in this long run into the short run, leaving no effect of E on e in any of the three sectors. We do not assume perfect substitution or instantaneous market clearing in the empirical work, but rather assume that changes in the nominal rate move the U.S. real exchange rate in the short run and attempt to estimate the consequences.

An appreciation of the home currency (the U.S. dollar), reducing e, reduces the relative price of foreign to home goods. This tends to shift demand from home to foreign goods, reducing output and employment in all three producing sectors. Changes in home and foreign real income, Y and Y^*, respectively, also enter the demand for exportables, while we assume that only home income Y is relevant for importables and nontraded goods.

On the supply side, we assume that the output of each sector depends on its price relative to the nominal wage. As the real product wage falls, supply increases. We do not attempt to model intersectoral supply reactions as relative prices change, given the common nominal wage rate. The supply functions below should in theory contain all relative prices.

In the theoretical background to our empirical work, then, is a model of supply and demand in each of the three sectors, with supply sensitive to the product wage and demand sensitive to the relative price of home and foreign goods and the relevant income variable. A log-linear model of demand and supply of exportables is described below, with analogous results for import-competing goods and non-tradables.

9.2.1 Exportables

The demand for exportables is written in log-linear form as:

$$\text{(1)} \qquad \ln Q_x = \ln c_1 + d_x \ln (EP^*/P_x) + g_{x1} \ln Y + g_{x2} \ln Y^*.$$

Here Q_x is the quantity demanded, EP^*/P_x is the relative price of exportables and foreign goods, and Y (Y^*) is home (foreign) real income. The parameter d_x is the positive price elasticity of demand, and the g's are the income elasticities. The supply of exportables is assumed to be an inverse function of the product wage:

$$\text{(2)} \qquad \ln Q_x = \ln c_2 + s_x \ln (P_x/W).$$

Here W is the nominal wage rate and s_x is the price elasticity of supply. As P_x/W increases, Q_x supplied increases.

The demand and supply equations (1) and (2) can be solved to obtain the "reduced form" expressions for Q_x and P_x, given E, P^*, W, Y, and Y^*. The solution for Q_x, the output of exportables, is given by:

$$\text{(3)} \quad \ln Q_x = A_{1x} + \frac{s_x d_x}{s_x + d_x} \ln \frac{EP^*}{W} + \frac{s_x}{s_x + d_x} [g_{x1} \ln Y + g_{x2} \ln Y^*],$$

where $A_{1x} = \dfrac{s_x c_1 - d_x c_1}{s_x + d_x}$ is the constant term.

Both coefficients in the reduced form are positive, given the way d_x was defined in equation (1). An appreciation of the dollar, expressed as the fall in the exchange rate E, reduces competitive prices EP^* relative to domestic costs W, reducing Q_x. Growth in Y or Y^* increases demand and production.

The estimating equations in section 9.3 below follow equation (3). The real exchange rate EP^*/W is inverted in those equations, since the data use the inverse IMF definition of the exchange rate. This makes the estimated coefficients for the real exchange rate negative. The domestic income variable is broken into trend and cyclical components, and Y^* is dropped due to colinearity with Y.

The equation for employment N_x in the exportable sectors takes the same form as the output equation, with the two tied by a production function. If the production function is $Q = Q(N,K)$, with the capital stock K fixed in the short run, variations in output are given by $dQ = Q_n dN$, where Q_n is the marginal product of labor. Then the employment equation in variation terms would be the output equation (3) divided by Q_n, which is positive. Since all the estimated equations below have a separate trend term, differential productivity growth trends across sectors are included in the controlled variable set. The employment equations are the same as the output equations with $\ln N_x$ replacing $\ln Q_x$ on the left-hand side of equation (3).

In a later phase of research, we will estimate the effects of movements in the real exchange rate on real wages and profits in the manufacturing sectors. It will be useful then to have the solution for P_x from (1) and (2):

$$(4)\quad \ln P_x = A_{2x} + \frac{1}{s_x + d_x}[g_{x1}\ln Y + g_{x2}\ln Y^* + d_x\ln(EP^*) + s_x\ln W],$$

where $A_{2x} = \dfrac{\ln c_1 + \ln c_2}{s_x + d_x}$ is the constant term.

The usual small-country results can be obtained from equations (3) and (4) by setting the price elasticity of demand d_x at infinity. In (3), this eliminates income effects and sets the relative price coefficient equal to s_x. The output of exportables reacts along the supply function as the real exchange rate moves exogenously. In the price equation (4), setting d_x at infinity sets the coefficients of Y, Y^*, and W at zero and the coefficient of EP^* at unity. Exportable prices are fixed by the world market in the small-country case. The assumption maintained in the empirical work is that the United States is not a small country, in the sense of being a price taker on world markets.

9.2.2 Import-Competing and Nontraded Goods

The basic demand and supply equations for import-competing and nontraded goods will have exactly the same form as (1) and (2) for exportables, so the quantity and price solutions will have the same form as (3) and (4). For both sectors we will eliminate the foreign output variable from the demand function, although in principle it (and many others) should be included. In both sectors supply is again an inverse function of the product wage, and demand depends on the price of own output relative to competing foreign goods, represented in general by EP^*. As EP^* rises, we expect substitution towards both domestic production of import-competing goods and nontraded output, and vice versa as EP^* falls and the dollar appreciates.

Again, in principle we should include all product wages in each supply function, to catch supply-side substitution as any relative price changes. And we should include all relative prices in each demand function for a similar reason. In the empirical work, we focus on the exogenous event of a major swing in E, producing a swing in the real exchange rate. The maintained hypothesis expressed in the exclusion of the other relative prices is that there was no significant exogenous shift amongst them during the sample period, or that shifts over time are captured by a trend variable. The obvious exception is the energy price, which is included explicitly in the empirical work.

With Y^* excluded from the demand functions, and m and n subscripts denoting import-competing and nontraded output and price, respectively, the reduced-form solutions for Q_m, P_m, Q_n, P_n are equations (3) and (4) with no term in Y^* and with the subscripts on the elasticities altered appropriately. The employment equations, again, are similar to the output equations via a production function. Trend terms will adjust for differences in productivity growth across sectors. The presumed difference in demand substitution against foreign goods among exportable, import-competing, and nontraded goods should come out in the estimated values of the demand elasticities, d_x, d_m, and d_n.

9.3 The Model to be Estimated

In the next section we report the empirical estimates of the relationship between movements in the real exchange rate and employment in manufacturing. We take the manufacturing sector to represent both import-competing and exportable goods. Initial estimates for nontraded goods are reported in Branson and Love (1986, table 2). Employment within the manufacturing sector is disaggregated by the 20 industries defined by the Standard Industrial Classification (SIC) system. We have not modeled each industry within the manufacturing sector individually, taking into account the special sectoral demand shocks and cost effects that may be important. A general reduced-form model is applied to all industries sectors, disaggregated again by type of worker.

The left-hand dependent variable is the natural logarithm of employment. The right-hand independent variables include a constant, three variables to capture secular, cyclical, and structural changes in demand, and the real exchange rate. The secular and cyclical variables are time (*TREND*) and the natural logarithm of the national unemployment rate (*LURT*). Inclusion of the national unemployment rate in the estimating equation catches the effect of fluctuations in aggregate demand. The coefficients of the real exchange rate therefore give the distributive effects of exchange-rate movements adjusted for cyclical movements in total demand. These coefficients are the effects of relative price changes of traded and nontraded goods, compensated for income effects.

The structural variable is the natural logarithm of an index to measure the real price of energy (*LRENGY*). This is the ratio of the energy component of the CPI to the total CPI. This variable catches the effects of shifts of energy costs on employment by sector. The net effect of a given change in the real exchange rate is therefore the coefficient of the exchange rate plus the coefficient of the relative energy price times the effect of the movement of the exchange rate on the energy price. The exchange rate variable is the natural logarithm of an index that measures the real U.S. trade-weighted exchange rate (*LREX*).[1] The exchange rate used here is the IMF index of relative unit labor costs. We considered the inclusion of a foreign demand variable, but found that deviations from trend growth in foreign demand were so highly correlated with changes in domestic demand that no additional explanatory power came from foreign demand.[2] The form of the estimating equation is

$$y_{it} = \beta_0 + \beta_1 t + \sum_{j=0}^{4} \beta_{2j}\, LURT_{t-j} + \sum_{k=0}^{4} \beta_{3k}\, LRENGY_{t-k} + \sum_{l=0}^{6} \beta_{4l}\, LREX_{t-l} + \epsilon_t, \tag{5}$$

where:

y_{it} = the log of employment or output in sector i,
t = the *TREND* variable time,
LURT = the log of the unemployment rate,
LRENGY = the log of the relative price of energy,
LREX = the log of the IMF real exchange rate index, adjusted for changes in relative unit labor costs,
ϵ_t = the stochastic error term,
and the β's are the parameters to be estimated.

The data used to estimate equation (5) are quarterly. The equations are estimated over a period that ends in first quarter 1986.[3] In most cases the equations were estimated over the periods beginning at first quarter 1970, although longer and shorter time periods were tested and are reported. The 1970:I to 1986:I estimates have 65 observations and 46 degrees of freedom.

The exchange rate variable *LREX* includes the current observation plus six quarters of lagged observations. The real energy price *LRENGY* and the unemployment rate *LURT* variables both include the current value plus four quarters of lags. Because the model is in log-linear form, the estimated coefficients have simple economic interpretations. The numbers we report are the sums of the coefficients on these log distributions and the test statistics on these sums.

The coefficient for the *TREND* variable (t) is the estimated exponential rate of growth or decline in employment that occurs due to secular changes in income, tastes, comparative advantage, or technology. A coefficient for *TREND* of −.001 means that, holding everything else constant, employment will decline at the percentage rate of 0.1% each quarter.

The coefficients for the real exchange rate, the real price of energy, and the unemployment rate variables can be interpreted as elasticities. For example, a coefficient of −.3 for the real exchange variable *LREX* means that a 10% increase in the exchange rate will lead to a 3% decrease in the number of workers employed. When coefficients are interpreted as elasticities it is not necessary to know the units which were used to measure the variables, and it is also easier to compare the coefficients across different industries. Because the estimated elasticities describe the percentage changes in the employment variable, it is necessary to make separate calculations of the number of jobs that will be affected by movements in the exchange rate. These calculations are described in greater detail below.

The source of the data on employment is the Bureau of Labor Statistics' (BLS) *Employment and Earnings*. The dependent variable is the natural logarithm of the number of employed workers. In most cases the employment variable includes all workers, although the results for production versus non–production workers are also reported for the 2-digit SIC manufacturing sectors.

The real exchange rate index is the IMF index of relative unit labor costs.[4] The real energy index is the CPI-Urban index for energy divided by the CPI-Urban index for all consumer goods. The unemployment rate is for all workers.[5]

9.4 Basic Results at the 2-Digit Level

Tables 9.1 through 9.4 report the results of the econometric estimates for the twenty 2-digit SIC manufacturing sectors. Table 9.1 provides the results from the equations that used all workers as the dependent variable, estimated over the period 1970:I to 1986:I. The table reports the first-order autocorrelation coefficient *RHO*, the coefficients for each of the independent variables, and a significance statistic. When independent variables are lagged, the coefficient represents the sum of all lagged coefficients. The significance measure (*SIG*) is the probability that the true value of the sum of the coefficients is zero, using a two-tailed *t*-test. The standard error (*SE*) for the sum of the exchange-rate coefficients is also reported.

The *RHO* is positive and large for most of the industries, indicating a high degree of serial correlation in employment. The variable *TREND* is positive for 12 of the industries and statistically significant at the .05 level in 16 of the regressions. The cyclical variable *LURT* measures the impact of cyclical movements in the national economy; the predicted

Table 9.1 Employment for All Workers, 1970:I–1986:I

	SIC	RHO	TREND	SIG	LREX	SE	SIG	LURT	SIG	LRENGY	SIG
					Nondurable Goods						
Food and kindred products	20	0.92	−0.001	0.03	−0.00	0.04	0.92	−0.05	0.01	0.01	0.87
Tobacco manufactures	21	0.70	−0.004	0.00	−0.07	0.06	0.27	−0.03	0.59	−0.03	0.86
Textile mill products	22	0.73	−0.006	0.00	−0.16	0.03	0.00	−0.09	0.00	0.01	0.84
Apparel and other textile prod	23	0.74	−0.004	0.00	−0.11	0.03	0.00	−0.09	0.00	0.05	0.48
Paper and allied products	26	0.84	0.001	0.19	0.00	0.03	0.91	−0.13	0.00	−0.00	0.98
Print and publishing	27	0.94	0.006	0.00	0.12	0.02	0.00	−0.13	0.00	0.02	0.52
Chemicals and allied products	28	0.93	0.000	0.90	−0.10	0.03	0.00	−0.11	0.00	0.10	0.02
Petroleum and coal products	29	0.47	−0.004	0.00	−0.25	0.06	0.00	−0.07	0.18	0.37	0.01
Rubber and misc plastics prod	30	0.73	0.007	0.00	−0.19	0.05	0.00	−0.27	0.00	−0.23	0.06
Leather and leather goods	31	0.93	−0.013	0.00	−0.14	0.11	0.21	−0.04	0.43	0.34	0.02
					Durable Goods						
Lumber and wood products	24	0.72	0.003	0.00	−0.13	0.05	0.01	−0.20	0.00	−0.28	0.01
Furniture and fixtures	25	0.88	0.004	0.00	−0.05	0.05	0.31	−0.21	0.00	−0.23	0.01
Stone, clay, and glass prod	32	0.88	0.000	0.74	−0.28	0.04	0.00	−0.19	0.00	−0.20	0.01
Primary metal industries	33	0.70	−0.007	0.00	−0.57	0.06	0.00	−0.35	0.00	0.14	0.28
Fabricated metal products	34	0.75	0.000	0.37	−0.29	0.03	0.00	−0.32	0.00	−0.03	0.63
Machinery, except electrical	35	0.69	0.002	0.00	−0.41	0.03	0.00	−0.37	0.00	0.32	0.00
Electrical and electronic equip	36	0.92	0.005	0.00	−0.03	0.05	0.53	−0.33	0.00	0.05	0.51
Transportation equipment	37	0.36	0.003	0.00	−0.19	0.04	0.00	−0.39	0.00	−0.09	0.32
Instruments and related prod	38	0.93	0.006	0.00	−0.15	0.04	0.00	−0.25	0.00	0.24	0.00
Misc manufacturing industries	39	0.77	−0.001	0.02	−0.28	0.03	0.00	−0.16	0.00	−0.12	0.10

Notes: Dependent variable is log of employment (all workers). Data are seasonally adjusted. Model: AR1(METHOD-MAXL) 70,1 86.1 DOF: 46. CONSTANT TREND LREX(0,6) LURT(0,4) LRENGY(0,4).

sign for this variable is negative, as high sectoral employment is associated with lower national unemployment rates. In the regressions, *LURT* is negative in all 20 industries and is significant at the .05 level 17 times.

The real price of energy variable *LRENGY* is positive 11 times and significant 8 times. The predicted sign of this variable is ambiguous. An increase in the relative energy price increases cost in all sectors, reducing employment. But some sectors produce outputs that substitute for energy or are inputs to energy-substitute products. In five of the eight cases where this variable is statistically significant, the sign is positive (*SIC* 28, 29, 31, 35 and 38).

The real exchange rate variable *LREX* is negative for 18 of the 20 industries and statistically significant at the .05 level 14 times. In 13 of the 14 industries where the exchange-rate coefficient is statistically significant, the sign of the coefficient is negative, the sole exception being print and publishing (*SIC* 27). The exchange rate has its greatest impact on primary metal industries (*SIC* 33), with an elasticity of −.57, and nonelectrical machinery (*SIC* 35), with an elasticity of −.41. Fabricated metal industries (*SIC* 34), petroleum and coal products (*SIC* 29), stone, clay, and glass products (*SIC* 32), and miscellaneous manufacturing (*SIC* 39) all have elasticities grouped between −.25 and −.30. We observe somewhat smaller, but important, effects on textiles and apparel (*SIC* 22 and 23), chemicals and allied products (*SIC* 28), rubber and miscellaneous products (*SIC* 30), lumber and wood products (*SIC* 24), transportation equipment (*SIC* 37), and instruments and related products (*SIC* 38).

The *LREX* coefficients for food and kindred products (*SIC* 20), tobacco manufactures (*SIC* 21), leather and leather goods (*SIC* 31), furniture and fixtures (*SIC* 25), and electrical and electronic equipment (*SIC* 36) are negative, but not statistically different from zero. Only paper and allied products (*SIC* 26) and print and publishing (*SIC* 27) have positive signs, and only the latter is statistically significant.

The model used in the basic estimates is, as noted above, a rather simple one, and it is certainly possible that the effect that is attributed to the exchange rate may an artifact of, among other things, the period used for estimation. The exchange-rate movements may be catching the effects of other structural changes in the economy or other omitted variables. One test of the robustness of these results is presented in tables 9.2 through 9.4. In tables 9.2 and 9.3, the regression results are reported for the same twenty industries, when the period of estimation is longer (beginning in first quarter 1963) and shorter (beginning in first quarter 1975) than was used in table 9.1 (beginning in first quarter 1970). In table 9.4 the three sets of estimated coefficients for *LREX*—those estimated from 1963, 1970, and 1975—are compared to each other.

Table 9.2 Employment for All Workers, 1963:I–1986:I

	SIC	RHO	TREND	SIG	LREX	SE	SIG	LURT	SIG	LRENGY	SIG
					Nondurable Goods						
Food and kindred products	20	0.92	−0.001	0.03	−0.01	0.03	0.75	−0.04	0.01	−0.04	0.40
Tobacco manufactures	21	0.60	−0.004	0.00	−0.06	0.05	0.18	−0.01	0.83	−0.03	0.71
Textile mill products	22	0.98	−0.002	0.06	−0.14	0.08	0.07	−0.10	0.00	−0.15	0.11
Apparel and other textile prod	23	0.97	−0.001	0.15	−0.13	0.07	0.05	−0.09	0.00	−0.11	0.24
Paper and allied products	26	0.97	0.002	0.00	0.02	0.04	0.59	−0.13	0.00	−0.09	0.08
Print and publishing	27	0.95	0.006	0.00	0.11	0.03	0.00	−0.12	0.00	0.02	0.55
Chemicals and allied products	28	0.99	0.002	0.01	−0.08	0.04	0.07	−0.13	0.00	0.02	0.71
Petroleum and coal products	29	0.59	−0.001	0.29	−0.28	0.07	0.00	0.02	0.74	−0.03	0.78
Rubber and misc plastics prod	30	0.78	0.009	0.00	−0.21	0.06	0.00	−0.21	0.00	−0.41	0.00
Leather and leather goods	31	0.98	−0.009	0.00	−0.14	0.10	0.18	−0.07	0.13	0.15	0.25
					Durable Goods						
Lumber and wood products	24	0.87	0.002	0.00	−0.08	0.06	0.18	−0.12	0.00	−0.26	0.02
Furniture and fixtures	25	0.87	0.005	0.00	−0.06	0.04	0.14	−0.20	0.00	−0.29	0.00
Stone, clay, and glass prod	32	0.91	0.001	0.08	−0.27	0.06	0.00	−0.17	0.00	−0.25	0.00
Primary metal industries	33	0.91	−0.004	0.00	−0.65	0.10	0.00	−0.31	0.00	−0.22	0.19
Fabricated metal products	34	0.98	0.002	0.00	−0.24	0.07	0.00	−0.31	0.00	−0.11	0.13
Machinery, except electrical	35	0.95	0.004	0.00	−0.45	0.06	0.00	−0.36	0.00	0.17	0.06
Electrical and electronic equip	36	0.90	0.005	0.00	−0.03	0.06	0.62	−0.32	0.00	0.06	0.45
Transportation equipment	37	0.57	0.002	0.00	−0.12	0.04	0.00	−0.37	0.00	0.12	0.06
Instruments and related prod	38	0.95	0.006	0.00	−0.13	0.05	0.01	−0.25	0.00	0.24	0.00
Misc manufacturing industries	39	0.88	0.000	0.67	−0.29	0.04	0.00	−0.15	0.00	−0.25	0.00

Notes: Dependent variable is log of employment (all workers). Data are seasonally adjusted. Model: AR1(METHOD-MAXL) 63,1 86.1 DOF: 74. CONSTANT TREND LREX(0,6) LURT(0,4) LRENGY(0,4).

Table 9.3 Employment for All Workers, 1975:I–1986:I

	SIC	RHO	TREND	SIG	LREX	SE	SIG	LURT	SIG	LRENGY	SIG
					Nondurable Goods						
Food and kindred products	20	0.14	0.001	0.05	−0.25	0.02	0.00	−0.03	0.05	−0.10	0.00
Tobacco manufactures	21	0.61	−0.002	0.41	−0.27	0.15	0.08	0.14	0.10	−0.21	0.26
Textile mill products	22	0.69	−0.004	0.00	−0.36	0.07	0.00	−0.01	0.86	−0.07	0.38
Apparel and other textile prod	23	0.31	−0.002	0.00	−0.27	0.05	0.00	−0.03	0.19	−0.01	0.87
Paper and allied products	26	0.69	0.001	0.06	−0.11	0.04	0.00	−0.11	0.00	−0.01	0.75
Print and publishing	27	−0.25	0.007	0.00	0.08	0.01	0.00	−0.14	0.00	0.02	0.07
Chemicals and allied products	28	0.92	0.001	0.33	−0.18	0.05	0.00	−0.09	0.00	0.09	0.08
Petroleum and coal products	29	0.04	−0.001	0.50	−0.55	0.14	0.00	−0.01	0.87	0.30	0.13
Rubber and misc plastics prod	30	0.64	0.007	0.00	−0.18	0.14	0.23	−0.28	0.00	−0.11	0.53
Leather and leather goods	31	0.84	−0.009	0.00	−0.58	0.15	0.00	0.10	0.26	0.24	0.17
					Durable Goods						
Lumber and wood products	24	0.59	0.004	0.02	−0.27	0.12	0.03	−0.20	0.01	−0.29	0.06
Furniture and fixtures	25	0.63	0.003	0.00	−0.06	0.06	0.37	−0.25	0.00	−0.10	0.17
Stone, clay, and glass prod	32	0.59	−0.001	0.07	−0.25	0.05	0.00	−0.27	0.00	−0.01	0.89
Primary metal industries	33	0.56	−0.010	0.00	−0.44	0.12	0.00	−0.48	0.00	0.44	0.01
Fabricated metal products	34	0.55	−0.000	0.71	−0.29	0.05	0.00	−0.37	0.00	0.08	0.22
Machinery, except electrical	35	0.62	0.000	0.83	−0.33	0.07	0.00	−0.43	0.00	0.45	0.00
Electrical and electronic equip	36	0.92	0.005	0.00	−0.11	0.07	0.14	−0.27	0.00	0.09	0.20
Transportation equipment	37	0.31	0.004	0.00	−0.20	0.06	0.00	−0.35	0.00	−0.14	0.07
Instruments and related prod	38	0.94	0.006	0.00	−0.25	0.07	0.00	−0.18	0.00	0.20	0.01
Misc manufacturing industries	39	0.69	−0.001	0.36	−0.38	0.08	0.00	−0.12	0.01	−0.14	0.14

Notes: Dependent variable is log of employment (all workers). Data are seasonally adjusted. Model: AR1(METHOD-MAXL) 75,1 86.1 DOF: 26. CONSTANT TREND LREX(0,6) LURT(0,4) LRENGY(0,4).

Table 9.4 Employment for All Workers, 1980–85

	SIC	1963			1970			1975		
		LREX	SE	SIG	LREX	SE	SIG	LREX	SE	SIG
					Nondurable Goods					
Food and kindred products	20	−0.01	0.03	0.75	−0.00	0.04	0.92	−0.25	0.02	0.00
Tobacco manufactures	21	−0.06	0.05	0.18	−0.07	0.06	0.27	−0.27	0.15	0.08
Textile mill products	22	−0.14	0.08	0.07	−0.16	0.03	0.00	−0.36	0.07	0.00
Apparel and other textile prod	23	−0.13	0.07	0.05	−0.11	0.03	0.00	−0.27	0.05	0.00
Paper and allied products	26	0.02	0.04	0.59	0.00	0.03	0.91	−0.11	0.04	0.00
Print and publishing	27	0.11	0.03	0.00	0.12	0.02	0.00	0.08	0.01	0.00
Chemicals and allied products	28	−0.08	0.04	0.07	−0.10	0.03	0.00	−0.18	0.05	0.00
Petroleum and coal products	29	−0.28	0.07	0.00	−0.25	0.06	0.00	−0.55	0.14	0.00
Rubber and misc plastics prod	30	−0.21	0.06	0.00	−0.19	0.05	0.00	−0.18	0.14	0.23
Leather and leather goods	31	−0.14	0.10	0.18	−0.14	0.11	0.21	−0.58	0.15	0.00
					Durable Goods					
Lumber and wood products	24	−0.08	0.06	0.18	−0.13	0.05	0.01	−0.27	0.12	0.03
Furniture and fixtures	25	−0.06	0.04	0.14	−0.05	0.05	0.31	−0.06	0.06	0.37
Stone, clay, and glass prod	32	−0.27	0.06	0.00	−0.28	0.04	0.00	−0.25	0.05	0.00
Primary metal industries	33	−0.65	0.10	0.00	−0.57	0.06	0.00	−0.44	0.12	0.00
Fabricated metal products	34	−0.24	0.07	0.00	−0.29	0.03	0.00	−0.29	0.05	0.00
Machinery, except electrical	35	−0.45	0.06	0.00	−0.41	0.03	0.00	−0.33	0.07	0.00
Electrical and electronic equip	36	−0.03	0.06	0.62	−0.03	0.05	0.53	−0.11	0.07	0.14
Transportation equipment	37	−0.12	0.04	0.00	−0.19	0.04	0.00	−0.20	0.06	0.00
Instruments and related prod	38	−0.13	0.05	0.01	−0.15	0.04	0.00	−0.25	0.07	0.00
Misc manufacturing industries	39	−0.29	0.04	0.00	−0.28	0.03	0.00	−0.38	0.08	0.00

Notes: Dependent variable is log of employment (all workers). Data are seasonally adjusted. Model: AR1(METHOD-MAXL). CONSTANT TREND LREX(0,6) LURT(0,4) LRENGY(0,4).

In each of the three sets of estimates, the signs of the *LREX* coefficients are overwhelmingly negative, in 18 of 20 industries in the 1963 and 1970 estimates and in 19 of 20 industries in the 1975 estimates. The 1963 and 1970 *LREX* coefficients are very similar. In the 1963 estimates the *LREX* coefficient is statistically significant at the .05 level for 11 industries. The 9 industries with insignificant coefficients include all 6 that were not significant in the 1970 regressions, plus 2 that would be significant at the .07 level. The sizes of the coefficients are also very similar. In all 20 of the industries the differences between the 1963 and the 1970 estimated *LREX* coefficients are less than twice the standard error (*SE*) from the 1970 regressions, and one cannot reject the hypothesis that the 2 coefficients are the same. In 16 of 20 industries the differences are less than one standard error. In most cases the coefficients are so similar that they are nearly identical.

The 1975 regressions are less similar to the 1970 estimates than the 1963 estimates, although for several industries there is little difference. Overall, 16 of the 20 industries have statistically significant coefficients, compared to 14 for the 1970 regressions. Three industries with insignificant coefficients in the 1970 regressions are significant over the shorter time period, including food and kindred products (*SIC* 20), paper and allied products (*SIC* 26), and leather and leather goods (*SIC* 31). One industry, rubber and miscellaneous plastics products (*SIC* 30), that has a significant coefficient in the 1963 and 1970 estimates is no longer significant for the 1975 regressions. Most of the industries that had the largest *LREX* coefficients in the 1970 estimates have roughly similar coefficients in the 1975 regressions. The estimated coefficients for a number of industries are quite different, however. Overall, for 14 of the 20 coefficients, the difference between the 1970 and the 1975 regressions is more than twice the 1970 standard error.

In most cases where there is a large difference between the 1963–70 regressions and the 1975 estimates, the *LREX* coefficient is larger in absolute value (more negative) for the 1975 regressions than for the 1963–70 estimates. The 1975 regressions place a much larger weight on the period 1978 through 1985, which experienced the greatest movement in the real exchange rate. The more recent period is also one in which the U.S. economy may have become more open and sensitive to international trade. On the other hand, the shorter period has fewer degrees of freedom and may overfit the data or place too much weight on periods that are unrepresentative because of shocks to the economy, such as the deep 1982 recession or the 1979 increase in oil prices.

For 16 of the 20 2-digit SIC industries, the 1970 regressions have the smallest estimated standard error for the *LREX* coefficient. For this reason, and also because it seems to be a good compromise between a longer history and the most recent experience, this time period is used hereafter as our base case. The choice of the time period, however, as well as many of the features of this or other models, remains inherently arbitrary, and caution should be used before too much reliance is placed on the individual industry estimates provided here.

9.5 Effects on Employment

The estimated coefficients presented in tables 9.1 through 9.4 provide one measure of the importance of the exchange rate to the manufacturing sector. These estimated elasticities give the percentage changes in employment that are the predicted percentage change in the exchange rate. As noted above, however, it is often helpful to have estimates of the number of jobs that will be affected by exchange rate movements. Table 9.5 provides these estimates.

Columns (3) and (4) in table 9.5 report the number of workers, in thousands, employed in each of 20 2-digit manufacturing industries in 1980 and 1985, respectively. For the manufacturing sector as a whole, employment declined from 20.29 million to 19.32 million, a loss of some 970,000 jobs. To decompose this employment change into the components attributed to the real exchange rate and other factors, the estimated model is used to predict the 1985 employment, given historical values for the four independent variables, *TREND, LRENGY, LURT,* and *LREX*. These numbers are reported in column (6).

Next, the predicted 1985 employment is recalculated four times, each time using the historical data for three of the series, but substituting the average 1980 values for the fourth independent variable. These new calculations represent the predicted value for employment, given the counterfactual case where the values for one of the independent variables remained at its 1980 level. The differences between the predictions based on the actual and the counterfactual values for the independent variables are the changes in employment that are attributed to the independent variables. These components of the change in employment are reported in columns (8), (9), (10), and (11), for each of the four independent variables. Column (12), which is labeled *RESID,* for the unexplained residual change, is the difference between the actual change and the change attributed to the four independent variables.[6]

According to these estimates, the appreciation of the dollar from 1980 to 1985 resulted in the loss of more than 1 million jobs for the manufacturing sector as a whole, or 5.3% of the work force employed in manufacturing in 1985. The *TREND* variable was associated with an increase of more than 400,000 jobs. The energy and unemployment

Table 9.5 **Change in Employment for All Workers, 1980–85 (Employment in Thousands)**

	Employment						1980–85 Employment Change[a]					Employment Change (%)[b]
(1)	SIC CODE (2)	1980 (3)	1985 (4)	Change (5)	Pred 1985 (6)	1985 Pred-Actual (7)	TREND (8)	ENERGY (9)	URATE (10)	EXCH (11)	RESID[c] (12)	(13)
	Nondurable Goods											
Food and kindred products	20	1,708	1,608	−100	1,623	15	−37.0	−3.0	−1.3	−8.6	−50.1	−0.5
Tobacco manufactures	21	69	65	−5	65	0	−5.2	0.4	−0.1	−0.4	0.8	−0.6
Textile mill products	22	848	704	−144	710	6	−83.9	−3.1	1.7	−42.6	−15.9	−6.1
Apparel and other textile prod	23	1,263	1,126	−138	1,134	9	−82.6	−6.6	3.4	−47.3	−4.7	−4.2
Paper and allied products	26	693	682	−11	689	6	7.2	−1.8	0.0	0.7	−16.6	0.1
Print and publishing	27	1,252	1,435	183	1,434	−1	158.6	−2.8	−2.6	52.9	−22.8	3.7
Chemicals and allied products	28	1,108	1,046	−62	1,054	8	1.1	−9.9	−1.5	−30.5	−20.9	−2.9
Petroleum and coal products	29	198	178	−21	179	2	−14.2	−4.1	−0.4	−16.6	14.8	−9.4
Rubber and misc plastics prod	30	727	790	63	799	10	109.9	12.3	0.2	−44.8	−15.1	−5.7
Leather and leather goods	31	233	166	−67	171	5	−50.3	−5.3	0.7	−9.6	−2.0	−5.8

	Durable Goods											
Lumber and wood products	24	691	701	10	704	3	41.8	13.7	3.3	−31.0	−18.3	−4.4
Furniture and fixtures	25	466	493	27	493	−0	37.7	8.2	0.8	−10.3	−9.2	−2.1
Stone, clay, and glass prod	32	663	591	−72	593	2	2.2	8.4	−0.3	−56.5	−25.6	−9.6
Primary metal industries	33	1,142	813	−330	816	3	−128.5	−9.7	−2.3	−158.2	−30.8	−19.5
Fabricated metal products	34	1,613	1,468	−146	1,470	3	11.6	3.8	−3.2	−133.9	−24.1	−9.1
Machinery, except electrical	35	2,494	2,182	−312	2,179	−3	64.8	−58.1	−12.1	−300.6	−6.3	−13.8
Electrical and electronic equip	36	2,091	2,207	117	2,212	5	205.4	−12.9	−5.4	−21.8	−48.8	−1.0
Transportation equipment	37	1,900	1,971	72	1,966	−5	131.0	22.4	−5.3	−101.0	24.4	−5.1
Instruments and related prod	38	711	724	12	735	12	79.1	−15.7	−2.8	−34.3	−14.1	−4.7
Misc manufacturing industries	39	419	369	−50	374	6	−10.7	3.5	0.1	−33.3	−9.3	−9.0
Total		20,287	19,316	−972	19,399	84	438	−60	−27	−1,028	−295	−5.3

[a]Change in 1985 predicted value when 1980 values are used.

[b]Due to exchange rate as percentage of 1985 employment.

[c]Employment change 1980–85 not attributed to the four variables.

variables together predicted an employment decline of less than 90,000, less than 0.5% of the work force employed in the manufacturing sector.

The unexplained decline in employment (*RESID*) is 295,000 jobs. This can be contrasted to the 84,000 difference between the predicted and actual employment for 1985. The apparent inconsistency between these figures is due to the lag structure of the model and the fact that the counterfactual assumptions use average values for 1980 rather than the particular history of values for the independent variables, including lagged quarters from 1979 and 1978.[7]

Among the individual sectors, two-thirds of the jobs lost because of the appreciation of the dollar are in four durable-goods industries: primary metals (−158,000), fabricated metal products (−134,000), nonelectrical machinery (−301,000), and transportation equipment (−101,000). Other durable-goods industries that experienced large job losses include lumber and wood products (−31,000), stone, clay, and glass products (−57,000), and instruments and related products (−34,000). Big losers among the nondurable goods industries include food and kindred products (−50,000), textile mill products and apparel and other textile products (−90,000), chemicals and allied products (−31,000), and rubber and miscellaneous plastics products (−45,000).

On a percentage basis, the big losers are primary metals, where the job losses represented nearly 20% of the 1985 work force, nonelectrical machinery (−13.8%), stone, clay, and glass products (−9.6%), fabricated metal products (−9.1%), petroleum and coal products (−9.4%), and miscellaneous manufacturing (−9.0%).

The industries that experienced the largest job losses are divided fairly evenly among industries that were experiencing secular decline and secular growth. Among the durable goods, three of the four largest losers in terms of the exchange rate show employment gains due to the *TREND* variable, but the largest percentage loser, primary metals, shows employment declines due to *TREND*. Among the nondurable goods sectors, six industries show employment declines due to *TREND*, and four of these show exchange-rate job losses that represent more than 5% of 1985 employment. Of the four nondurable goods industries that have positive growth in employment due to *TREND*, two have employment gains from the exchange-rate movement and two have declines. Overall, the two industries with the greatest *TREND* rate of growth are rubber and miscellaneous products and instruments and related products, and they experienced exchange-rate employment declines equal to 5.7% and 4.7%, respectively. The two industries with the most negative *TREND* growth rates are leather and leather goods and primary metal industries, and they experienced exchange-rate employment declines equal to 5.8% and 19.5%, respectively.

9.6 Production Workers and Non–Production Workers

The empirical results presented above relate to total employment. The Bureau of Labor Statistics also provides a series for the employment of production workers. The complement of this series, all workers minus the production workers, will be referred to here as "non–production workers." Production workers include employees who are directly engaged in the physical processes of production of manufactured goods—workers on assembly lines. The non-production series includes workers who are involved in research and development, marketing, transportation, secretarial and clerical tasks, and management activities.

If the market structure is such that the industry has a fixed ratio of production to non–production workers, and if production and non–production workers are both domiciled in the United States, then a movement in the real exchange rate would have the same percentage impact on production and non–production workers. If, on the other hand, the industry was characterized by increasing returns to scale, or if the results of the production workers' activities are more tradable than is the case for non–production workers, then exchange rate movements may have very different impacts on the production and non–production workers.

In tables 9.6 through 9.11, the two time series are compared, first to the combined series for all workers and then to each other. In table 9.6 the estimated coefficients for production workers are presented. Table 9.7 presents the results from the simulated decomposition of employment change, using the methodology described above. Table 9.8 compares results for production workers with those for all workers. Table 9.9 presents the results for non–production workers, and table 9.10 presents the results of the decomposition of change for this series.

A comparison between the production and non–production worker results is presented in table 9.11. In 15 of the 20 industries, the difference between the *LREX* coefficients is greater than two standard errors for the production worker series. Moreover, the signs of the coefficients are different for 8 of the 20 industries.

Within the nondurable goods industries the results are mixed. For half of the industries, the exchange-rate elasticities are more negative for production workers than is the case for non–production workers. Within the durable goods industries, the *LREX* coefficients are more negative in nine out of ten sectors, suggesting that production workers provide services that are more tradable than the services provided by non–production workers. Indeed, for three durable goods industries—electrical and electronic equipment, transportation equipment, and

Table 9.6 Employment for Production Workers, 1970:I–1986:I

	SIC	RHO	TREND	SIG	LREX	SE	SIG	LURT	SIG	LRENGY	SIG
					Nondurable Goods						
Food and kindred products	20	0.88	−0.000	0.54	0.01	0.04	0.78	−0.06	0.01	0.00	0.96
Tobacco manufactures	21	0.74	−0.005	0.00	−0.14	0.08	0.10	−0.01	0.92	−0.17	0.36
Textile mill products	22	0.72	−0.006	0.00	−0.15	0.03	0.00	−0.10	0.00	0.02	0.80
Apparel and other textile prod	23	0.72	−0.004	0.00	−0.09	0.03	0.01	−0.10	0.00	0.07	0.38
Paper and allied products	26	0.80	0.001	0.29	0.03	0.03	0.26	−0.16	0.00	−0.00	0.94
Print and publishing	27	0.92	0.005	0.00	0.17	0.02	0.00	−0.17	0.00	−0.02	0.66
Chemicals and allied products	28	0.87	−0.001	0.09	−0.13	0.03	0.00	−0.12	0.00	0.09	0.08
Petroleum and coal products	29	0.39	−0.004	0.01	−0.40	0.07	0.00	−0.11	0.11	0.29	0.15
Rubber and misc plastics prod	30	0.74	0.008	0.00	−0.20	0.06	0.00	−0.29	0.00	−0.27	0.07
Leather and leather goods	31	0.92	−0.014	0.00	−0.17	0.11	0.11	−0.03	0.60	0.35	0.03
					Durable Goods						
Lumber and wood products	24	0.76	0.003	0.00	−0.12	0.05	0.03	−0.21	0.00	−0.33	0.01
Furniture and fixtures	25	0.85	0.004	0.00	−0.07	0.05	0.18	−0.23	0.00	−0.26	0.01
Stone, clay, and glass prod	32	0.79	−0.000	0.73	−0.31	0.04	0.00	−0.20	0.00	−0.27	0.00
Primary metal industries	33	0.68	−0.008	0.00	−0.62	0.06	0.00	−0.40	0.00	0.09	0.57
Fabricated metal products	34	0.71	0.000	0.46	−0.31	0.03	0.00	−0.35	0.00	−0.12	0.08
Machinery, except electrical	35	0.72	0.000	0.73	−0.55	0.04	0.00	−0.47	0.00	0.28	0.00
Electrical and electronic equip	36	0.93	0.003	0.01	−0.16	0.07	0.04	−0.35	0.00	−0.06	0.60
Transportation equipment	37	0.37	0.003	0.01	−0.32	0.05	0.00	−0.43	0.00	−0.30	0.04
Instruments and related prod	38	0.90	0.004	0.00	−0.34	0.06	0.00	−0.30	0.00	0.22	0.02
Misc manufacturing industries	39	0.67	−0.002	0.00	−0.33	0.03	0.00	−0.18	0.00	−0.17	0.03

Notes: Dependent variable is log of employment (production workers). Data are seasonally adjusted. Model: AR1 (METHOD-MAXL) 70,1 86,1 DOF: 46. CONSTANT TREND LREX (0,6) LURT (0,4) LRENGY (0,4).

Table 9.7 **Change in Employment for Production Workers, 1980–85 (Employment in Thousands)**

	Employment						1980–85 Employment Change[a]					Employment Change (%)[b]
	SIC CODE	1980	1985	Change	Pred 1985	1985 Pred-Actual	TREND	ENERGY	URATE	EXCH	RESID[c]	
(1)	(2)	(3)	(4)	(5)	(6)	(7)	(8)	(9)	(10)	(11)	(12)	(13)
	Nondurable Goods											
Food and kindred products	20	1,175	1,122	−52	1,133	11.0	−8.6	−1.9	−1.2	−2.1	−38.4	−0.2
Tobacco manufactures	21	54	49	−5	49	0.5	−4.9	1.0	−0.1	−1.5	0.5	−3.1
Textile mill products	22	737	608	−129	612	4.4	−76.1	−3.3	1.7	−35.9	−15.2	−5.9
Apparel and other textile prod	23	1,080	949	−131	956	7.4	−84.3	−7.1	3.1	−36.5	−6.0	−3.8
Paper and allied products	26	523	516	−7	520	4.1	5.0	−1.9	0.0	4.5	−14.6	0.9
Print and publishing	27	699	793	95	794	0.3	72.0	0.5	−1.8	41.9	−18.1	5.3
Chemicals and allied products	28	626	579	−47	584	4.6	−8.2	−5.5	−0.3	−23.3	−9.2	−4.0
Petroleum and coal products	29	125	108	−18	107	−0.1	−9.0	−1.6	−0.4	−16.2	9.7	−15.1
Rubber and misc plastics prod	30	559	610	51	621	10.2	88.3	11.0	0.9	−36.1	−13.1	−5.9
Leather and leather goods	31	197	138	−59	142	4.2	−44.5	−4.4	0.6	−9.9	−1.1	−7.2

(*continued*)

Table 9.7 (continued)

	Employment						1980–85 Employment Change[a]					Employment Change (%)[b]
(1)	SIC CODE (2)	1980 (3)	1985 (4)	Change (5)	Pred 1985 (6)	1985 Pred-Actual (7)	TREND (8)	ENERGY (9)	URATE (10)	EXCH (11)	RESID[c] (12)	(13)
	Durable Goods											
Lumber and wood products	24	578	587	9	589	2.0	34.1	14.0	3.2	−25.2	−17.6	−4.3
Furniture and fixtures	25	376	394	18	393	−0.9	27.0	7.4	0.8	−10.6	−6.4	−2.7
Stone, clay, and glass prod	32	514	453	−61	452	−0.4	−1.9	8.7	0.1	−49.4	−18.5	−10.9
Primary metal industries	33	878	615	−263	616	0.4	−101.5	−4.5	−1.7	−131.3	−23.5	−21.3
Fabricated metal products	34	1,195	1,085	−110	1,084	−1.6	8.2	10.7	−1.8	−107.4	−19.7	−9.9
Machinery, except electrical	35	1,602	1,311	−291	1,303	−8.0	6.3	−29.8	−8.4	−243.0	−16.1	−18.5
Electrical and electronic equip	36	1,329	1,305	−24	1,305	−0.2	80.8	3.9	−1.3	−63.9	−43.0	−4.9
Transportation equipment	37	1,233	1,251	18	1,243	−8.3	73.3	36.1	−1.2	−111.5	21.3	−8.9
Instruments and related prod	38	425	393	−32	402	8.9	30.5	−7.6	−1.5	−44.4	−9.1	−11.3
Misc manufacturing industries	39	313	266	−48	269	3.5	−13.4	3.5	0.2	−29.7	−8.1	−11.2
Total		14,217	13,132	−1,085	13,174	42	73	29	−9	−932.0	−246	−7.1

[a]Change in 1985 predicted value when 1980 values are used.

[b]Due to exchange rate as percentage of 1985 employment.

[c]Employment change from 1980 to 1985 that is not attributed to the change in the four variables.

Table 9.8 Production Workers and All Workers, 1970:I–1986:I

		Exchange Rate Elasticities						Employment Change(%)[a]	
		Production Workers			All Workers			Production Workers	All Workers
	SIC CODE	LREX	SE	SIG	LREX	SE	SIG		
		Nondurable Goods							
Food and kindred products	20	0.01	0.04	0.78	−0.00	0.04	0.92	−0.2	−0.5
Tobacco manufactures	21	−0.14	0.08	0.10	−0.07	0.06	0.27	−3.1	−0.6
Textile mill products	22	−0.15	0.03	0.00	−0.16	0.03	0.00	−5.9	−6.1
Apparel and other textile prod	23	−0.09	0.03	0.01	−0.11	0.03	0.00	−3.8	−4.2
Paper and allied products	26	0.03	0.03	0.26	0.00	0.03	0.91	0.9	0.1
Print and publishing	27	0.17	0.02	0.00	0.12	0.02	0.00	5.3	3.7
Chemicals and allied products	28	−0.13	0.03	0.00	−0.10	0.03	0.00	−4.0	−2.9
Petroleum and coal products	29	−0.40	0.07	0.00	−0.25	0.06	0.00	−15.1	−9.4
Rubber and misc plastics prod	30	−0.20	0.06	0.00	−0.19	0.05	0.00	−5.9	−5.7
Leather and leather goods	31	−0.17	0.11	0.11	−0.14	0.11	0.21	−7.2	−5.8
		Durable Goods							
Lumber and wood products	24	−0.12	0.05	0.03	−0.13	0.05	0.01	−4.3	−4.4
Furniture and fixtures	25	−0.07	0.05	0.18	−0.05	0.05	0.31	−2.7	−2.1
Stone, clay, and glass prod	32	−0.31	0.04	0.00	−0.28	0.04	0.00	−10.9	−9.6
Primary metal industries	33	−0.62	0.06	0.00	−0.57	0.06	0.00	−21.3	−19.5
Fabricated metal products	34	−0.31	0.03	0.00	−0.29	0.03	0.00	−9.9	−9.1
Machinery, except electrical	35	−0.55	0.04	0.00	−0.41	0.03	0.00	−18.5	−13.8
Electrical and electronic equip	36	−0.16	0.07	0.04	−0.03	0.05	0.53	−4.9	−1.0
Transportation equipment	37	−0.32	0.05	0.00	−0.19	0.04	0.00	−8.9	−5.1
Instruments and related prod	38	−0.34	0.06	0.00	−0.15	0.04	0.00	−11.3	−4.7
Misc manufacturing industries	39	−0.33	0.03	0.00	−0.28	0.03	0.00	−11.2	−9.0

Notes: Model: AR1 (METHOD-MAXL) 70,1 86,1 DOF:46. CONSTANT TREND LRENGY (0,4) LURT(0,4) LREX(0,6).

[a]Due to exchange rate as percentage of 1980 employment.

Table 9.9 **Employment for Non-Production Workers**

	SIC	RHO	TREND	SIG	LREX	SE	SIG	LURT	SIG	LRENGY	SIG
					Nondurable Goods						
Food and kindred products	20	0.97	−0.003	0.00	−0.03	0.03	0.34	−0.03	0.02	0.04	0.28
Tobacco manufactures	21	0.20	0.000	0.81	0.20	0.06	0.00	−0.14	0.02	0.59	0.00
Textile mill products	22	0.78	−0.004	0.00	−0.20	0.04	0.00	−0.04	0.16	0.01	0.94
Apparel and other textile prod	23	0.88	0.001	0.30	−0.21	0.05	0.00	−0.07	0.02	−0.02	0.81
Paper and allied products	26	0.89	0.000	0.49	−0.07	0.05	0.12	−0.04	0.17	0.03	0.66
Print and publishing	27	0.95	0.007	0.00	0.04	0.03	0.15	−0.07	0.00	0.06	0.14
Chemicals and allied products	28	0.96	0.001	0.10	−0.08	0.04	0.08	−0.10	0.00	0.12	0.02
Petroleum and coal products	29	0.78	−0.004	0.01	−0.06	0.08	0.47	−0.03	0.60	0.49	0.00
Rubber and misc plastics prod	30	0.57	0.007	0.00	−0.16	0.02	0.00	−0.21	0.00	−0.08	0.13
Leather and leather goods	31	0.89	−0.009	0.00	0.05	0.12	0.68	−0.13	0.06	0.49	0.01
					Durable Goods						
Lumber and wood products	24	0.75	0.004	0.00	−0.17	0.05	0.00	−0.14	0.00	−0.00	0.96
Furniture and fixtures	25	0.87	0.006	0.00	0.02	0.05	0.71	−0.12	0.00	−0.12	0.25
Stone, clay, and glass prod	32	0.94	0.002	0.05	−0.19	0.06	0.00	−0.15	0.00	−0.01	0.89
Primary metal industries	33	0.89	−0.006	0.00	−0.40	0.05	0.00	−0.14	0.00	0.29	0.00
Fabricated metal products	34	0.92	0.001	0.14	−0.21	0.03	0.00	−0.20	0.00	0.20	0.00
Machinery, except electrical	35	0.79	0.004	0.00	−0.20	0.03	0.00	−0.20	0.00	0.37	0.00
Electrical and electronic equip	36	0.80	0.007	0.00	0.19	0.02	0.00	−0.28	0.00	0.31	0.00
Transportation equipment	37	0.79	0.004	0.00	0.09	0.04	0.02	−0.34	0.00	0.33	0.00
Instruments and related prod	38	0.91	0.008	0.00	0.11	0.04	0.01	−0.18	0.00	0.32	0.00
Misc manufacturing industries	39	0.79	0.001	0.09	−0.14	0.04	0.00	−0.07	0.02	0.04	0.68

Notes: Dependent variable is log of employment. Data are seasonally adjusted. Model: AR1 (METHOD-MAXL) 70,1 86,1 DOF: 46. CONSTANT TREND LREX(0,6) LURT(0,4) LRENGY(0,4).

Table 9.10 **Change in Employment for Non-Production Workers (Employment in Thousands)**

	Employment						1980–85 Employment Change[a]					Employment Change (%)[b]
	SIC Code	1980	1985	Change	Pred 1985	1985 Pred-Actual	TREND	ENERGY	URATE	EXCH	RESID[c]	
(1)	(2)	(3)	(4)	(5)	(6)	(7)	(8)	(9)	(10)	(11)	(12)	(13)
	Nondurable Goods											
Food and kindred products	20	534	486	−48	489	3	−29.4	−2.0	−0.1	−5.2	−11.0	−1.1
Tobacco manufactures	21	16	16	1	16	−0	0.1	−0.9	0.0	1.0	0.3	6.3
Textile mill products	22	111	96	−15	98	2	−8.0	0.0	0.1	−6.7	−0.4	−7.0
Apparel and other textile prod	23	184	177	−7	178	1	2.6	0.4	0.2	−13.0	2.7	−7.4
Paper and allied products	26	170	167	−4	169	2	1.5	−0.3	0.0	−3.0	−1.7	−1.8
Print and publishing	27	553	642	89	640	−2	88.6	−3.1	−0.8	8.5	−4.5	1.3
Chemicals and allied products	28	482	467	−15	468	1	7.9	−4.6	−1.2	−8.3	−9.0	−1.8
Petroleum and coal products	29	73	70	−3	71	1	−5.3	−2.5	0.0	−0.5	5.3	−0.7
Rubber and misc plastics prod	30	168	179	12	179	−0	21.7	1.4	−0.6	−8.7	−2.3	−4.9
Leather and leather goods	31	36	29	−7	30	1	−6.0	−1.4	0.0	0.5	−0.4	1.8

(*continued*)

Table 9.10 (continued)

		Employment					1980–85 Employment Change[a]					Employment Change (%)[b]
(1)	SIC Code (2)	1980 (3)	1985 (4)	Change (5)	Pred 1985 (6)	1985 Pred-Actual (7)	TREND (8)	ENERGY (9)	URATE (10)	EXCH (11)	RESID[c] (12)	(13)
		Durable Goods										
Lumber and wood products	24	113	114	1	115	1	8.6	0.0	0.0	−6.5	−1.1	−5.7
Furniture and fixtures	25	90	99	9	99	0	10.6	0.7	0.0	0.2	−2.5	0.2
Stone, clay, and glass prod	32	149	138	−11	139	1	4.3	0.1	−0.3	−8.1	−6.8	−5.9
Primary metal industries	33	265	198	−67	200	3	−25.2	−4.9	−0.6	−26.0	−10.3	−13.2
Fabricated metal products	34	418	382	−36	385	3	4.8	−6.2	−1.4	−26.6	−6.3	−7.0
Machinery, except electrical	35	892	870	−21	873	3	62.7	−27.5	−3.4	−57.6	4.6	−6.6
Electrical and electronic equip	36	762	902	140	907	5	122.4	−24.5	−4.5	50.1	−3.6	5.6
Transportation equipment	37	667	720	54	722	2	57.9	−19.6	−4.2	15.2	4.2	2.1
Instruments and related prod	38	286	330	44	333	3	48.1	−9.6	−1.2	11.7	−4.7	3.5
Misc manufacturing industries	39	105	103	−2	105	2	2.5	−0.1	0.0	−3.5	−1.2	−3.4
Total		6,071	6,184	113	6,215	31	370.0	−105	−18	−87	−48.7	−1.4

[a]Change in 1985 predicted value when 1980 values are used.

[b]Due to exchange rate as percentage of 1985 employment.

[c]Employment change 1980–85 not attributed to the four variables.

Table 9.11 Production Workers and Non-Production Workers, 1970:I–1986:I

		Exchange Rate Elasticities						Employment Change(%)[a]	
		Production Workers			Non-Production Workers			Production Workers	Non-Production Workers
	SIC CODE	LREX	SE	SIG	LREX	SE	SIG		
		Nondurable Goods							
Food and kindred products	20	0.01	0.04	0.78	−0.03	0.03	0.34	−0.2	−1.1
Tobacco manufactures	21	−0.14	0.08	0.10	0.20	0.06	0.00	−3.1	6.3
Textile mill products	22	−0.15	0.03	0.00	−0.20	0.04	0.00	−5.9	−7.0
Apparel and other textile prod	23	−0.09	0.03	0.01	−0.21	0.05	0.00	−3.8	−7.4
Paper and allied products	26	0.03	0.03	0.26	−0.07	0.05	0.12	0.9	−1.8
Print and publishing	27	0.17	0.02	0.00	0.04	0.03	0.15	5.3	1.3
Chemicals and allied products	28	−0.13	0.03	0.00	−0.08	0.04	0.08	−4.0	−1.8
Petroleum and coal products	29	−0.40	0.07	0.00	−0.06	0.08	0.47	−15.1	−0.7
Rubber and misc plastics prod	30	−0.20	0.06	0.00	−0.16	0.02	0.00	−5.9	−4.9
Leather and leather goods	31	−0.17	0.11	0.11	0.05	0.12	0.68	−7.2	1.8

(continued)

Table 9.11 (continued)

		Exchange Rate Elasticities						Employment Change(%)[a]	
		Production Workers			Non-Production Workers			Production Workers	Non-Production Workers
	SIC CODE	LREX	SE	SIG	LREX	SE	SIG		
					Durable Goods				
Lumber and wood products	24	−0.12	0.05	0.03	−0.17	0.05	0.00	−4.3	−5.7
Furniture and fixtures	25	−0.07	0.05	0.18	0.02	0.05	0.71	−2.7	0.2
Stone, clay, and glass prod	32	−0.31	0.04	0.00	−0.19	0.06	0.00	−10.9	−5.9
Primary metal industries	33	−0.62	0.06	0.00	−0.40	0.05	0.00	−21.3	−13.2
Fabricated metal products	34	−0.31	0.03	0.00	−0.21	0.03	0.00	−9.9	−7.0
Machinery, except electrical	35	−0.55	0.04	0.00	−0.20	0.03	0.00	−18.5	−6.6
Electrical and electronic equip	36	−0.16	0.07	0.04	0.19	0.02	0.00	−4.9	5.6
Transportation equipment	37	−0.32	0.05	0.00	0.09	0.04	0.02	−8.9	2.1
Instruments and related prod	38	−0.34	0.06	0.00	0.11	0.04	0.01	−11.3	3.5
Misc manufacturing industries	39	−0.33	0.03	0.00	−0.14	0.04	0.00	−11.2	−3.4
Total								−7.1	−1.4

Note: Model: AR1 (METHOD-MAXL) 70,1 86,1 DOF: 46. CONSTANT TREND LRENGY(0,4) LURT(0,4) LREX(0,6).

[a]Due to exchange rate as percentage of 1980 employment.

instruments and related products—the coefficients are negative and statistically significant for production workers, and positive and statistically significant for non-production workers. Thus for the instruments and related products industry, for example, the dollar appreciation from 1980 to 1985 is estimated to have caused a decrease of 11.3% for production workers, but an increase of 3.5% for non–production workers. Since the level of overall unemployment is controlled for in the estimates, the relative increase in non–production workers is not surprising.

These results suggest that a dollar appreciation may cause U.S. firms to move production facilities out of the United States, thus leading to a larger proportional reduction in production workers. This may mean that the jobs will not return to the United States now that the real value of the dollar has declined relative to foreign currencies. This may also imply that to some extent our model may be mis-specified, because of hysteresis effects.

Hysteresis reflects the dependence of present employment not only on the levels of the independent variables, but also on the path of those variables over the past. Industries or sectors where hysteresis effects may be important include industries where economies of scale or learning by doing are important, and where there are "sunk" costs for research and development (R&D), relocation, marketing efforts, capital investments, or other items that could represent a strategic barrier to entry in a market. It may be that once the initial costs of relocating production workers in foreign countries have been incurred, it will not be cost-effective to relocate the workers back in the United States after the dollar depreciates. Thus, while our model is useful in decomposing the causes of the changes in employment from 1980 to 1985, for some industries it may not be a good predictor of the employment changes that will occur in the more recent period of dollar depreciation.

Notes

1. The IMF defines the exchange rate as the inverse of EP^*/W from section 9.2. An increase of the index is an appreciation of the dollar.

2. We further considered the inclusion of a real interest rate variable, but found, surprisingly, that it had little explanatory power and did not significantly change the estimated exchange rate elasticities. The lack of explanatory power may be due to multicolinarity between the interest rate variable and the three variables *TREND*, *LURT*, and *LRENGY*.

3. The Beach-MacKinnon (1978) maximum likelihood procedure for correcting first order autocorrelation was used.

4. In an early version of this paper (Branson and Love 1986) we used a six-country index of exchange rates deflated by consumer prices. We have also experimented with an index based on wholesale prices, and we have used different weighing methods for the countries in the index. In general, changes

in the country weights or the price deflators have changed the metric of the estimates but not the ranking of the coefficients. The index based on unit labor costs tends to fit the data better than indexes based on wholesale or consumer prices.

5. Detrending of the unemployment rate to account for secular changes in labor force participation rates (a higher "natural rate") changes the estimated coefficient for the *LURT* variable and the *TREND* variable, but does not change the other coefficients.

6. The calculations reported in table 9.5 are the average of quarterly values, simulated as described in the text. The predicted values for 1985 are based on lagged values for the independent variables, and calculations based on the summed lagged coefficients reported in table 9.1 will lead to somewhat different answers from those in table 9.5, which are based on the particular lag structure estimated by the model.

7. If the model is true, then the first-quarter 1980 employment is a function of third-quarter 1978 real exchange rate and the first-quarter 1979 unemployment rate and price of energy, and not simply the average values for 1980 that are used in the counterfactual simulations. The values for the exchange rate, the unemployment rate, and the relative price of energy all underwent substantial changes between 1979 and 1980. The relative price of energy index rose from 114 in 1979:I to 144 in 1980:I, the civilian unemployment rate averaged 5.8% in 1979 and 7.1% for 1980, and the IMF relative unit labor cost index increased about 7% in 1980 over the value for 1979:I. The increase in the real exchange rate and the unemployment rate would suggest that the use of average 1980 values would understate the employment decline in the simulations, which explains both the additional 200-job loss in the residual category and the fact that the *RESID* column is negative for 18 of the 20 sectors. The use of the appropriately lagged series from 1978 to 1980 in the counterfactual simulations would result in a larger job loss associated with both the unemployment and the real exchange rate variables and a smaller job loss for the residual category.

References

Beach, C., and J. MacKinnon. 1978. A maximum likelihood procedure for regression with autocorrelated errors. *Econometrica* 46:51–58.

Branson, W. H. 1985. Causes of appreciation and volatility of the dollar. In Federal Reserve Bank of Kansas City, ed., The U.S. dollar—Recent developments, outlook, and policy options. Kansas City, pp. 33–54.

Branson, W. H., and James P. Love. 1986. Dollar appreciation and manufacturing employment and output. NBER Working Paper no. 1972, July.

Comment Robert M. Stern

Theoretical Considerations

Branson and Love begin with a theoretical framework in which three sectors are distinguished: exportables, import-competing goods, and

Robert M. Stern is a professor of economics and public policy in the Department of Economics and the Institute of Public Policy Studies at the University of Michigan, Ann Arbor.

nontradables. In the short run, with nominal wages and/or aggregate expenditure fixed, an exchange rate change will alter the value of the nominal variables relative to those abroad and thus bring about changes in output and employment. In terms of comparative statics, these changes in output and employment will depend on the magnitude of the change in the exchange rate and on the economic characteristics of the individual sectors, in particular the elasticity of supply of exports, the elasticity of substitution between imported and home-produced goods, and the input-output structure that will govern how individual sectors will respond to changes in the costs of intermediate inputs due to the exchange rate change itself and the secondary effects of the changes in outputs.

Since in their theoretical discussion Branson and Love rely on a partial equilibrium model, they can only provide a start toward understanding what the sectoral effects of exchange-rate changes may be. The full effects must include a variety of general-equilibrium interactions. Thus, for example, in their analysis of the sectoral impact of exchange-rate changes based on the Michigan Model of World Production and Trade, Deardorff and Stern (1986, esp. pp. 139–51), distinguish the following effects:

1. Export effect, which will depend on the elasticity of supply of the industry and the share of exports in total production
2. Import substitution effect, which will depend on the elasticity of substitution between imported and home-produced goods and the share of imports in total demand
3. World price effect, which will depend on the country's exports and imports as shares of the corresponding world supply and demand
4. Interindustry sales effect, which will depend on the share of final demand in total demand for an industry
5. Interindustry purchases effect, which will depend on the labor share of value added in an industry
6. Expenditure effect, which will depend on the size and direction of the change in consumer expenditure resulting from the change in the exchange rate

Branson and Love focus their presentation on the export and import substitution effects and also note that the United States is to be considered a large country in world trade. But they do not take into account the interindustry effects noted, and they do not explain if and how expenditure may be affected by the change in the exchange rate. Finally, they assume a common nomimal wage across all sectors, thus abstracting from differences and adjustments to changes in intersectoral wages.

The determinants of employment in each sector are assumed to be the same as the determinants of output, with employment and output being tied together by a production function. What form the production function takes is not stated explicitly in the paper, however. Presumably some allowance should be made in the production function for capital-labor substitution, as in the Michigan Model, but Branson and Love apparently abstract from such substitution.

Since there is reason to believe that sectors may differ substantially in their output and employment responses because of direct and indirect changes in relative prices as a consequence of a variety of general equilibrium interactions, it would thus be useful if Branson and Love were to be more explicit on what they were leaving out of their partial framework and how the omissions might affect the subsequent estimating equation and interpretation of results.

Estimating Equation

Branson and Love work with an estimating equation in which the log of employment in sector *i* over a given period of time is to be explained by lagged values of the log of the real exchange rate and domestic real income. The real exchange rate is supposed to capture changes in the relative prices of traded and nontraded goods. Changes in demand are presumed to reflect secular, cyclical, and structural influences, and the authors use a time trend, the log of the unemployment rate, and the log of the relative price of energy to capture these influences.

While the estimating equation bears a broad resemblance to the equations and discussion in the theoretical section of the paper, some of the links involved are not made clear. For example, in 9.2, the "real" exchange rate is $e = EP^*/P$, where P (P^*) is the relevant home (foreign) price. The key word here is "relevant." The authors apparently experimented with three different versions of the exchange rate based on relative movements in consumer prices, wholesale prices, and unit labor costs. They chose the latter measure on the basis of fit, although it is not clear if this particular measure is an accurate reflection of the relative price changes in tradables and nontradables. They assume that sectoral supply responds to the product wage (P/W), but as noted above, the wage is taken to be identical across industries, and no allowance is made for intersectoral wage differences which may in fact be fairly important.

An alternative procedure for decomposing the real income measure would be to fit a time trend and to measure the cyclical component of income in terms of deviation from trend. Presumably this would reflect the different elements of real income. Since they use a time trend and the unemployment rate, it is not clear that the two components of real income are being measured precisely. Further, the authors interpret the trend variable as measuring (9.4) "secular changes in income, tastes, comparative advantage, or technology." Since there are so many different influences included, it is not obvious what the trend variable is supposed to represent. Moreover, there is no allowance made for secular changes that could be important at the industry level.

Branson and Love use a four-quarter lag for the unemployment rate and the relative price of energy and a six-quarter lag for the real exchange rate index. They do not state how they selected these lag lengths. I imagine that it may have been after some previous experimentation with lags of different length.

Results

Even though the authors set up their theoretical analysis in terms of exportables, import-competing goods, and nontradables, they estimated single equations for 20 2-digit manufacturing industries without distinguishing the tradable characteristics of the different industries. It is not stated why they did not estimate equations as well for the agricultural sector and for the nontradables in order to provide a comprehensive set of estimates for all the major sectors in the economy. Not only would this be interesting in its own right, but it would call attention to the effects that the real appreciation of the dollar may have had in redistributing employment, especially between tradable and nontradable sectors. As it is, Branson and Love talk about "job losses" in manufacturing without considering whether the displaced workers may have been absorbed elsewhere in the economy.

Branson and Love ran their regressions for three different periods (1963:I–1986:I, 1970:I–1986:I, and 1975:I–1986:I) in order to "test the robustness" of the results. The best fits were for the period 1970:I–1986:I, and these were preferred over the longer and shorter time periods. It is not obvious why one would want to experiment with these different time periods, except that it may be worthwhile knowing how the coefficients may have been affected by the different events that took place. But distinguishing the results according to time period is not, despite what the authors suggest, a convincing test of the robustness of the results in terms of other structural changes that may have occurred or of omitted variables.

The ordinary-least-squares method is used for each of the 20 industries, with a correction for first-order autocorrelation. This assumes that the error terms are independent across equations. However, this may well not be true and, if not, the coefficient estimates may not be efficient. The equations should then be reestimated using generalized least squares to determine if the results may change.

For reasons that are not made clear, the industries are classified in the tables of results according to whether they represent nondurable or durable goods. However, there is only limited discussion of how the results differ. For example, it is evident that the durable goods sectors are more cyclically sensitive than the nondurable sectors in terms of the unemployment rate and relative energy price variables. The nondurable goods sectors especially show evidence of negative employment trends, which we would expect, and primary metals has a negative employment trend as well. The real exchange rate results appear on the whole to be larger for the durable goods sectors, especially primary and fabricated metals, nonelectrical machinery, stone, clay, and glass products, and miscellaneous manufactures. This may reflect in part the relatively homogeneous products involved, but there could be interindustry effects at work as well. In any event, some further interpretation of the results in terms of the economic factors at work would be useful.

Effects on Employment

Branson and Love use their empirical results to calculate the components of the sectoral changes in employment between 1980 and 1985. They conclude (9.6) that more than 1 million jobs were lost in the manufacturing sector as a whole because of the appreciation of the dollar. But, as mentioned above, since they do not include the agricultural and nontradable sectors, it is not clear how to interpret this calculation. Presumably the workers either became unemployed or they were absorbed in the nontradables sectors. To say that manufacturing jobs were "lost" may therefore be misleading. There were of course sizable impacts on employment in the tradables sectors due to the dollar appreciation. In this respect, the largest actual employment declines between 1980 and 1985 were in primary metals, nonelectrical machinery, fabricated metals, textiles, and apparel. The impact of the exchange rate was most pronounced in nonelectrical machinery and primary and fabricated metals. Primary metals also had a substantially negative trend effect, as did textiles and apparel. Printing and publishing, electrical machinery, and transport equipment had sizable positive employment trend effects, while transport equipment had a noteworthy decline in employment associated with the dollar appreciation.

Worker Characteristics

Branson and Love repeat the foregoing estimation for production and non–production workers in each of the 20 manufacturing industries. They show that the exchange-rate effects are much larger with respect to the employment of production workers, suggesting that the services of these workers are more tradable than the services of non–production workers. It would be interesting if they had made an effort to relate the employment results to the export and import-competing characteristics of the different industries and to a more detailed breakdown of the workers involved. Thus, for example, as Katz (1987, p. 7) and others have shown using cross-section data, import-competing industries "tend to have low wages, low value added per worker, and large concentrations of women, immigrants, and production workers relative to the typical manufacturing industries. . . . the opposite is true for . . . export . . . industries . . . [which] also tend to be more R&D intensive and to have more educated labor forces." The industry categories used by Branson and Love are perhaps too highly aggregated to identify clearly the major U.S. import-competing and export industries, and the industry labor force characteristics are not available on a continuous basis for all years. It would appear, nonetheless, that a richer and more complete portrayal of the employment impact of changes in the real exchange rate is possible than the one presented by the authors.

In their conclusion, Branson and Love note that their results suggest that dollar appreciation may cause U.S. firms to move production facilities abroad, to the detriment of U.S. production workers, and further, that because of hysteresis effects it may be difficult to reverse this process after the dollar depreciates. They view hysteresis as a possible source of misspecification of their model, which may possibly be the case. But one should not overemphasize hysteresis effects, especially in import-competing industries that are undergoing structural change because of relatively more abundant, and greater efficiency in the use of, factor endowments abroad. Thus, many U.S. industries would in any event be seeking out lower-cost sources of foreign supply. Dollar appreciation may have hastened this process, although to the extent that foreign investment in the United States was encouraged, there could be some offset to the employment declines associated with U.S. firms relocating abroad. Finally, the authors do not mention the difficulties that U.S. export industries may have in regaining markets. As implied above, this could work to the detriment of the relatively more skilled workers in the export industries.

References

Deardorff, Alan V., and Robert M. Stern. 1986. *The Michigan model of world production and trade: Theory and applications*. Cambridge: MIT Press.

Katz, Lawrence F. 1987. International trade and the wage structure in U.S. manufacturing. In process.

10 Long-Run Effects of the Strong Dollar

Paul Krugman

The fall of the dollar has now brought the U.S. real exchange rate down to roughly its level of the late 1970s. Against the yen and the deutsche mark, the dollar is at record real lows. Yet monthly trade numbers continue to report near-record trade deficits. Although some improvement in the U.S. trade position over the next few quarters is widely expected, few who have studied the issue believe that the depreciation of the dollar so far is sufficient to bring about anything approaching a return to current account balance.

Why does current account balance seem so unattainable, when the United States ran a current account surplus as recently as 1981? Pronouncements by Paul Volcker and some other officials suggest that the problem is inadequate growth in U.S. export markets, but this factor seems quantitatively of insufficient importance (see Krugman and Baldwin 1987). Congressional sentiment would like to blame the persistence of the U.S. trade deficit on unfair foreign trade practices, but few economists believe that these have gotten sufficiently more damaging since 1981 to account for the inability of the United States to restore current account balance. Business observers place weight on a decline in U.S. "competitiveness," a blurry term that refers among other things to a declining U.S. technological and productivity advantage; as we will see, there is at least rough empirical evidence that indeed supports the view that declining relative U.S. productivity has contributed substantially to the size of dollar decline required to restore a sustainable external balance. Finally, we are beginning to see assertions that a

Paul Krugman is a professor of economics at the Massachusetts Institute of Technology and a research associate of the National Bureau of Economic Research.

large part of the U.S. current account deficit is "structural" and insensitive to dollar devaluation.

All of these explanations seem, however, somewhat like ex post rationalizations. It would be intellectually much more appealing to make the growth of the U.S. trade deficit in the first half of the 1980s and its persistence in the second half part of the same story. That is, one cannot help but suspect that the stubbornness of the U.S. trade deficit in the face of a falling dollar is related to longer-term effects of the same causes that led to the emergence of that deficit in the first place. Or to put it a different way: is there some way in which a large and sustained trade deficit gets built into an economy, making it difficult to return to trade balance?

Now the idea that under certain circumstances adverse shocks to an economy produce long-term structural change has recently become popular in macroeconomics under the name of "hysteresis." (See Sachs 1986 and Blanchard and Summers 1986). It has been argued that hysteresis can occur in the unemployment rate if, for example, prolonged recession leads to a reduction in the capital stock, or if workers who have been long unemployed either come to be regarded as unemployable or are excluded from the wage bargain. It is not difficult to imagine several ways in which hysteresis might similarly arise in the current account balance. A prolonged trade deficit might lead to a large foreign debt, and restoration of the current account balance will then be made more difficult by the necessity of paying interest on that debt. A prolonged period during which a country's tradable sectors are uncompetitive may lead to disinvestment in those sectors, which may in turn mean that capacity contraints block restoration of trade balance when normal relative prices are restored. Finally, a prolonged deviation of a currency from its steady-state value misalignment may induce foreign firms to make, and domestic firms to abandon, invisible investments in market position, such as distribution networks and long-term customer reputation.

The purpose of this paper is to provide both an overview of theoretical reasons why a sustained dollar appreciation might lead to a sustained problem of international competitiveness and some quantitative assessments and evidence that bear on the issue. The paper begins by offering a simple measure of the extent of sustained overvaluation, which shows that if there indeed are long-term effects of sustained misalignment, then they are potentially of large magnitude indeed. Three main sources of long-term effects of a strong dollar are then considered. First is the effect of the strong dollar on the U.S. international investment position, with the dramatic shift of the United States from the world's largest creditor to its largest debtor. Second is the influence of dollar overvaluation on the allocation of capital between internationally competing and noncompeting sectors. Third is the possibility that foreign firms may have invested (and U.S. firms disinvested) in invisible assets such as reputation and distribution networks, leading to a loss in U.S. market share that cannot be regained simply through a return of the dollar to its previous levels. A final section of the paper pulls the evidence together.

To preview the verdict: while there are a number of plausible reasons why a period during which a country's currency is extremely strong might require a subsequent period of compensating undervaluation, there is not much evidence that any of these arguments has in fact been operating very strongly. Despite the massive overvaluation of the dollar, U.S. debt accumulation will probably not be enough to pose substantial additional difficulties in restoring a sustainable U.S. external account; there is surprisingly little evidence of a reallocation of capital away from tradable sectors, and there is no solid evidence of the kind of disinvestment in invisible assets that would shift the U.S. trade balance adversely for any given real exchange rate.

This does not mean that the United States faces no threats from the dollar's prolonged overvaluation. The country has grown accustomed to living beyond its means, and the adjustment down to living within its means will be painful even if there are no complications. Furthermore, if international investors decide to reduce the amount of U.S. debt that they hold willingly to levels comparable to those of six years ago, the United States will be forced into running a string of current account surpluses comparable to the deficits it ran in the period 1982–86, greatly aggravating the medium-term adjustment problem. Finally, the United States does appear to have suffered a major loss in competitiveness due to its lagging productivity growth, requiring a weaker dollar and worse terms of trade to cope with foreign competition. However, clear-cut evidence that the strong dollar itself has done lasting damage to U.S. competitiveness is surprisingly absent.

10.1 The Extent of the Potential Problem

We will be considering several alternative stories about how the strength of the dollar may have done long-term damage to the U.S. competitive position. Even if these stories are true, this does not mean that the United States will never return to current account balance: there is always some real exchange rate at which current account balance can be achieved, and the budget constraint will insure that the dollar is sooner or later driven down enough that the United States begins to pay its way in international markets. The point is instead that if the strong dollar has had long-run adverse effects, these will show up in the future path of the exchange rate. Each of the stories we will consider implies that a temporary period of dollar strength either permanently lowers the steady-state value of the dollar or requires that the dollar experience a period of compensating undervaluation to work off the effects of its initial overvaluation.

Figure 10.1 illustrates the possible senses in which a temporary deviation of the exchange rate from its steady-state value might be said to have long-run effects. The figure indicates the initial steady-state real exchange rate as $\bar{E}$. For some reason the exchange rate is pushed up temporarily. Most standard discussions have envisaged a subsequent path for the exchange rate like that illustrated as path (1): a gradual convergence of the exchange rate back to its long-run level. The concern of this paper is with possible reasons why the dollar might instead follow a path like (2) or (3). In case (2) the dollar depreciates below its original level, settling into a new steady state. In case (3) the dollar depreciates sharply below its original level, providing the compensating undervaluation needed eventually to restore the steady state.

Obviously it is crucial to specify the mechanism producing long-term effects of the strong dollar to determine both the nature of the path and the size of either the reduction in the steady-state exchange rate or the corrective undervaluation that will be necessary. All of the models suggested below, however, will relate the size of the long-term effect to the magnitude of the deviation from steady-state values that has occurred. As a preliminary step, it is therefore useful—and somewhat awe-inspiring—to contemplate the size of the deviation of the U.S. exchange rate from any likely estimate of its steady state during the 1980s to date. Figure 10.2 shows a comparison of the actual U.S. real exchange rate (Council of Economic Advisors estimate; the CEA series uses CPIs as price deflators) with a rough estimate of a steady-state value of the dollar from 1973 to 1986.[1] The difference between the two represents the cumulative deviation from the steady state since 1980: a total of 187 point-years of deviation. Some, though not all, stories about long-term effects of misalignment indicate that the dollar must go through a compensating undervaluation equal in extent to its initial

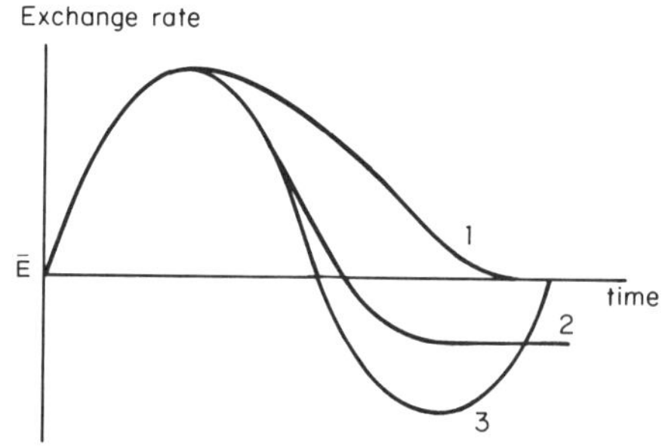

Fig. 10.1 Alternative paths for the dollar.

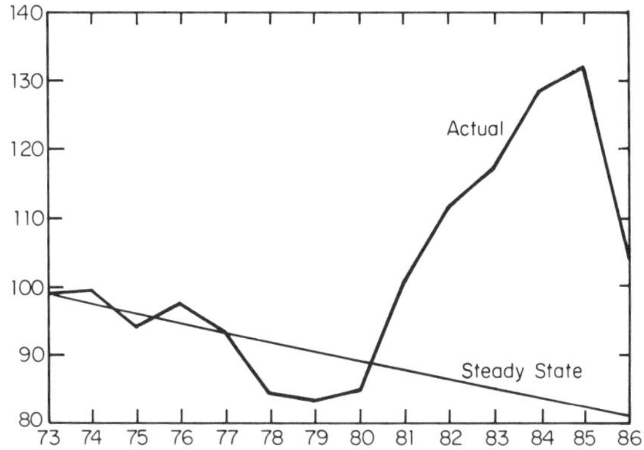

Fig. 10.2 Deviation of dollar from steady state.

point-years of misalignment. The extent of dollar weakness implied is startling.

10.2 The Debt Burden

The most easily measurable long-run effect of the strong dollar has been to transform the United States from a creditor to a debtor nation. The effect of debt accumulation in producing long-term effects of a temporary strong currency has been stressed by Branson (1985) in particular.

A reduced-form version of Branson's analysis may be given as follows. First, at any point in time the U.S. real exchange rate will depend negatively on U.S. net foreign indebtedness, because as foreign debt grows, foreign investors will perceive the United States as increasingly risky. On the assumption that it is foreign debt relative to U.S. GNP that matters, we may write this as

$$(1) \qquad E = E(d,z) \qquad \partial E/\partial d < 0,$$

where d is the ratio of foreign debt to GNP, and z is a vector of other factors.

Let r be the nominal interest rate, π the inflation rate, and g the growth rate of the U.S. economy. Then the growth of the U.S. debt-GNP ratio will be

$$(2) \qquad \dot{d} = -b + (r - \pi - g)d$$

where b is the ratio of the noninterest current account to GNP.

Finally, the noninterest current account will depend on the real exchange rate. Linearizing, we can write this as

$$(3) \qquad b = -\beta(E - \bar{E}).$$

Figure 10.3 illustrates how this small model works. On the vertical axis is the real exchange rate and on the horizontal axis the ratio of U.S. external debt to GNP. The line *EE* shows how the exchange rate depends at any point in time on the level of external debt. It is downward sloping because as U.S. debt grows, foreign investors will perceive greater risk and will demand a higher expected rate of return on U.S. assets. The line $\dot{d} = 0$ shows how the exchange rate consistent with a constant debt-GNP ratio depends on the level of external debt. It is downward sloping because as long as the real interest rate exceeds the growth rate, an increase in the level of debt will require an increase in the trade surplus to avoid explosive debt growth.

Now suppose that for some reason there is an increase in the exchange rate consistent with any given level of foreign debt. This might result from any of the explanations currently offered for the dollar's rise: a fall in U.S. national saving that raised real interest rates, a rise in investment demand brought about by changes in tax law, an exogenous shift in portfolio preferences due to renewed confidence in America or political instability abroad, or a simple speculative bubble. Whatever the source, the initial effect will be to shift *EE* up, say to *E'E'*. If the exchange rate is initially in equilibrium at point *R*, it will now shift to point *S*. However, over time, debt accumulation will gradually push the dollar down, as indicated by the arrows.

What happens next depends crucially on whether the shift in *EE* is permanent. If it is, the system will gradually converge to a long-run equilibrium at point *T*—that is, to a new steady-state exchange rate that is below the original level. This would be a story corresponding to path (2) in figure 10.1. On the other hand, suppose that the shift in *EE* is reversed—the speculative bubble that made foreigners willing to enlarge their claims on the United States bursts, the U.S. savings rate rises, and so forth. Then the economy will return to point *R*. To get there, it will have to experience a period of low real exchange rates so

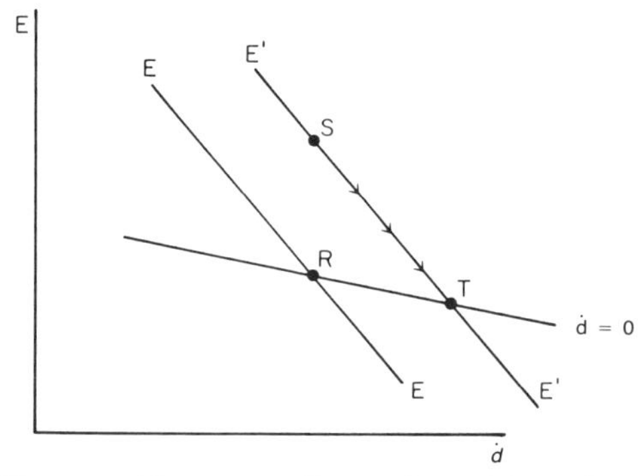

Fig. 10.3 Short- and long-run effects of portfolio shift.

as to run trade surpluses large enough to work off the debt. Specifically, if the initial shock comes at time O we must have[2]

$$(4) \qquad \int_0^\infty \dot{d}\, dt = -\beta \int_0^\infty (E_t - \bar{E}) e^{-(r - \pi - g)t}\, dt = 0.$$

That is, the initial deviation of the exchange rate from its steady-state level, measured in point-years, must be offset by a subsequent deviation on the other side that, as long as $r - \pi > g$, actually contains even more point-years.

How important are the long-term implications of the accumulation of U.S. external debt? The answer depends crucially on whether international investors remain willing to hold the stock of claims on the United States they have accumulated so far, or whether there is a demand for a return to the debt position of 1980. If the debt position need only be stabilized, the debt accumulation, though huge in absolute terms, will produce only a small drag on the U.S. current account. If the debt must be worked off, however, the burden of doing so will be large indeed.

Figure 10.4 shows actual and projected values of the U.S. net international investment position as a share of GNP. From 1978 to 1986 the numbers are actual (within the generous uncertainty of the data). From 1987 onwards they are based on the assumption of a linear return of the United States to current account balance, together with a combination of 2.5% real GNP growth and 3% inflation.[3] The United States can plausibly be expected to move from a net creditor position of almost 4% of GNP at the end of the 1970s to a net debtor position of 12% or more by the early 1990s—even if the current account does adjust steadily from this point onwards.

Viewed in absolute terms, the actual, and even more so the prospective, U.S. debt accumulation is daunting. (The nominal debt value

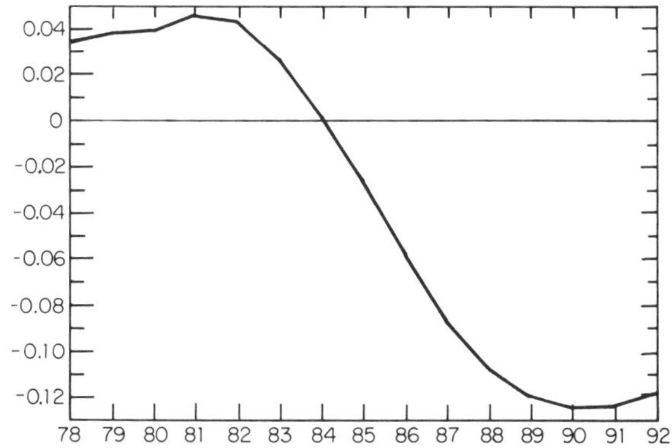

Fig. 10.4 U.S. external debt as percentage of GNP.

corresponding to the 1992 ratio of 12% of GNP is \$700 billion.) However, the United States is a huge country in an even-huger world. We need to be careful before getting alarmed about the size of even an apparently overwhelming debt accumulation. If foreign investors do not demand that the United States work off the debt it has run up and are content to allow the United States to stabilize its ratio of debt to GNP, then the debt buildup by itself will be relatively minor. On the other hand, if international investors decide not merely to end but to reverse the buildup of U.S. external debt, this would be a serious matter.

The relative ease with which the United States could stabilize the debt-GNP ratio despite the size of the debt accumulation is readily seen. To keep debt from rising faster than GNP, the United States must run a noninterest current surplus equal to $r - \pi - g$ times the value of the debt. The debt ratio d was approximately $-.04$ at the end of the 1970s, and may plausibly rise to .12 by the early 1990s; while the future of both the long-term real interest rate and the U.S. growth rate is uncertain, centrist guesses might be .04 and .025. This implies that the real resource transfer necessary to stabilize U.S. external debt would have been $-.06\%$ of GNP had there been no increase in the debt ratio since 1980, while it may have risen to $+.18\%$ of GNP by the early 1990s—a net swing of about .25% of GNP (about \$10 billion currently).[4] This is not a negligible amount, but it is not very large. If this were the whole story, the U.S. plunge into external debt would have to be considered no more important a factor in external adjustment than, for example, the trade policies of foreign governments, which have been widely dismissed as of secondary importance by economists.

Now it is possible that the direct burden of the debt will in fact be somewhat larger than this. Not all international claims consist of interest-bearing securities, and the rate of return on other investments is significantly higher. In 1985 the United States, although it had a roughly zero net investment position, ran a surplus of \$25 billion on investment income. This was at least partly because direct investment made up a higher share of U.S. assets than of U.S. liabilities (23 vs. 15%). It also reflected the fact that U.S. banks accepted foreign deposits and relent the money at higher interest—which may represent a miscounting as investment income of services provided by the U.S. financial system. To the extent that the growing debtor position of the United States is financed in future by a reversal of the U.S. position as more of a home than a host country for foreign direct investment, the burden of servicing foreign claims may be larger than would be calculated based on real interest rates for securities.

Nonetheless, it seems clear that the direct burden of growing U.S. debt, in the sense that restoring a sustainable external position will become much harder because of the need to pay interest on the debt, is in fact a relatively minor issue. This does not, however, mean that the growth in the debt is irrelevant. Similar calculations were made by many economists for less-developed debtors in the late 1970s and early 1980s, suggesting that LDC (less developed country) debt should not pose serious problems. These studies turned out to be wrong, because they failed to take into account the possibility that foreign investors would revise downward the quantity of debt they were willing to hold, forcing debtor nations into rapid shifts into trade surplus. If there is a major consequence of the accumulation of foreign debt by the United States, it must be the exposure of the United States to a similar risk.

Suppose that the willingness of foreigners to greatly increase their claims on the United States during the past five years turns out to have been a temporary aberration, and that starting sometime later in this decade the United States experiences capital outflows large enough to restore it to a positive net international investment position. The necessary concomitant of this restoration would be a very weak dollar. To work our way up to net debtor status took a massively strong dollar: from 1981 to 1986 the dollar was on average 31% above the level consistent with a stable net investment position. There is no reason why we might not now be faced with a period of comparable dollar weakness.

Now one might argue that such an extremely weak dollar will not happen because of the investment opportunities it would offer. A dollar so weak as to yield large current account surpluses would offer an opportunity to buy dollar-denominated assets with the expectation of large capital gains, and this would tend to mitigate the dollar's weakness. However, after the experience of the 1980s so far it is difficult to be so sanguine about financial markets. A cool appreciation of the long-run unsustainability of a very strong dollar did little to keep the dollar from rising to what in retrospect were thoroughly unjustified levels in 1984–85; there is no guarantee that the desire of investors to reduce claims on the United States will not lead to a similarly large undershooting of the dollar in the years ahead.

In summary, then, the growth in U.S. foreign debt does not pose a long-run problem for U.S. adjustment in the sense that the interest burden will make it difficult to achieve a sustainable balance of payments. Instead, the risk is that the run-up of debt in the 1980s will now be run in reverse, implying a dollar as weak relative to the steady-state level as the dollar of 1985 was strong.

10.3 Capital Reallocation

A second possible source of long-term effects of the dollar's overvaluation might be a reallocation of capital away from exporting and import-competing sectors. Press reports surely suggest that many U.S. manufacturing industries have retrenched or shifted production abroad; one would expect to find that this has been associated with a decline in the capital stock in these industries. To restore U.S. trade balance may therefore require a period of rebuilding, thus requiring a compensatory period of undervaluation to induce the necessary investment movement. There is a good deal of journalistic evidence for major movement out of tradable sectors by U.S. firms in the first half of the eighties; not only were there numerous complaints about "deindustrialization" and the emergence of the "hollow corporation," but stories about individual industries seem to fit the hypothesized pattern of shrinkage in the face of competition. Again and again, restoration of profitability in U.S. industries faced with foreign competition is said to have hinged crucially on closing of inefficient plants. Thus it seems plausible that capital reallocation should turn out to be a major long-term effect of the dollar's strength.

10.3.1 A Model of Capital Reallocation

The simplest model one can set up of capital reallocation is one that draws on the specific factor models of Neary (1978) and Mussa (1974, 1978). In this model a given stock of capital must be allocated between two sectors; it is costly to reallocate capital, so that capital moves only gradually to the sector of highest profitability. It would be more realistic, of course, to model a capital stock that grows over time, so that the choice is one of the allocation of investment at the margin rather than an actual movement of existing capital from one sector to another; but the simple capital reallocation model is sufficient to make the point.

Consider, then, an economy consisting of two sectors, one producing tradables and the other producing nontradables. Output in each sector is a constant-returns function of capital and labor. Labor is instantaneously mobile between sectors, while capital can be reallocated between sectors only at a cost that is increasing in the rate of reallocation. In order to focus on the issue of capital reallocation, let us assume full employment. Finally, in order to focus on the supply side, the trade balance will be taken to be exogenously given by international investment decisions.

First we consider the static relationships. Let K be the economy's total capital stock; it is divided at any point in time between the capital allocated to tradables, K_T, and that allocated to nontradables, K_N, so that

$$K_N = K - K_T. \tag{5}$$

Let P be the relative price of nontradables (which is one measure of the real exchange rate). Given our full-employment assumptions, this price will move so as to clear the market for nontraded goods. The supply of nontraded goods depends on their relative price and on the allocation of capital. The demand for nontradables will depend on their relative price and on real domestic expenditure. However, domestic expenditure is by definition equal to national income minus the trade balance, while national income depends on the allocation of capital and on relative prices. Thus we can write a reduced-form equation for P as a function of K_T and the real trade balance B:

(6) $$P = P(K_T, B) \qquad \partial P/\partial K_T > 0,\ \partial P/\partial B < 0.$$

Also, the rental rate on capital in each sector, measured in terms of the tradable good, depends on relative prices and the allocation of capital. Since relative prices in turn depend on the allocation of capital and the trade balance, we can write the reduced-form equations

(7) $$\rho_T = \rho_T(B, K_T)\ \partial\rho_T/\partial B > 0,\ \partial\rho_T/\partial K_T < 0.$$

(8) $$\rho_N = \rho_N(B, K_T)\ \partial\rho_N/\partial B < 0,\ \partial\rho_N/\partial K_T > 0.$$

Now consider the pricing of capital in each sector. Let us assume that there is a given world interest rate r in terms of the traded good, and that risk can be ignored. Then in each sector the rate of return on capital, including capital gains or losses, must be equal to r. Let q_t, q_N be the prices of capital in the two sectors. Then we must have

(9) $$r = \rho_T/ q_T + \dot{q}_T/q_T.$$

(10) $$r = \rho_N/q_N + \dot{q}_N/q_N.$$

Define $\tilde{q}$ as the difference between the value of capital in place in the two sectors, $q_T - q_N$. Then it is immediately apparent that $\tilde{q}$ will obey the law of motion

(9) $$d\tilde{q}/dt = H(\tilde{q}, K_T, B) \text{ with } H_1 > 0,\ H_2 > 0,\ H_3 < 0.$$

Capital will be reallocated to the sector with the higher price of capital. With convex costs of adjustment, the rate at which capital is reallocated will be an increasing function of the difference in prices of capital in place:

(10) $$\dot{K}_T = G(\tilde{q}).$$

This defines the dynamic system illustrated in figure 10.5. In the absence of any anticipated shocks, the allocation of capital will converge along the indicated saddle path.

10.3.2 Effects of a Temporary Trade Deficit

Now suppose that for some reason our economy is temporarily induced to run a trade deficit, say for N years. Suppose for simplicity

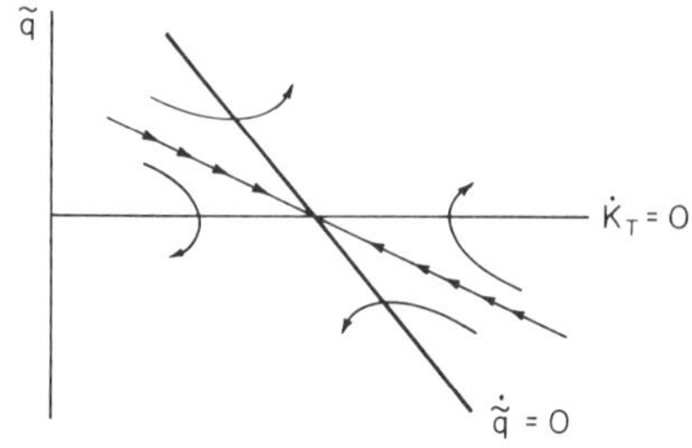

Fig. 10.5 Dynamics of capital reallocation.

that the length of time for which the deficit will persist is perfectly anticipated from the beginning. Then the dynamics will follow the path illustrated in figure 10.6. While the trade deficit persists, the line $d\tilde{q}/dt = 0$ will shift down, to the position indicated by the broken line. The capital stock allocated to tradables will therefore decline at first. Some time before the end of the trade deficit is anticipated, however, the capital in tradable industries will begin to rise again, so as to place the economy on the saddle path at the instant of transition.

If we look at the implied behavior of the relative price of nontradable goods, we will see that it first rises above its steady-state level, then falls below that level, before eventually returning to its original level. Thus the capital reallocation model implies that a temporary strong exchange rate must be followed by a corrective undervaluation along the lines of path (3) in figure 10.1.

Need this corrective undervaluation be equal in point-years to the original deviation from the steady-state exchange rate? The answer is no: because the reallocation of capital from tradables to nontradables tends to lower the relative rental in the nontradables sector even at a given real exchange rate, not all the incentive to return to the original allocation of capital need be supplied by the subsequent undervaluation. However, the effect of capital reallocation on the relative rental for a given relative price depends, as Neary has pointed out, on the difference in capital intensity in the two sectors. If the two sectors were of equal capital intensity, there would have to be a full corrective undervaluation. This suggests that the actual undervaluation would have to be fairly close to full compensation for the previous overvaluation.

The capital reallocation story thus seems to give a highly plausible reason why a strong dollar would have to be followed by a weak dollar before long-run equilibrium could be restored. However, the evidence on actual capital reallocation is puzzling and does not on the face of it support the view that the United States has in fact reallocated capital away from tradable production.

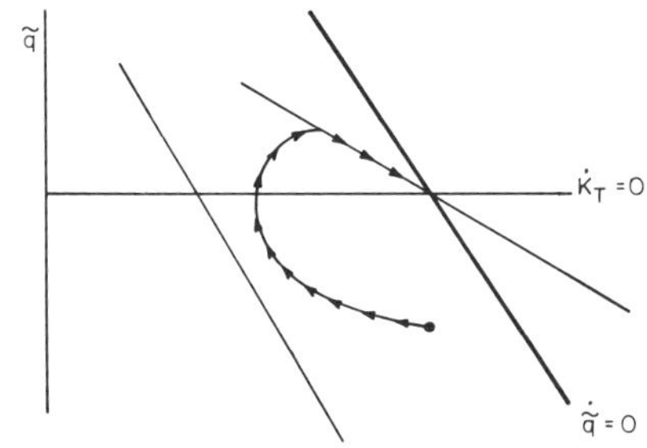

Fig. 10.6 Effects of a temporary trade deficit.

10.3.3 Capital Reallocation in the United States, 1979–85

It is a common approximation to treat tradables as equivalent to goods-producing industries, and nontradables as equivalent to services, on the grounds that goods are much more easily traded than services. Within the goods-producing sector, agriculture and mining have special problems that make it desirable to exclude them from the story. Thus the capital reallocation story should be apparent in a comparison of manufacturing with service sectors. Indeed, the rise of the U.S. trade deficit has been matched one-for-one by a rise in the manufacturing deficit, and there has been widespread concern that international competition has been undermining U.S. manufacturing.

Given these presumptions, it is surprising to discover that there is essentially no evidence of a reallocation of U.S. capital away from the manufacturing sector. Table 10.1 shows two measures of the allocation of U.S. investment between manufacturing and other sectors: the share of manufacturing investment in GNP and its share in total fixed investment. Neither measure shows any notable trend.

Table 10.1 **Indicators of Capital Reallocation: Fixed Investment in Manufacturing as a Share of GNP and Total Fixed Investment**

	GNP	Total Fixed Investment
1977	.034	.315
1978	.035	.303
1979	.038	.317
1980	.041	.348
1981	.041	.343
1982	.038	.329
1983	.034	.326
1984	.037	.333
1985	.038	.335
1986	.034	.316

This finding is part of the broader puzzle of what has been happening to U.S. manufacturing. The perception of massive deindustrialization does not arise purely from journalistic hype: employment in manufacturing has indeed been falling, with a 1.4% annual rate of decline from 1979 to 1985, compared with a 0.5% annual increase from 1973 to 1979. However, output growth has not slowed as much as one might have expected, given the surge in the manufacturing trade deficit: the growth rate dropped from 2.8 to 2.0% from 1973–79 to 1979–85. Correspondingly, productivity growth has accelerated, from 2.3 to 3.4% annually.[5]

It appears that the emergence of a manufacturing trade deficit has been accompanied by two other developments that blur the picture: a shift in the composition of domestic demand toward manufactures that has sustained the growth of manufacturing despite growing trade deficits, and a surge of capital deepening investment. The shift in domestic demand may be due in part to the military buildup, and the change in investment patterns to the incentives created by changes in the tax law. Whatever the reason, it is difficult to find any evidence of a shift of capital out of the manufacturing sector during the period of the strong dollar.

This does not, however, mean that capital shortage will not be an issue as the United States attempts to move back toward current account balance. If the shift of demand toward manufactures turns out to be permanent, then a reversal of the manufactures trade deficit will imply that manufactures output will have to grow substantially more rapidly than in either the seventies or the early eighties. One estimate puts the rate of growth over the next five years at 4.3% annually (Krugman and Hatsopoulos 1987). To grow this fast, manufacturing will need investment substantially above recent levels—and this will not be forthcoming unless the dollar falls sufficiently below its long-run level to make such an accelerated pace of manufacturing investment profitable. So there is still a case to be made that capital reallocation is an issue: if the dollar had not been so strong, there would have been a shift of investment toward manufacturing, and we may need a weak dollar to induce this investment in future. However, the clear-cut evidence that one might have expected of disinvestment in manufacturing is not there.

10.4 Invisible Assets

The market positions of firms do not depend simply on price and installed capacity. They also depend crucially on invisible assets of firms, such as distribution networks and customer loyalty. These invisible assets, like physical capital, can be built up through investment. It seems plausible to suppose that such invisible investment is an important factor in international trade flows.

At a fundamental level, invisible assets like reputation should be treated in the same way as more tangible investments. In practice, however, there are three reasons for treating them differently. First, invisible investment cannot easily be measured directly and thus must be inferred from its results. Second, since trade statistics measure flows of goods, while the invisible assets of firms tend to affect the perception of the value of these goods to consumers, invisible assets may show up as shifts in demand rather than supply. Finally, it seems plausible that in many cases investment in distribution, marketing, and so forth, has a strong fixed-cost aspect; a foreign firm must decide either to establish itself in the U.S. market, at substantial fixed cost, or not. These differing aspects suggest the need for a separate treatment of the possible long-term effects of the strong dollar that arise from foreign investment, and U.S. disinvestment, in the invisible aspects of international competitiveness.[6]

Recently Richard Baldwin and I (Baldwin and Krugman 1986) have offered a model that captures the fixed-cost aspect of investment in marketing and distribution. The most important conclusion of that model is that there should be a quantum effect: large and/or sustained deviations of the exchange rate from its historical norm will produce sustained effects on trade, where smaller deviations will not.

A crude test for the presence of such sustained effects is to ask whether trade equations show any adverse shift in U.S. exports and imports compared with what might otherwise have been expected given the trends in more conventional determinants of the trade flows. Table 10.2 presents some simple trade-flow equations for the United States, estimated for the period 1973–86. The equations are in log-linear form,

Table 10.2 Export and Import Equations

Dependent Variable	Export Volume	Export Volume	Import Volume	Import Volume
GNP	2.15	1.79	2.14	2.13
	(2.52)	(2.23)	(6.61)	(6.56)
Relative productivity	−1.14	−0.91	0.64	0.62
	(1.32)	(1.16)	(2.20)	(2.11)
Relative prices[a]	−0.65	−0.72	−0.98	−0.95
	(3.55)	(4.23)	(10.21)	(8.27)
Dummy[b]	—	0.05	—	0.02
		(1.97)		(0.49)
R^2	0.99	0.99	0.99	0.99
ρ	0.83	0.76	0.50	0.49

[a]Eight-quarter distributed lag.
[b]For period following 1984:II.

with the dependent variables being the volumes of U.S. nonagricultural exports and nonoil imports. The explanatory variables are GNP in the United States or the rest of the world, a distributed lag on the price of the traded good relative to either CPIs (in foreign markets) or the GNP deflator (in the United States), and—crucially—a measure of U.S. productivity in manufacturing relative to that of other industrial countries.[7] This last index is necessary to account for the apparent secular decline in the U.S. real exchange rate consistent with current account balance during the 1970s; a theoretical justification for the role of relative productivity in the trade equation is given in Krugman and Baldwin (1987).

The basic equations turn out fairly plausible, with price and income elasticities of plausible magnitude and relative productivity having the expected sign. However, two of the equations also include dummy variables designed to capture any structural shift as a result of the strong dollar. These dummies are zero before the third quarter of 1984, one afterwards; this somewhat arbitrary choice was made because it was in mid-1984 that financial markets seem to have concluded that the dollar could defy the laws of gravity indefinitely, and the final surge in the value of the dollar took place. Thus it seems a reasonable guess that firms making investment decisions would have decided to give up on waiting for a lower dollar at about the same time.

The result is somewhat surprising: there is no evidence of an adverse structural shift. If anything, the equations suggest a favorable shift in export performance. Thus the worry that the strong dollar has permanently impaired U.S. market position does not seem to be supported.

If this is the case, why does the return of the dollar to its 1970s level not lead to expectations of a great surge in U.S. trade performance? The answer lies in the relative productivity term: according to these estimates, it is the long-term decline in the U.S. productivity edge, rather than the damage done by the strong dollar, that requires that the dollar fall well below its historical levels in order to reverse the deficits of the mid-1980s.

10.5 Conclusions

This paper has reviewed several reasons why the strength of the dollar in the period 1981–86 might have long-term adverse effects on U.S. competitiveness. While it is easy to construct stories in which sustained deviations of a currency from its long-run sustainable level do have long-term effects, the evidence for such effects in the case of the United States is surprisingly weak. The burden of stabilizing the debt-GNP ratio will not be greatly exacerbated by the rise in that ratio, because the real interest rate does not greatly exceed the U.S. growth rate. There has been no visible reallocation of capital out of the U.S.

manufacturing sector. And there is no evidence of adverse structural shifts in U.S. trade flow equations.

This does not mean that the United States will be able comfortably to return to the equilibrium of 1980. There may still be a shortage of capital in manufacturing as the United States attempts to restore capital account balance. The trade flow equations embody, through a relative productivity term, a secular decline in the equilibrium real exchange rate that has continued through the 1980s. Finally, stabilizing the debt-GNP ratio may not be enough: if international investors attempt to reverse their buildup of claims on the United States, the United States may be forced into a period of capital outflow and a correspondingly weak dollar—which would be our version of a Latin-style debt crisis. Nonetheless, the basic message of this paper is cautiously optimistic: on the basis of preliminary evidence, the long-term damage from the strong dollar is less than one might have feared.

Notes

1. This estimate was derived as follows: the actual exchange rate in 1973 was assumed to represent a steady-state value; the steady-state value in 1980 was assumed to be 5% logarithmic above the actual; this reflects the widespread belief that the 1980 dollar was if anything somewhat undervalued. The steady-state exchange rate in fourth quarter 1986 was assumed to be 20% below the actual, reflecting a conservative guess about how much further dollar depreciation would have been needed to stabilize the U.S. debt-GNP ratio. The intervening steady-state rates were then filled in by log-linear interpolation. The decline in the steady-state exchange rate from 1980 to 1986 presumably reflects a combination of slow growth of foreign demand and secular trends in U.S. competitiveness, as discussed later in the paper.

2. If the debt-GNP ratio is eventually to return to its original level, then the integral over time of changes in that ratio must equal zero.

3. The U.S. current account, which equals the increase in net debt, declines $28 billion per year from $140 billion in 1986 to zero in 1991. The nominal debt is simply the cumulative current account to each year's end; the debt ratio is calculated as this nominal debt divided by nominal GNP, extrapolated from the 1986 GNP using the assumed inflation and growth.

4. If long-term U.S. growth should turn out to be 2% and the real interest rate 5%, the required resource transfer would double; if the numbers were 1.5 and 6, it would triple; but even in this extremely pessimistic scenario the resource transfer required to stabilize debt would not be overwhelming.

5. A good example of what seems to have been the typical case for U.S. manufacturing is the case of the tire industry, described in the *US Industrial Outlook* for 1986. There import competition led to closing of many plants and a 35% decline in employment from the 1970s to 1985; yet the industry invested heavily in improving the remaining plants. Real output, which fell 20% from 1973 to 1979, was stable from 1979 to 1985. From the point of view of workers,

this was an industry in decline; to someone who looked at either capital investment or productivity, the industry was actually doing quite well.

6. The picture is complicated to some extent by multinational firms, for whom the problem is one of choosing a location of production rather than deciding whether or not to be in the market. However, location decisions also involve substantial invisible investment commitments, so that the qualitative behavior of trade flow originating from multinationals need not be very different from that originating from competing national firms.

7. The index is based on interpolation and extrapolation of the relative productivity numbers provided by Data Resources, Inc. (DRI) (1985), with foreign countries weighted by bilateral trade with the United States in 1984.

References

Baldwin, Richard, and Paul Krugman. 1986. Persistent trade effects of large exchange rate shocks. NBER Working Paper no. 2167.

Blanchard, Olivier, and Lawrence Summers. Hysteresis and the European unemployment problem. NBER Working Paper no. 1950 (June).

Branson, William. 1985. Causes of appreciation and volatility of the dollar. In Federal Reserve Bank of Kansas City, *The U.S. dollar: Prospects and policy options*.

Data Resources, Inc. 1985. The competitiveness of U.S. manufacturing industry: International comparisons of labor, energy, and capital costs.

Helkie, William L., and Peter Hooper. 1987. The U.S. external deficit in the 1980s. Presented at the Brookings Workshop on the U.S. Current Account, January 1987.

Krugman, Paul, and Richard Baldwin. 1987. The persistence of the U.S. trade deficit. *Brookings Papers on Economic Activity* 1:1987.

Krugman, Paul, and George Hatsopoulos. 1987. The problem of U.S. competitiveness in manufacturing. *New England Economic Review* (Jan.–Feb.).

Mussa, Michael. 1974. Tariffs and the distribution of income. *Journal of Political Economy* (82):1191–1204.

———. 1978. Dynamic adjustment in the Heckscher-Ohlin-Samuelson model. *Journal of Political Economy* (86):775–94.

Neary, J. Peter. 1978. Short-run capital specificity and the pure theory of international trade. *Economic Journal* (88):488–510.

Sachs, Jeffrey. 1986. High unemployment in Europe: Diagnosis and policy implications. NBER Working Paper no. 1831 (Feb).

U.S. Department of Commerce. 1986. *U.S. Industrial Outlook*. Washington, D.C.: Government Printing Office.

Comment   Kala Krishna

Krugman presents a number of models which cast light on the consequences of the strong dollar. As he rightly points out, it would be

Kala Krishna is assistant professor of economics at Harvard University and a faculty research fellow of the National Bureau of Economic Research.

desirable to have the strong dollar of the recent past and the currently weak dollar to be part of the same story. The exogenous shift which caused the strong dollar should also be a reason for its current weakness. This is preferable to having both events be the result of unspecified exogenous shocks.

He examines three models which try to do this. The first one focuses on the role of debt on the long-run effects of a strong dollar. The second focuses on specific capital and movement of such capital across sectors in response to shocks. The third one focuses on the effects of entry and exit costs on the long-run effects of a strong dollar. I shall comment on each of these models and on the empirical evidence presented on the relevance of their insights.

The first model is similar to that presented by Branson, and since it aroused a number of comments, I will not dwell on it at length. The basic idea in this model is that an exogenous shock occurs which causes a strong dollar in the short run, which in turn creates an increase in debt over time. This increase in debt requires a weak dollar to service the debt in the long run if the shock is not reversed. If the shock is reversed, then a weak dollar will be required to run trade surpluses large enough to work off the debt. If the shock is not reversed, the increase in debt does call for a weaker dollar, but if the shock is reversed, the increase in debt calls for an even weaker dollar to pay off the debt. Krugman then argues that the former scenario should not cause much concern about the extent of dollar weakness required, while the latter should, on the basis of some simple calculations. This makes a good deal of sense. The question remains, however, as to which scenario is more appropriate in the current context, and the paper has less to say about this aspect of the dollar problem. Speculations on this would be a welcome addition to the paper. Another point which could be made clearer concerns the motivation for equation (1), which postulates that an increase in the debt-to-GNP ratio, d, lowers the real exchange rate, E, at any time. The motivation given is that an increase in d makes foreign investors perceive the United States to be increasingly risky. However, little is said about what the risk is. It could be a risk of repudiation—not only explicit repudiation, but implicit repudiation by inflation. It might also involve riskiness due to possible consequences of attempts by the holders of debt to use it strategically. For example, a decision by the Japanese banks not to hold T bills would probably have a large effect on the market today, and concern about Japanese actions could raise the perceived riskiness of U.S. investments. The model in the paper could be built upon to specify such a basis for such perceptions.

The second model focuses on the reallocation of capital between tradables and nontradables implied by a change in the real trade balance. The model suggests that an increase in the trade deficit will be accompanied by an increase in demand for nontradables, which results in an increase in the relative price of nontradables—that is, an appreciation of the dollar. This causes a reallocation of specific capital towards nontradables. The shift in specific capital raises the supply of nontradables, reducing their price.

For this reason, an increase in the trade deficit which it is anticipated will disappear in the future would result in an initial increase in the price of nontradables, *p,* and cause a strong dollar. As capital moved across sectors to this nontraded sector, the price of nontradables would fall. The anticipated disappearance of the increase in the trade deficit would require that capital be moved back to the traded sector. This would require an increase in the price of tradables—that is, an even weaker dollar in the interim period before the relative price stabilized to the original level. The basic idea in this model is thus that the strong dollar and the weak dollar were caused by a temporary exogenous shock which raised the trade deficit. The strong dollar was the result of the increase in demand for nontradables implied by the trade deficit. This reallocated capital to nontradables. The weak dollar was the result of having too much capital in nontradables when the shock disappeared, which required a reallocation of capital back into tradables and a weak dollar.

Krugman studies whether we can see such a reallocation of capital between services (K_N) and manufacturing (K_T) in 1979–85. He does not find such a reallocation in the aggregate data he looks at. However, it would be surprising if the reallocation had been apparent in the aggregate. It is likely that such evidence would only be forthcoming in a more detailed study.

In addition, an implication of the model is that $\tilde{q} = q_T - q_N$, the difference in the valuation of capital in the two sectors, falls and then rises to fall again. Do such differences in the valuation of capital in the two sectors arise in the data?

In order to be convincing empirically, a more careful industry-level study which identifies "open" industries, is needed. It would also be a good idea to omit military industries from the sample, since the growth of defense expenditure in this period could bias the results, and to examine both movements in capital stock across sectors and movements in the valuation of assets in the two sectors.

The third model focuses on the effect of entry and exit costs faced by firms, on the long-run effects of a strong dollar. The basic idea is that once Japanese firms are in the U.S. market, a large dollar depreciation is needed to drive them out. Hence, if a strong dollar caused entry of Japanese firms, we should expect to see a structural change in the import-export performance equations. Krugman tests whether a dummy variable, which is zero before the third quarter of 1984 and

1 after this, is significant. He finds that there is little evidence of such a structural shift. Once again, it seems unlikely that one would see such a shift in aggregate data, and one should look for such evidence at the industry level, focusing on industries where such costs are likely to be significant and which have foreign competition.

The drawback of using aggregate data in a country such as the United States which is not as open to trade as are a number of smaller countries is that the effects of trade shocks tend to be less obvious in the data.[1] This makes it important that aggregate evidence not be the only kind analyzed.

Another reason that long-run effects of the strong dollar may exist might be related to recent work on pass-through or pricing to market, mentioned by Johnson and Loopesko in this conference. Imports may adjust slowly to a depreciating dollar if the price of imports on foreign exchange also changes so as to keep the dollar price stable—that is, a pass-through of zero. The obvious point about the extent of pass-through is that a pass-through of unity is not necessary in any market structure, since exchange rate changes act like ad valorem taxes/subsidies, and it is well understood that the incidence of such taxes rarely falls on only one side of the market.[2] However, this does not have much to say about the long-run consequences of a strong dollar.

The presence of adjustment costs—such as costs of hiring and firing labor—do give long-run effects of a strong dollar. Such adjustment costs tend to have two implications. First, they tend to stabilize employment by making firms choose to employ fewer workers in good states and more in bad states. This stabilizes output, and if most output is exported to the United States, this stabilizes the dollar price. In addition, adjustment costs make employment and output decisions contingent on both expectations about the future and on previous employment levels, which of course depend on the entire history of previous states. They tend to create large regions of inertia in the choice of employment. Thus, if a strong dollar raised the employment and output of firms exporting to the United States, only a very weak dollar which is expected to remain weak would induce such firms to cut employment and exports. For smaller depreciations of the dollar, employment, output, and exports by such firms would be maintained. Thus, a strong dollar, by adjusting upwards the existing labor force in firms exporting to the United States, would have long-run consequences by requiring very large depreciations to combat low pass-through. While simple models of such phenomena exist, work in this area is at a relatively

1. The ratio of exports to GNP in the United States is only about 10%.

2. A number of such models are constructed in Krugman 1986, which also has several references to recent work in the area.

immature state, and testable predictions of models with adjustment costs are only beginning to emerge.[3] This seems like a very promising area for future research.

References

Caplin, A., and K. Krishna. 1986. A simple dynamic model of employment. Harvard University (mimeo).

Krugman, P. 1986. Pricing to market when the exchange rate changes. National Bureau of Economic Research Working Paper no. 1926.

3. A simple model of such labor market dynamics can be found in Caplin and Krishna (1986).

11 New Directions for Research

Rudiger Dornbusch

In the 1960s, Robert Mundell and Marcus Flemming worked out the formal framework for open-economy macroeconomics that would reign for more than a quarter of a century. The Mundell-Flemming model, built on the assumption that prices move slowly relative to exchange rates and that international capital mobility is a central factor in the transmission of business cycles, continues virtually unchallenged today. Of course, the models we use today have gone further in separating short run and long run, in allowing a role for expectations, and in taking into account the consequences of trade imbalances for asset accumulation. Even the stock market has now become part of the wider model. But the conclusions remain close to those of the Mundell-Flemming model. When we ask what the impact of monetary expansion is on the exchange rate and the balance of trade, the answer continues to be that increased money induces a real depreciation and hence an improvement in the external balance. Where then is the fruit of research in the past ten or fifteen years? These recent advances, even though they are only starting to show all their implications, will significantly advance our understanding of open-economy macroeconomics.

I want to highlight here three separate directions of research. The first is models of imperfect competition with their implications for price adjustment to exchange rate or commercial policy disturbances. The second direction of research is concerned with models of adjustment built around the notion of irreversible investments and the value of waiting. The third research program deals with apparently excessive

Rudiger Dornbusch is Ford International Professor of Economics at the Massachusetts Institute of Technology and a research associate at the National Bureau of Economic Research.

movements in exchange rates in response to disturbances. I will consider these in turn.

11.1 Pricing

There are two models of open-economy macroeconomics. One model assumes a small country that faces given prices in world trade and adjusts, under conditions of perfect competition, to those prices. Depreciation raises prices equiproportionately, and tariff liberalization reduces import prices by the full amount of the tariff cut. The other model, which is used as the pricing assumption in Mundell-Flemming, has prices as a fixed markup over unit labor costs. Wages are assumed fixed in nominal terms and so accordingly are prices. In this model, depreciation brings about an equiproportionate gain in competitiveness or loss in the terms of trade.

The new direction of research considers explicitly an industrial-organization pricing approach as part of the macroeconomic model. Pricing depends on market structure, market segmentation, and the domestic-versus-foreign cost base of participating firms. This approach has obvious fruits in two areas of application. Consider first exchange rate movements. When a currency is depreciated, with wages fixed at home and abroad, foreign firms experience a cost increase in home currency while home firms have no change in their cost. Industry equilibrium is disturbed by the unfavorable cost shock experienced by foreign firms, and industry price must change. The adjustment in price will depend on a host of factors. An example will make this point. Using a partial equilibrium approach to a particular industry, suppose that the product is diversified and that the Salop-circle model describes well the diversification. Assume that consumers are uniformly distributed along the product circle (in terms of their tastes) and that there are four firms, two domestic and two foreign. They alternate so that firms 1 and 3 are foreign, while firms 2 and 4 are domestic. Initially spatial competition has established a symmetric location pattern where firms share the market equally, so that each firm serves an equal number of customers to the left and right.

We now explore the effects of a home depreciation, given fixed unit labor costs in each country.[1] Consider firm 1. The depreciation of, say 10%, raises foreign firms' costs in dollars and raises marginal cost relative to the unchanged marginal revenue of competing the marginal customer away from firm 2 or firm 3. The equilibrium relative price structure will change as firm 1 raises its price and firms 2 and 4 match the increase partially. Figure 11.1 shows the reaction functions of the typical domestic (*DD*) and foreign firms (*RR*). The equations are, respectively:

(1) $$p = (p^* + c/n + w)/2$$

and

(2) $$p^* = (p + c/n + ew^*)/2,$$

where w and w^* are unit labor costs in the respective currencies, c is the consumers' transport cost per unit distance away from the preferred product, and n is the total number of firms supplying the market. The price structure is determined by the Nash equilibrium at point A. The level of prices is higher, relative to unit labor costs, the lower the substitutability and the smaller the number of firms.

Home depreciation, by raising foreign suppliers' marginal cost in home currency, shifts the foreign reaction function from RR to $R'R'$. The relative price of foreign products increases at A', and the price charged by domestic firms also increases. The elasticity of price with respect to the exchange rate depends on the number of firms in the industry and on the substitutability between alternative suppliers. The range of customers served by foreign firms contracts as a result of their increased relative price, as does their profitability. Home firms expand.

The model can be made more realistic by inclusion of two further considerations. The first is entry and exit. In the above discussion we assumed implicitly that there are no fixed costs and that firms have a fixed location in the product space. The second concerns capacity constraints. Each of these will affect pricing strategies and hence the impact of exchange rate movements on equilibrium prices.

In the postdepreciation equilibrium, the increased profitability of firms whose cost base is in the home market may bring about entry of new firms. These entering firms will select a location that places them optimally between existing firms. The entrants cause industry price to decline relative to the equilibrium at point A'. But they may also force

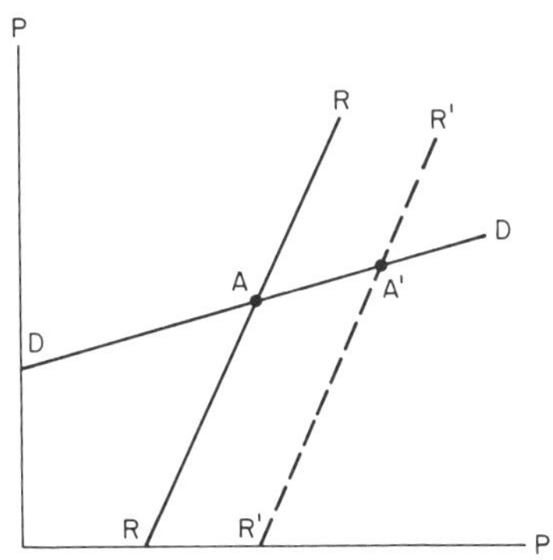

Fig. 11.1 The effect of exchange rate depreciation on relative prices.

high-cost foreign firms altogether out of the market. Of course the possibility of entry will influence the pricing policy of existing firms and hence limit in the first place the price response to depreciation.

Capacity constraints also influence the response of pricing to exchange rate shocks. Suppose that in the initial equilibrium at point A all firms are almost capacity constrained. The move to A' with a reduction in the relative price of domestic products is therefore not possible, since it would involve an expansion of sales by home firms. In the presence of capacity constraints, domestic firms price so as to maintain constant their volume of sales. Thus they will fully match foreign firms' price increases. The large price response in turn raises the issue of entry of new firms with a domestic cost base or expansion of capacity by existing firms.

These examples already show that there is a fruitful application of industrial organization approaches to open economy price responses. These ideas are important for the discussion of exchange rate effects and for the international transmission of price disturbances. But they apply equally to commercial policy questions. Suppose a small country liberalizes imports. We would expect that with fixed costs in setting up distribution networks, the smaller the country, the smaller the number of diversified products that can profitably be marketed. But that has radical implications: even under free trade we would not expect pricing at the world level. Except for the threat of entry, the size of the market creates an oligopoly structure. Changes in commercial policy such as tariff reduction are unlikely to be passed on fully. In the competition on the circle model, for example, the elasticity of final prices charged by foreign firms with respect to the tariff is less than two-thirds and that of home firms less than one-third. Moreover, if there are few firms and substitution is poor, these elasticities fall off sharply. These conclusions have immediate implications. Most important among these is the finding that opening the economy to induce price discipline will work poorly in very small countries and in industries where there are significant fixed costs and entry costs.

11.2 Waiting

Many investments have the property that they are almost irreversible, except via depreciation or at a significant loss. Pindyck (1986), following a number of earlier authors, has explored the optimal timing of such irreversible investments when the return on the investment project evolves stochastically.

Suppose, concretely, that a firm faces a stochastic demand

$$p = x - aQ, \tag{3}$$

where x denotes the state of demand which follows a Wiener process with drift and has a standard deviation s. Pindyck derives for this case the investment rule drawing on option pricing. The key idea is that the decision to invest amounts to the exercise of an option. The option will be exercised only when the state of demand is sufficiently favorable. Even though a unit of installed capital may already be profitable at a given level of demand, it may be profitable to postpone investment. The irreversibility of investment and the possibility of adverse states of demand place a premium on waiting for sufficiently favorable demand conditions. The optimal capital stock will depend on, among other determinants, the state of demand, x, as well as the variability of demand, s.

$$K' = K'(x,s, \ldots). \tag{4}$$

The investment rule is to choose at any point the larger of K' and K, the actual capital stock in place. In figure 11.2 I show the schedule $K'(x, \ldots)$ upward sloping. At a given time there will be a realization of demand x_0 and a given capital stock K_0. At a point like A the firm will not add to capacity. But if demand improves to a level x_1 the firm would add to the capital stock to reach point A'. Thus, small changes in demand, in the region below $K'(\text{x}, \ldots)$, do not affect investment, while large increases in demand lead to investment. The location of the schedule $K'(x, \ldots)$ will depend on the variability of demand. Increased variability reduces the desired capital stock at each level of demand.

This option-pricing approach to near-irreversible investments has many applications in open-economy macroeconomics. I will sketch here only two. Consider first the issue of European unemployment. Unemployment is commonly attributed to an excessively high real wage. It is argued that real wage increases in the 1970s outpaced pro-

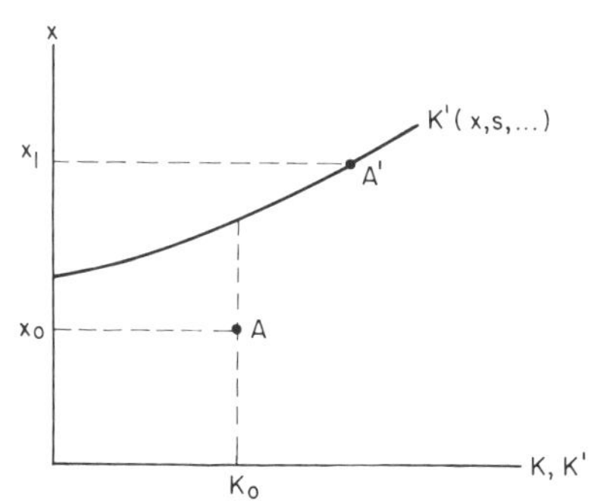

Fig. 11.2 Investment decisions and the value of waiting.

ductivity growth and the adverse effects of energy price increases. Hence unemployment is classical. The option-pricing approach to irreversible investments suggests an alternative interpretation. We can think of labor as an almost-irreversible investment. Attrition of the labor force or severance pay are the only ways in which a firm can relinquish labor.

With a suitable reinterpretation of the Pindyck problem, we can derive as in figure 11.3 the employment problem of the firm. The hiring and firing lines are *HH* and *FF*. If demand falls sufficiently low, given the variability and trend growth of demand relative to the rate of labor force attrition through retirement, the firm will fire workers. This defines the line *FF*, which is the maximum employment level the firm will sustain for a given low-demand level. The schedule *HH* shows the employment level to which a firm will move in favorable demand states. The corridor in between defines the area where demand changes do not influence employment. If the firm is initially at point *A*, a fall in demand below x_1 will lead the firm to fire workers, and a rise in demand above x_2 will lead to new hires. Smaller changes in demand have no effect.[2]

The location of these hiring and firing lines depend on all the parameters that govern the evolution of demand, on labor force attrition, and on severance pay. For that reason the model can help explain how the shift in the stochastic environment from the sixties to the seventies has led to the sharp increase in unemployment. The stochastic environment has deteriorated, since trend growth of demand has declined while the variability of demand has increased. Firms accordingly find that they have excessive labor, and they respond by shedding labor through attrition. In terms of figure 11.3, the corridor widens. The counterpart, of course, is an increase in youth unemployment and long-term un-

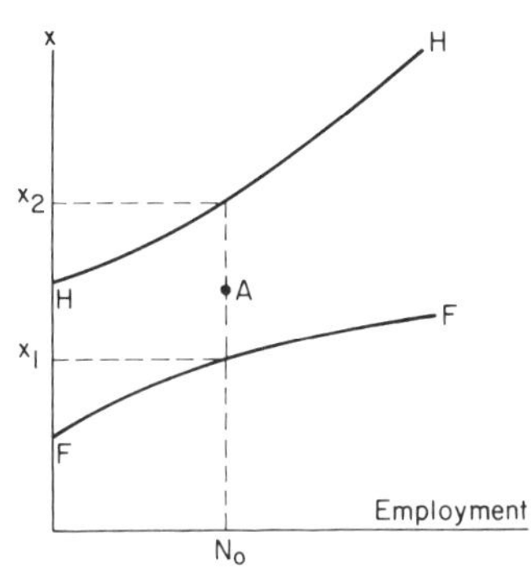

Fig. 11.3 Hiring and firing decisions when employment is quasi-irreversible.

employment. The model also predicts that firms will not show a significant response to a small increase in demand.

The same model can be used for any of a number of investment decisions. Obvious candidates are investment responses to real exchange rate changes. If real exchange rates move randomly, at what point do firms invest to expand capacity or scrap capital? A different kind of question that can be asked in this setting is that of the return of flight capital. The experience is that the return of flight capital tends to be very slow, except when the threat of bankruptcy forces firms to repatriate funds. This issue fits well into the spirit of the quasi-irreversible investment model. The risk of returning capital too early is that conditions deteriorate again, and that a renewed outflow can only occur at a high penalty cost. Hence the investment climate must become sufficiently favorable so that the immediate payoff on returning capital overshadows the prospect of a subsequent deterioration. But that poses a policy problem, because front-loading the benefits to a return of flight capital may run counter to fiscal stabilization and a favorable investment climate, or it may involve a politically unacceptable income redistribution.

11.3 Expecting

The third direction of research which I find particularly fruitful deals with expectations and their impact on portfolio choices and hence exchange rates. In Dornbusch (1976), I showed how once-and-for-all changes in the money stock, with sticky prices in goods and markets and perfect foresight in asset markets, lead to an overshooting of exchange rates. Lyons (1987) and Engel (1987) have rightly pointed out that the once-and-for-all model is not very interesting as a policy experiment. In a much richer model of a stochastic money supply process and rational expectations, they show that innovations in money growth, because they are extrapolated into cumulative increases in money, lead to sizable short-run movements in exchange rates in response to even small changes in money.

This is a promising direction for modelling exchange rate responses, putting the emphasis on the extrapolation of current events. A simple example can explain what is involved. Suppose that innovations in money are serially correlated, and suppose that inflation adjusts only gradually. A positive innovation in money is extrapolated into a cumulative accumulation of money relative to the trend growth. This implies that in the long run, the exchange rate will have moved to a higher path, as will the price level. Because inflation is not fully flexible, in the short run the real money stock is seen as growing, and hence nominal interest rates will be declining for some time before inflation

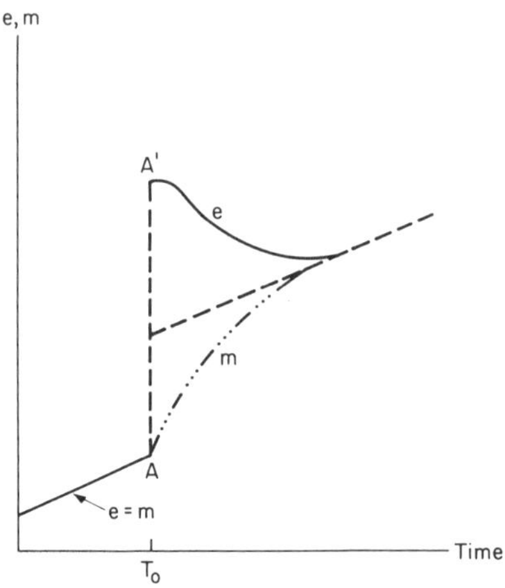

Fig. 11.4 The effect of a monetary innovation on money supply expectations and the exchange rate.

builds up to erode the growth in nominal balances. Ultimately the system returns to the initial rate of inflation, money growth, and depreciation.

Figure 11.4 shows the exchange rate path in response to this experiment. Initially, up to time T_0 the economy moves along the solid line. At T_0 the innovation occurs and is extrapolated. The public recognizes that asymptotically the economy will converge to the higher exchange rate path reflecting the cumulative increase in money relative to trend shown by the dashed line. But there will be an immediate depreciation of the exchange rate from A to A'. The overshooting reflects the fact that forward-looking asset holders anticipate the cumulative depreciation and will only hold domestic assets, in the face of reduced interest rates, if the exchange rate is appreciating. Along the new exchange rate path, the rate of appreciation, following the initial jump, will accelerate for some time as nominal interest rates initially decline. The basic point of this analysis is that the forward-looking expectations about the evolution of money, extrapolating the serial correlation of disturbances, must find their way immediately into the spot exchange rate. The analysis has obvious extensions to fiscal policy and other determinants of the exchange rate.

11.4 Concluding Remarks

The common trend of the three developments I have reviewed is to take open-economy macroeconomics away from a simple and mechanistic model. These new ideas do not change the qualitative direction of basic messages. In fact, they are not even surprising. But they do bring with them much more qualified comparative static properties. The response of investment to real exchange rates depends not only on current profitability but also on the anticipated persistence. The effect of innovations in money depends on how the public extrapolates the money innovation. Exchange rate impacts on prices and trade flows depend on the conditions of entry and on the number of firms. I believe these new ideas force us also to modify our testing of hypotheses. Case studies seem a suitable approach to try to start capturing this broader picture.

Notes

1. The discussion here draws on Dornbusch (1987).
2. For a complete model see Bentiola and Bertola (1987).

References

Bentiola, S. and G. Bertola. 1987. Firing costs and labor demand. How bad is Eurosclerosis. Unpublished ms. Cambridge, Mass.: MIT.

Dornbusch, R. 1976. Expectations and exchange rate economics. *Journal of Political Economy* 84 (December): 1161–76.

———. 1987. Exchange rates and prices. *American Economic Review* 77: 93–106.

Engel, C. M. 1987. Reliability of policy announcements and the effects of monetary policy. *European Economic Review* 29 (November): 137–55.

Krugman, P. 1986. Pricing to market when the exchange rate changes. NBER Working Paper no. 1926.

Pindyck, R. 1986. Irreversible investment, capacity choice and the value of the firm. NBER Working Paper no. 1980.

Lyons, R. 1987. Exchange rates and money supply expectations. Unpublished manuscript, Massachusetts Institute of Technology, Cambridge, Massachusetts.

Contributors

Joshua Aizenman
Graduate School of Business
University of Chicago
1101 East 58th Street
Chicago, IL 60637

Charles R. Bean
London School of Economics
Houghton Street
London WC2A 2AE, U.K.

Stanley W. Black
Department of Economics
The University of North Carolina at Chapel Hill
Gardner Hall 017 A
Chapel Hill, NC 27514

William H. Branson
Woodrow Wilson School
Princeton University
Princeton, NJ 08544

Willem H. Buiter
Department of Economics
Yale University
37 Hillhouse Avenue
P.O. Box 1972, Yale Station
New Haven, CT 06520

Paul De Grauwe
Centrum voor Economische Studien
Van Evenstraat 2B
B 3000 Leuven, Belgium

Rudiger Dornbusch
Department of Economics
E52-357
Massachusetts Institute of Technology
Cambridge, MA 02139

Alberto Giovannini
National Bureau of Economic Research
1050 Massachusetts Avenue
Cambridge, MA 02138

Dale W. Henderson
Department of Economics
Georgetown University
Washington, D.C. 20057

Robert A. Johnson
International Division
Board of Governors of the Federal Reserve System
Constitution Avenue and 20th Street, NW
Washington, D.C. 20551

Louka T. Katseli
Tsakalof 28
Athens 10673
Greece

Kala Krishna
National Bureau of Economic Research
1050 Massachusetts Avenue
Cambridge, MA 02138

Paul Krugman
Department of Economics
Massachusetts Institute of Technology
E52-383A
Cambridge, MA 02139

Robert Lawrence
Department of Economic Studies
The Brookings Institution
1775 Massachusetts Avenue, NW
Washington, D.C. 20036

Bonnie Loopesko
International Finance Division
Stop 23
Federal Reserve Board
Constitution Avenue and 20th Street, NW
Washington, D.C. 20551

James P. Love
Woodrow Wilson School
Princeton University
Princeton, NJ 08544

Richard C. Marston
3404 Steinberg-Dietrich Hall
The Wharton School
University of Pennsylvania
Philadelphia, PA 19104-6367

Jacques Melitz
21 rue Michel Ange
75016 Paris
France

Maurice Obstfeld
Department of Economics
University of Pennsylvania
3718 Locust Walk
Philadelphia, PA 19104-6297

J. David Richardson
Department of Economics
University of Wisconsin
1180 Observatory Drive
Madison, WI 53706

Robert M. Stern
Department of Economics and Institute of Public Policy Studies
Lorch Hall
The University of Michigan
Ann Arbor, MI 48109-1220

Stephen J. Turnovsky
Department of Economics
University of Washington
301 Savery Hall
Seattle, WA 98195

Guy Verfaille
Centrum voor Economische Studien
Van Evenstraat 2B
B 3000 Leuven, Belgium

John Williamson
Institute for International Economics
11 Dupont Circle, NW
Washington, D.C. 20036

Name Index

Subject Index